The effectiveness of the European Court of Justice

MANCHESTER
1824
Manchester University Press

The effectiveness of the European Court of Justice

Why reluctant states comply

Diana Panke

Manchester University Press
Manchester and New York
distributed in the United States exclusively
by Palgrave Macmillan

Published by Manchester University Press
Oxford Road, Manchester M13 9NR, UK
and Room 400, 175 Fifth Avenue, New York, NY 10010, USA
www.manchesteruniversitypress.co.uk

Distributed in the United States exclusively by
Palgrave Macmillan, 175 Fifth Avenue, New York,
NY 10010, USA

Distributed in Canada exclusively by
UBC Press, University of British Columbia, 2029 West Mall,
Vancouver, BC, Canada V6T 1Z2

British Library Cataloguing-in-Publication Data
A catalogue record for this book is available from the British Library

Library of Congress Cataloging-in-Publication Data applied for

ISBN 978 0 7190 8306 8 hardback

First published 2010

Typeset
by Action Publishing Technology Ltd, Gloucester
Printed in Great Britain
by CPI Antony Rowe Ltd, Chippenham, Wiltshire

Contents

List of tables and figures

Tables

Figures

Preface

This book is based on my PhD dissertation. It would have been written completely differently without the socialization I obtained in the process of getting the degree. After having written a non-empirical master thesis, I planned to write a purely theoretical PhD dissertation as well. When I first started to work with my supervisor, Prof. Tanja Börzel, I expected that I wouldn't have to bother about empirics at all and could spend all my energy in the theoretical realm – even if I ran the risk of theorizing 'unimportant stuff'. This resulted in a theoretically coherent but 'slightly' over-determined research design, with not less than 36 hypotheses. After Tanja invested a lot of energy in talking me out of a purely theoretical thesis (including the manipulation of my screen saver's slogan), empirics hit me. I searched for an empirical puzzle, developed a research question, reduced the number of hypotheses and, most importantly, adopted a theory-driven, methodological, sound empirical understanding of political science, which I am convinced of now and which this book reflects. Thus, I am extremely grateful for Tanja's commitment in acting as an agent of socialization.

Acknowledgements

In more than one respect, I am very much indebted to my supervisor Tanja Börzel. I profited tremendously from her highly dedicated supervision, her continuing support and optimism, her almost supernatural energy in pushing the project further and motivating me even in the wake of long empirical 'to do' lists and – of course – from her immense expertise. I would also like to thank Jeffrey Checkel and Thomas Risse. Their constructive comments on earlier versions of the manuscript and to papers on various conferences and workshops helped greatly to situate the work and sharpen the argument.

Moreover, I am grateful to my friends and former colleagues, in particular Nicole Bolleyer, Evelyn Bytzek, Carina Sprungk, Vera van Hüllen, and Tobias Hofmann for their support with quantitative, empirical, and general issues. I owe thanks also to Suzanne Mulcahy, Niall Morris and Michael Anderson who helped with language editing.

I presented parts of this study at various colloquia, conferences, and workshops. I would like to thank the participants and commentators for their sometimes 'nasty' questions which greatly helped to develop my argument and from which my work benefited enormously. These are: Karen Alter, Karen Anderson, Andrè Bächtiger, Tanja Brühl, Lisa Conant, Thomas Christiansen, Nicole Deitelhoff, Klaus Eder, Gerda Falkner, Anna Holzscheiter, Christoph Humrich, Markus Jachtenfuchs, Peter Katzenstein, Mareike Kleine, Andrea Liese, Altetta Mondré, Jürgen Neyer, Christine Reh, Martin Rhodes, Shawn Rosenberg, Frank Schimmelfennig, Jonas Tallberg, Daniel Thomas, Cornelia Ulbert, Antje Wiener, Bernhard Zangl, and Michael Zürn.

Last but not least, I would like to say thank you to my friends, and especially to Nicole and Tanja, for always being there for me and for cheering me up whenever necessary.

Abbreviations

ASEAN	Association of Southeast Asian Nations
ASF	Arbeitsgemeinschaft Sozialdemokratischer Frauen (German social-democratic women's forum)
BAA	British Agrochemical Association
BDA	Bund Deutscher Arbeitgeber (German Employer Association)
BDI	Bund Deutscher Industrie (German Industry Association)
BGA	Bundesgesundheitsamt (German Federal Health Authority), responsible for drinking water quality (now UBA)
BGB	Bürgerliches Gesetzbuch (German Civil Code)
BGBL	Bundesgesetzblatt (federal publication of legal acts)
BSE	Bovine Spongiforme Enzephalopathie
BUND	Bund Naturschutz Deutschland (German environmental organization)
CACM	Central American Common Market
CBI	Confederation of British Industry
CDU	Christdemokratische Partei Deutschlands (German Christian Democrats)
COM	European Commission
COMESA	Common Market for Eastern and Southern Africa
CRD	Collective Redundancy Directive
DEFRA	Department for Environment, Food and Rural Affairs
DFG	German Research Council
DGB	Deutscher Gewerkschaftsbund (German Trade Union Association)
DNR	Deutscher Naturschutzbund (German environmental organization)
DVU	Deutsche Volksunion (German Peoples Party)
DWD	Drinking Water Directive

DWP	Drinking Water Provision
DWR	Drinking water regulation
EAC	East African Community
EC	European Community
ECHR	European Court of Human Rights
ECJ	European Court of Justice
ECOWAS	Economic Community of West African States
ECT	European Communities Treaty
EFTA	European Free Trade Association
EG	Europäische Gemeinschaft (European Community)
EIA	Environmental Impact Assessment
EOC	Equal Opportunity Commission
EPA	Employment Protection Act
EqD	Equal Access Directive
EU	European Union
FDP	Freiheitliche Demokratische Partei (German Liberals)
FKST	Fachkommission Soforthilfe Trinkwasser (Drinking Water Task Force)
FoE	Friends of the Earth
GATT	General Agreement on Tariffs and Trade
GDP	Gross Domestic Product
GP	Green Party
IACHR	Inter-American Commission of Human Rights
ICC	International Criminal Court
IMF	International Monetary Fund
IR	International Relations
MAFF	Ministry of Agriculture, Fisheries and Food
MERCOSUR	Mercado Común del Cono Sur (Southern Common Market)
NABU	Naturschutzbund (German environmental organization)
NAFTA	North American Free Trade Agreement
NFU	National Farmers' Union, UK
NitD	Nitrates Directive
NPD	Nationaldemokratische Partei Deutschlands (German National Democrats)
NVZ	Nitrates Vulnerable Zone
OFWAT	Office of Water Services, UK
POST	Parliamentary Office of Science and Technology
RFWD	Residence of Foreign Workers and their Families Directive
SDA	Sex Discrimination Act, UK
SPD	Sozialdemokratische Partei Deutschlands (German Social Democratic Party)

TUC	Trade Unions Congress
TURERA	Trade Union Reform and Employment Rights Act
UBA	Umweltbundesamt (Federal Environmental Office)
UGB	Umweltgesetzbuch (German environmental code)
UN	United Nations
UVPG	Umweltverträglichkeitsprüfungsgesetz (German Environmental Impact Assessment Law)
WFD	Water Framework Directive
WIA	Water Industry Act
WSR	Water Supply Regulations
WTO	World Trade Organization
WWF	World Wide Fund for Nature

Part I

Introduction

1

Relevance and research question

After the Second World War, states increasingly cooperated in international institutions. This brought about a rich and ever-increasing body of law beyond the nation-state. Although 'almost all states comply with almost all international norms almost all the time' (Henkin 1968), non-compliance is a common problem of international institutions, affecting all states and taking place in all policy areas. Violations of international law delimit its strength, undermine the precondition for its effectiveness, and eventually thwart the very purpose of cooperation among states. Thus, international institutions have reacted to compliance deficits with various compliance management systems. Hard cases of non-compliance, in which member states persist in their initial positions and continue to violate law, are frequently referred to international courts. Unlike domestic courts, however, they cannot resort to the legitimate use of force as a last resort to abolish norm violations. Yet international courts can talk states out of non-compliance. To this end, they can apply judicial discourses, judgments, and threats of penalties. These instruments are widespread, as the increasing number of recently created or strengthened international courts, such as the European Free Trade Association (EFTA) Court, the European Court of Human Rights (ECHR), the International Criminal Court (ICC), the Court of the Economic Community of West African States (ECOWAS), the European Court of Justice (ECJ) or the Court of the Common Market for Eastern and Southern Africa (COMESA), demonstrates (Smith 2000).

Despite the empirical relevance of non-compliance and the wave of international legalization, we know very little about how these courts operate and under which conditions they succeed in effectively restoring the power of international law. While a growing body of literature investigates why states comply and why they violate international law,[1] studies

[1] Examples are Börzel 2000, Börzel 2001, Börzel 2003b, Cameron, Werksman and Roderick 1996, Checkel 1999, Fearon 1998, Fisher 1981, Hill 1997, Jönsson and Tallberg 1998, Krämer 1989, Mitchell 2003, Raustiala and Slaughter 2002.

rarely focus on how detected rule violations can be transformed into compliance (for exceptions see Tallberg 2002).

This book seeks to close these gaps. It analyzes how and under which conditions international courts can successfully end norm violations, and thereby, induce domestic changes – even against the initial resistance of affected states. This study basically shows that judicial discourses, judgments and threats of penalties are only sometimes effective in talking states into compliance. The presence of an elaborated toolbox of compliance instruments is only the necessary, but not the sufficient condition for international courts to abolish detected instances of norm violations. Issue-variables, such as the interpretational scope of the disputed issue, the fit between court judgments and domestically institutionalized norms, the compatibility of policy frames, and the seriousness of the infringement, crucially influence the prospects to transform detected norm violations into compliance. The book further shows that the success of judicial discourses, judgments and sanction-threats is not determined by states' characteristics such as political and economic power, financial, administrative, or political capacities, or judicial and legal cultures as prominent theories would predict.

This study draws on the European Union (EU) as an example of an international institution with a legalized compliance management system, encompassing the very prominent compliance instruments of judicial discourses, judgments and sanction-threats. As with any other international institution, member states are responsible for the legal and practical implementation, so that the EU faces non-compliance problems that hamper the effectiveness of European law (e.g. Mastenbroek 2003). Once cases are referred to the ECJ, the latter can apply judicial discourses, judgments, and sanction-threats, in order to talk states into compliance. Some infringements are very quickly settled after they reach the ECJ. The German drinking water or the UK collective redundancy cases show that the governments incorrectly transposed EU law in the first place in order to save expenses, but adapted legal acts during the ongoing judicial discourse. Others, such as the German and the UK equal access cases, require considerably more time and a judgment, before compliance is achieved and the discrimination of women can be stopped. For yet another group of cases judicial discourses and judgments fail to further compliance and the states continue the norm violations at the expenses of others. In these instances of severe resistance to the ECJ, sanction-threats can help to achieve compliance, as shown by the British nitrates case in which the government shied away from a penalty.

In all these instances, non-compliance severely interferes with the effectiveness of supranational law. This is all the more severe if it persists for long periods of time. Yet norm violations cannot always be resolved very quickly through judicial discourses or quickly through judgments, particularly if states strongly resist further legal adaptations to EU demands. In some cases, member state governments are very reluctant to introduce domestic changes even after ECJ judgments so that sanction-threats come into play. Penalties are the last resort in restoring compliance and have since their introduction in 1993, up to 2009 been exercised in only nine cases. Among those nine cases, there are only four instances in which member states incorrectly legally transposed EU law.[2] The other five cases are instances of incorrect implementations.[3] This indicates that the EU infringement procedure is a story of success, since sooner or later all member states can be talked into compliance. However, this might take a total of 19 years as in the British drinking water case, during which states save considerable compliance costs at the expense of affected individuals and of other member states. Thus, it is important to investigate why not every applied compliance instrument is equally successful. Why can states only sometimes be talked into compliance during a judicial discourse? Why are some judgments effective, while others fail to induce domestic changes? Why must the threat of sanctions sometimes be looming before states abolish non-compliance?

This study analyses how international courts operate and under which conditions they facilitate compliance – even against the strong resistance of states. The following questions are crucial in this regard: Under which

[2] The cases are: Case C-304/02 in which France incorrectly transposed fishing regulations (Council Regulations (EEC) No 2057/82, No 2241/87, No 2057/82, No 2847/93) and was ordered in 2005 to pay a lump sum of €20,000,000 as well as €57,761,250 for each period of six-month delay; Case C-177/04 in which the ECJ ruled in 2006 that France had to pay a daily penalty of €31,560 for the incorrect transposition of the product liability directive (85/374/EEC); Case C-121/07, in which France incorrectly transposed the directive on genetically modified organisms (directive 2001/18/EC) and was ordered in 2008 to pay a lump sum of €10,000,000; Case C-109–08 in which Greece incorrectly transposed the information directive (98/34) and was ordered by the ECJ in 2009 to pay a daily penalty of €31,798.80 as well as a daily lump sum of €9,636 for each day of continued non-compliance.

[3] These cases are: Greece had been issued with a penalty of €20,00 per day in 2000 for violating the waste framework directive (C-38791); Spain got a daily penalty of €45,600 in 2003 for incorrectly implementing the bathing water directive (C-278/01); Italy violated Article 48 (C-119/04) and got a daily penalty of €309,750 in 2006; Germany incorrectly implemented the waste disposal directive in two instances and got daily penalties of €31,680 and €123,7204 in 2007 (C-503/04); and the ECJ penalised Greece in 2009 for granting unlawful aid to Olympic Airways with a daily penalty of €53,611 and a lump sum of €10,512 for each of the days in which non-compliance continued (C-369/07).

conditions are judicial discourses successful? When do they fail? How and under which conditions do judgment instruments facilitate compliance? Why are states sometimes willing to transform non-compliance and introduce domestic legal changes after ECJ rulings and sometimes not? How do sanction-threats operate? Under which conditions can they deter states from continuing non-compliance?

1.I Non-compliance in the EU: the empirical puzzle

International institutions all face instances in which states violate laws. Since this reduces the effectiveness of the law and juxtaposes in the very extreme the initial purpose of cooperation between states, international institutions seek to transform detected norm violations into compliance. To this end, they apply argumentative means, such as bilateral dialogues between the parties or judicial discourses, and bargaining means, such as threats of judgments or financial penalties (Keohane, Moravcsik and Slaughter 2000, Smith 2000). However, it is unclear under which conditions these instruments succeed. In order to shed light on this often neglected issue, this study draws on the EU as an empirical example of a highly legalized international institution and investigates the operation of compliance restoring instruments. The EU is a good institution to study in order to learn something about the function of judicial discourses, judgments and sanction-threats, because the European Commission collects and disseminates comprehensive infringement data. In the EU, as in any other international institution, member states are ultimately responsible for the legal implementation of law beyond the nation-state. Thus, the insights that this book presents on the operation of the three compliance instruments and their scope conditions for success are also applicable to other international institutions with a similarly high degree of legalisation (see also section 8.V).

The EU infringement procedure consists of several steps. If the European Commission suspects a violation of primary or secondary European law, it initiates an infringement proceeding against the respective state, during which several compliance instruments are subsequently applied. Firstly, parties engage in a bilateral dialogue. If cases cannot be settled, the Commission refers them to the Court. The ECJ starts judicial discourses, which are followed by binding judgments and, if non-compliance still prevails, by financial penalties. While threats of penalties take place in about ten per cent of all ECJ cases, up to now, the ECJ has imposed financial penalties in only three instances (Commission of the European Communities 2005).

Given the possibility of pre-judicial settlements, ECJ referrals are among the least likely cases for the prospect of ending norm violations. In these instances, states' resistance to compliance is extremely strong, otherwise a common understanding regarding the interpretation of the disputed norm would have been developed in earlier stages and the case would already have been closed. Such instances of persistent non-compliance severely threaten the effectiveness of European law, since states safeguard their constituency and save high amounts of domestic compliance costs at the expense of other private and public actors within and beyond the affected state. Hence, studying how the ECJ operates and under which conditions non-compliance is quickly abolished through judicial discourses, after some time through judgments, or even more slowly through sanction-threats, is important. This study focuses exclusively on Court cases and inquires into the following research questions: How does the ECJ succeed in talking states out of norm violations? When are judicial discourses, judgments, and sanction-threats effective in facilitating compliance?

An empirical analysis of 1,792 ECJ cases on incorrect legal transpositions of EU law between 1978 and 2000 reveals an interesting pattern. On the aggregate level, the more compliance restoring instruments are applied the more inclined all states are to give in and shift towards compliance. Yet neither the mere presence of compliance instruments, nor their application, can explain the transformational dynamics. When it comes to ECJ cases, there is no clear leader-laggard pattern, since there are rather few differences between states, but significant variation within each state. Every member state has successful and failed judicial discourses, judgments and sanction-threats. A judicial instrument is sometimes effective and sometimes not, even against the same government and even within the same policy field. From the perspective of prominent compliance theories, which would expect that success of individual compliance instruments depends on country-specific variables, such as power, capacities, or culture, the high intra-state variation poses an empirical puzzle that these theories cannot sufficiently explain.

1.II The argument

In order to cope with problems of persistent norm violations, international institutions possess several compliance instruments. In the last fifteen years, we observe a wave of legalization on the international level, with many international institutions either strengthening existing international courts and tribunals or creating new ones (see also Busch and

Reinhardt 2003, Smith 2000). Yet although only hard cases of non-compliance, in which states' preferences are very strong, are referred to international courts, and although we witness a wave of legalization, we know very little about how these courts operate and under which conditions they effectively facilitate compliance with international law. In order to close this gap, this study draws on the EU and analyses how the ECJ talks states out of norm violations.

This book shows that unlike domestic courts, international courts, such as the ECJ, lack a monopoly of legitimate force, but can nevertheless be successful in fostering compliance if they possess compliance instruments, such as judicial discourses, judgments, and threats of sanctions. Yet the application cannot explain why an instrument sometimes succeeds and sometimes fails in settling infringement cases.

The book shows, secondly, that the success of compliance instruments is influenced by very specific scope conditions. The most prominent instrument, judicial discourses, is only effective if the advocates of the parties do not talk at cross purposes but develop a common norm definition and thereby argumentatively entrap the governments. This requires that both advocates actively participate in the discourse, focus on the same legal act, and apply methods of judicial interpretation that fit the complexity of the interpretational problem at hand. If this scope condition is present, judicial discourses foster a judicially superior norm definition from which governments cannot deviate any longer with good arguments, which in turn induces compliance with international law. The scope conditions for effective judgments and sanction-threats also depend on issue-specific constellations. For example, judgments create publicity, provide an authoritative norm definition and diffuse new ideas, which differentially empower domestic compliance constituencies. Domestic compliance constituencies can push their governments into compliance from below via shaming or reframing campaigns. Shaming campaigns are only successful if judgments resonate well with other deep-seated domestic norms, and reframing succeeds if judgments reduce the complexity of the contested issue, allowing developing and linking of a new policy approach to a complementary prominent frame. Finally, sanction-threats facilitate compliance only if they act as deterrents. This requires that infringements are serious so that the proposed penalties are high and that European authorities already introduced first steps towards enforcement so that governments can expect to become subject to penalties during their incumbency.

Thirdly, the effectiveness of compliance instruments is not biased by state characteristics. The share of votes in the Council of Ministers (political power) or the strength of the national economy (economic power), the training and motivation of the administrative staff (administrative capacity) or the number of domestic veto players (political capacity), as well as the judicial culture of states, do not determine their willingness or their ability to transform non-compliance into compliance in response to the ECJ. States with a continental-Roman legal culture, such as Germany, are not more responsive to ECJ judicial discourses than states with a common law tradition, such as the UK. Powerful states cannot deter the ECJ from rulings to a greater extent than weak states. Likewise, weak states are not more likely to shy away from ECJ penalties than their stronger counterparts. Finally, federal states with many veto players and a respectively low political capacity, such as Germany, are not more constrained when reacting to the ECJ than the unitary UK.

Fourthly, this study demonstrates that instruments are successful in some cases and unsuccessful in others, even for one and the same government. As a consequence, the proper mix of tools is essential to an effective political and legal community. The EU infringement procedure is an example of an effective compliance restoring system. Although it might take up to almost two decades after the detection of non-compliance until it is finally abolished, and although it might require judicial discourses, judgments and sanction-threats, in the end, all states respond to the ECJ and comply with EU law.

1.III Prominent (non-)compliance research and its shortcomings

With the enormous proliferation of international institutions in the twentieth century, liberal theories in particular on international cooperation mushroomed (Keohane 1984, Keohane and Nye 1989). It is remarkable that those theories overwhelmingly assume compliance with international norms to be the rule. They argue that states agree to norms in the first place only if they reflect their interests to an extent that is proportional to their bargaining power. If, in turn, international norms are results of states' preferences, it should prevent states from violating them.

However, this line of reasoning does not take into account some important sources of non-compliance: 1) Theories of incomplete contracting point towards the uncertainties of the future (Garrett 1995). The interests of states might change over time, reflecting alterations in domestic or environmental contexts. This provides incentives for defection and non-compliance; 2) Norms often require domestic change, which brings about compliance costs. Hence, free-rider problems emerge in all situations in which a state seeking to avoid compliance costs can reap benefits as soon as other states comply (Axelrod 1984, Hardin 1986); 3) Defections can be involuntary, due to the limited capacities of states, restricted deadlines for the implementation of norms, or the ambiguities of norms (Chayes and Handler-Chayes 1991).

Against this background, several theories discuss strategies for reducing instances of norm breaches. Neo-realists highlight how hegemons ensure compliance in deterring weaker states (Fearon 1998, Gilpin 1981: 210). Informed by these theories, legalization approaches point to hard law with high obligation and precision and to institutional transparency-creating mechanisms, such as centralized or decentralized monitoring systems (Abbott *et al.* 2000: 408–12; Goldstein *et al.* 2000: 386–7, Mitchell 1996: 17–20). At the same time, several empirical studies show that non-compliance cannot be completely prevented (e.g. Zürn and Joerges 2005). Hence, legalization approaches emphasize the importance of dispute settlement procedures for transforming non-compliance into compliance. These mechanisms are thought to be especially effective if many actors have standing and can issue complaints, if adjudication is obligatory and if third parties are independent and can refer to binding rulings instead of recommendations (e.g. Abbott *et al.* 2000: 401–16, Keohane, Moravcsik and Slaughter 2000: 461–2).

Despite this rich scholarship there are several gaps, which this book closes. Firstly, current research puts strong emphasis on the frequency and detection of non-compliance and the role of non-compliance bargaining in early stages of the EU infringement procedure (e.g. Reinhardt 2001, Tallberg 1999). In contrast, hard cases of persistent non-compliance that reach international courts are less well researched. Secondly, despite the recent wave of legalization (e.g. Abbott *et al.* 2000), we know very little about how international courts operate and under which conditions different compliance instruments are successful. How does high delegation to courts affect non-compliance patterns? Why are compliance instruments of courts only sometimes effective? Thirdly, prominent compliance and legalization approaches are state-centric. They overwhelmingly focus on country-variables in explaining non-compliance patterns,[4] but hardly ever draw attention to policy factors. Power and capacity of states are important to explain why states violate law (Börzel *et al.* 2007, Downs 1998, Martin 1992, Martin and Simmons 1998). Yet this study demonstrates that these variables lose their explanatory power

[4] e.g. Chayes and Handler-Chayes 1991, Downs 1998, Downs, Rocke and Barsoom 1996, Martin 1992, Martin and Simmons 1998, Mendrinou 1996, Tallberg 2002, Tallberg and Jönsson 2001.

for cases referred to courts and that the operation and the success of judicial discourses, judgments, and sanction-threats are not biased by country-variables. Finally, international courts lack a monopoly of legitimate force as a last resort to restore compliance and, therefore, rely on communicative means to abolish violations of international law. Current theories provide insights into different compliance instruments, but focus either on the argumentative power of discourses or on the bargaining power of threats of sanctions. Thereby, they overemphasize either the effectiveness of discursive means and argumentative power or of compliance bargaining and the power of costly threats, and arrive at different and incompatible propositions regarding compliance restoring dynamics. In contrast, this study incorporates rationalist and constructivist pathways within one framework, without biases towards bargaining processes and bargaining power on the one hand or towards discursive processes and argumentative power on the other.

1.IV Outline of the study

Despite judicial discourses, judgments and sanction-threats are very prominent in international institutions and despite the increase of hard law and the tendency to create new international courts and strengthen present ones, we know relatively little about when and under which conditions international courts succeed in fostering compliance. Hence, this study inquires into the effectiveness of compliance instruments applied to hard cases of norm violations that could not be resolved in pre-judicial negotiations. The argument proceeds in the following steps. Chapter 2 puts the EU in comparative perspective, sheds light on the EU infringement procedure and formulates the empirical puzzle. Why is it that each of the compliance instruments is only sometimes effective, even vis-à-vis one and the same state and vis-à-vis one and the same government? Chapter 3 theorizes the operation and success of judicial discourses, judgments, and sanction-threats in order to explain why they are always applied in the same order but significantly vary in their effectiveness within states. It develops competing rationalist and constructivist hypotheses on the three compliance instruments. Chapters 4, 5, and 6 empirically test the developed hypotheses via a series of qualitative case studies on environmental and social policy cases in the UK and Germany, selected according to a most similar systems design. Chapter 4 presents a German and a UK case in which judicial discourses, but not judgments or sanction-threats, successfully resolved non-compliance. It illustrates that governments can become argumentatively entrapped through judicial discourses, if the advocates do not talk at cross purposes but engage in judicial argumentation, focus on the same legal act, and apply a judicial technique of interpretation fitting the complexity of the issue at stake. Chapter 5 features four Court cases, in which judgments ended norm violations while judicial discourses and sanction-threats failed to do so. Judgments do not directly restore compliance in a top-down manner, but operate in a two-stage process. They increase publicity, provide authoritative norm definitions, and reduce the complexity of issues at stake. This empowers societal norm proponents vis-à-vis opponents, and allows them to use these ideational resources in pushing reluctant governments into compliance from below. In one of the German and in one of the UK cases, judgments resonated well with domestic norms and shaming campaigns created threats of potential reputational losses, to which governments responded with domestic changes. In the other two German and UK cases, societal actors argumentatively reframed domestic debates, launched a new policy approach, linked it to a complementary frame, and thereby incrementally fostered compliance. Chapter 6 illustrates the success of sanction-threats, which came into play after the two other instruments proved ineffective. The threat of penalties facilitated compliance in the British nitrates and the German environmental impact assessment cases, in both of which the infringement was very serious and the corresponding potential penalty high. Chapter 7 compares the UK and the German cases with a special emphasis on the role of country variables such as power, capacities and judicial cultures. This reveals that the operation of the three compliance instruments, as well as the conditions under which they successfully resolve norm violations, are not influenced by country-variables. Even though capacity, power and culture are constant in the four German cases and in the four UK cases respectively, the effectiveness of judicial discourses, judgments, and sanction-threats varies. The UK and Germany are relatively similar in terms of economic and political power in the EU and in terms of financial and administrative capacities, but differ in their political capacities (number of veto players) and in their judicial cultures. Nevertheless, both states responded in the same way to the stimuli of the three compliance instruments: whenever the issue-specific scope conditions for its success are present, an instrument succeeds in promoting compliance. Chapter 8 summarizes the major findings of this study and elaborates on its contributions to compliance and legalization research in general. It highlights that the insights into the operation of the ECJ and the effectiveness of judicial discourses, judgments, or sanction-threats can be applied to other states, other policy fields, and also to some of the other international institutions.

Part II

The puzzle and the argument

This section outlines the empirical puzzle (Chapter 2) and develops a set of hypotheses on the operation and scope conditions for the success of judicial discourses, judgments and sanction-threats (Chapter 3).

Similar to many other international institutions, the EU possesses an elaborated toolbox with sequentially applied *compliance instruments: judicial discourses, judgments*, and *threats of penalties.* A judicial dis-course is the first instrument that becomes applied and, if successful, settles cases very quickly. Judgments are used after judicial discourses and, therefore, require more time to effectively end norm violations. The same applies to sanction-threats that come into play if neither judicial discourses nor judgments foster compliance.

A glance at the empirical record of the ECJ reveals that infringement cases cannot always be quickly settled through judicial discourses, but might require several years and eventually also a sanction-threat before states stop saving on compliance expenditures at the expense of affected individuals and possibly also other states. The success of the ECJ varies significantly across cases. Most remarkably, each of the compliance instruments is only sometimes effective vis-à-vis the same state and even vis-à-vis one and the same government. At the same time, there is no significant leader and laggard pattern between member states. How can we explain that governments yield vis-à-vis the Court in some cases quickly after judicial discourses, in others after judgments, and yet in others only if sanction-threats are looming?

Within the EU, the institutional design, in which the three instruments are embedded, is more or less constant. Since the instruments are always applied in the same order, their application cannot explain why they are sometimes successful but fail to end norm violations in other instances. So, how can the ECJ induce states' compliance with European law? Under which conditions are judicial discourses, judgments, and threats of sanctions successful in ending norm violations and fostering domestic changes? In order to account for the puzzle that compliance instruments are only sometimes effective, the third chapter develops a set of alternative hypotheses. In a nutshell, it argues that judicial discourses are only effective in facilitating compliance if the advocates of the parties do not talk at cross purposes, but develop a common, judicially superior norm interpretation, which argumentatively entraps the respective government because norm violations can no longer be justified with valid arguments. Judgments create publicity, provide authoritative norm-definitions, and spread new ideas, which empower societal norm proponents to push their governments into compliance from below. This induces compliance, if reframing strategies are successful, which requires that new frames complement old ones. Alternatively, shaming strategies facilitate compliance, if the judgment resonates well with other domestic norms. Finally, the threat of penalties ends norm violations if external non-compliance costs exceed domestic benefits, which depends on the seriousness of the infringement and the likelihood that sanctions will be exerted while the government is still in office.

2

The puzzle: non-compliance and the varying success of compliance instruments

Although the EU has subsequently expanded its legislative competencies, member states are responsible for the implementation and transposition of European law. Through secondary law in the form of directives or regulations, the EU formulates legally binding demands for domestic changes. If there is a mismatch between European and domestic law, member states must instigate domestic change in order to achieve compliance (Börzel and Risse 2000, Falkner *et al.* 2005, Knill 2001). In principle, states can violate EU and international law in three ways. Firstly, they can abstain from transposing it into national law altogether or not notify the European Commission or the responsible international secretariats of measures undertaken (delayed transpositions). Secondly, law beyond the nation-state is violated if governments and parliaments incompletely or incorrectly transpose it into national law (incorrect transposition). Thirdly, due to administrative malpractices at central, regional, or local levels, member states can fail to practically implement European or international law correctly (incorrect implementation).

If the European Commission as the guardian of the treaties suspects a member state of violating EU law in one of the three manners outlined above, the Commission can open an infringement proceeding against the respective state (Art. 226 ECT). In doing so the Commission sends letters of formal notice to the respective government and governments react with written statements. If this unofficial step cannot solve the compliance problems, the Commission initiates the first formal steps of the infringement procedure by issuing reasoned opinions (Art. 226 ECT). This is followed by bilateral negotiations, in which the Commission and the state exchange clarifications and political considerations (Tallberg 2002). If compliance problems persist, the Commission refers the case to the ECJ. The ECJ is highly independent and can resort to *judicial discourses* and *judgments* as the two judicial compliance instruments. Once a case reaches the ECJ, it starts a judicial discourse (Art. 226 ECT). State and European advocates exchange judicial arguments in an oral and a written procedure. After both stages of the discourse have ended, since the two parties have exchanged all legal arguments, the European Advocate General prepares a written opinion for the ECJ, summarizing the arguments and developing his own views on the case. In the next step, the ECJ issues binding judgments on how to interpret the disputed norm (Art. 226 ECT). Should governments still refuse to comply and abstain from domestic legal changes after both judicial compliance instruments have been applied, the enforcement phase follows the adjudication stage and expands the toolbox through *sanction-threats* as the third available compliance instrument (Smith 2000: 142–3, Tallberg 1999). The European Communities Treaty (ECT) of 1957 entailed no provisions for centralized but only for decentralized sanctions.[1] If states did not comply with rulings, the ECJ referred to a violation of Art. 171 ECT. Through these references, instances of persistent non-compliance became transparent and opened windows of opportunity for informal sanctions by other states.[2] The Maastricht Treaty introduced a centralized sanctioning mechanism in 1993. If states fail to comply with judgments, the Commission will send second letters of formal notice[3] followed by second reasoned opinions based on Article 228 ECT. Thereby, a second infringement procedure is initiated that resembles the first procedure with one exception. As the Commission refers the case to the ECJ, it additionally proposes daily penalties and lump sums (Commission of the European

[1] The treaty basis for the infringement procedure, the European Communities Treaty (ECT), was changed in 1993 and in 1997. The European Economic Community Treaty of 1957 provided the legal framework for the infringement procedure (Arts. 169, 170 and 171) and Art. 171 had no second paragraph allowing for financial sanctions until 1993. If member states did not comply with ECJ rulings, the ECJ could only refer to a violation of Art. 171, which stated that member states are obliged to comply with ECJ rulings. Since the Treaty of Amsterdam, the infringement procedure is regulated by Articles 226–228 ECT (which correspond to the old Arts. 169, 170 and 171). For reasons of simplicity, this study refers to the newer numbers even for cases before 1997, when it would for example be formally correct to refer to Art. 169 instead of Art. 226 ECT, or to Art. 171 instead of Art. 228 ECT.

[2] Examples of informal sanctions are losses of reputation or credibility, which could negatively affect a state's bargaining power in policy-making processes.

[3] However, as for the first letter of formal notice, the European Commission keeps no publicly available track of the letters. Thus, it is not possible to acquire comprehensive data on second letters of formal notice.

Communities 2005). In its second judgment, the ECJ then imposes monetary sanctions (European Court of Justice 1991, European Court of Justice 2006).

None of the elements of the EU infringement procedure and none of its compliance instruments is unique. The provision that non-state actors can initiate infringement procedures without the consent of affected governments can be found in a similar manner in the WTO and the EFTA (Reinhardt 2001). There are more similarities: the two judicial compliance instruments, judicial discourses and judgments, are common to the EFTA Court, the European Court of Human Rights (ECHR), the Andean Tribunal of Justice, and the Inter-American Commission of Human Rights (IACHR) as well (Keohane, Moravcsik and Slaughter 2000: 461). Finally, the possibility of threatening states with centralized or decentralized sanctions is not unique to the EU, but can also be found in the COMESA, the ECOWAS, the NAFTA, and the MERCOSUR to name but a few (Smith 2000). Hence, the EU infringement procedure (Art. 226) and its embedded compliance instruments are not *sui generis* features of the EU. The ECJ is an instance of an international court that lacks the legitimate monopoly of force as a last resort for restoring compliance, but possesses instruments that are empirically widespread and common features of highly legalized international institutions.

Unlike many international institutions, the EU has a well-documented record of infringement cases. Since 1978, the European Commission has published annual reports on the transposition and implementation of Community law, which give an overview of open cases in each year and the stage of the procedure. The data used in this book is even more detailed than the annual reports of the European Commission, since it includes additional information on which directive is violated in which way, by whom, for how long and over which stages of the infringement procedure (see also Annexe).

How successful is the ECJ in fostering compliance? Figure 2.1 shows the secondary law infringements from the first published annual report of the European Commission in 1978 up to 2000 for the EU-12 member states. Of the almost 17,000 proceedings that the Commission opened through a letter of formal notice between 1978 and 2000, 6,043 cases reached the first official stage. Less than a third of the cases in which the Commission had sent a reasoned opinion were referred to the ECJ in order to be subject to a *judicial discourse*. Of those 1,792 referrals, the ECJ issued *judgments* in 736 cases. In 19 out of 20 occasions, the ECJ sided with most of the complaints of the European Commission and not with the member states. Only 34 cases became subject to a second infringement proceeding and *threats of sanctions* (reasoned opinions based on Art. 228 ECT). In only eight instances were cases referred to the ECJ for a second time. Up to 2000 the ECJ had not imposed a single financial penalty for incorrect legal transpositions.[4] Hence, overall the ECJ is very successful in ending norm violations through applying its toolbox of judicial and enforcement instruments. Yet the figure also indicates that the judicial compliance instruments in particular are not effective in inducing compliance in all cases to which they are applied.

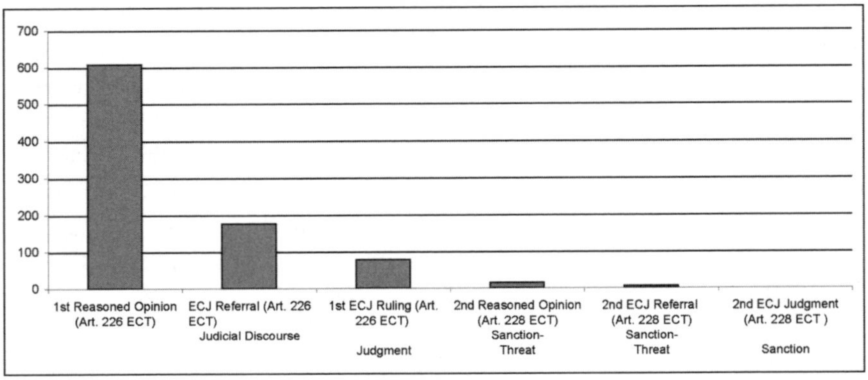

Figure 2.1 Secondary law infringement cases 1978–2000, EU-12

Sources: Annual Reports of the European Commission (see also Annex)

Figure 2.1 further shows that the majority of cases are settled in the early stages of the EU infringement proceedings, in which the parties engage in a political bilateral dialogue and compliance bargaining (see also Mendrinou 1996: 4–6, Tallberg 2002, Tallberg and Jönsson 2001). Nevertheless, this study exclusively focuses on the role of the ECJ, since all Court cases are hard cases for the prospects of international institutions to talk states into compliance. Commonly, states' resistance to domestic changes is extremely strong for ECJ referrals. Otherwise a consensus or compromise regarding the interpretation of the disputed norm would have emerged in earlier stages. Moreover, the current trend towards the increasing legalization of international institutions reflects a widely shared belief that this increases compliance rates and the effective-

[4] Up to 2009, the ECJ has imposed financial penalties in nine cases, of which four are instances of incorrect legal transpositions (see also footnotes 2 and 3 in chapter 1). Until 2000, the ECJ issued financial penalties in only one case: Greece was convicted in 2000 for incorrectly implementing the waste framework directive (C-38791).

ness of law beyond the nation-state (Alter 2003). Yet we know very little about the conditions under which these newly created or strengthened international courts facilitate compliance. Thus, this book examines how international courts succeed in talking states out of norm violations. How and under which conditions are the widespread instruments of judicial discourses, judgments, and sanctions effective?

If we take a closer look at the effectiveness of the ECJ in instances of delayed or incorrect transpositions,[5] we see again that judicial compliance instruments are always applied in the same order, but are only sometimes successful (Figure 2.2). Moreover, the variation of the effectiveness of judicial discourses, judgments and sanction-threats is very limited between states. In absolute terms, we can observe a leader-laggard pattern on failed transpositions of EU secondary law. If we look at the number of opened infringement cases, Italy, Belgium and Greece are the poorest compliers, while Denmark, the Netherlands, and the United Kingdom are compliance leaders (Figure 2.2). This distribution is relatively stable over the different stages of the infringement procedure, but becomes less pronounced with each additional stage, since all instances of non-compliance get settled in the end. It is remarkable that in each of the cases the ECJ applies its instruments in the same order, but their effectiveness of inducing compliance varies. While some judicial discourses and some judgments foster compliance in each of the states, some judicial discourses and some judgments fail to have this effect – even vis-à-vis the same state. It is simply not the case that a particular compliance instrument, for example a judicial discourse, is highly effective for one group of states, but not if it is applied to another group.

The very fact that compliance instruments are applied in the same order to all cases alike, but are not equally effective in settling cases is puzzling for legalization approaches (Abbott *et al.* 2000, Goldstein *et al.* 2000, Lutz and Sikkink 2000). Legalization approaches focus on the institutional design and in particular on the role of legal institutions (e.g. hard vs. soft law, monitoring institutions, dispute settlement procedures) for compliance with law beyond the nation state (e.g. Abbott *et al.* 2000). Informed by neo-liberal theory, they regard the free-rider problem as the central obstacle for international cooperation. While some states comply

[5] This book exclusively focuses on cases of delayed and incorrect transpositions. This limits the number of crucial actors to governments as respondents to compliance instruments of the ECJ and, depending on whether a judgment is transposed by executive decrees or laws, also national parliaments, instead of also including central-state, regional, and local administrations (see also Annexe).

with international law, others abstain from investing costs and fail to legally implement it. In order to prevent norm violations, legalization approaches point to hard law and its high degree of obligation and precision (Goldstein *et al.* 2000: 386–7) and to institutional transparency-creating mechanisms such as centralized or decentralized monitoring systems (Mitchell 1996: 17–20). Yet breaches of law beyond the nation-state cannot be completely prevented (e.g. Conant 2002, Falkner *et al.* 2005, Mendrinou 1996). Hence, legalization approaches emphasize the importance of institutionalized infringement and dispute settlement mechanisms for restoring compliance. Institutions are highly legalized if third parties (and not only states) have the right to file complaints (Alter 2006, Reinhardt 2001), if dispute settlement is not voluntary (Steinberg 2002), if judicial discourses take place, if courts can issue binding rulings (Abbott and Snidal 2000: 401–16, Smith 2000: 142–3) and if judges are independent (e.g. tenure, payment) (Keohane, Moravcsik and Slaughter 2000: 461–2). Most of the legalization approaches argue that high legalization of an international institution translates into higher compliance rates with its laws (Alter 2003, Chayes and Handler-Chayes 1995, Keohane, Moravcsik and Slaughter 2000).[6] Applied to the toolbox of compliance instruments, legalization approaches would expect that the more legalized that compliance instruments are in the toolbox of an international institution, the less likely it is that non-compliance prevails. At first glance, the very fact that the number of open cases in the EU infringement proceeding drops from stage to stage supports this expectation (see Figures 2.1, 2.2). Yet every case passed on to the next stage indicates that a particular compliance-restoring instrument has been ineffective. However, since legalization approaches focus on institutional design variables and seek to explain compliance differences across international institutions, they cannot explain why institutionalized instruments, such as a judicial discourse or a judgment, are sometimes effective, but fail to end the norm violation in other cases – possibly even against one and the same government.

On the aggregate level, the success of the highly legalized EU and its compliance toolbox is good news for the effectiveness of EU law and indicates that the EU is truly a political and legal community. While the broader picture looks promising, we do not know how and under which conditions cases in which states' non-compliance preferences were very strong and prevented early settlements, can be transformed into compli-

[6] Others argue that compliance is higher if international courts are less independent from the constituting states (Posner and Yoo 2005), since less independent courts tend not to issue too many norm interpretations unfitting to state preferences.

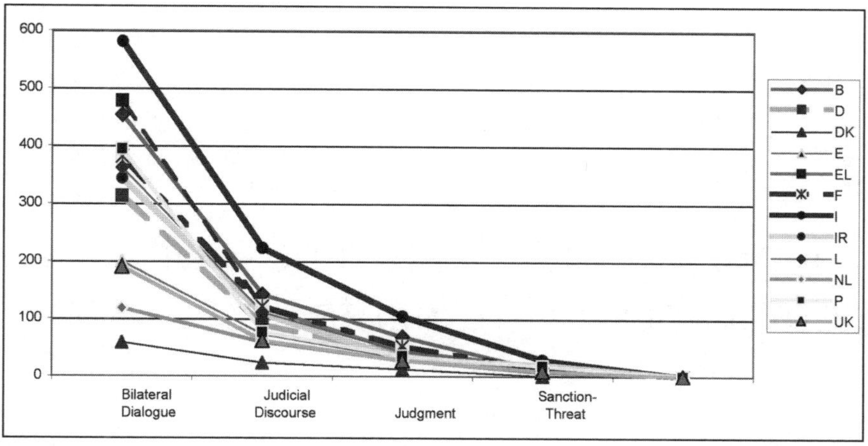

Figure 2.2 Absolute number of infringements on delayed and incorrect transpositions, 1978–2000

Sources: EURLEX database, Annual Reports of the European Commission, European Commission 2000 (see also Annexe)

Key:
B – Belgium; D – Germany; DK – Denmark; E – Spain; EL – Greece; F – France; I – Italy; IR – Ireland; L – Luxembourg; NL – Netherlands; P – Portugal; UK – United Kingdom

ance. More precisely: *Under which conditions are the instruments of judicial discourses, judgments, and sanction-threats effective in ending norm violations?* Several important issues are subsumed under this question: What role do judicial discourses play in restoring compliance? Why are governments in some cases more easily talked into compliance than in others? How do judgments operate and why do they only sometimes end norm violations? How important is the shadow of sanctions? Are some cases only settled because states shy away from the possibility of future financial penalties?

3

Theorizing the effectiveness of compliance instruments

We have seen that judicial discourses, judgments and sanction-threats are always applied in the same order to hard cases of non-compliance that have been dragged to the ECJ. Yet the two judicial instruments in particular are not always equally successful in abolishing non-compliance. Some judicial discourses succeed in quickly fostering compliance, others fail and require judgments to end norm violations and yet others even need an additional looming sanction-threat before cases can be settled. In order to solve the empirical puzzle why one and the same instrument is sometimes effective, but fails to end norm violations in other instances, even for the same state and the same government, this chapter examines how judicial discourse, judgments, and sanction-threats operate and inquires into the scope conditions for their success.

3.I Rationalist and constructivist pathways to compliance

In principle, social phenomena, including the operation of compliance instruments, can be reconstructed in a rationalist or in a constructivist manner. For example, judicial discourses can be characterized either as exchanges of legal arguments in Court that accelerate persuasion processes and compliance (constructivism), or as bargaining in the shadow of the Court that induces adaptations of strategic preferences and compliance compromises (rationalism). Although both pathways to compliance are theoretically possible, rationalist and constructivist action-theoretical assumptions matter, due to two crucial differences that they bring about. Firstly, the scope conditions for the effectiveness of compliance instruments differ, depending on whether a particular instrument operates on a constructivist or on a rationalist logic. Secondly, compliance instruments operating according to a constructivist logic facilitate persuasion processes related to normative ideas and a comprehensive form of compliance, while instruments operating according to a rationalist mechanism foster cost-related adaptations and a minimalist form of compliance (see 3.II).

Rationalism is based on a methodological-individualist concept of rationality, according to which actors are prior to and can be studied independent of social structures. They have substantial interests that are exogenous and fixed, while preferences over strategies on how interests should be pursued can change during interactions (Snidal 2002). Interactions are conceptualized as bargaining processes, in which strategic rational actors exchange information on costly constraints (Scharpf 1989a, Schelling 1978). Thereby, they adapt preferences on how to best pursue their given substantial interests to new information on costly constraints. In rationalist accounts, scope conditions for the effectiveness of compliance instruments are related to calculations on benefits and costs associated with different actions. If compliance instruments manage to increase non-compliance costs so that they exceed domestic benefits arising from norm violations, states adapt strategic positions and shift into compliance. Thus, judicial discourses, judgments, and sanction threats are successful, if bargaining acts are exchanged that considerably increase non-compliance costs, e.g. through threats of procedural costs during judicial discourses, threats of reputational losses on the EU level concerning judgments, or financial costs regarding sanctions. Since costs have to outweigh the benefits of non-compliance, the instruments are expected to be more effective the lower the issue salience or the weaker the non-compliance constituencies are.

By contrast, scope conditions for the effectiveness of compliance instruments differ considerably if they operate according to a constructivist mechanism. Constructivism rests on the ontological assumption that intersubjective meaning is embedded in institutions and influences identities as well as the development of substantial policy interests (Wendt 1999). Intersubjective meaning is reproduced but can also change in interactions in which communicative action takes place. If actors alter their beliefs on truth, righteousness and appropriateness in the wake of better arguments, substantial policy interests will change endogenously (Habermas 1995a, Müller 1995, Risse 2002). Thus, compliance instruments end norm violations, if arguments are exchanged according to which previously upheld norm interpretations are less true, rightful or appropriate. Consequently, the scope conditions facilitating compliance could relate to either the nature of the arguments, such as the superior expertise of advocates in judicial discourses, or the openness of state actors to be persuaded.

Table 3.1 Rationalist and constructivist pathways to compliance

	Rationalist approaches	*Constructivist approaches*
Rationality	Strategic rationality (means – ends calculations govern actions)	Communicative rationality (actions are embedded in social contexts, interests are at disposal of the better argument)
Typical speech acts in interactions	Bargaining acts (demands, threats, concessions, eventually linked to reasons related to the subjective world)	Arguments (propositions with reasons related to the inter subjective world)
Potential impact of communicated ideas	Adaptation of strategic preferences to costly external constraints	Adaptation of policy-related ideas to norms of appropriateness
Outcomes	*Minimalist compliance*	*Comprehensive compliance*

3.II Types of compliance

There is a second important difference between rationalist and constructivist causal reconstructions: the nature of domestic changes varies depending on whether an instrument operates on a rationalist or on a constructivist basis.

Effective bargaining processes facilitate not only changes of strategic positions, but also an *undemanding form of compliance.* If costs exceed non-compliance benefits, states adapt strategic preferences. In order to avoid prohibitive costs arising from norm violations, they engage in legal adaptations. At the same time, their policy interests are not altered and still point towards non-compliance. In this situation, it is strategically rational for states to incompletely change legal acts that define only vaguely what constitutes norm-reproducing and norm-violating action. States can do so by using ambiguous concepts, complex exceptional clauses, or introducing overlaps with other norms. On the one hand, legal changes that do not obviously violate EU law avoid non-compliance costs (e.g. in forms of penalties). On the other hand, undemanding transpositions with lots of ambiguous concepts, and overlapping complex and conflicting rules, create windows of opportunity to shift back into lax and less costly norm definitions in the stage of practical implementation, as soon as external constraints lessen and non-compliance costs decrease, for example after the Commission closes a case (*minimalist compliance*). In contrast, demanding and comprehensive legal changes that clearly and unambiguously define what constitutes compliance and what does not (*comprehensive compliance*) would not be strategically rational: abstaining from imprecise and ill-defined concepts, from broad and complex exceptions, and from creating overlaps with other legal norms pre-empts future lax, cost-saving norm applications, which become strategically rational once external costly constraints decrease.

Compliance instruments based on constructivist causal mechanisms can account for a *demanding form of compliance. Comprehensive compliance* is characterized by underlying normative or policy-related ideational changes that trigger complete legal adaptations, allowing for the full and comprehensive reproduction of the norm. During processes of argumentation in judicial discourses, in judgments, or through sanctions, states can learn that their interpretations of disputed norms were less true, apt or correct than a new one and that initial policy positions can no longer be justified with good and valid arguments. This form of argumentative entrapment changes the parameters for action: continuing non-compliance would be inappropriate for affected states, violating integrity and consistency norms. States can only attain normative consistency and integrity through comprehensively adapting legal acts removing the possibility of using backdoors to violate the formerly contested norms in the future again. By contrast, shifting into minimalist, cost-saving forms of compliance risks or even invites inappropriate norm violations in the implementation stage and is therefore not an option.

In the absence of effective arguing and effective bargaining processes, compliance instruments should fail to be effective in ending norm violations so that the null hypothesis expects continued non-compliance.

Why should we bother investigating whether a case ends in minimalist or in comprehensive compliance? The answer is simply that the nature of domestic change affects the effectiveness of EU law. The more comprehensive domestic legal changes are, the fewer legal uncertainties and norm divergences can emerge in the process of practical implementation. As a consequence, domestic law that was subject to comprehensive legal changes is better equipped to fulfil its regulatory or protective purpose. On the other hand, minimalist transpositions are more likely to still entail a high number of legal uncertainties leading to applicatory margins of manoeuvre for implementation authorities. Such minimalist transpositions foster less effective and less coherent applications of EU law and restrain some of its regulatory ambitions. As a consequence, infringement cases that end in comprehensive compliance are less likely to be subject to subsequent domestic court cases on the issue that was at stake in Court, as well as being less likely to be referred to the ECJ again for specifications via the preliminary ruling procedure (Art. 234 ECT). Cases ending in comprehensive compliance, by contrast, are less prone to domestic legal conflicts, which reduces the probability that they be referred to the ECJ via the decentralized preliminary ruling procedure (Art. 234) in subsequent years (see also Chapter 8).

The dependent variable of this study, the nature of domestic change, entails ideational and legal adaptations. Accordingly, it is operationalized via a two-step indicator.

Ideational change cannot be directly observed and is therefore measured by changes in the rhetoric of governments in response to compliance instruments. Before the case reached the ECJ, we will analyse how governments and involved ministries framed the issue at stake: Which normative, scientific and cost-related arguments did they make in order to justify their initially preferred transposition of the EU law in question? After a compliance instrument had been applied, we examine possible changes in the rhetoric: Do they highlight normative aspects and positive elements of the EU directive and stick to that even after domestic cost or external sanctions cease to cast a shadow over the government (e.g. because the Commission closed the case)? If this is the case, the involved actors undertook changes of substantial policy ideas as expected by constructivist hypotheses on compliance instruments.[1] By contrast, if governments focus on the cost implications of the EU law in question and its national adaptation and do so in particular after the successful application of a compliance instrument, it is very likely that changes of strategic positions took place – as expected by the rationalist approach.[2] If

[1] In response to compliance instruments operating according to a constructivist logic, states adjust normative ideas, but not cost–benefit related ones. Hence, governments and lead ministries should refer to the appropriateness, truth and righteousness of an issue, apply the same policy frame before *and* after domestic or external sanction-threats cast a shadow over the government (e.g. after the Commission closed cases or public and media attention declined). Moreover, governments that adapted normative ideas should not blame the ECJ or the EU as being ultimately responsible for the domestic adaptation, in order to justify new policies vis-à-vis non-compliance constituencies and to avoid electoral ex-post sanctions.

[2] If states adapt strategic ideas to increasing domestic or external non-compliance costs, governments do not apply a positive normative language of righteousness, appropriateness, or truth in the longer run. Rather, they refer to high compliance expenditures and mention costs associated with demanding norm interpretations. If external sanction-threats have been effective, governments highlight costs or benefits of non-compliance and blame the EU as being ultimately responsible for domestic changes. Through tied hands references, governments prevent domestic damages of reputation vis-à-vis non-compliance constituencies. As soon as costly external constraints decline, for example because the Commission closed infringement cases,

a compliance instrument fails to end norm violations, there are no ideational changes and non-compliance persists. Hence, governments stick to the old rhetoric, repeat their initial beliefs and do not adjust language games.

Legal changes into comprehensive or minimalist compliance can be directly observed by analysing the affected legal acts. What issues were problematic in the initial transpositions? Do lead ministries introduce legal changes and were they comprehensive or incomplete? Are all issues at stake in the Court case legally transposed? Does the new legal act introduce new and undefined concepts, complex interconnections within the norm, or broad and complex exceptional clauses? How does the new act fit into the domestic legal landscape? Are there many or few overlaps with other legal acts and do they create ambiguities and legal uncertainty?

Ideational changes in which actors adapt to norms of appropriateness facilitate comprehensive legal changes that foster the full reproduction of a demanding norm interpretation in avoiding ambiguous and underspecified concepts, extensive exceptional clauses, and overlapping incompatible legal acts. Strategic ideational changes in which actors adapt to costly constraints facilitate incomplete legal adaptations, which use underspecified or ambiguous concepts, introduce several overlaps with other legal acts, and extensively rely on exceptional clauses. In contrast to comprehensive legal changes, incomplete ones create windows of opportunity to pursue less demanding and less costly norm interpretations in future stages (e.g. during the stage of practical application), once costly constraints decline and norm violations become again more beneficial than compliance. If a compliance instrument is not effective at all, governments do not engage in legal adaptations, but continue non-compliance.

In order to obtain the information to reconstruct ideational and legal changes, we draw on a broad variety of data sources. These include protocols of parliamentary debates, committee sessions, written and oral parliamentary answer sessions, interviews with involved stakeholders and their staff, and newspaper reports on public speeches, as well as several legal databases.[3]

---

governments readjust strategic positions and shift back into opposing norms at stake. If domestic sanction-threats were successful, governments highlight the benefits of a certain norm in a window dressing manner for a very brief period. As soon as domestic threats cease to exist, governments shift into criticisms of the contested norm and apply cost-benefit calculations.

[3] For information on data sources, see Annexe.

3.III ECJ compliance instruments

Do state-actors follow a strategic cost–benefit oriented logic of action or are they guided by norms of appropriateness and communicative action? The question on the 'correct' micro foundation of social science approaches became prominent in the 1990s when social constructivism was on the rise and rationalist assumptions became challenged by a social conceptualization of actors' behaviour (e.g. Onuf 1989, Wendt 1987). At first, both assumptions were treated as incompatible, mutually exclusive alternatives: either states act according to a strategic or to a communicative/normative rationality. In this stage, constructivist research focused on the question of whether communicative action actually takes place in international affairs (e.g. Müller 1994, Risse 2000). After it became clear that this was the case, but that most often arguments and bargaining acts are exchanged, bridge-building approaches became prominent and sought to identify conditions under which one of the micro-foundations can more adequately explain observed behaviour in order to integrate bargaining and arguing within one framework (e.g. Checkel 2004, Müller 2004). They inquired into questions such as: Under which conditions is arguing effective and when does it facilitate persuasion processes? This brought about a rich set of competing hypotheses and insights, drawing on the Habermasian discourse theory (e.g. Deitelhoff and Müller 2005) and social psychology (e.g. Checkel 2006), such as that variables increasing the quantity of argumentative speech acts are conducive to effective arguing or that actors with few prior beliefs are more open to persuasion, in particular under conditions of uncertainty. The third wave of dealing with both action-theories pragmatically reconciled them in assuming that one and the same actor can principally shift from strategic into norm-guided action and vice versa (e.g. March and Olsen 1998). Repertoires for action are rich and actors exchange arguments as well as bargaining acts. Accordingly, it is essential to test competing rationalist and constructivist hypotheses against each other, while it is not necessary to stick to either one action-theoretical micro foundation for a theoretical framework that sequentially encompasses several elements.

This chapter follows the latter approach in assuming that bargaining and arguing dynamics can in principle take place in all cases and for all compliance instruments, but some institutional settings induce the exchange of arguments (e.g. judicial discourses) and other instruments foster bargaining acts (e.g. sanction-threats). It is thus likely that actors are sequentially exposed to argumentative dynamics and normative considerations as well as to bargaining dynamics and cost–benefit calculations, in particular if different compliance instruments accelerate different modes of interaction. During bargaining processes, an actor might adapt policies to changing costs and might shift into minimalist compliance. Yet if argumentative dynamics take place in another case, the same actor might adapt policies to changes in the normative structure and shift into comprehensive compliance.

Although actors are capable of both modes of action, in which way they behave is not completely arbitrary. Some contextual variables (and some compliance instruments, such as the judicial discourse) foster the exchange of arguments so that constructivist theorizing might be better able to capture real-world dynamics and explain outcomes than rationalist accounts. Other contextual variables (and some compliance instruments, such as sanction-threats) accelerate bargaining dynamics so that rationalist accounts might be better able to capture real-world dynamics and explain outcomes than constructivist ones. In analysing whether a particular compliance instrument is conducive to arguing or to bargaining dynamics, we get a glimpse of which causal reconstruction, rationalism or constructivism, is more adequate to theorize action in a particular context. In applying this reasoning, this chapter advances a constructivist hypothesis on the operation of judicial discourses, a rationalist as well as a constructivist one on judgments and a rationalist hypothesis on sanction-threats. Yet since the acceleration of one type of speech act (e.g. arguments) does not deterministically exclude the exchange of the other type of speech act (e.g. threats), we also formulate alternative hypotheses for each of the instruments.

Judicial discourses

Are judicial discourses more conducive to arguing and comprehensive compliance than to bargaining and minimalist compliance? Do judicial discourses facilitate the use of one type of speech acts? Are states more exposed to argumentative than to bargaining dynamics? Under which conditions are judicial discourses effective and which type of compliance do they facilitate? This section argues that judicial discourses induce the use of arguments over bargaining speech acts and tend to foster a comprehensive form of compliance. Since not every judicial discourse is effective, although arguments are exchanged in all cases, we examine in a second step the scope conditions under which judicial discourses successfully induce policy changes and the conditions under which non-compliance is likely to be maintained. Thirdly, this section formulates two alternative rationalist hypotheses on the operation and the scope conditions for the success of judicial discourses and finally discusses the operationalization of its hypotheses.

Once cases are referred to the ECJ, judicial discourses start and end on average two years later with either a Court judgment or the withdrawal of the case. Judicial discourses take place between European and national advocates in a two-stage written and oral procedure. Once all judicial arguments and arguments related to matters of facts are exchanged in writing, a rapporteur summarizes the first stage of the discourse for the ECJ. Thereafter, an oral procedure takes place, in which both advocates concentrate on the remaining contested issues of the norm at stake. Once all legal points are exchanged, the European Advocate General prepares a written opinion for the ECJ, which then decides the case by consensus (European Court of Justice 1991, European Court of Justice 2006).

After the European Commission opens an infringement proceeding, political aspects are at the centre of debates between the European Commission and the respective state (Snyder 1993: 40, Tallberg and Christer 1998). By contrast, judicial discourses are not prone to bargaining but conducive to the use of argumentative speech acts. Judicial aspects rather than political considerations become increasingly important and legal arguments related to legal acts in question dominate the debates (see also Alexy 1983, Onuf 1989, Rasmussen 1986: 75, also interviews ECJ#1, 09–03–05, ECJ#2, 16–03–05; COM#2, 02–03–05, Federal Ministry#, 08–10–04). Professionalization additionally reinforces the use of judicial reasoning based on legal arguments since advocates are trained to apply a set of judicial techniques for the interpretation of disputed norms ('judicial methods') (Gulmann 1980, Rasmussen 1986: 171–4).

According to judicial positivism there is a single correct interpretation of a norm, which judicial reasoning has to uncover (Hart 1961, Kelsen 1966). However, the 'true' interpretation of a norm is not just out there.[4] Instead, an intersubjectively valid interpretation of a disputed norm has to be developed in a process of social construction. This process is a judicial discourse. It is structured by professional norms: in judicial discourses the advocates of the parties exchange legal arguments based on the canon of interpretational techniques which they have acquired through their professional training, in order to defend their positions and to persuade the other legal experts involved (Dewey 1924, Fiss 1982, Habermas 1998). Hence, the institutional context of judicial discourses favours speech acts of arguing over bargaining, because the latter are contextually

[4] Judicial reasoning sometimes refers to other values and norms than the issue in question. It is this value-laden nature which hampers objectivism (Klare 1998, Wheeler Cook 1927). Moreover, the selection and presentation of relevant 'facts' introduces subjectivity (Brest 1982, Dewey 1924, Fiss 1982, Habermas 1998).

inappropriate in front of the ECJ (interview ECJ #2, 16–03–05; see also protocols, e.g. Advocate General 1998b, Advocate General 2000). Consequently, the compliance instrument 'judicial discourse' is likely to operate according to a constructivist logic, which would mean that it is conducive to comprehensive compliance. Although judicial arguing takes place in all judicial discourses, not all of them effectively end norm violations. Exchanging arguments alone is not sufficient to change ideas underlying a country's initial non-compliance position: not every argument is per se good, convincing, and suited to persuade others. Therefore, crucial questions are: What characterizes a good judicial argument and how does this trigger compliance? Under which conditions can judicial discourses foster compliance and when do they fail?

The next paragraphs will argue that judicial discourses are only effective if the advocates of the parties do not talk at cross purposes but develop a common, intersubjectively valid norm definition and thereby argumentatively entrap the governments.[5] This requires that both advocates:

- actively participate in the discourse,
- focus on the same legal norm, and
- apply a method of judicial interpretation that fits the complexity of the interpretational problem at hand.

If those conditions are not met, the advocates talk at cross purposes and cannot develop a norm interpretation that they regard as professionally superior. As a consequence, governments and lead ministries cannot become argumentatively entrapped and non-compliance prevails.

Active engagement is a very precondition for successful judicial discourses, since two parties are required to develop an intersubjectively as opposed to a subjectively valid interpretation. This requires that both participants exchange judicial arguments, rather than either being silent altogether or making pragmatic or political claims instead of using the canon of judicial interpretational techniques. Another important precondition for successful processes of social construction is that the actors are not talking at cross purposes. This requires that the advocates in judicial discourses are analysing the same legal act, instead of each focusing on different ones. For example, if the European advocate exclusively analyses the EU directive in question and the national advocate only focuses on the

[5] If judicial discourses end in dissent, advocates do not argumentatively entrap national governments, and the compliance instrument 'judicial discourse' fails to be successful so that non-compliance continues even after the judicial discourse ends.

domestic legal act concerned, they cannot arrive at a common understanding of how to best resolve the interpretational issue at stake. The last important condition for an effective judicial discourse, namely that the advocates have to use a method of legal interpretation that matches the complexity of the issue at stake, is the most difficult one. A good and persuasive argument has to be intersubjectively valid. This presupposes that the participants of a discourse share a yardstick for the evaluation of the quality of speech acts so that they can commonly filter good and convincing from bad and unconvincing claims and thereby incrementally arrive at a consensus on how the norm should best be interpreted. If a common yardstick for the measurement of the goodness of claims is lacking, the actors simply talk at cross purposes during the discourse and cannot establish a norm definition which both sides accept as right, appropriate, true, or – in the case of a judicial discourse – professionally superior.

In general, truth, rightness and appropriateness are possible yardsticks to assess the quality of argumentative speech acts. If actors share them, they are able to incrementally develop consensual perspectives, because they can commonly filter good and convincing from less compelling ideas and incrementally arrive at a consensus. The standard of truth encompasses epistemological and methodological principles as well as ontological elements. Argumentative interactions, in which the quality of arguments can be measured based on standards of truth, are conducive to a consensual norm definition when the actors share expertise on the subject matter. However, truth-related reasoning becomes meaningless when there is no consensus on whether an effect reproduces or reinforces the norm proper to its content and scope. Thus, a necessary condition for the consensual development of a norm definition is the presence of a consensus on the common general interest which the norm reflects (Habermas 1995a: 42, Habermas 1992b, Habermas 1995b). For incorrect transpositions of EU secondary law, however, this is most likely disputed. Yet actors are not trapped in the dilemma that they can only develop a consensual norm definition when they consent on a common interest that the norm reflects as well as on the general meaning of the norm, while the very fact that the case has been carried on to the Court indicates that such a consensus is absent. The judicial discourse offers an expedient: It aims at the clarification of the contents and scope of disputed norms and, thus, of the standard of rightfulness itself. In order to clarify contested issues, judicial techniques of interpretation serve as additional yardsticks to assess the quality of arguments. In applying the *historical method* of judicial interpretation (as the broadest interpretational instrument), the ECJ defines the scope and content of directives through reference to the will of the norm-creators. The *teleological method* is the second broadest instrument, since it aims at defining the content and scope of a disputed norm or paragraph by analysing the general aim of the norm at hand or the broader legal context: What is the purpose of the treaties and how does it relate to the norm in question? The *systematic method* is less broad than the teleological method. It solves interpretational questions by analysing the paragraph or article in question in the context of other, similar legal norms: What can we learn from other norms for the disputed element in a particular norm? Do other norms have a similar internal logic and if so how are issues similar to the contested one interpreted in their contexts? The *teleological method* can also be used within the legal norm itself (*directive-immanent teleological method*). This technique is less broad than the non-directive-immanent methods of legal reasoning. In applying the directive-immanent teleological method, an advocate inquires into the purpose of the norm and analyses how far a particular interpretation of the element in question can positively contribute to the fulfilment of the norm's purpose or whether it would juxtapose the norm's aim. The *systematic method* can also be applied within one legal norm (*directive-immanent systematic method*) and solves interpretational questions by analysing the paragraph or article in question in the context of the whole legal norm: Are new concepts introduced in other paragraphs that define or delimit the issue in question? Are exceptions in other parts of the norm named and enumerated and do they impact scope and content of the interpretational issue? The narrowest interpretational device is the *wording method* which aims at solving interpretational differences by analysing the exact phrasing of the paragraphs in question: Are new concepts introduced? How are they defined? Are exceptions named and enumerated?[6]

Judicial discourses can only be effective if the advocates actively participate in the discourse, focus on the same legal act, and apply methods of judicial interpretation that fit the complexity of the interpretational problem at hand. Only under these conditions is it likely that the

[6] An empirical analysis of the ECJ protocols reveals that participants of judicial discourses have almost never applied the historical method of judicial reasoning and the broad teleological method that refers to basic aims of European integration (Gulmann 1980). Instead, European and state advocates extensively rely on more specific directive-immanent techniques of legal reasoning that facilitate less far-reaching readings of the disputed norm such as wording, systematic and directive-immanent teleological methods of interpretation (see also Chapters 4–6). In front of the ECJ, advocates often start with a narrow interpretational technique, such as wording method, and often refer to broader ones, such as the directive-immanent teleological method of interpretation if the wording instrument fails to provide a single reading of the disputed element (Gulmann 1980).

advocates of the parties do not talk at cross purposes but can equally assess the quality of their claims, which allows them to possibly arrive at the same professional conclusion of how to best interpret the issue at stake.[7] Yet, similar to the fact that a shared yardstick for truth claims cannot help to solve questions of appropriateness and vice versa, not every method of judicial interpretation is suited to solve every interpretational problem. Some disputed issues are complex and characterized by imprecise, new or ill-defined concepts concerning aims, procedure and applicatory scopes, many and vague cross-references, several relevant paragraphs or articles, and complex exceptional clauses. Other interpretational problems have narrow interpretational scopes and are highly specific and characterized by relatively precise concepts, few cross-references and detailed or even no exceptional rules. In order to select a single interpretation out of the variety of possible norm readings, a high goodness of fit between the complexity of the interpretational problem at hand and the shared judicial method is required. If the phrasing of a norm specifically addresses the interpretational problem and the actors commonly apply the wording device to this paragraph, the match is high and a single interpretation can be funneled out of the variety of possible norm interpretations. For complex interpretational problems, in which the issue at stake is not directly addressed, because concepts are vague or not defined, broad and complex exceptional clauses apply, or different paragraphs or articles are relevant, a narrow interpretational method

---

It is not surprising that the very broad historical and the also very broad teleological methods are not often used. Since states and not the ECJ were prominently involved in European policy-making, arguments related to 'the original will' of the norm creators will most likely be evaluated as 'not right', if the norm creators themselves have diverging memories of the 'original will' or if the ECJ doubts that states correctly recall the original will of states for disputed norms (since the norm creation is often more than 8 years ago). This prevents historical arguments from being persuasive and hinders effective arguing, changes of substantial policy interests and transformations into comprehensive compliance. Moreover, sometimes non-accused states join in the judicial discourse in order to support the accused state. If those states also doubt the correctness of the reconstruction of the original will, changes of substantial policy interests are additionally unlikely.

The ECJ has often been criticized for its dominant pattern of pro-Commission and, thus, pro-integration rulings (Garrett, Kelman and Schulz 1998). Prominent cases, such as the Costa case, in which the ECJ developed the doctrine of supremacy of European law, reveal that ECJ rulings can have an enormous impact on further dynamics of European Integration. In such rulings, the ECJ strengthens the supranational character of the integration project based on the very broad teleological method (Gulmann 1980: 189, 199, Rasmussen 1986: 149, 173, 180, 264, Snyder 1993: 40).

[7] Most often, infringement cases deal with two to four interpretational aspects (e.g. on applicatory scopes, procedures, aims) of the norm in question.

cannot generate a single interpretation. If a legal norm does not explicitly address the interpretational problem, but mentions the debated issue in different paragraphs or articles, the wording technique of legal reasoning fails to provide only one reading. This is because different articles or paragraphs, interpreted according to their wording, can lead to completely different interpretations of the whole norm, while the wording method provides no answer to the question of which article or paragraph should be given priority. Moreover, if the phrasing of the norm is silent with regard to the contested issue, it also fails to provide one interpretation. Two conclusions are possible: firstly that the interpretation is up to the states; secondly that a specific obligation was not enumerated, since it is obvious that it has to be subsumed under the contested norm. In contrast, disputes with broad interpretational scopes are better dealt with by broader interpretational methods (teleological, systematical), because they allow for developing a comprehensive reading of the whole norm. Interpretational problems with narrow scopes are best dealt with by narrow methods, since they are best for dealing with problems of detail. Broad legal methods of interpretation applied to a dispute with a narrow interpretational scope multiply the number of possible readings. This broadens content and scope ex-post and is not conducive to the incremental development of a consensual norm definition.

In short, successful judicial discourses require that the advocates of the parties exchange legal arguments, focus on the same legal act in question and use a judicial method of interpretation that matches the complexity of the interpretational problem at stake. If these conditions are met, the advocates of the parties will not talk at cross purposes but jointly sort good from less convincing judicial arguments so that they can agree on a particular norm interpretation as professionally superior.

But how does a professionally valid norm interpretation of a judicial discourse foster compliance within a state? In the course of the one to two years that a judicial discourse lasts on average, national advocates are in contact with the affected ministries and translate their concerns and preferences into judicial arguments. At the same time, they disseminate new ideas on judicial interpretations, as developed in the interaction with the European advocate to their governments. The process of two-level judicial arguing can incrementally trigger processes of ideational entrapment leading to compliance. If the advocates of the parties apply different judicial methods of argumentation or refer to different parts of the norm, they will talk at cross purposes and won't agree on how to best interpret the contested norm. By contrast, if the advocates of both parties happen to apply a judicial method of interpretation that fits with the interpretational scope of the problem at hand, the chances that they professionally disagree on how to best interpret the norm decline and they are more likely to arrive at the same conclusion. In such instances, national advocates will seek to convince the responsible ministries to accept the developed norm interpretation and abandon non-compliance. To this end, they can draw on their legal expertise and highlight the superiority of the new as compared to the old norm interpretation or argue that non-compliance can no longer be justified with good arguments vis-à-vis European enforcement authorities and domestic pro-compliance actors. If the involved ministries at a minimum accept the legal expertise of their own advocate, they are likely to become ideationally entrapped and convinced that they can no longer pursue their old non-compliance policies – either because the latter rested on a inferior norm interpretation, or simply because the old non-compliance policies cannot be justified with good arguments without violating norms of appropriateness, consistency and integrity. Hence, ideationally entrapped ministries and governments should strive to quickly reconcile policies with logics of appropriateness and normative consistency and integrity. Comprehensive compliance ensures that the logic of appropriateness and of normative consistency and integrity are not violated in the implementation stage. By contrast, minimalist compliance entails built-in uncertainties as windows of opportunity to shift into lax and less costly norm interpretations in the future, and invites practical violations of the new norm definition. This would again lead to violations of appropriateness, consistency and integrity norms, which argumentatively entrapped actors seek to avoid. Thus, in response to successful judicial discourses, states should shift into comprehensive compliance and should do so as quickly as possible.[8]

[8] Judicial discourses can have ideational entrapment effects even for strategic rational governments that are not consciously motivated to change ideas in the light of the better argument. According to the institutional logic of judicial discourses, a party can only win a case if its judicial arguments succeed in persuading the other party or, more importantly, the ECJ, of the superiority of a particular norm interpretation. To this end, advocates apply judicial methods, usually moving from narrow to broad ones. If states would oblige their advocates to use only a judicial method of legal interpretation that definitely supports the initial interests of a government, the national advocate would be forced to stick to one claim and could not respond properly to argumentative dynamics during the judicial discourse. This would severely reduce the chances of successfully convincing the Court or preserving initial national interests at least to some extent. Hence, forcing their advocates to use only a specific method of legal interpretation that safeguards the original interests of states is not at all a rational strategy for governments – and is empirically uncommon in front of the ECJ, as the eight case studies in this book show.

The constructivist hypothesis focuses on ideational entrapment according to which actors learn that their initial positions can no longer be defended with compelling arguments so that they are likely to adapt policies to norms of appropriateness, integrity and consistency in reaction to effective judicial discourses. Hence, it states: *Judicial discourses are likely to foster comprehensive compliance, if the advocates actively engage in the judicial discourse, if they analyse the same legal norm, and if they use a judicial method of interpretation with a high goodness of fit to the complexity of the interpretational problem at stake* (H1).

There are two versions of the rationalist alternative hypothesis on judicial discourses.

Firstly, the affected ministries and the government could perceive an emerging consensual norm definition as a costly external constraint to which they adapt strategically with minimalist compliance. If the actors maintained their old policies and continued non-compliance despite an emerging consensual judicial norm definition, they might face costs. Judicial discourses do not bring about financial costs or economic disadvantages, but a government that violates EU law although the legal experts have resolved the former interpretational difficulties might face reputational costs. If states continue to violate the norm in question despite the presence of a norm definition that advocates regard as legally correct, they might lose reputation in the eyes of the Commission and the European Court of Justice. This could have negative consequences for the cooperation with the Commission in the numerous negotiations on the creation of new EU law or for future infringement proceedings.[9] In order to avoid these negative implications, states could strategically adapt to an emerging judicially superior norm definition in shifting into minimalist compliance. On the one hand, minimalist policy changes that entail loopholes and ambiguities could pacify the Commission and the ECJ, but would allow states to shift back into less demanding norm implementations once the case is closed and the attention of the Commission and the ECJ has declined. Hence, the first rationalist alternative to the constructivist hypothesis on judicial discourses states: *Judicial discourses are likely to create a threat of reputational losses and foster minimalist compliance, if the advocates actively engage in the judicial discourse, if they analyse the same legal norm, and if they use a judicial method of interpretation*

[9] At the same time, it is unlikely that the government faces losses in reputation and electoral support by domestic norm proponents, since the latter have no access to ongoing judicial discourses and no information about an emerging consensual norm definition prior to the ECJ judgment.

with a high goodness of fit to the complexity of the interpretational problem at stake (H2a).

The second version of the alternative rationalist hypothesis on judicial discourses focuses on compliance bargaining. Bargaining speech acts are rarely if at all used in Court (see also Gulmann 1980, Rasmussen 1986).[10] However, informal compliance bargaining could take place between the state and the European Commission in the shadow of ECJ judicial discourses. States could approach the Commission outside the Court in order to negotiate a compromise. This is most likely to be successful if both sides share a conception of what constitutes bargaining power so that they avoid talking at cross purposes but instead meaningfully relate to each others' demands, concessions, offers and threats and incrementally establish a compromise norm interpretation. In such a setting, there is no formalized bargaining power, for example in the form of voting rights. Instead, bargaining power rests on a social construction of competencies for threats and concessions. The bargaining asset of the European Commission is its discretion to withdraw the case before the ECJ issues a ruling, if the Commission thinks that the respective state has ended the norm violation during the ongoing judicial discourse. The power of the Commission to not withdraw the case would be a bargaining threat. The state, on the other hand, cannot easily threaten the Commission in the shadow of the formal infringement procedure. The only obvious concession which states can offer to the Commission is to shift quickly into a less costly form of compliance instead of delaying domestic changes for several additional years until they eventually adopt policies reflecting a more demanding norm interpretation.

Hence, the second rationalist alternative to the constructivist hypothesis on judicial discourses states: *Informal compliance bargaining in the shadow of judicial discourse fosters quick legal adaptations and minimalist compliance, if the European Commission and the state mutually accept their bargaining capacities and incrementally arrive at a compromise norm interpretation* (H2b).

How do we know whether a judicial discourse should successfully end a norm violation or whether it should be doomed to fail?

[10] The advocates lack a shared standard for what constitutes bargaining power in judicial interactions and would therefore talk at cross purposes without reaching a compromise. The European advocate cannot threaten states with adverse ECJ judgments, since he or she cannot determine the decision of the judges. States have almost no bargaining powers either, because the ECJ is highly independent regarding its composition, tenure, payment, and terms of recall (see also Abbott *et al.* 2000: 419, Keohane, Moravcsik and Slaughter 2000: 460).

To operationalize the constructivist and the first rationalist hypotheses, we have to analyse whether both advocates actively made judicial arguments, whether they focused on the same legal norms, and which judicial techniques the advocates of the parties use, how broad the interpretational scope of the issue at stake is, and whether used methods of interpretation match the complexity of the contested problem. In the course of judicial discourses, advocates can use a variety of judicial techniques, which differ in the questions they raise and the specificity of the answers they can provide on how to best understand the purpose, aim, procedures and scopes of a norm. The narrow wording method aims at solving interpretational differences by analysing the wording of the paragraphs in question: Are new concepts introduced? How are they defined? Are exceptions named and enumerated? The broader systematic technique of interpretation solves interpretational questions by examining the paragraph or article in question in the context of the whole legal norm: Are new concepts introduced in other paragraphs that define or delimit the issue in question? Are exceptions in other parts of the norm named and enumerated and do they have an impact on the scope and content of the interpretational issue? The broad teleological methods of legal reasoning aims at defining the content and scope of a disputed norm or paragraph by analysing the broader legal context: What is the purpose of the treaties and how does it relate to the norm in question? Similar to judicial methods, contested issues also differ concerning their interpretational scope. A complex interpretational issue is characterized by different articles and paragraphs that apply to it, by unspecified concepts in the legal norm, by complex exceptional clauses, and by overlaps with other norms. A disputed issue with a narrow interpretational scope is less ambiguous concerning essential and applicable paragraphs or articles, and is characterized by well-defined crucial concepts, few and very specific exceptional clauses without ambivalent scope conditions, and has few overlaps with other legal norms that create legal uncertainty. Not every judicial method is suited to solve every interpretational question, but their interpretational scopes have to match. The narrow and highly specific wording technique cannot produce a single interpretation for complex issues. This is because the wording of different articles or paragraphs of a norm can lead to completely different conclusions of what the whole norm is about, which procedures it requires, and in which circumstances it should be applied. At the same time, there is no way of deciding which article or paragraph should be given priority out of the variety of wording-based interpretations. Moreover, issues with broad interpretational scopes might lack a definition of core concepts so that a wording-based interpretation is impossible. Yet for very specific interpretational problems, in which concepts are defined and the complexity of the issue is limited, a narrow wording-based interpretation can easily provide a professionally acceptable conclusion of how the norm should be understood. Issues with broad interpretational scopes are better dealt with by broader teleological or systematic methods. Broad judicial techniques of interpretation allow the development of a comprehensive reading of the whole norm, without stumbling over the fact that individual elements of a norm are not at all or hardly specified, or mentioned in several paragraphs, but are incompatible. Hence, if both parties apply the same judicial means of interpretation and if this additionally fits the complexity of the disputed issue, we expect that national advocates argumentatively entrap the responsible ministries,[11] which change normative ideas and bring about comprehensive legal changes. If the compliance instrument of 'judicial discourse' fails, because the advocates share no judicial method or because the only shared judicial method of interpretation does not match the issue at stake, non-compliance should prevail.

The constructivist judicial discourse hypothesis is confirmed if we observe firstly that the advocates of the parties do not argue at cross purposes but both engage in judicial argumentation, focus on the same legal norm and use a judicial method that fits the interpretational scope of the problem at stake. Secondly, if the consensual norm interpretation deviates from the initial position of the state, we should observe that state actors adapt their rhetoric to changes in policy ideas (e.g. portray the EU norm or the new policy positively and do so also after the case is closed) and quickly introduce comprehensive policy changes (e.g. adapt legal acts comprehensively).[12] The hypothesis would be falsified if the judicial discourse fostered comprehensive compliance, although the advocates did not both engage in judicial argumentation (e.g. one party is completely silent, or one party makes only political or pragmatic arguments), did not focus on the same legal act (e.g. one party focuses only on the EU directive

[11] Normative entrapment cannot be directly observed since the interactions between ministries and national advocates do not leave publicly accessible paper trails. In addition, ECJ cases are sensitive political issues. Thus, the interviewees gave no information on the micro-processes underlying ideational and legal adaptations in response to judicial discourses although all case studies included a time-lag of several years.

[12] Note that comprehensive legal changes might take time. Hence, in some cases of successful judicial discourses, legal changes might have been initiated but not yet completed so that the ECJ would issue a judgment. In cases in which the judicial discourse was effective but a judgment was nevertheless ruled, already initiated domestic changes are usually completed within only a couple of months of the judgment.

in question, while the other party focuses only on the national legal act in question), and did not use a method of legal interpretation fitting to the complexity of the issue at stake (e.g. applying a narrow method to a complex issue). Secondly, the constructivist hypothesis would be disconfirmed if the advocates actively engaged in judicial arguments, focused on the same legal act, and used a method of interpretation that fits the complexity of the issue at stake, but the judicial discourse did not foster ideational and legal change reflecting comprehensive compliance.

The first rationalist hypothesis is confirmed if the advocates of the parties both exchange judicial arguments, focus on the same legal act and use a judicial method that fits the interpretational scope of the problem at stake, and if we observe that states adapt their strategic positions and shift into minimalist compliance. In this case, we expect that states do only temporarily but not consistently change their rhetoric and shift back into criticizing the EU directive or into praising the old policy approach and the underlying frames once the Commission has closed the case so that the threat of reputational losses ceases to exist. Similarly, we expect states to pursue only minimalist legal changes, so that ambiguities, overlaps with norms, and broad and complex exceptional clauses can be used to pursue a less demanding practical norm implementation once the case is closed and reputational losses are unlikely since the attention of the Commission and the ECJ declines.

The operationalization of the second rationalist hypothesis is more challenging, simply because the publicly available documentation on the case entails no information on compliance bargaining. In addition, since none of the actors revealed any information on compliance bargaining in interviews,[13] we cannot directly analyse the exchanged threats, concessions and promises and make inferences as to whether it is likely that both parties could relate to each other meaningfully and foster a compromise. Instead of analysing exchanged bargaining acts, we focus on the dynamics that successful compliance bargaining should trigger on the way to a minimalist legal adaptation. If bargaining were successful in fostering a compromise, the state's obligation would be to quickly adapt legal acts before the judicial discourse ends, while the Commission should withdraw the case before the ECJ issues a judgment. If both observable dynamics lead to ideational and legal adaptation resembling minimalist compliance, the rationalist hypothesis would be confirmed. By contrast, the hypothesis would firstly be falsified if Commission and state actors show bargaining

[13] Infringement cases that reach the ECJ are politically very sensitive so that information on underlying dynamics if often confidential (see also Annex).

dynamics and quickly adapt legal acts and withdraw the case, but the outcome reflects comprehensive compliance, and secondly not be confirmed if the judicial discourse fosters minimalist compliance, although the Commission did not withdraw the case or the state did not quickly adapt legal acts before the judgment.

The data on the independent variables stem from publicly available protocols of the cases, from a Commission database on compliance with EU secondary and primary law, from newspapers and from interviews with involved state and European actors.[14]

Judgments

While some states comply with a European directive, others abstain from investing resources and fail to legally implement it. In order to prevent norm violations, legalization approaches point to hard law and its high degree of obligation and precision (Goldstein *et al.* 2000: 386–7) and to institutional transparency-creating mechanisms, such as centralized or decentralized monitoring systems (Mitchell 1996: 17–20). Breaches of law beyond the nation-state cannot be completely avoided and every international organization grapples with instances of non-compliance (e.g. Conant 2002, Falkner *et al.* 2005, Mendrinou 1996). Hence, legalization approaches emphasize the importance of judicial procedures for restoring compliance. Such mechanisms are highly legalized if third parties (and not only states) have the right to file complaints (Alter 2006, Reinhardt 2001), if dispute settlement is not voluntary (Steinberg 2002), if courts can issue binding rulings (Abbott and Snidal 2000: 401–16, Smith 2000: 142–3), and if judges are independent (e.g. tenure, payment) (Keohane, Moravcsik and Slaughter 2000: 461–2). According to these criteria, the EU is a highly legalized institution. The ECJ is composed of independent judges and can issue binding rulings.

Yet the empirical pattern showed that not all ECJ judgments foster compliance. This is a puzzle for legalisation approaches, which cannot explain why one and the same state might end non-compliance in response to an ECJ judgment, while other cases are dragged on and require the application of sanction-threats. Against this background, this section

[14] The protocols of the European Advocate General and the ECJ are available in the EU Eurlex database (http://eur-lex.europa.eu/en/index.htm). The data on non-compliance (including on withdrawal cases) was provided by the European Commission to the 'Compliance. Wenn Staaten sich (nicht) an die Regeln halten' ('Compliance. Member States' (Non-)Compliance with EU Law'), which was led by Prof. Dr Tanja A. Börzel and funded by the German Research Council (DFG) (project number 0015031102; BO 1831/1–2, duration 2002–2007). For additional information see also Annexe.

examines how judgments work and under which scope conditions they effectively facilitate comprehensive compliance or minimalist compliance respectively. It presents a rationalist and a constructivist hypothesis and discusses their operationalizations.

On average, judicial discourses take about two years. If the Commission has not withdrawn the case in this period, because the state already achieved compliance in the meantime, the ECJ issues a binding judgment. Judgments summarize the major cleavages of the cases, authoritatively define the content and scope of contested norms, and reduce the complexity of the disputed issues. While the written and oral stages of the judicial discourse exclude the public, judgments are openly accessible and increase the publicity of cases. Thereby they disseminate new ideas into the domestic sphere and clarify how the state concerned violated EU law. This differentially empowers domestic compliance constituencies vis-à-vis domestic compliance opponents (Börzel 2006, Conant 2002, Dai 2005, Finnemore and Sikkink 1998). Norm proponents gain additional attention, new ideas on the issue-matter, and the normative backing of the Court. At the same time, non-compliance proponents are disempowered through authoritative norm definitions of the ECJ because they can no longer use the legal uncertainty for their purposes, can no longer claim to be in line with EU law and can hardly argue for ignoring the ECJ (Alter and Vargas 2000, Börzel 2006, Cichowski 2006, Dai 2005).

Differentially empowered societal actors, most notably interest groups, can use judgments to push their states into compliance via two pathways. Firstly, compliance constituencies can threaten their respective governments with losses of reputation and support in future elections. Successful shaming campaigns change governmental cost–benefit calculations and facilitate minimalist compliance. Alternatively, domestic norm proponents can use judgments in order to argumentatively reframe domestic debates, establish new ideas on how to deal with an issue appropriately, and induce comprehensive compliance. While it is ultimately contingent whether societal compliance reframing or shaming campaigns take place, the scope conditions for the success of both societal strategies can be theorized.

In shaming strategies societal norm proponents refer to domestically institutionalized norms of appropriateness, link them to governmental non-compliance, publicly shame the government for its insufficient policy and thereby create social sanctions in the form of reputational losses (Checkel 2001: 560, 568). Such threats with reputational costs and eventual electoral losses are effective if societal actors and the government have a common conception of what constitutes a costly threat. In democracies, actors know that re-election requires public support. Hence, the greater the match between the judgment and already domestically institutionalized norms and the greater the public attention, the more likely it is that a costly bargaining threat to the government can be generated. For example, if an ECJ judgment on the equal access of men and women resonates well with already institutionalized ideas on the protection of women as the weaker sex or on the country's self-perception as being an equality leader, societal norm proponents can publicly highlight that governmental non-compliance violates domestic norms and is inappropriate. Thereby, societal compliance constituencies create threats of potential reputational and electoral losses through maintaining non-compliance. Successful shaming increases domestic non-compliance costs and renders norm violations less favourable. In order to avoid electoral losses, in particular with a view to upcoming elections, governments react by adapting strategic positions, while their policy interests continue to point towards non-compliance. Consequently it is strategically rational for governments to engage only in minimal, incomplete legal changes. Ambivalent, vaguely defined norms or overlapping scopes serve as built-in windows of opportunity for future norm violations. This creates opportunities to pursue less demanding norm interpretations in the application phase, once public attention has declined and costs of non-compliance have again decreased. For a second reason, governments exposed to shaming strategies pursue minimalist rather than comprehensive domestic changes. Once domestic non-compliance costs exceed the benefits of norm violations, governments have an incentive to act quickly in order to avoid being sanctioned. In this context, minimalist legal transpositions are better suited than comprehensive changes, because the former can be completed much faster and thus have higher chances of pacifying the compliance constituency and effectively avoiding losses in reputation and electoral sanctions.

Summing up, shaming strategies facilitate minimalist compliance and are most likely successful where the resonance between the judgment and domestic norms is high. Thus, the rationalist hypothesis on judgments states: *ECJ rulings strengthen societal norm proponents to the disadvantage of opponents. This is conducive to successful shaming and a minimalist form of compliance, if the judgment resonates well with domestically institutionalized norms* (H3).

While shaming campaigns rest on rationalist processes of signalling threats, reframing strategies are based on constructivist dynamics of arguing. Societal actors could get new ideas on the subject matter through the publicly available ECJ judgments. Nevertheless, the prospects of successful arguing are limited if domestic norm proponents merely repeat the points made in the judicial discourse, which have not persuaded the government during the judicial discourse in the first place. Re-framing is an argumentative alternative to merely restating legal arguments. In putting an issue into a different cognitive context, which exhibits new implications for the policy concerned (Payne 2001, Rein and Schön 1993: 146, Snow and Benford 1992), reframing can foster policy changes resembling a comprehensive form of compliance. Reframing primarily changes the normative and cognitive underpinnings of a particular issue, instead of instrumentally manipulating cost–benefit calculations. As a result, states that adopted a new frame lack incentives to pursue minimalist legal changes with built-in ambiguities that allow switching back into less costly forms of compliance in the implementation stage.

Judgments provide authoritative norm definitions and thereby reduce the complexity of contested issues. This makes it easier to subsume them under new policy-frames, which require different and more demanding handling of the subjects concerned. For example, drinking water issues can be framed as a matter of environmental protection or of public health. The latter approach is less demanding than the former because it encompasses only specific water sources, fewer quality parameters and no precautionary protective measures beyond public health requirements. Hence, the framing of drinking water issues matters: it can promote less (public health) or more encompassing (environment) water quality approaches. In launching new or alternative frames, societal actors put the judgment, or elements thereof, into another ideational context with which it had not before been associated. This has consequences for compliance: while non-compliance was in line with the old frame, it is not in line with the new frame.

Under which conditions can new frames be successfully launched? As for other argumentative strategies, reframing will have high prospects for success, if actors share a reference system for the evaluation of the quality of arguments. Yet frames are in themselves reference systems for the assessment of ideas, and influence which ones are regarded as compelling (Jachtenfuchs 1996, Payne 2001). Nevertheless, policy frames constantly compete with each other and the quality of arguments for a new frame can be assessed by all other prominent frames (Mörth 2000, Snow and Benford 1992, Surel 2000). Thus, reframing strategies are more successful, the better the new frame fits with other, already prominent frames. For example, the frame of drinking water as an environmental rather than a public health matter can be launched more easily if societal actors highlight how good an environmental approach (introducing a polluters-pay principle) complements a dominating economic frame, according to which the costs for water quality should neither put a burden on customers nor on the water supplying industry. Likewise, new frames are more easily adopted if competing ones are already in processes of degeneration, which is, for example, likely in instances of rapid environmental change or ongoing incremental societal, economical or political transformations (Payne 2001, Snow and Benford 1992, Surel 2000).

If a new frame is successfully launched, it induces comprehensive compliance. Reframing alters scientific and normative underpinnings of a policy and affects the very beliefs of how a certain issue should be dealt with, while strategic cost–benefit calculations are not at the centre. Consequently, governments do not pursue minimalist legal changes in order to create windows of opportunity for future norm violations. Instead, they introduce policy changes in line with the logic of appropriateness, as defined by the new frame. Thus, the respective constructivist hypothesis on the compliance instrument of 'judgments' states: *Judgments reduce the complexity of the issues at stake. This is conducive to societal reframing strategies that induce comprehensive compliance, if new frames fit with other prominent, complementary frames* (H4).

When none of the bottom-up strategies is successful, governmental actors have no incentives to change legal acts and therefore non-compliance continues.

Which indicators allow the disentangling of shaming and reframing mechanisms and under which conditions are the two judgment hypotheses confirmed or falsified?

The chances of whether differentially empowered societal actors use the publicity boost of judgments to threaten reluctant governments with potential sanctions and successfully shame them into minimalist compliance crucially depend on the match between judgments and domestically institutionalized norms. The resonance is high, if judgments can easily be linked to at least one prominent institutionalized domestic norm of appropriateness or rightfulness in the affected policy field. If the judgment either violates domestically institutionalized norms or cannot be linked to a prominent institutionalized norm in the affected policy field because it is based on different conceptions of what is appropriate, fair or scientifically sound, the resonance is low. The shaming hypothesis would be disconfirmed if process-tracing showed that the judgment did not fit with domestic norms so that non-compliance costs were low, but that the government nevertheless reacted to public shaming campaigns with legal adaptations. It would also be falsified if domestic non-compliance costs were very high because of a high resonance and upcoming elections, but shaming strategies nevertheless failed to induce minimalist compliance. By contrast, the hypothesis would be confirmed if a judgment resonated well with some domestic norms so that governments shifted into minimalist compliance in reaction to organized interests, who considerably increased non-compliance costs through publicly highlighting the inappropriateness of governmental conduct and demanding policy changes.

The reframing hypothesis captures how concepts embedded in ECJ judgments are used, in order to redirect domestic debates and, thereby, promote comprehensive compliance. It focuses on the possibility of linking new, alternative policy frames to complementary prominent ones, with which the issue matter had not been previously associated. Frames constantly compete with one another, so that the quality of arguments for a new frame can only be assessed by other prominent ones. Thus, reframing strategies are all the more successful, the better the new one fits with already prominent complementary approaches. If such linkages cannot be made, the actors lack a shared reference system for the evaluation of arguments and talk at cross purposes. Hence, similar to the shaming hypothesis, we operationalize the independent variable dichotomously: the compatibility between frames is high if a new frame and its embedded central assumptions, core concepts and essential policy aims are complementary to the ones of prominent policy frames, so that they reinforce each other, while competing policy approaches become isolated. The fit of new and old frames is poor, if central assumptions, concepts and policy aims are conflicting. The reframing hypothesis would be confirmed if process tracing showed that societal norm proponents promoted an alternative policy approach, which was conducive to a demanding norm interpretation, linked it to an embedded fitting policy frame, and thereby fostered a shift into comprehensive compliance. It would be falsified if the launching of a new well-resonating frame failed to induce comprehensive compliance or if comprehensive compliance was achieved despite a low fit of the new frame.

In order to acquire the information necessary to trace shaming and reframing processes in case studies and to put the two hypotheses to the test, we use a mix of different sources for public statements of involved societal compliance proponents and opponents as well as governmental reactions. These include newspaper articles,[15] strategy papers,

[15] The newspaper selection encompassed 19 of the prominent as well as smaller, conservative/liberal and social-democratic papers, and regional as well as national papers. All newspapers were accessed in their electronic version, as available through the Lexis-Nexis database (http://web.lexis-nexis.com/professional/). For further information see Annexe.

parliamentary debates, and interviews as well as a series of questionnaires on perceptions of involved organized interests regarding the case, their own role, the role of ECJ compliance instruments and their domestic impact.

Sanction-threats

If judicial discourses and judgments fail and member states do not even induce first steps towards legal transpositions with two years, sanction-threats will come into play. Enforcement theories prominently feature sanction-threats and penalties as compliance instruments. In line with rationalist action theoretical foundations, states' policy interests are assumed to be exogenous to interactions, while they are capable of adjusting preferences over strategies in response to changes in external contexts. Consequently, enforcement approaches claim that states unwilling to bear compliance costs violate international law (Downs, Rocke and Barsoom 1996, Martin 1992, Martin and Simmons 1998). Against this background they argue that compliance can only be induced if external constraints in the form of sanction-threats or penalties increase non-compliance costs to an extent that they outweigh the incentives to continue with the norm violation. Legalized international institutions increase non-compliance costs and render norm violations less attractive (Powell 1994, Victor, Raustiala and Skolnikoff 1998). They do so with two types of enforcement instruments. In decentralized systems (e.g. WTO, GATT), monitoring and transparency-creating mechanisms allow the identifing of free-riders. In instances of norm violations, third parties can issue binding rulings, but it is up to other states to carry out enforcement measures (decentralized enforcement). In centralized enforcement systems, by contrast, international institutions themselves impose penalties (e.g. the EU since 1993).

Prior to 1993, the ECJ could threaten governments with references to Article 171 ECT and highlight that a particular state is a free-rider. This opened a window of opportunity for informal sanctions through other states (e.g. losses in credibility). The Maastricht Treaty strengthened the enforcement system in 1993, so that the ECJ can issue a second judgment and impose financial penalties on non-compliant states. As with any other bargaining threat, sanction-threats are only effective in abolishing norm violations if states take them seriously and regard then as a deterrent. This requires that states perceive the costs for future non-compliance as exceeding the domestic benefits of continued norm violations (Fearon 1998, Horne and Cutlip 2002), which will depend on the remoteness of sanction-threats and the amount of anticipated sanctions. Governmental gains from non-compliance are also very important. Yet for all cases that reach the enforcement stage because judicial discourses and judgments were ineffective, governmental non-compliance benefits are most likely very high, not least because the governmental constituency strongly opposes compliance.

Within the first year after the ECJ judgment, the shadow of possible sanctions is not imminent. Since European actors do not introduce first enforcement measures in this period, but allow states time to initiate transpositions, governments do not shy away from potential future sanctions immediately after the ECJ ruling (Panke 2006). Even highly risk-averse governments value non-compliance benefits of today more strongly than avoiding non-compliance costs in the remote future, when they might not even be in office anymore. Hence, remote threats of sanctions are most likely too weak to facilitate the adaptation of strategic positions and minimalist compliance within the first year after ECJ rulings.

As the shadow of financial penalties is looming, due to the introduction of first measures towards enforcement by the European Commission (after 1993) or the ECJ (prior to 1993), we have to distinguish between centralized and decentralized enforcement systems. Comparing the implications of a reasoned opinion based on Article 228 ECT (after 1993) and a referral to Article 171 ECT (before 1993), the likelihood that non-compliance costs exceed non-compliance benefits is lower for decentralized sanctions. It is uncertain whether other states will indeed react to the ECJ and consider free-riding states as less credible partners in future negotiations. Also, it is unclear in which negotiations in the Council of Ministers losses of reputation negatively affect the bargaining power of norm-violating states. Moreover, decentralized sanctions might take place with a time lag, thus punishing subsequent governments rather than those responsible for breaching EU law in the first place. The consequences for non-compliant governments are more tangible in centralized enforcement systems. If states do not adapt legal acts within the average period of one and a half to two years after the first ECJ judgment, the European Commission sends a second reasoned opinion to the respective state (Commission of the European Communities 2005). This increases the likelihood of being severely sanctioned within the next twelve months, although there are still two further steps, the second ECJ referral and the second ECJ judgment, before stubbornly non-compliant governments face financial penalties.

The credibility of the sanction-threat increases additionally if the European Commission recommends a concrete daily penalty to the ECJ.

The amount of potential penalties is based on the economic strength of the respective country, because the daily flat rate of €600 is multiplied by coefficients measuring the economic power: the factors range between 0.36 (Malta) and 25.40 (Germany) (Commission of the European Communities 2005: 9–10).[16] Besides the GDP, two other determinants influence the amount of daily penalties and lump sums. Just as in domestic courts, the Commission and the ECJ also take the damages that norm violations caused for others into account for the ultimate decision on the extent of sanctions. In the EU, the basic penalty of €600 is multiplied by coefficients measuring the seriousness of infringements and their duration (Commission of the European Communities 2005: 6, 8–12). This ensures that sanctions can deter all states and also respect 'both the principle of proportionality and the principle of equal treatment among the Member States' (Commission of the European Communities 2005: 2). The duration of infringements influences lump sums and daily penalties but is relatively low (a long duration can multiply penalties up to three times). The seriousness of the infringement[17] is much more important in determining the amount of penalties, since it affects lump sums with a coefficient between one and 20 (Commission of the European Communities 2005: 8). In effect, economically weak and powerful states could be subject to the same sanction, if the norm violation of the less wealthy state was more severe. Also, economically powerful countries cannot per se more easily afford to be penalized than less wealthy states, since the amount of sanctions is considerably higher for the former. Consequently, the economic power of states cannot determine whether a looming sanction-threat renders non-compliance prohibitively expensive, since the penalty already includes a proxy accounting for economic power differences between states.

Taken together, the higher and the more credible sanction-threats are,

[16] So far, Greece has been ordered to pay a penalty of €20,000 a day (Case C-387/97). Spain had to pay €34,200 a day (Case C-278/01) (its penalty was set as €624,150 a year for every 1% of the bathing water that violates the directive – the estimation was that it affected 20% of the Spanish bathing waters (European Court of Justice 2003)). France was punished with €320,895.83 a day and an additional lump sum of €20,000,000 (The ECJ issued a penalty of €57,761,250 for each period of six months (European Court of Justice 2005)) (Case C-304/02) European Court of Justice 2000b, 2003, 2005).

[17] The Commission defines the seriousness of infringements based on the importance of the Community affected provisions (e.g. if they impact fundamental rights or the four freedoms) and the effects of the infringement on general and particular interests (e.g. impact on Commission's resources and functions, harm for people, involved financial gains, relative economic importance, etc.) (Commission of the European Communities 2005: 6–7).

the more effective they become in fostering minimalist compliance. The mere possibility of sanctions in the remote future barely increases non-compliance costs. Once the Commission sends a second reasoned opinion to reluctant governments, the likelihood of being punished during a governmental incumbency increases, which considerably increases the credibility of the threat. The amount of possible sanctions matters as well. Controlling for the economic power of states, sanction-threats are higher the more serious the infringements are and the longer they endure (Commission of the European Communities 2005: 2–12).

If external costs for norm violations exceed its domestic benefits in the perception of the government, the latter will adapt strategic positions accordingly and pursue minimalist legal adaptations. Minimalist compliance simultaneously allows the government to avoid sanctions and to fall back into a less demanding and less costly norm interpretation, once the Commission has closed the case. In addition, minimalist legal adaptations can be more quickly achieved than comprehensive legal changes. This more effectively prevents the ECJ from issuing a second judgment and financial penalties. Thus, the rationalist hypothesis on the compliance instrument 'threats of sanctions' states: *Minimalist compliance can be expected if anticipated sanction costs exceed domestic non-compliance benefits. This is all the more likely if sanction-threats are looming and if the amount of sanctions is high due to the seriousness of the infringement* (H5).

Although the European Commission and the ECJ are unlikely to additionally employ argumentative means while using sanction-threats, we develop a constructivist alternative to the above hypothesis. In this line of argumentation, sanction-threats support norm definitions as provided in judgments, since they underline that non-compliance is inappropriate. This differentially empowers those lead ministries which would have favoured a policy shift towards compliance long ago, but abstained from doing so because of strong domestic non-compliance proponents. If ministries would have preferred a change of policies in line with a demanding norm interpretation from early on or at least since after an ECJ ruling, but continued the norm violation in order to avoid domestic electoral sanctions through a compliance-averse public or because other ministries opposed legal adaptations, an immediate and credible external sanction-threat might change equations. Once sanctions are looming, lead ministries can argue that they have to shift into compliance because sticking to norm violations has become unbearably costly and thereby rules itself out. Sanction-threats provide the window of opportunity for compliance-prone lead ministries to finally pursue demanding policy changes in line with the ECJ judgment – even against the will of domestic constituencies or other ministries. Since comprehensive legal changes need time to be finalized, we would expect that lead ministries initiate them relatively quickly after ECJ judgments as soon as European enforcement authorities undertake first steps to restore compliance (letter of formal notice, Art. 228 ECT). Hence, the constructivist alternative hypothesis expects the following: *Sanction-threats differentially empower lead ministries and induce comprehensive compliance, if the lead ministry preferred compliance from the outset but was prevented from proposing or passing demanding policies by domestic veto players* (H6).

How can we measure looming sanction-threats and how can we empirically disentangle the two different causal mechanisms? The rationalist version of the sanction-threat hypothesis focuses on the credibility and the size of the sanction-threat. Sanction-threats are not deterrent directly after the ECJ judgment and are not sufficiently imminent if the European Commission only sent a second letter of formal notice to the affected state. In order to be a credible threat in the sense that governmental actors can safely assume to be punished during their incumbency, it is necessary that the Commission has also opened the official stage of the second infringement procedure in sending a reasoned opinion to the reluctantly non-complying state (Art. 228 ECT). The sanction-threat must additionally be sufficiently high to deter a state from persistent non-compliance. This variable is crucially influenced by the seriousness of the infringement, which the European Commission measures according to pre-defined criteria. The seriousness is determined by whether a case affects the four fundamental freedoms or basic rights and by a catalogue of criteria, encompassing more than ten measures such as

> the loss of Community's own resources, the impact of the infringement on the way the Community functions, serious or irreparable damage to human health or the environment, economic or other harm suffered by individuals and economic operators, including intangible consequences, such as personal development, the financial sums involved in the infringement, any possible financial advantage that the Member State gains from not complying with the judgment of the Court, the relative importance of the infringement taking into account the turnover or added value of the economic sector concerned in the Member State in question, the size of the population affected by the infringement (...), the Community's responsibility with respect to non-member countries, whether the infringement is a one-off or a repeat of an earlier infringement (for example, repeated delay in transposing directives in a certain sector). (Commission of the

European Communities 2005: 6–7)

In addition, it is important to consider whether the EC law in question was very precise or rather ambiguous, or whether the violated norm belongs to already established case-law (Commission of the European Communities 2005: 6). For the purpose of this study we consider an infringement as serious if five or more out of the above criteria are fulfilled. The rationalist sanction-threat hypothesis would be confirmed if states shied away from external sanctions and shifted into minimalist compliance, if a reasoned opinion (based on Art. 228 ECT) was sent to the respective ministry and if the infringement was serious. It would be falsified if states were deterred and pursued minimalist compliance even though either the threat was not looming (no second reasoned opinion) or the amount of anticipated sanctions was not sufficiently high (only four or less criteria fulfilled). The rationalist sanction-threat hypothesis would also be disconfirmed if comprehensive rather than minimalist compliance were achieved.

The constructivist version of the sanction-threat hypothesis conceptualizes sanction-threats as windows of opportunity for pro-compliance ministries to pursue demanding legal changes against the preferences of other ministries or domestic constituencies. Since comprehensive transpositions are more time-consuming than minimalist ones, we expect that lead ministries would initiate them after the European Commission has sent a second letter of formal notice (Art. 228 ECT) to the respective state. The hypothesis would be confirmed if we observed a shift into comprehensive compliance after the European Commission issued a second letter of formal notice. Accordingly, the constructivist version of the hypothesis would be falsified if this compliance instrument fostered minimalist instead of comprehensive compliance or if steps towards comprehensive compliance were initiated after a second reasoned opinion or even after sanctions had been issued.

In order to put these hypotheses to an empirical test, the study will draw again on the compliance database on EU law, on newspaper articles, on parliamentary debates, and interviews with involved actors.

3.IV Overview of the core hypotheses and case selection

This book applies qualitative methods in order to empirically test the hypotheses on the three compliance instruments. This has two advantages. Firstly, many of the independent variables cannot be quantified. Secondly, process tracing allows for reconstructing the complex underlying causal mechanisms. The case selection seeks to comprehensively test the four featured hypotheses and each of the case studies also tests for all developed alternative explanations. The four main hypotheses are: the constructivist judicial discourse hypothesis (H1), the rationalist as well as the constructivist judgment hypotheses (H3, H4), and the rationalist sanction-threat hypothesis (H5).[18] The case studies are selected according to a most similar systems design. It systematically varies the independent variables of the four featured hypotheses, while other alternative country-specific explanations are kept constant (for discussions of country-based explanations see Chapter 7).

In the EU, as in any other infringement procedure, compliance instruments are sequentially applied and the order is constant for all cases. Judicial discourses are started once cases reach the Court. On average, they last 620 days before the ECJ issues rulings. After judgments, differential empowerment effects require additional time, until the domestic compliance constituency pushes governments into compliance.[19] In instances in which non-compliance is continued, since states did not even introduce first steps towards domestic change within the first one and a half years after the judgment, threats of potential sanctions as the third compliance instrument come into play and are issued after a second ECJ referral and a second ECJ judgment. Although European actors strictly apply the three compliance instruments in a sequential order, the impact of an instrument on outcomes can have time lags, both for ideational change to be observed and for legal change to be completed. For example, states might anticipate future sanction-threats in earlier stages (e.g. immediately after judicial discourses) so that this instrument could have an impact on compliance dynamics, although it has not yet been applied. Since the impact of compliance instruments might overlap, this book isolates the effects of judicial discourses, judgments and sanction-threats. The case selection ensures that one and only one instrument should be effective in each of the cases. In the *first two cases*, parties actively engage in judicial argumentation, focus on the same legal norms, and use a

[18] The constructivist judicial discourse hypothesis is selected as the main explanation, because arguing is much more likely in this social context than compliance-bargaining and threats. Hence a constructivist reconstruction of the judicial discourse mechanism seems to be more plausible than a rationalist once. Conversely, arguing and persuasion are unlikely to dominate the interactions leading to domestic adaptations in situations in which the sanction instrument comes into play. Here, a rationalist reconstruction of the underlying dynamics is more plausible.

[19] Empirically, this study observes that shaming restores compliance faster than reframing strategies, because the latter requires not only fundamental ideational but also more comprehensive legal changes.

judicial method of interpretation with a high compatibility to the complexity of the interpretational issue at stake. The precondition for the first featured hypothesis (judicial discourses) is present, while effective shaming and reframing strategies are unlikely and sanction threats remain weak. The *third and fourth cases* are characterized by a high resonance between the judgment and already domestically institutionalized norms, while the preconditions for effective judicial discourses (all three hypotheses), reframing campaigns, and threats of penalties (the rationalist and the constructivist hypotheses) are not present. Thus, boh cases should exemplify effective shaming strategies and we expect minimalist compliance. Successful reframing strategies and comprehensive compliance are to be expected in the *fifth and sixth cases*, in which a new frame fits to

Table 3.2 Case selection

Hypothesis and scope condition	*Cases 1, 2 (Chapter 4)*	*Cases 3, 4 (Chapter 5)*	*Cases 5, 6 (Chapter 5)*	*Cases 7, 8 (Chapter 6)*
(H1): active judicial argumentation focusing on the same norm and high fit of judicial method and issue at stake	**Present**	Absent	Absent	Absent
(H3): resonance between ECJ judgment and institutionalized norms	Low resonance	**High resonance**	Low resonance	Low resonance
(H4): complementary frame to which the new frame can be easily linked	Absent	Absent	**Present**	Absent
(H5): serious infringement and looming penalties	No	No	No	**Yes**
Expected effective compliance restoring instrument	Judicial discourse	Judgment/ shaming	Judgment/reframing	Sanction-threat
Expected pathway and outcome	Constructivist mechanism: comprehensive compliance	Rationalist mechanism: minimalist compliance	Constructivist mechanism: comprehensive compliance	Rationalist mechanism minimalist compliance

prominent complementary frames, while the scope conditions for the effectiveness of the other pathways to compliance are absent. In the *seventh and eighth cases*, neither judicial discourses nor judgments should have ended norm violations. In response to continued non-compliance, sanction-threats came into play. Once they become credible and sufficiently high, the featured rationalist hypothesis expects that affected states shy away and shift towards minimalist compliance.

This study analyses two environmental and two social policy directives for Germany and the UK respectively.[20] The two policy fields cover areas with many (environment) and few (social policy) EU competencies, in which the EU is very (environment) or less (social policy) active. The selected social policy directives are the equal treatment directive (76/207), which aims to promote equal treatment of men and women in occupational activities, the collective redundancy directive (75/129), which protects workers in instances of collective redundancies, and the directive on the residence of foreign workers and their families (90/364), which seeks to increase the reliability of residence entitlements for foreign workers. In the environmental policy field, the cases concern the quality of water intended for human consumption (80/778), which defines quality parameters for drinking water, the nitrates directive (91/676), which aims towards the reduction of nitrates in fresh water and in groundwater and the environmental impact assessment directive (85/337), which seeks to protect air, water and soil from environmental damage resulting from construction projects.

The ECJ issued rulings in all the cases listed in Table 3.3.[21] In the German drinking water and in the UK collective redundancy case, the parties both actively engaged in judicial argumentation, and both focused on the same legal acts and used judicial methods with a high goodness of fit to the interpretational problems at hand so that the constructivist hypothesis expects that judicial discourses facilitate comprehensive compliance (see also Chapter 4). Differential empowerment effects of ECJ judgments should allow for successful shaming campaigns in the case on

[20] In order to test all hypotheses in a most similar systems design, one would ideally select only one policy field and choose cases on identical directives for both states. However, there are not four directives within one policy field which both states violated and which have been referred to the Court. This is not problematic, because the independent variables for the effectiveness of compliance instruments are issue-specific and not directive-specific.

[21] The qualitative study does not include cases that have been referred to the ECJ, but withdrawn prior to the judgment, since protocols of judicial discourses are only publicly available for cases in which the ECJ issues judgments.

the EqD in the UK and the RFWD in Germany because of a high resonance between the judgments and already institutionalized norms (see also Chapter 5). In the British drinking water and in the German equal access case, reframing should successfully induce comprehensive compliance, since new policy frames fit complementary prominent ones (see also Chapter 5). In the German EIA and in the UK nitrates cases high and looming sanction-threats should induce minimalist compliance in line with the rationalist hypothesis (see also Chapter 6).

Table 3.3 Overview of selected directives and Court cases

	Collective Redundancy Directive (CRD)	*Residence of Foreign Workers and their Families (RFWD)*	*Equal Access Directive (EqD)*	*Drinking Water Directive (DWD)*	*Nitrates Directive (NitD)*	*Environmental Impact Assessment Directive (EIA)*
Celex-number	75/129	90/364	76/207	80/778	91/676	85/337
Policy field	Social policy	Social policy	Social policy	Environment	Environment	Environment
Aim	Protection of workers in processes of collective redundancies	Increasing reliability for foreign workers and their families concerning residency	Equality of men and women in work-related matters (jobs, career, etc.)	High quality of water intended for human consumption	Reduction of nitrates in groundwater and freshwater, environmental protection	Protection of all media (air, water, soil) from the impact of projects
Means	Consultation and information requirements for employers	Criteria for residence entitlements of foreign workers and their families	Not specified	Quality parameters for water quality, means for measurement	Designation of nitrate vulnerable zones, action plans	Procedures to measure the potential impact of projects prior to their approval

Court cases	C-383/92	C-095/96	C-248/83 C-165/82	C-237/90 C-340/96	C-069/99	C-301/95
Main issues at stake before the ECJ	Acceptance of workers' representatives and concept of consultation unclear, sufficient penalties for employers. Scope: all redundancies?	Lack of transparency hinders the achievement of the directive's aim	D: scope – inclusion of public administration and independent professions, transparency and communication UK: scope – occupational activities and collective agreements	D: communica-tional require-ments of exceptions, state of emergency as exception UK: system of undertakings broadens exceptions	Scope of the NitD: designation of action programmes and vulnerable zones insufficient	Scope of the directive, are the projects of Annex II obligatory or voluntary?
ECJ judgment	UK 1994	D 1997	D 1985, UK 1983	D 1992, UK 1999	UK 2000	D 1998

Part III

Evidence

This section puts all main and all alternative hypotheses on the three compliance instruments to a comprehensive empirical test. To this end, it presents case studies featuring effective judicial discourses (Chapter 4), judgments (Chapter 5) and sanction-threats (Chapter 6). Firstly, each of these studies examines the role of all three instruments and tests for the respective alternative rationalist or constructivist pathways to compliance. The empirical tests basically reveal that judicial discourses talk member states into compliance when the advocates of the parties do not argue at cross purposes. None of these studies, by contrast, found empirical evidence for the rationalist alternative of compliance bargaining in the shadow of the ECJ. Secondly, the empirical chapters also show that judgments differentially empower domestic norm advocates, who can either shame the government into compliance, if the judgment resonates well with pre-existing institutionalized domestic norms, or reframe domestic debates if they can link a new policy approach to complementary frames. Thirdly, the studies reveal that sanction-threats foster domestic changes if high penalties are looming due to the seriousness of the infringement. By contrast, the alternative constructivist approach, according to which sanction-threats differentially empower pro-compliance ministries vis-à-vis domestic veto-players, found no empirical support in any of the eight case studies. Thus, all four of the featured hypotheses find empirical support, while the alternative hypotheses are not confirmed.

Each of the empirical sections is laid out as follows. Firstly, it provides background information on the infringement cases, reconstructs governmental rationales for violating the European norm, outlines the domestic legal context and shows how it has changed over time. Secondly, since the European authorities apply the instruments in the same order in all infringement cases, each chapter discusses the role of judicial discourses, followed by an analysis of the judgments and a test of the sanction-threat hypotheses.

4

Effective judicial discourses

The following two case studies qualitatively test for the effectiveness of the ECJ compliance instruments. They reveal that, in line with the constructivist judicial discourse hypothesis, even formerly reluctant governments can become ideationally entrapped through judicial discourses.

4.1 The UK collective redundancy case

The collective redundancies directive (75/129) is part of the early European employment policy. The directive introduces protective measures for employees in the event of collective dismissals. It prescribes a set of information and consultation procedures between employee representatives and employers. The directive seeks to ensure that workers subject to collective redundancies can make their voices heard on positions and problems in the event of a collective dismissal. The collective redundancy directive was politically contested among the EU member states and not supported by all states equally. Although the actors at the Council negotiation table agreed that the collective redundancy directive contributes positively to the functioning of the common market, they disagreed on the extent to which the Community and states should interfere in economic policy. This found expression in the preface of the collective redundancy directive, which states that 'it is important that greater protection should be afforded to workers in the event of collective redundancies while taking into account the need for balanced economic and social development within the Community'.

The redundancy directive entered into force in February 1975 and had to be legally implemented by all of the EC member states.[1] The EU

[1] Directive 1975/129 expired in August 1998 and was substituted by a new one (31998L0059), which further extended workers' rights.

directive did not have a legal predecessor in UK law, not least because the regulation of labour relations through law was rather uncommon in the UK (Ashford 1981: 101, 140–3, Harrison and Crossland 1950). While the Conservative Party and the Liberals opposed protective legislation, the Labour Party welcomed the EU directive. Hence, even before the deadline of transposition expired, the Labour government passed the Employment Protection Act (EPA) in order to completely transpose the directive. The 1975 EPA specified the appointment and recognition of employee representatives and their rights in cases of collective redundancies (K.W.W. 1976: 174–5). When the Conservatives came into power in 1979, the Thatcher government abolished these trade union and other collective rights with the 1980 Employment Act and the 1985 EPA (Docksey 1986). As a consequence, the UK shifted from initial comprehensive compliance into violating the redundancy directive. From 1980 onwards, many of the protective measures of the directive were de facto at the disposition of employers. The 1980 and 1985 Acts left workers affected by a collective redundancy without the protection prescribed by the directive and allowed employers to save costs to the disadvantage of their employees.

Fifteen years after the adoption of the directive, the European Commission prepared a report on the status quo of the implementation and the effectiveness of the directive with a view to its eventual revision (European Commission 1991). This process revealed that the Thatcher government had substantially altered the 1975 EPA in 1980 and 1985 (European Commission 1991). Since the Commission suspected that the 1985 EPA transposed the directive only partially, it opened an infringement procedure against the UK and issued a reasoned opinion in March 1991. Yet the Conservative Major government claimed to be in compliance with EU law. They regarded the Commission's interpretation of the directive as too demanding, especially concerning the full recognition of workers' representatives, their bargaining power in consultations, the applicatory scope of the directive to all collective dismissals and rules on sanctions for non-compliant employers.

During the early stages of the EU infringement procedure, the principled and causal beliefs of the government as well as its strategic priorities pointed strongly towards a narrow collective redundancies approach and non-compliance with a demanding reading of the European directive. Adhering to the idea that the freedom of enterprise and deregulation are the best means to ensure economic growth in Great Britain, Conservatives opposed market interventions (Ashford 1981: 101–14, House of Commons 1989a: 475, House of Commons 1991: 476, House of Commons 1992b: 172). Consequently, they did not support collective rights and individual protective rights, other than work safety measures (House of Commons 1991: 476, House of Commons 1992b: 172). In line with this governmental orientation, employer associations, the most important societal compliance opponents, constantly highlighted that workers' rights constituted direct and indirect employment costs, diminished employers' abilities to react to the market and placed a burden on the economy (Ashford 1981: 22, 152–3, Brainard 1960, Docksey 1986, House of Commons 1993b).

Since the norm violation of the subsequent Thatcher (1979–1990) and Major governments (1990–1997) was rigid, the Commission referred the redundancy case to the ECJ in October 1992 (C-383/92). Before the Court, four issues were at stake: the applicatory scope (all redundancies or only redundancies for economic reasons); two procedures (compulsory or voluntary recognition of trade unions by employers; prohibitive penalties for non-compliant employers); and the aims (agreement between employer and employee representatives or mere information) of the directive. On 8 June, 1994 the ECJ ruled that the British legal transposition of the collective redundancy directive (75/129) was incomplete with regard to all four issues (European Court of Justice 1994: 45–6).

The pattern of legal change

The 1975 EPA was fully in line with the EU directive and specified the appointment and recognition of employee representatives and their rights in cases of collective redundancies. Yet the Conservative government changed the EPA in 1980 and shifted into non-compliance. The European Commission criticized the 1980 EPA for severely weakening workers' rights and opened an infringement proceeding. In this proceeding, the ECJ ruled that the 1980 EPA narrowed the applicatory scope of the directive and did not properly protect employees in the event of redundancies, for example because employers could de facto refuse to recognize worker representatives, could circumvent meaningful consultations through merely informing workers' representatives of developments and measures, and reduced the application of the directive to economic redundancies only.

The UK had already begun introducing changes to redundancy legislation during the ongoing judicial discourse. The 1993 Trade Union Reform and Employment Rights Act (TURERA) was mainly a measure that restricted collective trade union rights and strengthened individual protective rights. Nevertheless, the TURERA transposed three of the four contested issues: it included all collective redundancies, stated that consultations between workers' representatives and employers should aim for an agreement and introduced prohibitive sanctions for non-compliant employers. The only issue before the ECJ that was not accommodated by the 1993 TURERA was the question of whether employee recognition was voluntary or compulsory for employers. This issue was transposed within one year after the ECJ ruling with the 1995 Collective Redundancies and Transfer of Undertakings (Protection of Employment) (Amendment) Regulations.

Table 4.1 Collective redundancy legislation

Date	*Title*	*Initiated by*	*Outcome*
1975	Employment Protection Act (EPA)	Labour government	In line with the collective redundancies directive with regard to the role of employer representatives
1980	Employment Protection Act (EPA)	Conservative government	Violated the collective redundancies directive
1993	Trade Union Reform and Employment Rights Act (TURERA)	Conservative government	Compliance measure regarding the scope of the directive (not only economic, but all redundancies) and sanctions
1995	Redundancy Payments (Local Government) (Modification) (Amendment) Order 1995 (No. 1157 of 1995)	Conservative government	Not related to the ECJ case
1995	Collective Redundancies and Transfer of Undertakings (Protection of Employment) (Amendment) Regulations 1995 (No. 2587 of 1995)	Conservative government	Legal transposition of directive 75/129

The 1993 TURERA and the 1995 regulations clearly specified the formerly contested issues and considerably strengthened workers' rights in processes of collective redundancies. The legal acts introduced neither new concepts nor complex exceptional clauses, avoided overlaps with other legal acts, and reduced the legal uncertainty enormously.[2] Consid-

[2] An additional indicator of the ambiguity of legal acts is the number of national court cases on issues closely related to the directive at stake. Prior to the ECJ judgment in 1994, four national court cases dealt with the collective redundancy directive, neither of which had been referred to the ECJ for a preliminary ruling. After the ECJ ruling in June 1994, by contrast, not a single judicial proceeding dealt with the interpretation of the directive in the UK (see also Table 13, Annexe).

ered altogether, the reforms resemble comprehensive compliance: all formerly contested elements have been legally transposed without introducing or maintaining legal uncertainties stemming from new or ill-defined concepts, tensions within the newly created laws and regulations, complex exceptional clauses or overlaps with other employment law.

How did the ECJ manage to facilitate compliance against the strong resistance of the Conservative government? Which of the compliance-restoring instruments was effective in this case?

The judicial discourse in operation

The judicial discourse lasted from October 1992 until June 1994 (C-383/92). It covered four different interpretational questions related to the aim, the procedures and the applicatory scope of the directive. The UK transposed three of the four disputed elements during the ongoing judicial discourse with the 1993 TURERA and was in the process of transposing the one remaining issue relating to regulations on collective redundancies and transfer of undertakings in 1994. Since the UK did not complete the legal change during the ongoing discourse, the ECJ issued a judgment in June 1994, stating that the collective redundancy directive had not been legally implemented correctly (European Court of Justice 1994: 45).

This section tests the constructivist and the two alternative rationalist judicial discourse hypotheses in turn. Starting with the constructivist one, it firstly reconstructs the arguments exchanged during the judicial discourse with a particular emphasis on the type of legal interpretational techniques applied. Secondly, it analyses if the formerly compliance-averse actors had become argumentatively entrapped and shifted into comprehensive compliance (constructivist hypothesis, H1) or if they shifted into minimalist compliance to circumvent losses in reputation (rationalist hypothesis, H2a). In both regards, this section looks at each of the interpretational problems in turn. Afterwards, the focus shifts towards the second alternative rationalist explanation on judicial discourses, and analyses whether compliance bargaining in the shadow of the Court could have triggered quick legal adaptations (H2b). This shows that the judicial discourse succeeded in talking the UK into compliance as expected by the constructivist hypothesis, whereas threats of losses in reputation as well as compliance bargaining fail to account for the observed policy changes.

Judicial discourse: ideational entrapment or threats of reputational losses?

Does the directive apply to all or only to economic collective redundancies? The first disputed element concerned the applicatory scope of the collective redundancy directive. Against the backdrop of the UK Employment Protection Act (EPA) of 1975 (Sections 99 and 100), which applied only to economic collective dismissals, the parties disagreed on whether the directive encompassed all collective redundancies (European Commission) or only those for economic reasons (UK).

From the very beginning of the judicial discourse, the participants used the wording technique of legal reasoning to specify which types of redundancies the directive captures (Advocate General 1994: 33, European Court of Justice 1994: 30–2). Article 1 I b of the directive is very precise and states:

> For the purposes of this Directive: (a) 'collective redundancies' means dismissals effected by an employer *for one or more reasons not related to the individual workers* concerned where, according to the choice of the Member States, the number of redundancies is: – either, over a period of 30 days: (1) at least 10 in establishments normally employing more than 20 and less than 100 workers. (Article 1 I b, Collective Redundancy Directive; emphasis added)

In the UK collective redundancy case, the advocates of both parties actively engaged in making and exchanging judicial arguments, they focused on the same legal acts and did not talk at cross purposes. The shared narrow wording method fitted well with the interpretational problem at hand. Consequently, it unmistakably followed from the explicit phrasing of Article 1 that the directive covered all collective dismissals – regardless of their underlying reasons (European Court of Justice 1994: 30–2). Even if the wording method had not been applied to Article 1 I b, but to 1 II b instead, which also specified the applicatory scope of the EU directive, the result would have been the same: the directive regulates all collective redundancies and not only those for economic reasons (Advocate General 1994: 33; European Court of Justice 1994: 29–32).[3] Thus, the judicial discourse should be successful. The

[3] Other, broader interpretational devices would have been less suited for the development of a consensual norm definition, because they would have introduced additional ambiguity instead of clarifying the scope of the directive. For example, the directive-immanent teleological interpretation would allow the extension of the scope to include individual dismissals, since this would serve the directive's aim of providing protective rights for workers against employers.

constructivist hypothesis on ideational entrapment is confirmed if governmental policy ideas turned from a narrow interpretation into a broader one, encompassing all collective redundancies, and if the legal changes also reflect comprehensive compliance. The alternative hypothesis according to which the government shies away from the Commission and the ECJ in order to avoid a bad reputation would be confirmed if the government had adapted its strategic positions for a limited period of time and shifted into a minimalist form of compliance.

Despite several years of non-compliance, the lead Ministry for Competition and Consumer Affairs quickly abandoned its initial position. Prior to the judicial discourse their policy only covered reactive collective dismissals related to the termination or the reduction of a business due to a decline in demand of a particular type of work. It excluded active dismissals resulting from strategic managerial changes, although this type of redundancy is very common. This left many workers unprotected. Yet the judicial discourse revealed that there was no longer any way to restrict the directive's scope with good and valid political or legally valid arguments. Ideational entrapment took place. The Ministry for Competition and Consumer Affairs, the Department of Employment and the government accepted 'that this narrow scope constitutes a defective implementation of the directive' (Advocate General 1994: 33). The government did not respond to a potential loss in reputation vis-à-vis the Commission or the ECJ. Instead of temporarily paying lip service to these actors, the ideational change towards a more demanding policy was robust over time. The government stopped defending scope restrictions and did not shift into the old rhetoric after the case was closed and losses in reputation were no longer looming (e.g. House of Commons 1994d, House of Commons 1996b, House of Commons 1996d). Although the government had strongly opposed the directive for more than a decade, they quickly accepted that a narrow scope of application could not be justified and that the protective measures of the directive also applied to collective redundancies caused by active management strategies (Secretary of State for Employment, Mr Forsyth, in House of Commons 1995e: 805).[4]

In line with this ideational change, the UK declared as insufficient its

[4] The Ministry for Competition and Consumer Affairs not only quickly changed its policies after the judicial discourse revealed that the initial position can no longer be defended with good arguments. It also completely refrained from blaming Europe for this demanding policy shift, although the Confederation of British Industry (CBI) as the constituency of the Conservatives, opposed the European directive (*Financial Times* 1994a, House of Commons 1994b, House of Commons 1995a, House of Commons 1995d).

former legal transposition with the 1975 Employment Protection Act (Sections 99 and 100) in combination with the 1978 Employment Protection (Consolidation) Act (Section 81) (Advocate General 1994: 33). Both acts restricted the application of protective measures to redundancies caused by reductions of businesses or certain types of work, but this application was no longer compatible with the new policy ideas that were triggered by the judicial discourse. Accordingly, in 1993, only one year after the judicial discourse had started, the government pursued demanding legal changes. The TURERA explicitly broadened protective measures in line with the European directive and no longer restricted their applicatory scope to economic redundancies only. Although the TURERA also removed several rights from trade unions (e.g. membership fees: House of Commons 1993b: 327), it did not introduce ambiguous concepts and overlaps or complex exceptional clauses that would have allowed the practical application of the protective measures only to a limited group of redundancies.

In conclusion, the judicial discourse was effective. In line with the constructivist argumentative entrapment hypothesis, the Department of Employment and the Ministry for Competition and Consumer Affairs shifted into a comprehensive form of compliance, forestalling ambiguities that could invite future norm violations. The rationalist reputation hypothesis, however, does not find empirical support.

Are consultations between employers and employee representatives open-ended or should they aim for agreements mitigating the consequences for workers?

The UK and the Commission further disagreed on the aim of consultations. The British legislation in force (the EPA) merely prescribed that consultations should take place, but did not specify their aim. It did not state that consultations were a means of reaching an agreement. As a consequence employers could de facto reject all positions of workers' representatives, which did effectively reduce the consultation procedure to merely one of information provision. This issue affects the very heart of the directive: employees were less protected if workers' representatives only had a voice which employers could easily ignore. Prior to the judicial discourse, the British government defended its EPA, while the European Commission argued that meaningful consultations, which really protect employees, require more than just the exchange of information.

In the judicial discourse, the European advocate applied the wording technique of legal reasoning (European Court of Justice 1994: 34–6). According to this method of interpretation, Article 2 I of the collective redundancies directive precisely defined that reaching an agreement was the aim of information and consultation endeavours between employee representatives and employers (European Court of Justice 1994: 34). The subsequent paragraph (Article 2 II) stated that consultations 'shall, at least, cover ways and means of avoiding collective redundancies or reducing the number of workers affected, and mitigating the consequences'. Contrasted with this wording interpretation, it became obvious that Section 99 VII EPA was less demanding. Instead of giving workers' representatives real bargaining power in prescribing an agreement between both parties as the aim of consultations, the EPA allowed that employers could easily reject all positions of employee representatives as long as they stated reasons (Advocate General 1994: 34; European Court of Justice 1994: 34–6). The narrow wording instrument of judicial interpretation matched the limited complexity of the interpretational problem well. Only Article 2 of the directive was relevant. Both applicable paragraphs pointed in the same direction and did not create overlaps and they did not entail any ambiguous concepts or other uncertainties: Article 2 I and II of the EC directive precisely prescribe the aim of consultations between employee representatives and employers as reaching agreements (European Court of Justice, 1994: 34–6). Thus, regardless of whether one would start the legal analysis with article 2 I or with 2 II, the wording method suggests that merely providing information to workers' representatives is not sufficient and cannot qualify as consultation (European Court of Justice, 1994: 35).

Due to the high fit between the issue and the applied interpretational device, the norm interpretation developed in this very early judicial discourse made it impossible for the UK to defend their initial position any longer with sound arguments. Any attempt at denying that the directive explicitly requires that consultations should aim for an agreement would have failed. Hence we would expect that the leading ministry, the Ministry for Competition and Consumer Affairs, had either become argumentatively entrapped by the legal reasoning and adapted policies to norms of appropriateness and consistency or reacted with policy adaptations in order to avoid losing reputation vis-à-vis the Commission or the ECJ.

Conservatives had traditionally opposed collective protection rights of workers due to their liberal economic approach (House of Commons 1992b: 218). This changed in response to the early judicial discourse. After the legal reasoning had been put forward in the early written stage of the judicial discourse, the UK advocate no longer argumentatively defended the initial British position (Advocate General 1994: 34, European Court of Justice 1994: 35). At the same time, the departments of employment and of trade and industry pushed for a change in the affected legislation prior to the ECJ judgment (Advocate General 1994: 34, House of Commons 1993b: 327). Instead of emphasizing the almost imposed necessity to adapt policies, members of government and the responsible ministry publicly defended the policy changes as rightful and appropriate (e.g. *Financial Times* 1994a, House of Commons 1993b).[5] Although a threat of reputational losses vis-à-vis the European Commission and the ECJ was off the table after the former had closed the case, the government did not adjust its rhetoric and did not shift back into arguing in favour of a more limited collective redundancy approach (e.g. House of Commons 1996b). The Conservatives broadened their economic policy ideas to include protective measures, but managed to do so without strengthening trade unions (interviews Conservative Party#1, 11–10–06, organized interests#14, 20–03–06). The 1993 TURERA limited the legal rights of trade unions, but – fully in line with the norm interpretation as it had emerged during the judicial discourse – extended collective worker entitlements regarding collective redundancies (House of Commons 1993b). Most importantly, the TURERA incorporated the agreement between employer and worker representatives as the aim of consultations and, thereby, considerably broadened collective protective rights (House of Commons 1993b: 325ff, House of Commons 1994d). Although employers' associations, most notably the Confederation of British Industry, opposed collective rights of workers, the government quickly pursued comprehensive legal changes on redundancy matters during the ongoing judicial discourse (House of Commons 1993b: 327, interview organized interests#13, 13–09–05).

Hence, the judicial discourse succeeded in talking the UK into compliance. In response to very early legal arguments, the government changed its policy ideas and incorporated them into their macro-economic approach. Also they pursued a legal change based on a demanding interpretation of the collective redundancy directive and without loopholes for future norm deviations. While ideational entrapment has very likely taken place and fostered comprehensive compliance, there is no empirical evidence that the UK shied away from the ECJ and the European Commission in order to avoid losses of reputation. They did not shift into the old rhetoric once the case was closed and they did not opt for a cost-saving

[5] Also in line with the constructivist judicial discourse hypothesis, the Conservatives did not play two-level games, by blaming the ECJ for forcing them to make legal changes, in order to justify to their constituency the extension of collective rights concerning collective redundancies (House of Commons 1993b, House of Commons 1994d: 432).

minimalist transposition, which, for example, grants worker representatives bargaining power only on specific issues (e.g. which workers should be released first, which second) or which specifies conditions under which consultations can end without agreements.

Which sanctions are sufficient for ensuring the effectiveness of the directive? The third disputed issue concerned sanctions for employers who disobeyed the protective measures of the collective redundancy directive. The parties disagreed regarding whether the EPA entailed deterrent sanctions. The EPA allowed sanctions to be fully or partially offset against payments which the employer is obliged to make to the employee in any case (based on employment contracts). While the UK delimited sanctions for non-compliant employers, the European Commission favoured more costly penalties.

In the early stages of the judicial discourse, the advocates applied the narrow wording method of judicial interpretation to the EPA (Advocate General 1994: 35, European Court of Justice 1994: 38–41). This revealed that Article 102 III EPA allowed for the offsetting of sanctions against open payments (European Court of Justice 1994: 41). Focusing on the EPA alone cannot solve the question of which penalties are sufficient. Yet neither of the advocates used the wording instrument in relation to the collective redundancy directive. Even if they had done so, a consensual norm interpretation was unlikely to emerge because not a single provision deals with sanctions. Thus, given the high complexity of the interpretational problem at stake, the European advocate used the broad systematic method of judicial reasoning in the early stage of the judicial discourse. Based on this technique, he concluded that Article 5 of the EC Treaty required member states to:

> take all measures necessary to guarantee the application and effectiveness of Community law. For that purpose, while the choice of penalties remains within their discretion, they must ensure in particular that infringements of Community law are penalized under conditions, both procedural and substantive, which are analogous to those applicable to infringements of national law of a similar nature and importance and which, in any event, make the penalty effective, proportionate and dissuasive. (European Court of Justice 1994: 40)

In a further step, the European advocate turned to the EPA and investigated whether it guaranteed the effectiveness of the redundancies directive, in the sense of Article 5 ECT. This revealed that employers who did not properly inform and consult workers' representatives during processes of collective redundancies were not sufficiently penalized

(European Court of Justice 1994: 39). While the British advocate very actively engaged in many of the issues at stake, he did not put a single argument forward against the reasoning of the European side to defend the initial British position, but instead stopped disputing this complaint (e.g. Advocate General 1994: 35). 'The United Kingdom accepts that this second element, namely the set-off against other forms of compensation, has the result that the sanction is insufficiently effective and deterrent and that the United Kingdom has thereby failed to fulfil its obligations under the Treaty' (Advocate General 1994: 31). This is not surprising, since the systematic as well as the teleological method of interpretation would have led to the conclusion that a very mild penalty cannot support and might even thwart the very aim of the directive. Hence, the initial British position could no longer be defended with sound legal arguments.

Again, it is very likely that ideational entrapment took place, which stopped the UK from further making legal claims. The British government, as well as the Ministry for Competition and Consumer Affairs, stopped defending their initial, soft penalty-approach and, consequently, changed the relevant legal provisions through the TURERA during the early stages of the judicial discourse (European Court of Justice 1994: 39). According to this reform, sanctions for non-compliant employers may no longer be offset against other payments to affected employees (House of Commons 1993a). The leading ministry extended worker rights in relation to collective redundancies completely in line with the norm interpretation as it had emerged in the judicial discourse. The TURERA eliminated all ambiguities so that employers violating protective measures could no longer be punished according to the soft EPA rules. The government defended this comprehensive reform as appropriate, referred to the merits of penalties towards non-compliant employers, and claimed that prohibitive sanctions are crucial to protect employees in the event of redundancies (House of Commons 1993b). Similar to the previous disputes on the directive's scope (economic vs. all collective redundancies) and its purpose (voice of representatives vs. agreements between employers and employee representative), the government refrained from shifting the blame to the ECJ in particular, or the EU in general (e.g. House of Commons 1996b). Instead, the UK quickly responded in the early stage of the judicial discourse by pursuing a comprehensive form of compliance.

Again, there is no empirical evidence that the British government ended the norm violation in order to protect its reputation vis-à-vis the European Commission and the ECJ. Firstly, no key actor shifted into defending lax penalties for employers who do not comply with the protective redundancy measures in the TURERA after the Commission had closed the case and declining attention would have allowed for re-adjustments of strategic positions. Secondly, the legal change does not resemble minimalist compliance that would, for example, allow at least the offsetting of some parts of the payments or would introduce exceptions.

Voluntary vs. obligatory recognition of representatives

The fourth dispute at stake in the Court was the question of whether employers must recognize or can refuse to accept employees' representatives as a party in collective dismissal processes. This is an important issue. Without procedures ensuring the presence of employee representatives, many of the protective measures of the collective redundancy directive are ultimately at the discretion of employers.

The interpretational scope of this issue is broad, not least since several articles and paragraphs refer to it. Article 1 1 b provides a definition of representatives: 'the term "workers' representatives" means the workers' representatives provided for by the laws or practices of the Member States'. Article 2 of the collective redundancy directive defines information entitlements and consultation procedures for worker representatives: employers must supply all relevant information on collective redundancies (e.g. number of workforce employed and affected) and must provide reasons for them. Moreover, consultations shall mitigate the negative consequences of collective redundancies for affected workers (e.g. in reducing the number of dismissals). According to Article 3 of the directive, employers must notify the competent public authority of future collective redundancies and of consultations with workers' representatives.

Whereas the UK pursued a narrow approach, by arguing in effect that recognition of workers' representatives by employers was voluntary, the European Commission regarded it as obligatory. In order to make these claims, both parties began by applying different instruments of judicial reasoning. On the one hand, the UK advocate applied the wording method to Article 1 3 of the directive (European Court of Justice 1994: 14). It states that 'according to Article 1(1)(b) of the directive, the term "workers' representatives" is to be understood as meaning the workers' representatives provided for by the laws or practices of the Member States' (European Court of Justice 1994: 14). On the other hand, the British advocate stressed that the laws of the respective state should exclusively define what was meant by the concept of 'workers' representatives'. Yet, since the 1980 and the 1985 reforms, employee representations had not been regulated by British law, but had been based on a system of voluntary recognition by employers (Docksey 1986). No legal act obliged employers to accept workers' representatives. Consequently, trade union recognition was ultimately voluntary for employers. Hence, the UK advocate concluded that the collective redundancy directive, and in particular Articles 2 and 3, could not be applied to instances in which employers did not to recognize trade unions (Advocate General 1994: 8, European Court of Justice 1994: 14).

The European advocate disagreed and claimed that the recognition of workers' representatives was obligatory, by referring back to the wording (Advocate General 1994: 7) and by using systematic techniques of legal reasoning (European Court of Justice 1994: 13). Based on the wording method, the European advocate argued that the directive 'leaves it up to the Member States to define the term "workers' representatives" in accordance with their laws or practices' (Advocate General 1994: 7). The European advocate continued: 'there is, however, a huge difference between leaving Member States free to provide for workers' representatives in accordance with their own legal systems and leaving them free not to provide for any such representatives at all' (Advocate General 1994: 7). Furthermore, based on the somewhat broader systematic technique of legal reasoning, the European advocate drew on Articles 2 and 3 in order to understand the meaning of Article 1. Articles 2 and 3 regulate consultation procedures although neither address whether employers have to accept trade unions as a party in collective redundancy processes, but seem to take the presence of workers' representatives for granted. On this basis, the European advocate argued that the recognition of workers' representatives was not voluntary and not up to individual employers (European Court of Justice 1994: 13, 19).

At the beginning of the judicial discourse, both parties argued at cross purposes because the compatibility between the interpretational scopes of the narrow wording method and of the slightly broader directive-immanent systematic method of interpretation and the complex interpretational problem at hand was low and because the parties did not apply a method of legal reasoning that would have resolved the interpretational problem. Applying the wording instrument to the question of whether employers must accept workers' representatives or whether recognition can be voluntary and circumvented cannot produce a consensual norm definition. This is because the answers to the interpretational question change, depending on whether one uses Article 1 or Articles 2 and 3. Put simply, the wording method produced different interpretations, depending on whether Articles 2 and 3 or Article 1 was given priority. Also, the directive-immanent systematic method did not match the high complexity of the issue at stake, because Articles 2 and 3 do not address the question of whether employers have to recognize trade unions so that they can act as a party in collective redundancy processes. Thus, based on the directive-immanent systematic method, one could argue that consultation procedures can only be applied if two parties are already present in a particular enterprise (UK position), or that consultation presupposes the mutual recognition of employers and trade unions as parties so that it is not up to employers to decide whether they recognize trade unions or not (position of the European Commission).

In the course of the oral and written exchange of legal arguments, however, the advocates used the much broader directive-immanent teleological method of judicial reasoning (European Court of Justice 1994: 14, 20, 24–5). Based on this technique, advocates firstly inquire into the aim of the norm. Secondly they place every disputed paragraph in the context of the directive's purpose. Does an interpretation positively contribute to the directive's aim or does it thwart it? Based on this interpretational device, the advocates came to the same conclusion on the aim of the directive: the UK advocate emphasized that the collective redundancies directive did not harmonize systems of worker's representation, but intended the harmonization of protective legislation in cases of collective redundancies (European Court of Justice 1994: 14). He stated that the 'directive is limited to a partial harmonization of the rules for the protection of workers in the event of collective redundancies' (European Court of Justice 1994: 14). The European Commission did not claim that the directive gave way to a general harmonization, but argued that it aimed towards the protection of workers and emphasized that this cannot be effectively achieved if the very procedures to protect workers are undermined (Advocate General 1994: 7, European Court of Justice 1994: 1, 5). Based on these arguments, it logically followed that the directive could not accomplish partial harmonization of workers' protection in collective redundancies if workers were not represented at all (European Court of Justice 1994: 24–5).

The relatively broad directive-immanent teleological method matched the relatively high complexity of the disputed issue. Consequently, it led to only one conclusion: the recognition of representatives cannot be voluntary for employers, but must be mandatory (European Court of Justice 1994: 15, 23–5). The advocates of both parties actively engaged in the exchange of judicial arguments, focused on all relevant legal acts and used a broad technique of legal reasoning, which did match the broad interpretational scope of the issue at stake. Hence, the constructivist judicial discourse hypothesis (H1) expects that the government became ideationally entrapped, could no longer defend non-compliance with good arguments, and shifted into comprehensive compliance in order to bring their conduct in line with norms of appropriateness, consistency and integrity. Likewise, the alternative rationalist hypothesis (H2a) expects that the government feared reputational losses vis-à-vis the Commission and the ECJ in the event of continuing non-compliance despite a legally superior norm interpretation, and shifted into minimalist compliance. Which, if any, account holds true?

Despite severe criticisms of the Labour Party, the Conservative Major government defended voluntary recognition of trade unions by employers prior to the judicial discourse (House of Commons 1989e: 1108, House of Commons 1990: 64, House of Commons 1991: 476, House of Commons 1992b: 172). They interpreted the collective redundancies directive narrowly, since the voluntary recognition of trade unions fitted well with their liberal economic approach (House of Commons 1989a: 475). Moreover, employer associations, being the constituency of the Conservative party, opposed compulsory consultations because they considered collective rights to be indirect costs and a burden to their business (Skidmore 1995: 746). Thus, in the first months after the ECJ referral in 1992, the Minister of State, Department of Employment (Mr Forsyth) explicitly stated that 'employers will remain free as they are now to decide which, if any, trade union they want to recognise' (House of Commons 1992b: 240). During most of the judicial discourse, the government maintained its compliance-averse attitudes. Consequently, the TURERA did not include compulsory recognition procedures, although it regulated trade union issues (House of Commons 1993b: 360, Skidmore 1995: 745–6).

Only in later stages did the judicial discourse become effective. Once both advocates stopped talking at cross purposes since an interpretational technique had been applied which matched the complexity of the disputed element, the discourse pointed to only one professionally valid conclusion on whether the state had to legally ensure that employers could not simply disregard the protective measures of the directive by not recognizing workers' representatives. As we will see below, it is unlikely that the government adapted its policies in order to forestall losing its good reputation vis-à-vis the Commission and the ECJ if it continued non-compliance despite the interpretational problem having been resolved. Rather, the evidence points towards ideational entrapment, according to which the Department of Employment, the Ministry for Competition and Consumer Affairs and the government could no longer justify with valid arguments their initial narrow position on this issue and shifted into comprehensive compliance.

The judicial discourse revealed that voluntary recognition could not protect employees in the event of collective redundancies (European Court of Justice 1994: 15, 23–5). After the Major government had accepted as legitimate the collective redundancy directive and its aim to provide protective measures for employees and workers (House of Commons 1993b: 326–8, House of Commons 1994d: 431f., House of Commons 1996b: 205), there was no reasonable way to defend the voluntary recognition system any more with practical, legal or political arguments within a frame of appropriateness. Hence, after the late stage of the judicial discourse, the Major government no longer denied that the directive put an obligation on employers to consult and inform workers' representatives and stopped claiming that recognition was voluntary.

> We reached a point of considerable uncertainty where it looked as though an employer had to consult in cases of collective redundancy only if there were a recognised trade union. If there were no recognised trade union, the employer was apparently under no obligation to consult anyone, *which cannot be right*. The European Court of Justice must be supported in its judgment. Tonight we are trying to ensure that, in the case of collective redundancies, everyone is consulted, either through a recognised trade union or through an election. (Minister for Competition and Consumer Affairs, Mr John M. Taylor, in House of Commons 1996b: 205; emphasis added)

The UK had accepted the consultation and information obligations of employers and considered voluntary recognition no longer appropriate for collective redundancy issues. Even years after the judicial discourse had ended, the responsible minister explicitly stated that previous legal acts were insufficient and emphasized the significance of legal adaptations.

> The main point arising from those judgments is that there should be consultation of employees' representatives regardless of whether there is a recognised trade union. Most hon. Members who take an interest know that at present the only consultation required is consultation with a recognised trade union, if there is one. If there is none, there is no current obligation to consult at all. That is the deficiency in our law – laws that were put on the statute book by the Labour Party. The Government are now putting that right. (Minister for Competition and Consumer Affairs, Mr John M. Taylor, in House of Commons 1996b: 233)

The righteousness of the normative language and the positive attributes, which were repeatedly used also after the case had been closed, indicate that the Major government substantively changed its normative policy ideas on the recognition issue, in response to the judicial discourse. If, in contrast, the UK had simply adapted strategic positions in order to avoid a bad reputation for non-compliance vis-à-vis the Commission or the ECJ, we would have expected that the government would have shifted back into the old rhetoric after the Commission had shifted their attention to other states and cases and closed the case. Yet during the remainder of its incumbency, the government did not criticize the EU redundancy legislation (interview organized interests#14, 20–03–06). Moreover, if the UK had simply paid lip-service to the ECJ and the Commission, we would expect that they would have opted for a legal transposition that would have stated that the recognition of worker representatives is obligatory but would have introduced loopholes allowing employers de facto to dictate the terms of redundancies instead of offering meaningful protection to workers. For example, the UK could have used the 1995 regulations to weaken some of the 1993 measures and, thus, reduce the implementation costs for their compliance-averse constituency. Instead, in line with the constructive judicial discourse hypothesis, the UK finalized the legal changes in 1995 which resembled a comprehensive form of compliance (Collective Redundancies and Transfer of Undertakings Regulations). Accordingly, employers were no longer free to ignore workers' representatives, but had to recognize a trade union or other representatives elected by the employees (House of Commons 1996b, interview organized interests#13, 13–09–05). Consequently, even in the absence of trade unions in a specific company, workers were protected from negative consequences of collective redundancies. These rules allowed for the complete reproduction of the directive without including loopholes for lax implementations. Yet the government's reaction to the ECJ judgment was different to what a typical response of the Labour Party would have been. Labour favoured compulsory recognition of trade unions, while strengthening of trade union rights was not compatible with the Conservative party's programmatic core of deregulation and freedom of enterprise, especially since compulsory recognition would have had far-reaching consequences for other issues (e.g. wage bargaining) (House of Commons 1995e, House of Commons 1996b). Hence, the government sought a way to introduce obligatory consultations between employers and employees which did not necessarily strengthen trade unions. In moving from trade union rights towards individual and collective protective rights, the government opted for regulations that did not force employers to recognize specific trade unions, but obliged them to accept any elected workers' representatives (House of Commons 1996b). Thus, workers would profit from collective protective rights even in instances in which there were no trade unions. In instances in which trade unions were present, but in which employees additionally elected representatives for the collective redundancy situation, employers could negotiate the collective dismissals with elected representatives instead of trade unions.

The Labour Party criticized the transposition of the recognition issue as insufficient. They argued that the 1995 regulation allowed employers to choose between the recognition of trade unions and other elected employee representatives and that the regulations did not provide for election procedures for representatives (House of Commons 1996b: 198, 225). The Labour Party even claimed that the regulation was part of the Conservatives' 'campaign to achieve trade union derecognition by the back door' (House of Commons 1996b: 197). In response to such criticisms, the government stressed that the regulation left no loopholes for future norm violations:

> Regulations place a strict duty on the employer to consult appropriate representatives. If the employee representatives or a recognised trade union consider that the employer has not consulted them as required, or the employees affected have not been given a proper opportunity to elect representatives, they may present a complaint to an industrial tribunal. An employer will run a serious risk of an adverse finding if he fails to take such steps as allowing organisers access to the affected employees or providing a list of their names, and in appropriate cases allowing time off and access to facilities. (Minister for Competition and Consumer Affairs, Mr Taylor, in House of Commons 1996b: 204–5)
>
> The regulations now provide for consultation by an employer, whether or not the employer voluntarily recognises a trade union. (Minister for Consumption and Consumer Affairs, in House of Commons 1996b: 208)
>
> An employer may choose whether to consult a union or elected representatives, but he cannot choose not to consult anyone at all. (Mr Taylor, in House of Commons 1996b: 209)

Although the 1995 regulation did not resemble a comprehensive shift in the Conservative party programme, the collective redundancy policy substantively changed. Thus, the Conservative constituency and some Conservative members of parliament continued to oppose the concept of obligatory consultation (e.g. House of Commons 1996b: 215, 226).[6] They

[6] 'The regulations stem from the European collective redundancies directive of 1975, which was agreed to by the then Labour Government. I fear that the directive is a very good example of the kind of pettifogging European interference in the affairs of this country that so annoys so many of our constituents. We do not need Europeans to tell us how to regulate relations between employers and employees; we are perfectly well able to do that ourselves. It is about time that the Council of Ministers reviewed the matter and removed the directive altogether under the principle of subsidiarity. We have to compete in a global market and, to put it simply, the more the regulation, the fewer the jobs. I am interested in securing jobs for the people of this country' (Mr M. Stephen, in House of Commons 1996b: 215).

did not follow the government who had accepted a more demanding norm definition and applied a positive rhetoric (House of Commons 1996b: 205, House of Commons 1996f).[7] Instead of shifting the responsibility to the EU and referring to tied hands, in order to minimize reputational losses vis-à-vis their constituency, the government shifted the blame for the formerly incorrect transpositions to their Labour predecessors: 'That is the deficiency in our law – laws that were put on the statute book by the Labour Party. The Government are now putting that right' (Minister for Competition and Consumer Affairs Mr John M. Taylor in House of Commons 1996b: 233). Moreover, they undertook some efforts to convince their own party members and their constituencies of the merits of the 1995 regulation (House of Commons 1996a, House of Commons 1996f). To this end, the Major government referred back to its macroeconomic policy aims and emphasized that they had not been abandoned, but that the recognition issue had been incorporated in a manner fitting to the economic ideology. Mr Taylor stated:

> As the Government have said before and will continue to say, we believe in flexibility – in setting a framework, but leaving the details to the good sense of employers and employees. That is what gives our businesses the edge that enables them to compete in global markets. (Minister for Consumption and Consumer Affairs, in House of Commons 1996b: 209)

In sum, as expected by the ideational entrapment hypothesis, the Major government changed its normative ideas and the collective redundancy policies in response to the judicial discourse and pursued demanding legal changes. At the same time, the government did not introduce the 1995 regulations as a strategic response to safeguard its good reputation vis-à-vis the Commission and the ECJ.

The second rationalist alternative hypothesis: compliance bargaining in the shadow of the ECJ

This section investigates the rationalist alternative hypothesis on the operation of judicial discourses. Did the Major government strategically

[7] As expected by the ideational entrapment mechanism, the government stated that they were no longer willing to adopt different norm interpretations: 'I do not wish to place any interpretation on the judgment of the European Court of Justice, other than its reported judgment, which I have in my hand' (Mr Taylor, Minister for Competition and Consumer Affairs, in House of Commons 1996b: 210). Similarly 'I do not need to look behind the judgment to find out what the intention was, because I accept the judgment' (Mr Taylor, in House of Commons 1996b: 210).

shift into compliance as a result of a compromise, constructed via compliance bargaining with the European Commission in the shadow of the ECJ?

Information on possible bargaining encounters between the parties is not publicly available. Hence, we cannot directly analyse whether demands and concessions were exchanged, and if so which ones, and whether a common conception of bargaining power was present. However, since successful compliance bargaining should trigger a compromise, we would expect that it not only fosters quick compliance on the side of the affected state, but also results in a withdrawal of the case prior to an ECJ judgment. During the judicial discourse, the government publicly conceded that its transposition of the collective redundancy directive was insufficient concerning the limitation of the directive's scope, the restriction of the purpose of consultations and the nature of sanctions. For example, the European advocate noted in his summary of the case that 'The United Kingdom accepts that this narrowing of the scope constitutes a defective implementation of the directive and it has for that reason passed amending legislation designed to rectify the matter' (Advocate General 1994: 33). This could indicate that the UK acknowledged the power of the European Commission to withdraw the case beforehand, or pursue it until the ECJ issued a ruling. It would have been possible for the UK to make concessions on three of the contested elements and quickly abandoned the norm violations, hoping to get concessions from the Commission on the remaining issue of the recognition of trade unions by employers and to achieve a withdrawal of the case without an authoritative and binding Court judgment. However, even if this had been the bargaining chip and the underlying calculation of the UK, the European Commission did not accept this deal. Instead of withdrawing at least the three already resolved issues, or even the complete case, and instead of compromising in the debate on voluntary vs. mandatory recognition, the Commission explicitly insisted on not withdrawing the three resolved elements: 'The Commission has none the less requested the Court to hold that there was a failure to fulfil the obligation, and in view of the Court's case-law (...) the request ought to be upheld' (Advocate General 1994: 33). Thus, even if compliance bargaining had taken place between the parties, it failed to foster a compromise and could therefore not have triggered a shift into compliance. This is in line with the reasons for the policy changes that governmental members gave in public and the comprehensive nature of the legal adaptations. Rather than playing two level games, the government adopted a language of normative righteousness (e.g. Minister for Competition and Consumer Affairs, Mr John M.

Taylor, in House of Commons 1996b: 233). Hence, the rationalist compliance bargaining hypothesis cannot explain the observed dynamics of ideational and legal change.

The compliance instrument 'judgment'

This section studies another alternative explanation for the policy change in the collective redundancy case: did the UK abolish the norm violations as a reaction to the ECJ judgment? Did the judgment differentially empower domestic norm proponents who invested their resources in shaming or re-framing campaigns in order to push the UK into compliance?

The judicial discourse started in October 1992 and ended in June 1994 with the ECJ judgment (European Court of Justice 1994). Since most but not all of the issues at stake in Court were already completely transposed by the end of the discourse, the ECJ issued a ruling. It publicly highlighted that the UK had lost the case (European Court of Justice 1994: 46) and presented a binding interpretation of all contested elements, basically siding with the arguments put forward by the European advocate, but not with the initial claims of the UK (European Court of Justice 1994: operative part 1). The ECJ stated that

> by failing to provide for the designation of workers' representatives where an employer does not agree to it, by laying down statutory provisions designed to implement Council Directive 75/129/EEC of 17 February 1975 on the approximation of the laws of the Member States relating to collective redundancies that are narrower in scope than the directive, by not requiring an employer contemplating collective redundancies to consult the workers' representatives with a view to reaching an agreement and in relation to the matters specified in the directive, and by failing to provide for effective sanctions in the event of failure to consult the workers' representatives as required by the directive, the United Kingdom has failed to fulfil its obligations under the directive and under Article 5 of the EEC Treaty. (European Court of Justice 1994: operative part 1)

Prior to the ECJ judgment, the government's constituency did not support demanding collective redundancy policies. The CBI and other employer associations opposed the directive and welcomed all liberal reforms that weakened trade unions (Ashford 1981: 140–3, House of Commons 1996b, Skidmore 1995). While the Trade Unions Congress (TUC) strongly supported a demanding collective redundancy approach (e.g. in favouring compulsory recognition), they were not part of the traditional constituency of the Conservatives, but instead sympathized with the Labour Party (Docksey 1986, House of Commons 1992b: 216f., see also

Trades Union Congress 2002: 4–5). Hence, the government had electoral incentives to opt for a narrow reading of the European directive. In addition, such a cost-saving implementation also fitted well with the government's deregulative economic approach.

In the period prior to the Court ruling, successful societal campaigns pushing the Major government into compliance from below were absent. Contextual conditions were not favourable for successful shaming or reframing campaigns and trade unions had few incentives to engage in collective redundancy affairs.

Effective shaming was difficult, due to the low media attention of the case and the widespread scepticism regarding European social policy (e.g. *Financial Times* 1985a, *Financial Times* 1991a). Moreover, prior to the judgment it was openly contested which obligations the European directive entailed and whether or not the UK already met its terms (*Financial Times* 1991b, *Guardian* 1992a). Without an authoritative and widely recognized judgment, the mobilization of criticism of the government for inappropriate norm violations would have been very difficult. Finally, the resonance between collective redundancy issues and domestically institutionalized ideas was low and would have made effective shaming very difficult: the employment law in place restricted collective worker rights in general and trade union rights in particular and the dominating economic paradigm was one of deregulation and liberalization.

The domestic context was equally unfavourable to reframing campaigns during the ongoing judicial discourse. Firstly, due to the uncertainty regarding the directive's content and scope, collective redundancy issues were widely perceived to be legally complex (e.g. *Daily Mail* 1992) and were, consequently, difficult to reframe. Secondly, liberal economic ideas were strongly institutionalized and reinforced a restrictive collective redundancy approach. Accordingly, the government and its constituency perceived collective protective rights as a costly burden to employers (House of Commons 1993b, House of Commons 1995b). Finally, complementary policy frames supporting market-intervention were not prominent so that an alternative approach promoting employee protection could not be linked with them.

In this unfriendly environment to effective shaming or reframing campaigns by trade unions, norm proponents did not invest significant resources in pushing for compliance. Apart from the low prospects of success, one reason for their inaction was the 1993 TURERA (Trade Union Reform and Employment Rights Act) that entailed both carrots and sticks for trade unions. While this law brought serious disadvantages in diminishing protective rights (relating to collective wage bargaining and to the financing of trade unions), it considerably strengthened collective rights on redundancies. Hence, trade unions protested against the cutbacks, but welcomed the legal chances related to the directives' scope (encapsulating all collective redundancies), aims (consultations shall achieve an agreement between employer and worker representatives) and measures (higher penalties for non-compliant employers) (e.g. *Financial Times* 1993).

In 1994, the ECJ judgment empowered trade unions as societal norm proponents in three respects. Firstly, it clearly and authoritatively stated that the UK violated the collective redundancy directive (European Court of Justice 1994). Secondly, the judgment provided a clear and unambiguous norm definition with regard to scope and content. Thirdly, it increased media attention and created publicity (*Financial Times* 1994a, *Guardian* 1994, *Independent* 1994, *Observer* 1994, *The Times* 1994a). However, there were not many opportunities for trade unions to conduct shaming or reframing strategies. In 1994, the government no longer pursued a minimal interpretation of the directive and most of the disputed issues at stake in Court were already completely transformed into compliance with the 1993 TURERA. Also the changes of the 1995 regulations were already on their way, so that there were almost no issues left for public shaming campaigns.

The prospects for successful reframing campaigns improved only slightly after the ECJ ruling 1994. On the one hand, the judgment reduced the complexity of the collective redundancy issues and the uncertainty as to what the best interpretation of the directive might be. On the other hand, liberal economic principles were still deeply institutionalized – especially since the government managed to include collective protective rights into the TURERA and created, thus, an alternative to trade unions (House of Commons 1993b, House of Commons 1996b). As in the phase before the ECJ judgment, a new, alternative policy-frame promoting market intervention to protect employees did not resonate with the deregulative approach of the government. Also, different complementary policies, to which a strong protection approach could have been linked, were still absent.

Thus, societal norm proponents did not push the Ministry for Competition and Consumer Affairs in particular, or the government in general, into compliance from below. Although the TUC welcomed the opinion of the European Advocate General and stated that 'once again, British workers have been shown to be denied rights that are accepted in law in all other European Union countries' (General Secretary of the TUC, in *The Times* 1994a), trade unions did not engage in shaming or reframing campaigns before and after the ECJ judgment (e.g. *Independent* 1994, *Observer* 1994). Instead of blaming and shaming the government for its reluctance to fully implement the collective redundancy directive, the TUC and also the Confederation of British Industry (CBI) constructively participated in consultations with the responsible ministers on options for the legal transposition of obligatory representation of employees (House of Commons 1996b: 197). While some members of the TUC strongly argued for compulsory recognition of trade unions (*Herald* 1992, House of Commons 1996b: 213–14, *The Times* 1994b), others supported the idea of extending workers' representation beyond trade unions. They prepared an interim document, and eventually sided with the Conservative government's solution of legally transposing the norm definition as developed in the Court (*Financial Times* 1994b, *Financial Times* 1994c). By the end of 1994, the TUC task force on workplace representation had developed a new approach towards workplace rights for all workers leading to a coexistence of collective trade union and individual protective rights (*Financial Times* 1994b) which resembled the Major government's policy in large parts. Yet it was difficult to win support for this approach within trade unions and the TUC itself. Notable exceptions were the TUC general secretary, Mr John Monks, who supported the workplace representation approach (*Financial Times* 1994b, *Financial Times* 1995b). It was not until autumn 1995, that the internal coherence of the TUC was restored and the TUC opposed the dissolution of collective rights and their incremental substitution by individual protective rights (*Financial Times* 1995a). By then, however, the legal changes had already been completed.

Thus, the judgment did not induce policy changes in 1993 and 1995 and did not trigger comprehensive compliance with the collective redundancy directive.

The sanction-threat

Did the government anticipate future sanction-threats and therefore comply with the collective redundancy directive relatively soon after the ECJ issued a judgment? This section examines whether the UK strategically adapted policies to increasing non-compliance costs associated with potential future sanctions (rationalist version) or shifted into compliance because a possible sanction-threat differentially empowered pro-compliance ministries (constructivist version).

The rationalist hypothesis: credible sanction-threats increase non-compliance costs

The rationalist sanction-threat hypothesis expects that governments adapt strategic positions to increasing costly, external constraints and quickly shift into a minimalist form of compliance once anticipated costs exceed benefits of maintaining the norm violation. This is especially likely if sanction-threats are looming and if the amount of penalties is high due to the seriousness of the infringement.

In 1993, the shadow of sanctions was not imminent, since the ECJ had not even issued a first ruling. Thus, we would not expect the UK to adapt policies in 1993 and 1995 in an attempt to shy away from eventual penalties. If the Ministry for Competition and Consumer Affairs and the government had adapted strategic positions in anticipation of remote future sanctions, while their compliance-averse substantial policy interests had remained rigid, two strategies would have been rational. Firstly, introducing minimal legal changes would create windows of opportunity for future norm deviations once the case was closed and the sanction-threat had disappeared. Secondly, blame-shifting would have prevented a damage of reputation among employer associations as their compliance-averse constituents, by stressing that pressures emanating from the ECJ were ultimately responsible for policy changes. Yet the government opted for neither of these strategies. On the contrary, they emphasized that collective worker rights are just and appropriate (House of Commons 1993b: 326–7, House of Commons 1995b). Accordingly, they drafted legal acts without loopholes for future lax applications of the collective redundancy directive (e.g. through ambiguous and ill-defined concepts, complex and broad exceptional clauses, or overlaps with other legal acts). Also, no member of the cabinet publicly pointed to a potential ECJ judgment and to possible future non-compliance costs, even though the CBI opposed protective measures, such as information and consultation rights in cases of redundancy, and framed them as a costly burden for British employers (European Foundation for the Improvement of Working Conditions (Marc W. Gilman) 1997, *Financial Times* 1995a). Instead of blaming Europe for policy adaptations, the Ministry for Competition and Consumer Affairs and other governmental members defended ideational and legal changes vis-à-vis their constituency, highlighting how well the new policies fitted with the liberal economic approach (House of Commons 1994d).

In the months after the ECJ judgment in 1994, the shadow of potential future penalties loomed larger than in the period of the ongoing judicial discourse. However, the Commission did not undertake first measures towards enforcement (letter of formal notice, Art. 228 ECT) and the infringement was not very serious from a Commission perspective. The only element constituting a serious issue was the economic harm of workers who were dismissed in collective redundancies. Yet the size of the affected population was relatively small. The collective redundancy directive concerns important rights, but does not strongly affect the four fundamental freedoms of the movement of goods, services, people and capital. Concerning other criteria, the collective redundancy infringement was not very serious either. The Commission's own resources or the operation of the EU were not affected, it did not harm many people or the environment and the UK did not gain an important competitive advantage vis-à-vis other states. Hence, the extent of sanctions would have been rather low. Also, penalties were unlikely and certainly not expected to materialize during the incumbency of the Major government because the Commission did not introduce first enforcement measures. Consequently, we would not expect that the UK shied away from sanctions in the redundancy case. In line with this, the government initiated legal changes even prior to the judgment and completed them soon afterwards. The 1995 regulations abolished the highly contested issue of the recognition of trade unions and even allowed that alternative forms of collective workers' organization could represent employees' interests during collective redundancies: if multiple representations and trade unions are present, the employer can choose with whom he consults. This reform was not a response to the possibility of a future sanction-threat. Firstly, the government did not defend it in cost–benefit terms, but highlighted the obligatory recognition of employees' representatives as righteous (e.g. House of Commons 1996b: 205). Secondly, they never emphasized the role of the ECJ and potential financial penalties for continuing non-compliance, although two-level games strategies would have justified the policy shift and the 1995 reform vis-à-vis their compliance-averse constituency (House of Commons 1995b, House of Commons 1996b, House of Commons 1996c). Thirdly, the government and the Ministry for Competition and Consumer Affairs argued that Conservative core values had not been abandoned or violated, but that the 1993 and 1995 reforms incorporated the recognition issue in a manner which was compatible with the Conservative's liberal economic ideology (House of Commons 1995b).[8] Fourthly, during their incumbency, the government never shifted

[8] Mr Taylor, the Minister for Competition and Consumer Affairs, stated: 'When we framed the regulations, uppermost in our mind was the need to give proper effect to the directives in a way that gave employers flexibility in deciding how to meet their obligations. That has always been our intention: it was spelt out in our consultation paper last year, and we have acted accordingly. As the Government have said before and will

back into a narrow interpretation of the collective redundancy directive even when the shadow of sanctions had disappeared completely after the European Commission had closed the case. If the government had merely adapted strategic positions to external constraints based on cost–benefit calculations, it would have been rational to adopt less costly policies again as soon as the sanction-threat vanished. Yet the Major government did not introduce additional legal changes in order to create windows of opportunity for future lax applications of collective redundancy norms.

In sum, as expected, the remote sanction threat was not sufficiently high and credible to induce compliance in the collective redundancy case. The UK did not pursue the 1993 and 1995 reforms because they were shying away from the ECJ's enforcement instrument.

The constructivist hypothesis: sanction-threats empower pro-compliance ministries

According to the constructivist version of the sanction-threat hypothesis, sanction-threats underline the inappropriateness of non-compliance. This differentially empowers lead ministries and induces comprehensive compliance if the lead ministries were in favour of compliance from the outset but were prevented from proposing or passing demanding policies by domestic veto players. Hence, as a result of differential empowerment, pro-compliance lead ministries initiate legal changes, once the Commission undertakes the first steps towards enforcement (letter of formal notice, Art. 228 ECT).

Since the European Commission did not issue a second letter of formal notice (Art. 228 ECT), sanction-threats were absent and the lead ministry could not use this external intervention to push for a pro-compliance policy. Did the Ministry for Competition and Consumer Affairs instrumentalize the ECJ judgment, which clarified that breaching the collective redundancy norm was inappropriate, for compliance purposes and did they hint to a potential sanction-threat in this context? Becoming differentially empowered by the ECJ, either moderately through a judgment (which can be disregarded for at least one year without consequences) or strongly through sanction-threats (which have short-term effects), requires that the lead ministry is in favour of compliance, but cannot pursue comprehensive policy changes due to domestic or governmental opposition. In the collective redundancy case, the domestic

---

continue to say, we believe in flexibility – in setting a framework, but leaving the details to the good sense of employers and employees. That is what gives our businesses the edge that enables them to compete in global markets' (House of Commons 1996b: 208–9).

non-compliance constituency was strong throughout the infringement proceeding, since the CBI opposed the directive and the strengthening of worker rights (*Financial Times* 1994a, House of Commons 1995a). In line with them, the Conservative Party and the government also argued against interventions into employment affairs (Ashford 1981, House of Commons 1992b, House of Commons 1995d). The Ministry for Competition and Consumer Affairs was as liberal as the government and the CBI. For example, the Minister Mr Forsyth explicitly stated that 'employers will remain free as they are now to decide which, if any, trade union they want to recognise' (House of Commons 1992b: 240). This position did not change until the judicial discourse triggered ideational changes, in 1993 and 1994 respectively, which subsequently found expression in the 1993 and 1995 policy changes. Only after the UK government and the lead ministry adopted new policies in response to the judicial discourse and had already shifted from norm violation into comprehensive compliance for three out of four issues, did the Minister for Competition and Consumer Affairs refer at one point to the ECJ judgment in a positive, uncritical manner.[9] Implying that the policy change is right and appropriate and in line with ECJ judgment might have silenced parts of the domestic compliance-opposition. The main strategy to pacify the CBI was emphasizing that the new redundancy approach still fitted with the Conservative's liberal economic policies.[10] Since drawing on norms of appropriateness concerning the ECJ, as well as explaining the fit to the economic approach, were means to justify policy changes ex-post facto, differential empowerment did not causally induce compliance. In sum, the ECJ did not differentially empower the lead ministry, the Ministry of Competition and Consumer Affairs, and did not induce comprehensive compliance via this pathway.

[9] 'The main point arising from those judgments is that there should be consultation of employees' representatives regardless of whether there is a recognised trade union. Most hon. Members who take an interest know that at present the only consultation required is consultation with a recognised trade union, if there is one. If there is none, there is no current obligation to consult at all. That is the deficiency in our law – laws that were put on the statute book by the Labour Party. The Government are now putting that right (Minister for Competition and Consumer Affairs, Mr John M. Taylor, in House of Commons 1996b: 233).

[10] e.g. 'As the Government have said before and will continue to say, we believe in flexibility – in setting a framework, but leaving the details to the good sense of employers and employees. That is what gives our businesses the edge that enables them to compete in global markets' (Minister for Consumption and Consumer Affairs, in House of Commons 1996b: 209).

The collective redundancy case: a successful judicial discourse

In the UK collective redundancy case, governmental non-compliance interests were very strong and were upheld for several years. The Conservatives opted for liberalization and, therefore, opposed the idea that employers could be forced to recognize trade unions in the event of collective redundancies, had to negotiate the terms of redundancies and were penalized if they did not do so. As a consequence, they eliminated much of the protective legislation that their Labour predecessors had put in place during the 1970s. In one of these legal reforms, the government effectively abolished trade union rights as defined by the EC collective redundancies directive. After becoming aware of this, the Commission initiated an infringement procedure against the UK. Since the Conservatives did not give in, the case came before the ECJ. The first compliance instrument is the judicial discourse. European and UK advocates applied judicial methods matching the complexity of the interpretational problems at stake. In the course of about two years, the judicial discourse revealed that the initial narrow interpretations of the Conservative government were judicially far less convincing than broader definitions. These judicially superior norm definitions entrapped the government in Westminster and fostered the acceptance of a more demanding interpretation of scope and aim of the collective redundancy directive. Hence, they no longer argued against obligatory recognition of workers' representatives by employers or against an agreement as the aim of consultations rather than purely being for the purpose of information exchange. This incrementally facilitated policy changes that were stable over time. Contrary to its previous strong claims, the Conservative government introduced legal changes that allowed for the unambiguous and complete reproduction of the demanding reading of the European directive without loopholes for future norm violations.

In the British collective redundancy case, the judicial discourse helped to talk the government out of non-compliance while the shift into comprehensive compliance was neither induced by strategic adaptations to reputational loses or compliance bargaining in the shadow of the judicial discourse, nor by societal shaming or reframing endeavours after judgments or sanction-threats.

4.II The German drinking water case: an effective judicial discourse

In its preface, the drinking water directive of 1980 (DWD, 80/778) was framed as a means to address differences between member states and as a measure to harmonize the common market. The directive formulated a broad range of emission-based quality standards that water must fulfil to be suitable for human consumption. In doing so, the directive had a dual aim. It focused on public health and on environmental protection and consequently entailed more quality parameters (e.g. levels of ammonium and magnesium) than necessary for avoiding harm to human health. As with all EU directives, member states were required to transpose the directive into national law, which Germany did not do completely.

Overall, the German negotiation team was relatively successful in uploading their drinking water policies to the European level (Börzel 2003a: 77, Knill 2001: 153). The DWD largely resembled the 1980 German ordinance on drinking water, which focused exclusively on public health matters and was based on emission standards instead of procedural regulations. Thus, the misfit between the German legal acts and the DWD was relatively low. Yet the DWD incorporated some standards for environmental parameters that were not part of the German public health-oriented water legislation (Börzel 2003a: 76–81, Liefferink and Jordan 2004: 37–8, interview UBA#1, 18–02–05). In this sense, the directive created a demand for legal adaptation, to which Germany reacted with a four-year delay in issuing a drinking water regulation in 1986 (DWR). The CDU/FDP Kohl government and the leading health ministry were reluctant to comply not least because of the cost implications for water suppliers, who were ultimately responsible for achieving the quality standards (see also Börzel 2003a: 81, Bundestag 1989a). In addition, the European drinking water directive did not correspond to the governmental public health orientation in water quality matters (Bundesregierung 1987b, Bundesregierung 1988, Bundestag 1988c). Hence, environmental parameters exceeding public health protection were not transposed in 1986. In addition, the 1986 DWR allowed for broad exceptions and departures from several quality standards. This limitation of the applicatory scope of the DWD saved compliance costs for the provision of drinking water, but did not strictly ensure that the drinking water was to the high standard demanded by the European directive. This left consumers and the environment less protected than intended by the directive.

In 1987 the Commission opened an infringement proceeding (1987/0440) and accused the Federal Republic of breaching the DWD. Since both parties had strong interests, the dispute continued and the Commission referred the case to the ECJ in July 1990 (237/90). In November 1992 the Court ruled that Germany had incorrectly transposed the 1980 DWD, by interpreting the scope of application too narrowly and the exceptional clause too broadly, as well as by providing an insufficient reporting system for quality deviations.

The pattern of legal change

Germany legally transposed the DWD with a regulation in 1986 (the DWR). However, this legal act followed a public health approach and did not prescribe the same quality standards as the European directive. This affected especially environmental parameters as well as parameter values that were difficult to measure with the commonly applied technology. The Commission suspected that the DWR violated the DWD and opened an infringement proceeding which reached the ECJ. In Court, two issues were at stake. The first violation concerned the 1986 DWR, which allowed for exceptions from the quality standards, if public health was not at risk and if the quality parameters could only be met at the expense of unacceptable costs. This opened broad windows of opportunity for derogations from the directive's quality parameters in the stage of practical implementation (European Court of Justice 1992b: 11, Stathopoulos and Kaiser 1989: 1). In particular, the European Commission criticized Germany for not transposing 'states of emergency' as a necessary criterion for allowing exceptions. Secondly, the parties disagreed on the communicational and informational requirements for departures from the quality aims. It was contested whether informational channels had to be prescribed in legal acts, and whether the obligation to report bad water quality encompassed all derogations or only short-term exceptions.

Already in 1990, Germany had adopted a new drinking water regulation (DWR) that no longer entailed an extensive exceptional clause (e.g. considering events such as thunderstorms as qualifying for exceptions from the directive's quality standards). The 1990 DWR clearly prescribed 'events of emergencies' as a necessary precondition for granting exceptions and followed a preliminary ruling of the Court in another case, in which the concept 'events of emergencies' was further specified. The 1990 DWR did not introduce ambiguity through new and ill-defined concepts, it avoided overlaps with other legal acts and it no longer entailed a broad exceptional clause which prevented loopholes for lax application of the DWD. It resembled comprehensive compliance and resolved the first of the two disputed elements prior to the ECJ judgment.[11]

[11] Since the 1990 DWR entered into force in January 1991, the Commission expected failures in the practical implementation until January 1991. However, since the new complaint was introduced after the case had been referred to the Court, the ECJ dismissed this point as inadmissible (European Court of Justice 1992b: 21, 22).

The second disputed issue concerned communicational requirements in cases of failure to meet the quality parameters. At issue was whether communicational requirements must be outlined by domestic legal acts and whether all deviations had to be reported. As in the pervious regulation, the 1990 DWR required only reports on derogations if temporary events (e.g. floods) rather than the soil (geogen reasons) caused bad water quality (European Court of Justice 1992b: 31). In effect, temporary quality deviations were reported, but permanent failures in meeting quality standards were not. This issue was resolved with the 1992 Drinking Water Provision (DWP), which encompassed all derogations and no longer prevented comprehensive monitoring of the European Commission. The 1992 DWP completely transposed the norm interpretation as developed before the Court and closed loopholes for lax applications. It unambiguously stated that all derogations as defined by the DWD were subject to communicational requirements, abstained from imprecise concepts and reduced uncertainties and ambiguities through overlaps with other legal acts. Hence, the DWP also resembled a comprehensive form of compliance.[12] In line with this, the number of domestic court cases related to the issues at stake in the European infringement procedure dropped sharply from four to zero after compliance had been achieved (see also Annexe, table 1).

The government had been reluctant to transpose a demanding reading of the DWD that included all health and environmental parameters for almost ten years. While the 1986 DWR was based on a narrow approach, the legal changes in 1990 and 1992 were not. Why did the CDU/FDP coalition change policies? The following sections examine the role of the three compliance instruments. Did the German government abolish non-compliance in response to the judicial discourse? Was the judgment successful or did the threat of potential sanctions ultimately force the CDU/FDP coalition to change its drinking water policy?

The judicial discourse in operation

The judicial discourse took place between July 1990 and November 1992 (case 237/90). Two issues related to the scope of application were at stake (Advocate General 1992: 1, 8): the parties debated under which

[12] Yet even after 1992, the Commission was not satisfied with the German drinking water quality and criticised the application of the DWD. Especially in the new Länder, the pipe system was old and parameters of the DWD (e.g. on lead and iron) were not met. However, since the legal transposition reduced uncertainties and ambivalences concerning the necessary conditions for granting derogations and the communicational requirements, none of the preliminary references dealt with these elements afterwards.

conditions states could grant exceptions from the DWD and whether all deviations had to be reported to the Commission.

This section analyses the constructivist and the rationalist hypotheses in turn. It shows that the German government became ideationally entrapped through the judicial discourse and accordingly changed its policy ideas and legal acts into comprehensive compliance.

Judicial discourse: ideational entrapment or threats of reputational losses?

'States of emergency' as a precondition for exceptions?

The parties disagreed about the conditions under which states can grant exceptions from the quality parameters of the European directive. The German 1986 DWR allowed for exceptions that did not put the public health at risk, if the quality parameters could only be met at the expense of unacceptable costs. The European Commission regarded this as an intolerable limitation, violating the DWD, and emphasized that exceptions are permitted only under 'states of emergency'.

Already in the early stages of the infringement procedure, the European Commission claimed that a broad reading of the exceptional clause, ignoring the crucial precondition of 'states of emergency', could not qualify as compliance (European Court of Justice 1992b: 11). In court, the European advocate backed this argument with a mixture of wording and directive-immanent teleological techniques of legal interpretation. In a first step, the narrow wording method revealed that exceptions for temporary derogations from the quality parameters could indeed be granted. Article 10 I DWD stated:

> In the event of emergencies, the competent national authorities may, for a limited period of time and up to a maximum value to be determined by them, allow the maximum admissible concentration shown in Annex I to be exceeded, provided that this does not constitute an unacceptable risk to public health and provided that the supply of water for human consumption cannot be maintained in any other way. (European Court of Justice 1992b: 7)

Since this article was precise and directly addressed the preconditions for water quality exceptions, the wording method fitted well the low complexity of the interpretational problem. It clarified that exceptions are allowed 'in the event of emergencies', which is the opening term of Article 10 DWD and has the status of a necessary condition. But a wording interpretation gives no hint as to what the term 'event of emergencies' actually encompasses. Although this was not directly at stake before the Court since the initial German transposition completely disregarded this precondition for granting exceptions, the European advocate applied the directive-immanent teleological method as well. Based on that, he concluded that the effectiveness of the DWD would be in severe danger if emergencies were interpreted too widely (Advocate General 1992: 12, European Court of Justice 1992b: 11).

At the beginning of the judicial discourse, the leading Federal Ministry for Youth, Family and Health defended its broad reading of the exceptional clause of the DWD. To this end, the German advocate used a pragmatic argument linking the DWR to the DWD as well as to a broader German principle. Accordingly, the criterion of 'acceptable costs' in the 1986 DWR specified Article 10 I and Annex 1 of the DWD, which both regulate exceptions, via the German principle of proportionality (Advocate General 1992: 10–11, European Court of Justice 1992b: 12). The proportionality principle basically demands that means and ends should be in proper relationship: not every means is justified in reaching an end. According to this reasoning, quality exceptions are in line with the DWD as well as with the German proportionality principle as long as exceptions are only granted if they do not pose a risk to human health and if the cleaning of water to reach all DWD quality aims would be very expensive. In making this pragmatic argument, Germany did not address the question of whether 'states of emergency' are necessary preconditions for granting exceptions in the first place.

In the course of the judicial discourse, the interpretational problem became more and more clear: the parties did not generally dissent on whether exceptions are legitimate, but on the preconditions under which they can be invoked. Hence, responding to the European advocate's reasoning, the German advocate no longer ignored the meaning of 'states of emergency' and also used the wording instrument of judicial interpretation (Advocate General 1992: 11, European Court of Justice 1992b: 12). In a first step, Germany conceded that the wording of its 1986 DWR did not refer to 'states of emergency' at all (Advocate General 1992: 11). Once this was on the table, defending the initial German position, according to which 'unacceptable costs' are a good reason to grant exceptions from the DWD's quality parameters, with high-quality judicial arguments was very difficult. The interpretational scope of the issue at stake was very low and matched the narrow wording method pretty well. Since it was clear that article 10 DWD did not include 'unacceptable costs' as relevant criterion allowing for quality exceptions and because no other paragraph of the DWD would have allowed the incorporation of additional criteria for granting exceptions, the German advocate could not and did not defend the initial DRW with the narrow wording or any of the broader techniques of judicial reasoning (Advocate General 1992: 11, European Court of Justice 1992b: 12).

During the judicial discourse, the advocates stopped talking at cross purposes. Both advocates actively exchanged judicial arguments, focused on all relevant legal acts and applied the wording method of judicial interpretation (Advocate General 1992: 10–14, European Court of Justice 1992b: 7–12). It matched the low complexity of the interpretational issue at stake, and the advocates consented that 'events of emergency' are necessary preconditions for granting quality exceptions. Consequently, the constructivist judicial discourse hypothesis predicts that Germany became ideationally entrapped by this judicial discourse and, therefore, was persuaded that its initial policy could no longer be defended with sound and good arguments so that it shifted into a comprehensive form of compliance. At the same time, the alternative rationalist hypothesis expects that Germany adapted its strategic positions and shifted into minimalist compliance in order to circumvent losses in reputation vis-à-vis the ECJ and the Commission because it violates EU law despite the legal interpretational difficulties being resolved.

Prior to the judicial discourse, Germany opted for a narrow transposition of the DWD. The Minister for Youth, Family and Health, Wolfgang Schäuble, openly admitted that 'some parameters are not transposed; partially they are below the detectable sensitivity, partially measurement techniques are lacking' (Federal Ministry of Youth 1985: 1, translation DP). While environmental parameters were compromised, essential health-related parameters were not: 'the new drinking water regulations contain requirements, guaranteeing that life-long water consumption cannot harm human health' (Bundesregierung 1985: 6, translation DP). Thus, the 1986 DWR allowed for derogations from drinking water quality standards if public health was not jeopardized and if compliance with all quality parameters of the DWD led to unacceptable costs. Due to the scientific advice of the Federal Health Office, 'states of emergency' were not explicitly defined as a necessary criterion for granting exceptions.[13]

[13] The Federal Health Office argued that a narrow definition of 'states of emergency' and a restrictive exceptional clause were incompatible with water providers' public responsibility, since it could result in complete interruptions of water supply if certain parameters were not met. 'In such cases the water consumers are worse off than in cases of temporary provision of lower quality water, since they cannot even boil water before consuming it' (interview UBA#6, 06–05–05, translation DP). It convinced the Federal Health Ministry to adopt a restrictive water quality approach regarding environmental aspects. Since the term 'states of emergency' in the DWD referred to unforeseen natural incidents, the broad exceptional clause in the 1986 DWR affected primarily environmental issues.

This policy changed once the judicial discourse argumentatively entrapped the leading ministry. After it became evident that the legal experts concluded that states of emergency have to be necessary conditions for quality exceptions to be allowed, Germany realized that its initial broad interpretation of the DWD exceptional clause could no longer be defended with plausible and convincing judicial arguments. Just five months after the beginning of the judicial discourse, the health ministry accepted that the exceptional clause in the 1986 DWR was too broad. Consequently, they modified the formerly contested drinking water regulation in 1990 during the ongoing judicial discourse in line with what the ministry now regarded as being the correct and appropriate interpretation of the DWD. The 1990 DWR stated that 'events of emergency' are the necessary precondition for temporarily allowing water quality exceptions. Thus, in line with the norm interpretation favoured by the legal experts of both parties, the revised DWR entailed a narrow exceptional clause (European Court of Justice 1992b: 18, 21). It abolished all previous loopholes for saving compliance costs concerning environmental parameters and even emphasized clearly that exceptions are only granted temporarily. Thus the 1990 DWR transposed the demanding norm interpretation as developed during the judicial discourse.

The government pursued the legal adaptation, even though the domestic context was not favourable to it. In 1990 opponents of a demanding drinking water approach with few quality exceptions had emerged from an unexpected angle: the Green Party criticized the demanding drinking water approach on which the DWR was based for insufficiently distinguishing between drinking and non-drinking water (Green Party 1990: 1–2). They also emphasized that applying the DWD quality parameters could cause environmental damage since even toilets have to be operated with drinking water (Green Party 1990: 1–2). In response, a public debate evolved around the distinction between drinking water and water intended for other human needs which the draft DWR entailed (Bundesministerium für Jugend 1990b, UBA#2, 21–02–05). The pool of sceptics broadened, to include not only drinking water suppliers and the federal health office (interview UBA#5, 18–03–05), but also the general public. Rather than exploiting this compliance-averse context to abstain from legal changes altogether or at least postpone them until the ECJ issued a judgment, the health ministry emphasized that non-drinking water could still be used for watering private gardens and went on with their plans for the demanding DWR (Bundesministerium für Jugend 1990a). The 1990 DWR completely abolished the previous loophole for saving compliance costs. This cannot be explained from a rational choice perspective.[14] The latter would reduce judicial discourses to cheap talk, and would therefore expect that the compliance-averse government would use public sentiments against the DWR to either water it down or further delay the transposition. The very fact that the federal health ministry passed the DWR in late 1990, despite domestic scepticism and against their own, previous strategic preferences and policy interests (compare e.g. Bundesregierung 1987b, Bundesregierung 1988 with Bundesregierung 1990b, Bundestag 1991e) can only be explained by the constructivist argumentative entrapment mechanism, which prevented the government from defending their initial position with valid arguments and triggered comprehensive ideational and policy change.

The lead ministry and the government also adapted their policy ideas. In line with the newly identified logic of appropriateness and of consistency, they shifted from a narrow to a demanding approach. Both the ideational and legal changes reflected comprehensive compliance. Prior to the judicial discourse, governmental members applied a health and a cost frame to drinking water quality issues. According to both frames, drinking water quality was important because of public health concerns, but high compliance costs trumped the health issues and new environmental aspects could de facto be ignored (e.g. Bundesregierung 1988, Bundestag 1988c). This water quality approach was in line with the German principle of proportionality. Yet after the judicial discourse had produced a judicially superior norm definition, this framing changed. The government realized that the old, lax approach could no longer be defended with good arguments. Thus, from winter 1990 onwards, the government and the health ministry consistently argued in favour of the DWD and emphasized its merits instead of its compliance costs (Bundesregierung 1990b, Bundestag 1990a, Bundestag 1991c, Bundestag 1991e). Public health concerns no longer dominated drinking water quality debates and environmental issues were regarded as equally important (e.g. Bundestag 1991d, Bundestag 1991f). When costs for high water quality and for environmental protection were mentioned at all, the government now pointed to the righteousness of environmental protection (*Süddeutsche Zeitung* 1991). This ideational change remained stable over time, which also indicates that the German government did not change its policies in order to maintain its good reputation vis-à-vis the European

[14] This is all the more surprising, since even a drinking water task force (Fachkommission Soforthilfe Trinkwasser, FKST) suggested granting broad exceptions in order to maintain the water supply in the new Länder and would have supported the Kohl government in further delaying a demanding legal transposition of the DWD (interview UBA #1, 18–02–05).

Commission and the ECJ. Even several years after the case had been closed, the government did not shift back to undemanding water policies via a broad, cost-saving reading of the exceptional clause of the DWD (Bundesregierung 1993a, Bundesregierung 1994b, Bundestag 1993b, Bundestag 1994a).

In sum, in line with the constructivist judicial discourse hypothesis, Germany shifted into comprehensive compliance. In contrast to what the rationalist reputation hypothesis would have expected, the government did not adapt its strategic positions and did not shift back into the old rhetoric once the case was closed. Also, Germany did not opt for a minimal transposition that included loopholes such as allowing temporary derogations beyond the directive or ambivalently formulating the conditions under which exceptions can be granted to save implementation costs.

Communicational requirements for derogations from quality parameters

The second issue at stake concerned the reporting system in place for collecting and disseminating information on derogations from water quality standards (Le Moal-Ollive 1990). The German Drinking Water Regulation (DWR) of 1986 was the initial transposition of the European DWD and did not prescribe the exchange of information between the central state and federal states. Consequently, there was no legislation mandating the availability of comprehensive information on drinking water quality and derogations thereof. This constituted a window of opportunity for distributing low quality water behind the European Commission's back. Consequently, the Commission repeatedly stressed that drinking water quality must be comprehensively documented. In order to ensure that water providers systematically and comprehensively collected water quality and quality derogation information and passed it on to the European Commission, the Commission urged Germany to legally regulate its domestic water quality monitoring system. By contrast, Germany regarded its decentralized quality reporting system as sufficient, although it did not systematically and comprehensively require reports on implementation data and de facto excluded permanent deviations from reporting requirements.

The issue was debated in two stages. In the early judicial discourse, the parties focused on the legal obligation of information and dissented on the applied judicial techniques, but talked at cross purposes. In the later stage of the discourse (late 1991 and 1992), the parties held full debates on which substantive deviations had to be subject to reports. Here a judicial method with a high compatibility to the contested issue was applied and this fostered a consensual norm definition among the legal experts. Hence, while the advocates of both parties talked at cross purposes at the beginning of the judicial discourse, they shared a judicial method of interpretation matching the interpretational scope of the problem at stake later on.

Early in the judicial discourse, Germany defended its transposition by using the highly specific wording method of interpretation (European Court of Justice 1992b: 24). The wording of the DWD demands a 'wholesome communication' of failed parameters (Article 9 I, Article 10 III DWD). However, this concept was not further specified in the remainder of the European directive. The DWD also failed to specify whether the procedures ensuring wholesome communication had to be spelled out in a legal rule.[15] Based on the wording method of judicial interpretation, Germany argued that the DWD did not explicitly prescribe a national legal act on the collection of relevant information and the communication of derogations (European Court of Justice 1992b: 25, *Süddeutsche Zeitung* 1992d). The central concept 'wholesome communication procedures' is vague and not defined in the DWD so that the interpretational scope of the issue at stake was very broad. The narrow wording instrument was ill-suited to tackling the high complexity of the contested element. During the early discourse, Germany also pragmatically referred to a German legal institution, the 'states' loyalty towards the federation'. The German advocate argued that the Länder were practically obliged to report derogations to the central state, which rendered a secondary law on communicational requirements superfluous (European Court of Justice 1992b: 25).

Based on the wording method, the European advocate could not dismiss the German argument that the text of the directive was silent on whether procedures for the collection of water quality information and water quality derogations should be legalized (European Court of Justice 1992b: 23, interview COM#2, 02–03–05). Yet the wording of the DWD did not explicitly prescribe the German option and the European advocate did not conclude that the German transposition was in line with the directive. The European advocate also did not interpret the European directive and the German DWR in reference to the 'loyalty towards the federation'-

[15] 'The German Government goes on to argue that the directive does not require the incorporation in domestic legislation of the obligation of notification laid down by Article 9(1) and Article 10(3) of the directive on the ground that that obligation ensues directly from the directive. The obligation for the Länder to notify the Federal Government is not imposed by the directive' (European Court of Justice 1992b: 25).

principle, but regarded the latter as irrelevant to the case and as functionally inadequate (Advocate General 1992: 16, European Court of Justice 1992b: 23, 29). Instead, the European advocate applied the broad directive-immanent teleological method (Advocate General 1992: 16, European Court of Justice 1992b: 23). According to this line of reasoning, communicational requirements had to be legally prescribed to ensure the effectiveness of the European drinking water approach, since the Commission could not fulfil its monitoring function otherwise (Advocate General 1992: 16, European Court of Justice 1992b: 1–2, 29, interview COM#7, 07–02–06).

In this stage of the judicial discourse, arguing was not effective and the advocates talked at cross purposes. The text of the DWD lacked an explicit paragraph concerning whether or not states were required to make legal rules to ensure complete reports on bad water quality. Since the central concepts were vague, the interpretational scope of the problem was very high. Consequently, the narrow wording method could not produce an intersubjectively valid interpretation. Instead of facilitating a single reading, the wording instrument of judicial interpretation allowed for two conclusions. Firstly, that the DWD did not require certain legally binding communicational mechanisms so that the choice of how to achieve 'wholesome communication' was entirely up to the member states (German position). Secondly, that various monitoring and information mechanisms can be used, but each of them has to ensure 'wholesome communication' which implicitly presumes a legal framework to ensure effective implementation and compliance (position of the European Commission). Similar to the working method, the directive-immanent teleological method could also not intersubjectively resolve the interpretational problem. The directive-immanent teleological method was too broad and allowed for two instead of one answer to the question of whether the DWD requires legal procedures that prescribe how information on water quality derogations is collected. On the one hand, one can follow the European advocate. On the other hand, one could argue that while the Commission's monitoring function requires that the results of water quality measurements and derogations are transparent and this information is accessible to the Commission so that states can be held accountable, it is up to the member states how they create transparency and how they ensure that the Commission obtains the complete information. Hence, in the first stage of the judicial discourse the parties argued at cross purposes and dissent prevailed.

As the constructivist and the rationalist hypotheses predict, the early judicial discourse failed to produce an intersubjectively valid norm interpretation. Hence, Germany did not become argumentatively entrapped and did not shift into compliance. Also, in the absence of a legally superior norm interpretation, there was no need to pay lip-service to the Commission and the ECJ in order to avoid costs of reputational losses. In line with both predictions, the government continued to save on compliance costs and prevented major investments in 1990 and 1991 (Bundestag 1991h: 396). They opposed a demanding reporting system that comprehensively gathered all deviations form the drinking water quality – especially in the case of long-lasting and severe derogations. The government and the leading health ministry opposed a demanding proposal of the Social-Democratic opposition on the institutionalization of communicational channels (Social Democratic Party 1991), because of an overarching hesitation to increase transparency, in particular for environmental issues,. The draft proposal included a comprehensive reporting system to collect and disseminate information on drinking water quality to the public, the central state and the European Commission (Bundestag 1991a: 5455–68). The Federal Ministry for Youth, Family and Health neither highlighted the merits of the European DWD nor consented with the SPD that the German DWR was seriously lacking on the issue of communicational requirements (Bundestag 1991a: 5455–68). Instead, they shifted the responsibility to local authorities, claiming that the latter were solely responsible for monitoring the water quality and derogations (Social Democratic Party 1991). Hence, the health ministry had not been persuaded by legal arguments exchanged before the ECJ and continued to believe that the German position could be argumentatively defended. In line with the absence of changes of policy ideas and adaptations of strategic positions, Germany did not shift into compliance. The government did not introduce a comprehensive quality monitoring system, although a legal change concerning the first issue at stake in Court (necessary conditions for granting exceptions and the role of 'states of emergency') would have provided a window of opportunity to do so without much additional work. The Drinking Water Regulations of 1990 transposed the other contested issue and also specified reporting procedures on derogations in this context (Article 4 III). However, the government did not introduce a comprehensive quality reporting system. Communicational obligations for granted quality deviations were restricted to meteorological reasons associated with 'states of emergency'. The 1990 DWR did not require the collection and dissemination of information on derogations caused by permanent conditions, such as the soil (geogen reasons) (European Court of Justice 1992b: 31). Excluding this sub-type was important, since geogen quality deviations were more durable than short-term meteorological ones and consequently brought about more severe and costly drinking water quality problems. A comprehensive reporting system would have uncovered all instances of poor drinking water quality. This would have increased pressures on water suppliers and the government to invest additional resources and would have multiplied compliance costs (interview organized interests#7, 09–02–05). Thus, due to the unsuccessful early judicial discourse, the 1990 DWR entailed an incomplete quality monitoring system and required no reports for long-term derogations that were caused by the soil.

The 1990 DWR did not solve the issue on the proper communication procedure and the judicial discourse continued (European Court of Justice 1992b: 4–5). Yet due to the legal changes with the 1990 DWR (that had been introduced to transpose the other issue at stake in Court), the discourse shifted substantially. It moved from the abstract and complex question of whether reporting requirements should be legally prescribed in general, to the more concrete and far less complex issue of what to do with derogations caused by the soil (European Court of Justice 1992b). Since this issue was explicitly referred to in Article 9 I DWD and this Article did not introduce new and ambiguous concepts, complex exceptional clauses or linkages to other parts of the DWD, the interpretational scope of this problem was low. The parties debated whether geogen derogations must also be reported to the European Commission (position of the Commission), or whether the communicational obligations referred only to quality derogations that were caused by meteorological 'emergencies' (German position). Again, the implications were important, since the number of reported derogations and the potential costs for water providers were much higher for the former than for the latter option.

The wording of the crucial Article 9 I DWD states:

> Member States may make provision for derogations from this Directive in order to take account of: (a) situations arising from the nature and structure of the ground in the area from which the supply in question emanates. Where a Member State decides to make such a derogation, it shall inform the Commission accordingly within two months of its decision stating the reasons for such derogation; (b) situations arising from exceptional meteorological conditions. Where a Member State decides to make such a derogation, it shall inform the Commission accordingly within 15 days of its decision stating the reasons for this derogation and its duration.

The European advocate applied the wording method to the German DWR and the European DWD (Advocate General 1992: 18). Based on this, the European advocate argued that Article 9 DWD grants specific, but not general geogen exceptions and also that only specific exceptions from drinking water quality standards, which are caused by soil-related problems, can be approved (Advocate General 1992: 18). Consequently the wording of the DWD demands that information on all quality deviations has to be collected and communicated to the Commission (Advocate General 1992: 18, interview COM#5, 25–11–05).

Initially, the German advocate did seek to justify the exemption of soil-related quality deviations from strict communicational requirements and referred to the wording of Article 9 I DWD (Advocate General 1992: 19, interview COM#5, 25–11–05). Yet Article 9 DWD precisely addressed the issue of what to do with derogations and was not compatible with the 1990 DWR and the initial German position (European Court of Justice 1992b: 28). The wording method of judicial interpretation only allowed for one conclusion of how the communicational obligations of the DWD should be understood: all instances of poor quality have to be reported (Advocate General 1992: 20). Since the German advocate himself used the wording method at the beginning of the discourse, it was not possible to simply disregard this method and the argument of his European colleague later on, especially since it had a high match to the low complexity of the issue at stake. Consequently, in the late oral stage of the judicial discourse, the German advocate did not challenge the wording-based interpretation of his European colleague with arguments based on alternative methods of legal reasoning and no longer denied the necessity of comprehensive quality reporting requirements independent of the sources for quality problems (European Court of Justice 1992b, interview COM#5, 25–11–05). Furthermore, the German advocate no longer claimed that general exceptions were possible if they were caused by the soil so that they must not be reported to the Commission on a case-by-case basis (Advocate General 1992: 17, 19, European Court of Justice 1992b: 25f, interview UBA#2, 21–02–05). The non-communication of soil-related exceptions could not be justified with the wording instrument. Part a) and b) of Article 9 I DWD unmistakably specify the reasons for possible derogations as geogen or exceptional meteorological conditions (interview organized interests#7, 09–02–05). Consequently, the wording method of judicial interpretation demanded that information on both types of quality deviations must be reported.

In debating whether, and which, reporting requirements are in line with the European DWD, the parties shared the narrow wording method. This matched the limited interpretational scope of the problem at stake. Hence, as the constructivist hypothesis expects, Germany became argumentatively entrapped in the late stage of the judicial discourse and ended non-compliance in response. While the constructivist ideational entrapment hypothesis predicts comprehensive compliance, the alternative rationalist reputation hypothesis expects that Germany shifted into minimalist compliance in order to avoid losses of reputation vis-à-vis European authorities. Which of the two predictions is better suited to explain the compliance dynamics?

Towards the end of the judicial discourse, legal experts could not see any room to justify deviations from the consensual norm interpretation.[16] Once this became clear, the health ministry and members of the government changed their rhetoric on drinking water policies, initiated legal changes five months ahead of the judgment, and enforced complete implementation of the new demanding drinking water policy thereafter. Firstly, rather than focusing on costs associated with the European DWD and defending a minimalist drinking water quality approach, the government highlighted the merits of the DWD for preventing environmental and health damages (Bundestag 1992c). They even stated that environmental concerns were important for the maintenance of Germany's high water quality standards (Bundestag 1992c: 13027–48).[17] Prior to the judicial discourse, drinking water issues were debated in the Bundestag in terms of public health in line with an undemanding reading of the DWD. However after the judicial discourse, drinking water quality came to also be regarded as a matter of environmental protection, which matched a more demanding water quality policy (Bundestag 1994a, 21641–57, interview federal ministry#7, 08-03-05). The distinction between rightful health-related quality parameters and 'unnecessary' environmental quality parameters was no longer sustainable and the conviction that compliance expenditures for the latter should be reduced stopped being in vogue in the health ministry (Bundestag 1993b: 13027–48, interview UBA#6,

[16] The ministry could have relied on the (broader) systematic argument that the federal loyalty principle precluded the legalization of any explicit information rules (as argued in the early stage of the discourse), in order to defend its initial position. But this argument would not have addressed the precise issue at stake. It would also not have been compatible with the professional opinions of the advocates and was unlikely to be accepted by the European enforcement authorities. Hence, after the judicial discourse produced an interpretation that was intersubjectively valid among the advocates of the parties, it would have been irrational (since most likely unsuccessful) and inappropriate of the German government to use a deviating argument any longer.

[17] e.g. 'We always emphasized that water policy may not exclusively focus on drinking water aspects, but is also required for ecological purposes' (Hirsche, Parliamentary State Secretary, Bundestag 1996b: 3432; translation DP). Or 'for ecological reasons and reasons of health protection and health care the government puts strong emphasis on the modernization of drinking water facilities' (Bundesregierung 1993a: 10, translation DP).

06–05–05). This was in stark contrast to the arguments prominent in 1989, in which the scientific and technological basis of the DWD, and in particular of some of its environmental parameters, had been attacked from all sides in order to justify a minimalist, cost-saving transposition of the DWD (Bundesregierung 1988, Bundestag 1988c: 2799). Also, the ideational change was stable over time and the government did not shift into the old rhetoric after the Commission had closed the case.

Secondly, the government and the leading Federal Ministry for Youth, Family and Health not only changed the rhetoric, but also adapted legal acts in line with a comprehensive monitoring and information system. The health ministry had already drafted the Drinking Water Provision (DWP) during the late stage of the ongoing judicial discourse in July 1992 (Federal Ministry for Health 1992). The DWP was passed in December 1992 and entailed communicational requirements for all water quality derogations. In addition, the government invested DM 11,000,000 in laboratories of water providers and other institutes, in order to enable them to comprehensively check the quality of drinking water (Bundestag 1992a: 55, Bundestag 1992c: 4). As expected by the judicial discourse hypotheses, the 1992 DWR constituted comprehensive compliance, since it was based on a demanding and comprehensive interpretation of the DWD. Germany changed its drinking water policies, despite the strong non-compliance preferences of water providers (e.g. Bundesregierung 1993a, Bundestag 1993b: 13027–48) and despite the still huge compliance costs, in particular for the drinking water systems in the new Länder. For example, estimations went up to DM 100,000,000,000 (~€ 51,129,000,000) for improvement of the water supply and the sewerage disposal in the new Länder (Bundestag 1992b: 5971). The comprehensive and quick legal adaptation was remarkable for a second reason. The DWP draft required the approval of the Bundesrat, because implementation issues, as competencies of the Länder, were at stake. However, CDU-governed Länder in particular opposed comprehensive reporting requirements (Bayern 1992, Bundesrat 1992). Even the Bundesrat's Committee for Health proposed scope restrictions to the informational requirements in the governmental draft DWP (Bundesrat 1992: 487, Bundesratsausschuss für Gesundheit 1992: 2). The Kohl government managed to pass the DWP in spite of this scepticism and prescribed communicational requirements for deviations from all parameters for geogen and for meteorological reasons. The DWP ensured the comprehensive collection of information on exceptions and derogations from local authorities to the federal ministry for health. It did not leave windows of opportunity for less demanding norm interpretations in the future and did not entail unspecified or ambiguous new concepts. Nor did it create overlaps with other bodies of law, but resembled a demanding form of compliance (Federal Ministry for Health 1992: 1, 6).

Thirdly, in line with this policy change, the health ministry also strengthened domestic compliance monitoring and enforcement measures. The German Federal Health Authority (BGA) had extensive contacts with water providers in the Länder, and opposed the 1990 DWR and the 1992 DWP, campaigning for non-compliance with some of the drinking water quality parameters (Bundestag 1991g, Bundestag 1993e, interview federal ministry#7, 08–03–05). The BGA was concerned that comprehensive quality reporting systems would reveal all instances of poor drinking water quality, in particular in the new Länder. They thought that this would increase pressures on the BGA, local authorities, and water suppliers or even lead to additional EU infringement proceedings for failures of practical implementation of the DWD (interviews UBA#5, 18–03–05, UBA#6, 06–05–05). Neither the government nor the health ministry used the scepticism of the BGA as a window of opportunity to pursue a less demanding drinking water quality approach in the implementation stage. Instead, they reacted promptly with threats of dismissals, in order to bring the BGA in line with compliance and eradicate domestic norm violations (interviews UBA#5, 18–03–05, UBA#6, 06–05–05).

All these indicators point towards the effectiveness of the judicial discourse as predicted by the constructivist hypothesis. After a decade of violating the DWD, the judicial discourse developed a consensual norm definition which argumentatively entrapped the government since its initial position could no longer be defended with valid arguments. Thus, Germany finally abandoned its non-compliance rhetoric, adapted legal acts and achieved a comprehensive form of compliance very quickly after the ECJ judgment. In contrast to predictions of the rationalist reputation hypothesis, the Kohl government did not shy away from potential reputational costs imposed by the Commission and the ECJ. The change in policy ideas was stable over time, and the legal adaptation reflected comprehensive compliance; accordingly, Germany did not shift back into a less demanding approach after the Commission had closed the case and losses of reputational costs were no longer likely.

The second rationalist hypothesis: compliance bargaining in the shadow of the ECJ

According to the second rationalist hypothesis, informal compliance bargaining in the shadow of the ECJ can foster quick adaptations of policies resembling minimalist compliance. This is likely if compliance bargaining takes place and if both parties have a common conception of mutual bargaining power. Successful compliance bargaining ends non-compliance, because state parties make concessions in the timing and content of legal changes and the European Commission makes concessions by withdrawing the case of single disputed elements before the ECJ issues a judgment.

The official documentation shows no traces of compliance bargaining in the shadow of the judicial discourse (Advocate General 1992, European Court of Justice 1992b). Nevertheless, we cannot exclude that one delegation informally approached the other to avoid a judgment and foster a swift transformation of non-compliance. The 1990 adaptation of the DWR could indicate that Germany struck a deal with the Commission and therefore shifted into compliance during the ongoing judicial discourse. However, if bargaining took place and indeed fostered compliance, we would expect the European Commission to have withdrawn the case or the issue or at least to have made concessions on the second contested element. Yet the official protocols reveal no traces of the Commission making any compromises (Advocate General 1992, European Court of Justice 1992b). Moreover, if compliance bargaining had taken place and had triggered the 1990 policy shift, we would expect Germany to have responded to the Commission's breach of the deal in either readjusting policies to an undemanding approach again or at least in adapting its rhetoric to revert to criticism of the DWD again. This was not the case. Even some time after the European Commission had finally closed the case, the government as well as the ministry for health and the ministry for environment did not shift back towards a less demanding and less costly form of compliance, but maintained its new, demanding policies and its positive, normative rhetoric on drinking water quality issues (Bundestag 1993c: 12355C-21360D, Bundestag 1994e: 17766–96). Hence, compliance bargaining in the shadow of the judicial discourse did not end the norm violation in the drinking water case.

Judgments and differential empowerment

In November 1992, the ECJ ruled in favour of the European Commission. The judgment stated firstly that 'events of emergency' are a necessary condition for granting exceptions from the quality parameters of the DWD and that broad exceptions from maximum admissible concentrations were not in line with the directive (European Court of Justice 1992b: 16). Secondly, the ECJ also clarified that the DWD required complete reports of all water quality deviations and granted exceptions (European

Court of Justice 1992b: 29, 31). This section argues that the ECJ judgment of 1992 did not cause a shift into compliance.

Before the ECJ issued its judgment in 1992, the domestic context was by and large compliance averse. Due to high compliance costs, water suppliers opposed all the parameters beyond the already present German health-related regulations (*Süddeutsche Zeitung* 1992b). The agricultural lobby feared a shift towards a polluters-pay approach, according to which they would pay compliance costs associated with high water quality standards (Federal Government 1985: 6, Green Party 1989: 2). Environmental organizations, as compliance proponents, did not push the government towards a more demanding approach, but remained largely passive. They supported the incremental adaptation to the DWD and consequently cooperated with responsible authorities, instead of mobilizing the public (Börzel 2003a: 83). This is not too surprising. Ongoing contestation on the EU level about what the DWD was actually about made it very difficult for environmental activists to shame their government into a demanding drinking water approach. In addition, the media attention was relatively low and focused mostly on practical implementation problems (e.g. *Süddeutsche Zeitung* 1991). The context was also hostile to attempts to reframe domestic debates. The public health approach, and to a lesser extent the cost frame, on which the German drinking water approach was based, were deeply embedded at the beginning of the judicial discourse. Both conceptions reinforced each other and structured domestic debates (e.g. *Süddeutsche Zeitung* 1992c). In addition, reframing would have been very difficult, since environmental protection was based on a polluters-pay instead of an end-of-pipe approach, which farmers and the fertilizer and pesticides industry strongly opposed (e.g. Bundestag 1988d, Bundestag 1989d, Bundestag 1990c). In line with the two hypotheses on the compliance instrument 'judgment', there had been no successful shaming or reframing campaigns prior to 1992. The government in Bonn changed its policy ideas, but did so without being pushed from below, and in fact against broader public sentiments (e.g. Bundesregierung 1990b, Bundestag 1991c, Federal Ministry for Health 1992).

With the judgment in 1992, the ECJ empowered societal norm entrepreneurs by increasing publicity, providing an authoritative perspective on how to interpret the norm and simplifying the issue (e.g. *Süddeutsche Zeitung* 1992d). Yet this had no effect on the compliance dynamics (interview organized interests#7, 09–02–05). The legal adaptations were almost completed by the date of the judgment, so that societal norm proponents remained inactive afterwards. Even if shaming campaigns had taken place, they would have failed. The government had already committed itself towards a demanding drinking water quality approach and brought about legal changes that reflected comprehensive compliance. Hence, there was nothing left to blame and shame as inappropriate action, thereby creating reputational losses, to which the government could have responded with strategic concessions. By contrast, the contextual conditions for effective reframing strategies increased slightly, since public health and cost considerations had lost their importance (e.g. Bundestag 1993e, Bundestag 1994e: 17793). However, the Kohl government had already changed substantial policy interests, so that there was no point in reframing the drinking water debate after the judgment, in order to promote high quality standards.

Summing up, the legal changes in 1990 and 1992 were not induced through bottom-up campaigns of societal actors. Rather the opposite is true. The CDU/FDP coalition pursued legal changes in 1990 and 1992 against the backdrop of societal opposition. The water supply industry opposed the DWD due to anticipated implementation expenditures (Bundesregierung 1993a, Bundesregierung 1994b, Bundestag 1991i). Environmental organizations were sceptical about a demanding reading of the DWD in 1989 and 1990, because they feared that high drinking water quality standards could prevent citizens from using non-drinking water to save their resources (Bundestag 1989a, Green Party 1989: 2).

Sanction-threats

The third compliance instrument at the disposal of the ECJ is a sanction-threat. This section argues that the German government neither ended the norm violation in the drinking water case because they anticipated that they would be penalized nor because a sanction-threat differentially empowered the lead ministry vis-à-vis other ministries.

The rationalist hypothesis: credible sanction-threats increase non-compliance costs

Prior to the ECJ judgment, the possibility of sanctions was very remote. Firstly, issuing financial penalties was not possible prior to the Maastricht reforms of 1993. Secondly, even decentralized sanctions through a reference to the violation of Article 171 ECT would have required a Court judgment at the very least. Thirdly, neither the Commission nor the ECJ hinted at any forms of sanctions at all. Hence, at this stage of the proceeding, the Kohl government did not adapt strategic positions to anticipated rising non-compliance costs and did not shift into minimalist compliance (e.g. Bundesministerium für Jugend 1990b, Bundesregierung 1990b, Bundestag 1991b). Rather than referring to external costs and blaming the ECJ for forcing Germany into policy changes, the government opted for demanding policies and defended environmental issues, restrictive exceptional clauses and comprehensive reporting systems in terms of righteousness and appropriateness (e.g. Bundestag 1991b, Bundestag 1994e: 17792–3).

Possible sanctions did not even become credible threats after the judgment of 1992. Firstly, the shadow of sanctions loomed only slightly. In 1992, the ECJ did not refer to a violation of Article 171 ECT and in 1993 the European Commission initiated no second infringement proceeding based on Article 228 ECT. Hence, Germany could have continued non-compliance in order to avoid high domestic expenditures for the implementation of the DWD (e.g. of the agricultural industry), without being subject to immediate external compliance costs. Secondly, breaching the DWD was a serious infringement in only two respects: due to the strong German water legislation with regard to public health parameters, the German violation, while negatively affecting the environment, did not endanger public health. While non-compliance with the DWD allowed Germany to save costs at the expense of the environment, it did not negatively affect other states, the four freedoms, the resources of the European Commission, or the functioning of the Community. Hence, the amount of sanctions would not have been a deterrent in 1993 and did not end the norm violation.

In line with this, it was not the case that Germany was shying away from potential decentralized or centralized sanctions by strategically adapting preferences and policies in 1990 and 1992. Rather than making strategic concessions towards minimalist compliance in anticipation of future external threats, the government shifted into comprehensive compliance. They no longer maintained the health and the cost frames, but opted for restrictive exceptional clauses and for a demanding water policy including environmental as well as public health aspects (compare e.g. Bundesregierung 1987b with Bundesregierung 1994b, Mr Töpfer the Minister for the Environment in Bundestag 1994e: 17795). Even after the European Commission had closed the case, the government did not fall back into an undemanding, cost-saving water quality approach (Bundestag 1993c, Bundestag 1993e, Bundestag 1993f, Bundestag 1994e).[18]

[18] Moreover, if Germany had been counterfactually threatened by ECJ sanctions, while the domestic constituency still opposed the directive, it would have been strategically rational to justify policy changes by shifting the blame to the EU. Through references to the ECJ and the necessity of legally adjusting to EU law, the government could have externalized responsibility for policy shifts and avoided damage to reputation and electoral support. Yet blame-shifting was absent in the parliamentary debates before and after the ECJ ruling (e.g. Bundesregierung 1993a, Bundestag 1993a, Bundestag 1993e).

The constructivist hypothesis: sanction-threats empower pro-compliance ministries

According to the alternative constructivist hypothesis, sanction-threats strengthen logics of appropriateness according to which norm violations are unacceptable and thereby differentially empower pro-compliance ministries vis-à-vis domestic veto players. This mechanism presupposes that the leading health ministry would have preferred a demanding drinking water approach that entailed not only human health but also environmental parameters from the outset, but was prevented from successfully pursuing such policies by other, more sceptical, ministries. In the German drinking water case, neither the ECJ judgment nor a possible future sanction-threat differentially empowered the leading ministry vis-à-vis other ministries and fostered compliance. Although the Federal Ministry for Environment, Nature Conservation and Nuclear Safety was created in 1986, the health ministry continued to be primarily responsible for the case, since drinking water quality was regarded as a matter of public health. Prior to the judicial discourse, the leading health ministry strongly opposed a drinking water approach that included environmental elements Bundesregierung 1987b, Bundesregierung 1988, Bundestag 1988c, Federal Ministry of Youth 1985: 1). Early in the judicial discourse, the lead ministry as well as the government shifted their policy preferences (see also Bundesregierung 1990b, Bundestag 1991e, Federal Ministry for Health 1992). Accordingly, they pushed for legal changes even before a judgment or the remote possibility of a future sanction-threat came into play (Bundesregierung 1990b, Bundestag 1991e).

The German drinking water case in retrospect

In summary, the European Drinking Water Directive (DWD) of 1980 and especially its environmental parameters created a demand for legal adaptation. However, the Kohl government was reluctant to comply. They opposed environmental aspects of the directive and some of the measurement techniques mainly because of cost implications for the German drinking water sector and because of a misfit with their public health-based water approach. Both reasons for scepticism towards the DWD were reinforced through the scientific advice of the Federal Health Office (BGA) (Börzel 2003a: 81, Bundestag 1989a). Thus, non-compliance preferences were rigid and strong, so that the Commission referred the infringement case to the ECJ.

In a similar dynamic to the UK collective redundancy case, the judicial discourse was effective in talking Germany out of the norm violation and facilitated a swift change into comprehensive compliance. Both parties actively engaged in judicial argumentation and analysed all relevant legal acts. The judicial discourse developed dynamics of its own, during which several methods of legal reasoning were used, including those that fitted the complexities of the two interpretational problems at stake. This fostered the notion of one superior interpretation of the DWD among the involved legal experts and prevented the German advocate from continuously defending the initial German position, due to the lack of good judicial arguments. The advocate communicated the judicial arguments and the notion that there was a legally superior norm definition to the government. Thus, argumentative entrapment took place. The government and the leading health ministry could no longer justify its initial policies with convincing, high quality arguments and could not stick to their old policies within a logic of appropriateness and argumentative consistency. As expected, the leading health ministry altered policy ideas, abandoned its minimalist focus on public health issues, included environmental aspects and adopted a demanding water approach. The legal adaptations of the 1990 DWR and the 1992 DWR reflected these ideational changes and also resembled a comprehensive form of compliance. Accordingly, both acts did not introduce ambiguities and uncertainties, for example through undefined, new concepts, complex and broad exceptional clauses or overlaps with other legal acts that would have allowed for the circumvention of obligations on environmental parameters during the stage of practical implementation.

The judicial discourse was effective and entrapped Germany argumentatively in line with the constructivist hypothesis. By contrast, neither a threat of reputational losses due to the resolved interpretational ambiguities, nor compliance bargaining in the shadow of the judicial discourse, did further compliance. Also, the ECJ judgment did not abolish the norm violation – as expected by both judgment-hypotheses. Water suppliers, the BGA, and even environmental activists opposed the DWD while an active domestic compliance constituency was absent. Societal norm proponents remained inactive and the government was not pushed into compliance from below. Rather, the opposite dynamic took place: the Kohl government pursued demanding legal adaptations, especially the DWR in 1990, against the interests of the stakeholders (e.g. water companies), public opinion and the advice of the Federal Health Office. Similarly, the threat of potential sanctions did not induce compliance. This is in line with the predictions.

4.III Summary: the power of judicial discourses

The UK collective redundancy case and the German drinking water case confirmed that states can be talked out of non-compliance in judicial discourses. Ideational entrapment requires that the advocates of both parties do not talk at cross purposes. Instead they need to actively engage in judicial argumentation, analyse the same legal acts, and at least one party needs to apply a judicial method with a high fit to the complexity of the issue at stake. This produces a norm definition which legal experts regard as legally superior. Through repeated contacts between the national advocate and his or her ministries, the notion that the interpretational difficulty is resolved and that the initial position can no longer be defended with good and valid arguments gets disseminated. This triggers a shift into comprehensive compliance, because only this way can governments reconcile their policies with norms of consistency, integrity and appropriateness. Minimalist compliance invites future deviations form the norm definition as developed by the legal experts and consequently would also violate norms of consistency, integrity and appropriateness. The other six case studies of this book present many instances in which argumentative entrapment did not work since the scope conditions were not met. Should a party not engage in legal argumentation at all, should no actor use a method with a high fit to the interpretational scope of the contested issue, or should the advocates talk at cross purposes because they focus on two different legal acts and continue to contest the claims of the opponent, a consensual norm definition won't emerge. Judicial discourses are not the ultimate remedy for all norm violations, but face the risk of dissent. Firstly, if a government or ministry decides to not make judicial arguments in a case at all (the UK nitrates case is such an example, see also Chapter 6.I), argumentative entrapment cannot take place. However, at the same time, not actively participating in the discourse takes away the possibility of actively shaping the outcome and eventually persuading the Court of one's initial norm interpretation (as Germany managed for some of the issues at stake in the equal access case, see also Chapter 5.IV). Secondly, judicial discourses can end in dissent if simply none of the used methods of legal interpretation provide a clear norm definition but allow for two different conclusions on how to answer the question at stake. As the question on whether a domestic legal act has to describe requirements for the reporting of drinking water quality derogations in the German drinking water case demonstrated, it can even be the case that an interpretational issue is too broad to be solved with the narrow wording instrument (since the wording is silent on the issue), but not complex enough to be resolved with the broad directive-immanent teleological method of interpretation.

While the German drinking water and the British collective redundancy case studies found evidence for the constructivist judicial discourse hypothesis (H1), the rationalist alternatives cannot be confirmed in any of the eight case studies presented in this book (H2a,b). In none of the cases did states shift into minimalist compliance after the advocates had resolved the interpretational ambiguities during the judicial discourse in order to avoid losses of reputation vis-à-vis the European Commission or the ECJ (H2a). This is not too surprising, since all member states are from time to time dragged to court, usually seek to uphold their initial policies as long as possible, and often do not initiate legal changes before the ECJ issues judgments. Hence, a government that would not react to developments in ongoing judicial discourses would not negatively stick out. Also the link between a bad reputation in judicial proceedings and negative consequences is not too strong. The Commission is highly specialized. While its legal service is mainly involved in infringement proceedings, the policy-related directorates-general (DG) cope with the formulation of new proposals for EU law and the actual negotiations. Hence, even if the legal service is frustrated over a member state due to delaying compliance in a particular Court case, it is unlikely that a policy-DG punishes the respective state in withholding information on a policy proposal or in not accommodating its positions at all.

The second rationalist hypothesis (H2b) cannot be confirmed either. Compliance bargaining did not take place and quickly foster compliance. However, since effective compliance bargaining should lead to the withdrawal of issues or even of complete cases, the hypothesis cannot be rigorously tested because material on withdrawal cases is not public. Thus, while H2a is falsified, H2b is simply not confirmed.

5

Effective judgments

The following four studies illustrate how ECJ judgments trigger compliance. In two of the cases, norm violations were brought to an end in response to shaming campaigns of differentially empowered societal actors, while the other two cases are examples of how compliance was achieved through successful reframing of domestic debates.

5.I Equal access of men and women – shaming the UK into compliance

The European directive on the equal access of men and women to employment, occupational training, promotion, and working conditions (76/207) aims to promote equal treatment of men and women in employment related matters. The directive incorporates an anti-discrimination clause (Article 2), according to which 'there shall be no discrimination whatsoever on grounds of sex either directly or indirectly by reference in particular to martial or family status'. It specifies the applicatory scope of the equal access principle and makes way for positive discrimination measures, but also highlights that exceptions to the equality principle are possible in matters in which a certain sex is an indispensable prerequisite. The equal access directive is part of the early European employment and social policy and was conceptualized as a measure to harmonize living and working conditions in the EU.

In the 1970s, the UK was the self-proclaimed European leader in the fight against sex discrimination (e.g. House of Commons 1975c: 551). By 1919 the House of Commons had already passed a Sex Disqualification (Removal) Act, prohibiting the exclusion of women from public posts. The Equal Pay Act forbids wage discrimination on grounds of sex and originated in 1970. The Labour Party in particular considered the 'unequal status of women in our society an evil of great antiquity' (Secretary of State for the Home Department in House of Commons

1975c: 511). Thus, they promoted equal treatment with a Sex Discrimination Act (SDA) in 1975. Similar to the European equal treatment directive, the 1975 SDA aimed to reduce sex discrimination in the economic sphere and promoted the equal treatment of men and women. Hence, after the directive entered into force in February 1976, the UK notified the Commission that the SDA already implemented the directive. Although the legal misfit was lower in the UK than in many other EC member states (e.g. Germany), the European Commission suspected that the 1975 SDA had a narrower scope of application than the directive. After the transposition deadline had expired in 1978, the Commission sent a reasoned opinion to the UK.

In 1979 the Thatcher government came into office. They pursued a liberal economic policy and opposed the 1975 SDA and the equality directive. Instead of regulating the employment sector by legal means, the Conservatives emphasized that access of women to employment, educational training and career should be left to market forces or to voluntary agreements (Boston 1987, House of Commons 1975c: 542, 567, 570, 589–93, House of Commons 1975a: 567, 570). The Confederation of British Industry (CBI) opposed the equal treatment approach, as well as other protective rights, due to predicted increased employment costs. The Conservatives were sensitive to these demands and emphasized repeatedly that a deregulated market was the key to a successful economy and to economic growth in Great Britain (Ashford 1981: 101–14, House of Commons 1989a: 475). Thus, the UK saved compliance costs at the expense of women, who had fewer means of protection than women of other member states when faced with unequal treatment concerning access to vocational activities. In this sense, the UK did not fully support the promotion of equal living conditions across the EU member states and barred the harmonization of the common market, even though the preface of the equal access directive made clear that this was important.

As in the collective redundancies case, the Conservative government maintained its compliance-averse policies insisting that the UK had completely and correctly transposed the directive. Thus, in June 1982, the Commission referred the case to the ECJ (C-number 165/82).

The pattern of legal changes

Before the Court, three issues were at stake. Firstly, the parties disagreed on the issue of whether non-binding collective agreements were also subject to the directive. Secondly, it was unclear whether member states could exclude certain occupational activities (employment in private households and small undertakings) from the equal access principle.

Thirdly, the parties dissented on whether the activities of certain professions, such as midwives, might be exempt from the directive. On 8 November 1983, the ECJ stated in its judgment that the UK had insufficiently transposed the directive regarding the first and second issue (European Court of Justice 1983). This ruling created a demand for further legal changes because the 1975 SDA did not prohibit unequal treatment of men and women in non-binding collective agreements, in independent professions, in rules of undertakings, in private households and in small undertakings. In addition, the concept of sex discrimination was restricted to instances of intentional action and did not include instances in which sex discrimination was an unintended result of actions related to other aims (Bamfort 1993: 872–3, McGinley 1986).

Table 5.1 Legal changes on equal treatment measures

Date	*Title*	*Initiated by*	*Outcome*
1975	Sex Discrimination Act (SDA)	Labour government	Below the scope of the directive
1983	Equality Bill	Labour opposition	More demanding than the directive – but failed
1986	Sex Discrimination Act (SDA)	Conservative government	Amends the SDA of 1975, transposes most elements of the judgment
1988	Sex Discrimination Act 1986 Order 1988	Conservative government	Abolishes restrictions on night work of women in industrial undertakings, not related to the case
1989	Employment Act	Conservative Government	Amends the SDA, not related to the case

As a means to comply with the ECJ ruling of November 1983, the Thatcher government initiated consultations for a revised Sex Discrimination Act in 1985. It took one additional year to pass the bill (House of Commons 1986b: 617).[1] The new SDA broadened the applicatory scope of the anti-discrimination principle and incorporated the judgment with

[1] The draft and final version of the 1986 SDA were almost identical in substance (Fritzpatrick 1987). Proposals from the Labour Party on a strengthened enforcement system as stated in the proposed Equality Bill of 1983 (House of Commons 1983), or on the inclusion of private households (House of Commons 1986b: 538), would have been necessary for comprehensive compliance, but were not included (Fritzpatrick 1987: 943–5, House of Commons 1986b: 619).

regard to collective agreements, independent professions, and small enterprises. However, it still excluded private households and certain collective agreements from the equal treatment principle (House of Commons 1986b: 538). The 1986 SDA resembled a minimalist form of compliance because it transposed not all issues at stake in Court and because it entailed ambiguities and abstract, undefined concepts regarding the aims and applicatory scope of the legislation, as well as overlaps with other legal acts. This created interpretational uncertainties and loopholes for lax practical implementation and gave rise to several court cases. In a five-year period after compliance was achieved, no less than 38 national court cases dealt with interpretations of the EC directive; 10 of these cases were referred to the ECJ through a preliminary reference procedure (based on Article 234 ECT) (see also Annexe, Table 1).

The judicial discourse

The European Commission referred the equal access case to the ECJ in June 1982. The parties disagreed whether non-binding collective agreements, independent professions, rules of undertakings, private households, small undertakings, and the profession of midwives were subject to the equal treatment principle. After one and a half years of a written and oral judicial discourse, the ECJ ruled that the UK legislation in force incompletely implemented the equal access directive (European Court of Justice 1983). This section analyses the constructivist and the two rationalist hypotheses and shows that the compliance instrument 'judicial discourse' failed to end the norm violation through either ideational entrapment (H1), anticipated reputation costs (H2a) or compliance bargaining (H2b).

Judicial discourse: Ideational entrapment or threats of reputational losses?

Is the directive applicable to non-binding collective agreements, independent professions and rules of undertakings?

The first dispute concerned the applicatory scope of the equal access directive (European Court of Justice 1983: 3). The Commission argued that British law failed to declare as void all collective agreements, rules of undertakings and rules of independent professions that violate the equal treatment principle (European Court of Justice 1983: 3). The UK, by contrast, defended its transposition as correct, not least because it saved employers from compliance costs and fitted well with the Conservatives' liberal economic paradigm.

In order to defend the position of the British government, the advocate applied the wording technique of legal reasoning to the TURERA and the SDA, but did not engage in interpretations of the equal access directive itself. According to Section 18 of the TURERA 'any collective agreement made before 1st December 1971 or after the entry into force of the Act are to be presumed to not have been intended by the parties as legally enforceable, unless they are in writing and contain a provision in which the parties express their intention that the agreements are to be legally enforceable' (European Court of Justice 1983: 4). This meant that collective agreements were usually not legally binding in the UK, but exceptions were possible. The UK continued to apply the wording method to the SDA (Sections 6, 11, 13, and 77). Concerning collective agreements, rules of undertakings and independent professions, the SDA was very precise. For example, Section 6 explicitly prohibited discrimination on the basis of sex for independent professions and rules of undertakings. Hence, the British advocate argued that the SDA rendered as void all legally binding collective agreements, rules of undertakings and independent professions that entailed provisions violating the equal treatment principle (European Court of Justice 1983: 5, 6). Within this line of reasoning, the UK concluded that British legal acts did not violate the equal access directive.

The European advocate disagreed. In contrast to the British judicial argument, the European advocate analysed the wording of the SDA and of the equal access directive and additionally used on the directive-immanent teleological method of interpretation in relation to the directive (European Court of Justice 1983: 2, 3, 11). Firstly, the European advocate argued that the exclusion of collective agreements and rules of undertakings was incompatible with the wording of article 4b of the equal access directive, which included all collective agreements without further distinguishing between the natures of the legal effects (Advocate General 1983; European Court of Justice 1983: 10, 11). Additionally, in applying the directive-immanent teleological method, the European advocate inquired into the purpose of the directive. Article 1 states that the directive should promote the equal treatment of men and women in vocational activities, related to access to employment, promotion, vocational training, and working conditions as well as to social security matters in the member states. This aim is further specified through an anti-discrimination clause in Article 2, according to which 'equal treatment' requires that 'there shall be no discrimination whatsoever on grounds of sex either directly or indirectly by reference in particular to martial or family status' (Advocate General 1983: 15–6). In a second step, the European advocate argued that the equality principle was violated by excluding non-binding collective agreements, independent professions, and rules of undertakings from the directive (Advocate General 1983: 16; European Court of Justice 1983: 21). Since the purpose of the directive was thwarted by the UK's scope restrictions, it followed from this line of judicial reasoning that the SDA was not in line with the directive.

The advocates were talking at cross purposes because the wording method applied to the SDA did not match the complexity of the interpretational question[2] and because the UK focused on the British SDA only and did not analyse the European directive, although this would have been essential to develop an intersubjectively valid interpretation of whether the directive covers non-binding collective agreements, independent professions and rules of undertakings.[3] Hence, the judicial discourse failed. The UK did not become ideationally entrapped and did not shift into a comprehensive form of compliance. Likewise, the government did not strategically adjust towards minimalist compliance in order to avoid a bad reputation vis-à-vis the European enforcement authorities for continuing the norm violation despite legal uncertainties being resolved. In 1975, the Conservatives had already opposed broad applications of the equal treatment principle (House of Commons 1975b: 1448) and opted for a scope restriction in the SDA according to which cases involving less than 25 employees would not be subject to the SDA (House of Commons 1975a: 530). After the judicial discourse ended in 1983, the Conservatives upheld their compliance-averse ideas and policies and

[2] The analysis of the SDA with the too narrow wording method failed to resolve interpretational difficulties but allowed for two different conclusions (European Court of Justice 1983: 4, 8). Even if the UK had also applied the wording method of judicial reasoning to the equal treatment directive, a consensual norm definition would have been very unlikely, because the complexity of the interpretational issue was high. The equality directive does not state explicitly whether the equal access principle has to be applied to collective agreements, independent professions and rules of undertakings. The lack of an explicit reference to these questions in the directive (e.g. no annexe specifying the scope of application) could be interpreted in two ways. It could be interpreted either narrowly (as not being subject to the directive, since otherwise it would have been mentioned) or broadly (as being self-evidently subject to the directive, so that an explicit wording was not at all necessary). The wording technique had a weak fit with the scope of the contested issue.

[3] While the broader directive-immanent teleological method of legal reasoning had a high level of compatibility with the complex interpretational problem, it could not produce a consensual norm definition, since the UK advocate focused on the British and not the European legal act. By focusing on the aim of the directive, an evaluation of the suitability of competing scope assessments was possible. According to this technique of legal reasoning, the reading that positively contributes to the directive's aim is superior. If a restrictive interpretation (such as the British one) thwarts the very purpose of the directive, while a more demanding interpretation supports the directive's aim, the latter is the better one.

continued to oppose the equal access principle in the economic sphere (e.g. Chalmers 2000: 196, House of Commons 1985, House of Commons 1989b). Until 1985, the Thatcher government had been reluctant to change the SDA. During the debates on a revision of the deficient SDA in 1985 and 1986, the Conservatives stressed that barriers for the economy should be removed and emphasized the usefulness of scope restrictions for the equal access principle and problems regarding increases of employment costs resulting from the directive (House of Commons 1985, House of Commons 1986b). Governmental members also stressed the importance of flexibility in the labour market, which extensive protective legislation would diminish (House of Commons 1986b). At the same time, the Conservatives made no normative arguments in favour of a demanding equal treatment approach (e.g. House of Commons 1988, House of Commons 1989d, House of Commons 1989c: 933f.). The failure of the judicial discourse was also reflected in the lack of any legal changes during and in the immediate aftermath of the judicial discourse. The Conservative government even out-voted a proposal on an equality bill of the Labour opposition in 1983, which included more demanding equal access rules and had a broader applicatory scope – in line with the ECJ judgment.

Are private households and small undertakings subject to the exceptional clause of the directive?

The Commission also accused the UK of delimiting the scope of the directive by excluding private households and small undertakings with five employees or fewer from the equal treatment rule (European Court of Justice 1983: 2).

The UK conceded that undertakings with five or less employees and private households were not subject to the equality principle according to Section 6 III of the 1975 SDA (European Court of Justice 1983: 12). The British advocate justified these exceptions based on Article 2 of the directive. Article 2 II states: 'this directive shall be without prejudice to the right of member states to exclude from its field of application those occupational activities and, where appropriate, the training leading thereto, for which, by reason of their nature or the context in which they are carried out, the sex of the worker constitutes a determining factor'. The UK argued that the SDA excluded private households and small undertakings as instances of contexts 'in which sex is a determining factor' (European Court of Justice 1983: 12). Concerning private households, the UK made an additional argument. Based on the teleological technique of interpretation, the UK argued that the 1975 SDA aimed to balance the countervailing principles of equal treatment and respect for private life, and referred to the exceptional clause (Article 2 II) of the directive to that end (European Court of Justice 1983: 13). The UK applied the teleological method to British law only, and could not specify the meaning of 'the nature or the context of the work, in which sex is a determining factor' as a precondition to apply the exceptional clause of the European directive.

The narrow wording technique did not fit the high complexity of the interpretational problem on whether equal access has to be granted to small undertakings and private households as well. The wording of the exceptional clause in directive 76/207 did not elaborate on what was meant by the crucial concept of the 'nature or the context in which sex is a determining factor' and could, in turn, not help to solve the problem of how the directive's scope should be interpreted. Accordingly, the European advocate did not apply the wording method, but used the directive -immanent teleological method in interpreting the meaning of the directive's exceptional clause (Advocate General 1983). In a first step, directive-immanent teleological reasoning identified the aim of the directive as equal treatment of men and women in the economic sphere. The second step of interpretation revealed that the British legal acts that excluded private households and small undertakings from the equal access principle, reduced the effectiveness and, in turn, thwarted the very purpose of the equal access directive, while a broader applicatory scope would positively contribute to the directive's aim (Advocate General 1983: 19, European Court of Justice 1983: 16). While this broad interpretational device was better compatible with the complex inter-pretational problem at hand, it was not suited to analyse what the crucial phrase 'nature or the context in which sex is a determining factor', which specifies under which conditions exceptions to the equality principle are possible, actually means.

Since the advocates talked at cross purposes during the entire judicial discourse because neither side applied a very broad method of interpretation (e.g. the historical method) that would have allowed an explicit answer to what the question 'nature or the context in which sex is a determining factor' means, they did not commonly resolve the interpretational ambiguities. Thus, the ideational entrapment hypothesis and the reputation hypothesis expect that non-compliance prevails. Accordingly, the lead economic ministry and the government maintained their initial policy ideas after the judicial discourse had ended in 1983 and did not pursue any legal changes for over two years after the judgment. They continued to oppose the application of the equal treatment principle to firms with less than five employees (House of Commons 1975a: 530): 'we still question whether it is really appropriate to seek the objective of equal treatment by applying to all small firms a law designed to meet the circumstances of larger employers' (Minister for Employment, Mr Clarke, in House of Commons 1986b: 571). The lead ministry further argued that small firms lacked the administrative resources to deal with complex equality legislation (The Parliamentary Under-Secretary of State for Employment, Mr Lang, in House of Commons 1986b: 617). Also, with regard to private households, the Thatcher government did not change its position for over two years after the judicial discourse: 'we have no wish to bring the law governing public employment relationships into people's private living arrangements' (House of Commons 1986b: 570, also 617, see also Fritzpatrick 1987: 938–9). In sum, the judicial discourse failed to induce compliance. Since the advocates talked at cross purposes, the judicial discourse was not effective. Hence, the British government continued to publicly oppose demanding equality approaches as costly and unnecessary burdens on employers and the British economy and abstained from policy changes for over two years after the judicial discourse had ended (House of Commons 1986b: 571). The ECJ concluded that the general exception of private households and small undertakings from the 1975 SDA 'goes beyond the objective which may be lawfully pursued within the framework of article 2 II of the directive' (European Court of Justice 1983: 16, 21). Consequently, the ECJ ruled that the British legal acts were incompatible with the scope of the equal treatment principle as defined in directive 76/207 (European Court of Justice 1983: 21).

Is the profession of midwives subject to the exceptional clause?

The European Commission suspected that the SDA excluded the profession of midwives from the equal access principle and thereby violated the equality directive (European Court of Justice 1983: 3, 17). The UK disagreed and its advocate used the wording means of legal interpretation in order to defend the SDA, which allows training of male midwives only in specific places (European Court of Justice 1983: 17). The UK justified this equality limitation with respect to patients' sensitivities, by applying the wording instrument to Article 2. This article exempts some occupational activities from the equality principle (European Court of Justice 1983: 18). Yet the wording itself was silent on whether the profession of midwives was, by its nature, a 'context in which sex is a determining factor'. Since the interpretational problem at hand was broad, the phrasing of the exceptional clause (Article 2) alone could be interpreted in various manners. Hence, the UK and the European advocate both adopted a broader interpretational device (Advocate General 1983: 21–4, European Court of Justice 1983: 8, 20). Based on the directive-immanent systematic instrument, they put the exceptional clause (Article 2) in the context of Article 9 II of the directive. The latter specifies what qualifies as an exception based on Article 2 II in stating that social developments are crucial: 'Member States shall periodically assess the occupational activities referred to in article 2 (2) in order to decide, in the light of social developments, whether there is justification for maintaining the exclusions concerned. They shall notify the Commission of the results of this assessment.' It followed that exceptions were in line with Article 2 II if they were compatible with the current state of social developments (which included patients' sensitivities in 1983) (Advocate General 1983, European Court of Justice 1983: 18–20). Based on the broader directive-immanent systematic method it became clear that exceptions granted on the basis of Article 2 II should be kept under review and eventually changed in the future, if societal developments revealed ideational shifts (European Court of Justice 1983: 8). Thus, the advocates concluded that the exception of midwives was valid as long as it was subject to future review, in order to keep track with societal changes.[4]

The advocates both engaged in judicial argumentation, both analysed all crucial legal acts and jointly applied a judicial method with a good match to the complexity of the question of whether midwives could be exempt from the equal access principle. Due to the high compatibility, the actors developed a consensual norm definition and also the ECJ concluded that the 1975 SDA did not violate the directive concerning the treatment of midwives. Since this was exactly the initial position of the UK (Advocate General 1983), there was no need for the UK to adapt its policies in this regard. In line with that, the Conservatives did not fully apply the equality principle to the profession of midwives before and after the judicial discourse (compare House of Commons 1975c: 532 with House of Commons 1986b: 570) and did not increase or delimit the scope of the equal access approach concerning legal rules on midwives.

The second rationalist alternative: compliance bargaining in the shadow of the ECJ

Did compliance bargaining foster minimalist compliance because the parties involved mutually accepted their respective bargaining power and developed a compromise through reciprocal concessions? Again, there is

[4] The ECJ also joined this line of argumentation, acknowledging that the patient's sensitivity constituted grounds for an exception and dismissed the third complaint (European Court of Justice 1983: 20, 22).

no hard evidence of such negotiations taking place and we can only apply counterfactual reasoning. Did compliance bargaining in the shadow of the ECJ foster a compromise between the UK and the European Commission, thereby making the European Commission give in on the issue of midwives, thus saving the UK from legal changes in this regard, while the Commission gets concessions from the UK on the other issues? This scenario is implausible. Firstly, the European Commission did not give in on the issue of midwives. Instead of withdrawing it, the European advocate pursued it until the ECJ issued a ruling siding with the UK (European Court of Justice 1983). Secondly, the UK did not even start adapting their policies on the applicatory scope of the directive concerning non-binding collective agreements, independent professions, rules of undertakings, small undertakings and private households during the judicial discourse. Hence we can safely conclude that compliance bargaining did not end the norm violation.

Differential empowerment through judgments

In the equal access case, the judicial discourse, which was the first compliance instrument to be applied, failed to end the norm violation. Subsequently, the judgment, as the second instrument, came into play. Did the ECJ judgment differentially empower societal actors, thus helping to foster compliance?

In November 1983, the judicial discourse ended with the ECJ ruling. In this judgment, the Court clarified that the UK and the Commission had both been partially successful in their submissions (European Court of Justice 1983: 23–4). The Commission lost the claim that the UK was in violation of the directive concerning the profession of midwives, while the UK was found to have violated the directive by exempting non-binding collective agreements, independent professions, rules of undertakings, small undertakings and private households from the equal access principle (European Court of Justice 1983: operative part 1).

Prior to the ECJ judgment in 1983, bottom-up pressure on the government and the leading ministry of employment to comply with the European equality legislation was very weak. Societal opponents were better organized than proponents, who were also less numerous. Employers, trade unions, commercial undertakings, the professions and educational establishments were largely dominated by male workers and all opposed the directive (Duina 1999: 49–50, House of Commons 1975c: 524–5, 539, Povall 1992: 176). They anticipated increases in employment and wage costs if women were no longer bound to carry out the low-wage jobs (employee associations), more severe labour market competition (trade unions) or challenges of conservative role models (educational establishments) (House of Commons 1975c: 557). In contrast, societal norm entrepreneurs were much less numerous and organizationally weaker. Women's organizations, such as the National Federation of Women's Institutes or the Association of Catholic Women, focused less on legal than on societal aspects and complained, for example, that nurseries were insufficient although they constituted the infrastructure allowing mothers to seek employment in the first place (House of Commons 1975c: 573). Many women feared that equal treatment laws would abolish protective legislation and ultimately worsen their conditions (House of Commons 1975c: 545). Consequently, only a few organizations, such as the Fawcett Society and the Women's National Commission, were concerned with politics.[5] One of the most important politically active norm proponents was not a societal organized interest group, but the Equal Opportunity Commission (EOC). The EOC was founded with the 1975 SDA. Since then, it has been primarily financed by the British state and is responsible to the cabinet minister in charge of women's issues. As an independent, non-departmental public organization, the EOC has been responsible for monitoring the societal, economic and political conditions of women in the UK and for the provision of expertise (Equal Opportunity Commission 2006, Sacks 1986, Sifft 2003: 159).

Before the ECJ issued its ruling in 1983, the arguments of norm opponents resonated much better with the governmental agenda, with public opinion and with institutionalized norms than the arguments of compliance proponents. Conservatives sympathized with the economic fears of industry and employer associations (House of Commons 1975b: 1434). Also, in line with trade unions, the Conservatives argued that the 1975 SDA was disadvantageous to women because it would 'be so much cheaper to employ men than women' (House of Commons 1975b: 1435). Against this background, shaming strategies of women's organizations had low prospects of success prior to 1983. In addition to the organizational inequalities, public and media attention on anti-discrimination laws, the EC equal treatment directive and the infringement procedure against the UK were low. Also, the fit between a demanding interpretation of the equal treatment principle and domestically institutionalized norms was very limited. On the one hand, the tradition of

[5] The Fawcett Society was founded in 1866 and promoted female suffrage in the UK, but was, due to financial difficulties and internal organizational restructuring endeavours, less active in equal treatment campaigns in the late 1970s and early 1980s (The Fawcett Society 2006: 2–3).

anti-discrimination law dates back to 1919 and the share of (part-time) working women had been higher in the UK than in many other member states. In the 1970–1980s approximately 60 per cent of all British women were in employment (the highest rate in the EC during the 1970s except for Denmark) (House of Commons 1988: 326). At the same time, however, women were overwhelmingly employed in low-paid jobs (House of Commons 1989d: 343), public opinion widely opposed equal treatment in the economic sphere and the role model of female caregiver and male breadwinner were strongly institutionalized in the societal sphere (Sacks 1986: 565, 589). Furthermore, before 1983, it was contested what the directive was about and especially where it should be applied. Without an authoritative norm definition, there was uncertainty as to whether the UK was really violating the directive – especially considering that the 1975 SDA originated with the more progressive Labour government and was perceived to be a precursor of further equality legalization (Boston 1987, House of Commons 1975c: 511). All of these factors decreased the prospects for mobilization of the electorate against the governmental violations of EU law and of domestic standards of appropriateness, which might shame the government into compliance.

The contextual conditions were even worse for reframing the domestic debate. Before the ECJ judgment, the dominant role model conception was strongly institutionalized (Sacks 1986: 565). It was compatible with part-time (and poorly paid) jobs for women while equality regarding highly paid jobs would have damaged the male breadwinner role model (Boston 1987: 311). Hence, trade unions and employer associations reproduced the dominant framing. At the same time, a complementary frame, to which norm proponents could have referred in promoting a demanding interpretation of the equal treatment principle, was not available. Linking equal treatment to human rights was difficult, since the human rights discourse was dominated by 'first generation issues', such as civil and political liberties (see also Falk 2000). In addition, the issues at stake were not easy to reframe comprehensively prior to the ECJ ruling, which reduced the complexity of the issues at stake. Prior to 1983, there was uncertainty as to the instances in which the equal access directive should be applied and under which conditions exceptions could be granted. The dispute concerned the applicatory scope and the exceptional clause of directive 76/207 and focused on several unspecified concepts. It also affected a series of UK legal acts (most prominently the SDA) in the employment and social policy field. The complexity of these issues was very high. As a consequence, it was difficult to subsume all contested aspects comprehensively under one alternative frame that, additionally, launched a demanding norm interpretation.

In line with both hypotheses, societal norm proponents did not successfully push the reluctant Thatcher government into compliance from below before the ECJ could differentially empower a pro-compliance constituency with its judgment. Most norm proponents, such as the Fawcett Society or the Women's National Commission, remained inactive. An exception was the EOC, which proposed several legal changes but did not succeed in shaming the government into a demanding equality approach or in reframing the gender-related debates (Chairman of the EOC, in House of Lords 1986: 1193).[6]

After the ECJ ruling of November 1983, the domestic context became conducive to effective shaming campaigns. The judgment attracted public attention and authoritatively clarified that the UK was in violation of the equal treatment directive (European Court of Justice 1983, *Financial Times* 1983). Thus, employer associations, trade unions and the Thatcher government could no longer legitimately claim that the existing legal acts sufficiently promoted equality. Simultaneously, the judgment empowered the EOC, the Fawcett Society and the Women's National Commission. These compliance proponents not only gained additional arguments against discrimination on grounds of sex in general and new arguments for a broad applicatory scope of the equal treatment principles in particular, but could also refer to the authority of the ECJ in pushing for legal changes. The differential empowerment of societal norm proponents is not sufficient to facilitate successful shaming and minimalist compliance. Their success essentially depends on their willingness to invest resources and in the resonance between the judgment and domestically institutionalized norms.

In the equal access case, the ECJ ruling resonated well with already domestically institutionalized ideas, although it did not fit perfectly. On the one hand, the UK perceived itself as a front-runner in anti-discrimination law (House of Commons 1985). It had a high share of part-time working women (House of Commons 1988: 326, see also *Financial Times*

[6] A reason for the very limited role of the EOC was its organizational weakness in the late 1970s and early 1980s. This was due to the EOC's composition (the government prevented feminists from being appointed and favoured non-experts, Sacks 1986: 561), insufficient financial resources (the EOC gained only a third of the funding of other Commissions such as the Commission for Racial Equality, Sacks 1986: 565) and a lack of experience (until 1982 internal managerial problems dominated; after this period debates revolved predominantly around expenditures rather than policies until 1986, Sacks 1986: 562–3).

1988). Also, British society of the early 1980s supported protective legislation for women, because it was widely believed that women as the weaker sex required greater protection (House of Commons 1985, House of Commons 1986b: 572). On the other hand, male dominated trade unions and employer associations, as well as some elements of public opinion, were still sceptical concerning the equal treatment of men and women. They feared that this would increase competition, especially in well-paid jobs, and decrease the average wage because women would no longer primarily take (ill-paid) part-time jobs.

After the judgment, women's organizations shamed the government for their inappropriate norm violation. Firstly, the EOC publicly emphasized that the protection of women in the economic sphere was necessary because of the high employment rate in the UK and that protection would only be achieved if the scope of application of the equal treatment principle were broadened, as demanded by the ECJ.[7] In addition, other women's organizations, such as the Women's National Commission, as well as the EOC, argued that a minimalist equality approach was inappropriate for an equality-leader, which the UK had been for almost a decade (interview organized interests#16, 21–03–06).[8] They stressed potential reputational losses and actively lobbied for legal changes according to a more demanding equality approach (*Financial Times* 1986b, *The Times* 1986). These campaigns incrementally increased domestic non-compliance costs.

In 1985, the Thatcher government responded to the reputational costs imposed by the shaming endeavours in two regards (Boston 1987, *Financial Times* 1986b, House of Lords 1986: 1189–92). Firstly, negative value-laden arguments almost completely disappeared from public speeches (compare House of Commons 1975c[9] with House of Commons 1985, House of Commons 1986b, House of Lords 1986). Secondly, the government responded with a policy change aligning equal treatment

[7] See also Boston 1987, *Financial Times* 1986a, *Financial Times* 1986c, House of Commons 1986c: 132, House of Lords 1986: 1193, *The Times* 1985, *The Times* 1986.

[8] See also *Financial Times* 1985b, *Financial Times* 1986c, *Financial Times* 1986d, *Guardian* 1985, House of Commons 1985, House of Commons 1986a, Baroness Lockwood, former chairman of the EOC House of Lords 1986: 1198.

[9] A Conservative MP argued: 'differences between man and women are real (...) it can be seen in any aspect of the animal kingdom. It has not diminished but rather developed as man has grown more complicated. It has been presumed that it is right for women to specialize in certain aspects of life and men in others. A girl likes dolls because she will be a mother (...) No one starts off as a stereotype. These characteristics develop naturally (...) this Bill is not merely foolish and ridiculous but positively wicked and evil' (Mr Bill, in House of Commons 1975c: 191–3).

issues with liberalization. Two years before the ECJ judgment, the Thatcher government had already planned to deregulate the employment market. To this end, they initiated consultations on deregulation on issues such as working hours with the EOC, the TUC and the CBI. Yet until 1983, there was strong societal opposition to the Conservative deregulation agenda, especially from workers, who expected a weakening of protective individual rights and collective organizational rights, and from women, who feared that their protective rights might be restricted too. The consultations with the EOC, the TUC and the CBI were lengthy and a quick deregulation of the employment sector was not possible (interview organized interests#15, 20–03–06). Once the shaming strategies of the EOC and other women's organizations put pressure on the government, they realized that there was a window of opportunity to pacify the CBI with deregulations and the EOC with equality measures at the same time and avoid deadlock of the consultations (interview organized interests#15, 20–03–06). On the one hand, the government broadened the applicatory scope of the equal treatment directive and included collective agreements, independent professions and rules of undertakings in the proposal for the 1986 SDA. On the other hand, the Conservatives pursued their deregulation agenda: they removed bureaucracy, abolished protective measures for workers in general, but also for women, and created more flexibility for employers (House of Commons 1986a, House of Commons 1986b: 569, 598). This minimized domestic opposition to the 1986 SDA. Employers' associations embraced deregulation and accepted the extension of the equal treatment principle to small firms, collective agreements, and rules of undertaking as merely a negative side effect. For women, the carrot was the extension of the scope of the equal treatment principle; while the negative side effects were deregulation and the abolishment of parts of the protective legislation concerning shift work, working hours for women and night work. A majority within the EOC supported repealing protective legislation treating men and women differently and did not regard this as being in contradiction to the promotion of women's rights (e.g. Baroness Platt of Writtle, Chairman of the EOC, in House of Lords 1986: 1195–6). As a consequence, the biggest societal opposition against the 1986 SDA came from trade unions, who were the only ones who did not win through either deregulation or broadening the scope of the equal access principle (House of Commons 1986a, *Financial Times* 1986b). Also, the Labour Party claimed that most parts of the governmental draft worsened the status of women and were 'a direct consequence of the Government's determination to turn back the clock to pre-Victorian conditions of employment for men and women' (House of

Commons 1986b: 582, 610–13). Yet neither the parliamentary nor the societal opposition could prevent the SDA revision.

Non-compliance was transformed into a minimalist form of compliance in 1986. From the very beginning, the Conservative government framed the SDA as having a dual objective: deregulation and compliance with EU law. The bill removed 'needless bureaucracy' and made a 'modest contribution to Labour market flexibility and the ability of business to respond to changed economic and social conditions' (Minister for Employment, Mr Clarke, in House of Commons 1986b: 569, Fritzpatrick 1987, House of Commons 1986c: 1326, 1329–30). The second aim was 'furthering equal opportunities' and to 'bring us more closely into line with Community law' (House of Commons 1986b: 582). However, only the first two clauses were actually related to the ECJ judgment (small firms, independent professions and collective undertakings), while all others served deregulation purposes by abolishing legal differentiations between men and women for several issues. The revised SDA eradicated a number of protective measures for women (e.g. concerning night work, health protection, redundancy rights and working hours) (House of Commons 1986b: 582, 596, 610; House of Commons 1986c: 1330). The 1986 SDA was only a minimalist legal change. The equal treatment component relied on a narrow understanding of equal treatment and lagged behind both the opposition's and the EOC's proposals (Baroness Lockwood, former Chairman of the EOC, in House of Lords 1986: 1199).[10] In addition, not all aspects of the ECJ judgment were resolved by the 1986 SDA, since employment in private households and certain collective agreements were still exempt from the equal access principle: 'we still question whether it is really appropriate to seek the objective of equal treatment by applying to all small firms a law designed to meet the circumstances of larger employers' (Minister of Employment, in House of Commons 1986b: 571) and 'we have no wish to bring the law governing public employment relationships into people's private living arrangements' (Minister of Employment, in House of Commons 1986b: 570).

[10] For example, the government rejected the opposition's suggestion of a stronger enforcement system (Fritzpatrick 1987: 943–6, House of Commons 1986b: 619) and of inclusion of private households (House of Commons 1986b: 583–4). Moreover, the opposition criticized the governmental draft of Clause 2 of the Sex Discrimination Act 'to provide for the removal of discriminatory items in collective agreements and rules, which means that they will remain unless or until they are removed by renegotiation or as a result of individual complaints and a successful decision in a court or tribunal' (House of Commons 1986b: 584), defined Clause 1 as unnecessarily wide leading to conflicting rules (House of Commons 1986c: 1329), and perpetuated discrimination of women regarding redundancy rights in Clauses 2 and 3 (House of Commons 1986c: 1330).

As long as the Conservative government stayed in power, the context remained unfavourable for effective reframing. The ECJ judgment provided an authoritative norm definition and thereby reduced the complexity of the issue. However, the dominant male breadwinner and female caregiver approach was strongly institutionalized during this period (Sacks 1986: 565). Forty-three per cent of women and 52 per cent of men normatively adhered to this model in 1987 and did not wish for legal changes which would affect existing gender-related logics of appropriateness (The Fawcett Society 2005: 2). Moreover, the prominent liberal macro-economic frame was not compatible with a more demanding equal treatment approach allowing for state interventions to promote gender equality. Thus, new frames which might require demanding interpretations were not launched at all[11] and would have most likely not been successful. Consequently, the government and also the leading ministry of employment upheld the traditional role models, protected the market and the economy from 'over-regulation' and did not change their policy ideas towards a demanding equality approach. Even a decade after the ECJ ruling of 1983, Conservatives still opposed protective legislation and pursed deregulation, thus sacrificing the interests of women whenever economic concerns were at stake.[12] They repeatedly emphasized that the existing UK equal treatment legislation was sufficient and required no further changes (House of Commons 1994c: 438–40). Some Conservatives even denied the phenomenon of sex discrimination altogether (House of Commons 1994c: 467) or accused women of being responsible for the weakness of their positions, which, they claimed, was caused by a lack of self-confidence rather than by discrimination of any kind (House of Commons 1994c: 468).

Sanction-threats

This section examines an alternative explanation to successful shaming campaigns. Did sanction-threats foster the UK's shift into minimalist compliance in 1986? Did the ECJ manage to threaten the UK with a referral to Article 171 ECT and de-centralized sanctions and thus induce compliance as expected by the rationalist hypothesis? Did looming sanctions differentially empower a pro-compliance ministry and thereby foster compliance as expected by the constructivist hypothesis?

[11] For example, there was no single campaign in which societal norm proponents promoted equal treatment as a basic human right (e.g. *Independent* 1992, *The Times* 1991a, *The Times* 1991b, *The Times* 1992a, *The Times* 1992b).

[12] For example, the Conservatives opposed minimum wages in arguing that they would reduce the number of jobs for women (House of Commons 1994c: 464).

The rationalist hypothesis: credible sanction-threats increase non-compliance costs

After the ECJ judgment, the UK remained reluctant to adapt policies for two years, before they started to initiate changes in the SDA (see also House of Commons 1983, House of Commons 1994c: 471–2). The looming shadow of decentralized penalties (e.g. losses of reputation vis-à-vis other member states or the Commission) was not responsible for the shift into minimalist compliance in 1986. Most importantly, there was no credible and deterrent sanction-threat, because the ECJ did not even introduce any first decentralized enforcement steps with a referral to a violation of Article 171 ECT.

In line with this expectation, the Conservative government did not engage in blame shifting to the ECJ to limit damages of reputation and prevent electoral losses. Instead of signalling to their compliance-averse constituency that the ECJ was ultimately responsible for policy changes, the government publicly argued that they were not responsible for the judgment in the first place. They stressed that the ruling was the fault of the Labour Party who were in government in 1975 when the SDA was established (House of Commons 1986b: 616). 'The hon. Member . . . must realise that it is not this Government's record at the European Court that is bad. Rather it is the durability and adequacy of the previous Labour Government's legislation that is bad' (House of Commons 1986b: 616). Thus, the government mentioned the judgment not because it was deterred by threats of possible sanctions and pursued blame shifting to the ECJ in order to justify unavoidable policy adaptations. Instead they publicly emphasized that the ECJ ruling was ultimately caused by outdated legal acts from the previous Labour government. This allowed them to circumvent reputational losses vis-à-vis women's organizations and prevent shaming campaigns, since the Conservative government could hardly be accused of violating the reputation of the UK as an equality leader, given that they were not responsible for the deficient legal act in the first place.

The constructivist hypothesis: sanction-threats empower pro-compliance ministries

Did the ECJ judgment or the ECJ sanction-threat strengthen a logic of appropriateness and thereby differentially empower a pro-compliance ministry vis-à-vis domestic veto players in the equal access case?

In the course of legal adaptation, the leading employment ministry did not attack the ECJ, but highlighted that its ruling had to be acknowledged: 'Recognizing the judgment placed on us an obligation to amend the Act, we carried out an extensive consultative exercise last autumn to establish how this could be done in a manner best fitted to our national circumstances and practice' (Minister for Employment, Mr Clarke, in House of Commons 1986b: 569). Nevertheless, the ECJ did not differentially empower the employment ministry via its judgment or a potential remote sanction-threat and thereby induce compliance. Both the leading employment ministry and the government were compliance-averse before the ECJ referral, during the ongoing infringement proceeding and even after the Commission closed the case. Prior to the opening of the case, the Conservatives pursued a liberal economic policy, opposing intervention into market forces for the promotion of women's rights (Boston 1987, House of Commons 1975a: 567, 570, House of Commons 1975c: 542, 567, 570, 589–93). Consequently, they, for example, explicitly opted for a limited applicatory scope of the equal treatment principle on private households, small undertakings and midwives (House of Commons 1975c: 530–2). These convictions did not change over time, although the Minister for Employment stated in the process of legal adaptation that 'it is my desire that we pass this legislation in a way that actually improves and strengthens our law and protects us against unfair discrimination' (Mr Clarke, in House of Commons 1986b: 577). Rather than expressing a normative conviction, the employment ministry paid lip service to shaming actors. Consequently, the Minster continued his speech with, 'It is also my desire that we should not be led into absurdity in so doing' (Mr Clarke, in House of Commons 1986b: 577) and opted for a minimalist legal implementation of the judgment, purposefully leaving two out of five elements unresolved (House of Commons 1986b: 617).[13] Also after the case was closed, the Conservatives did stick to their parsimonious equality approach (House of Commons 1989c: 933f., House of Commons 1994c: 438–40, 467–8). Hence, the ECJ did not differentially empower the economic ministry vis-à-vis domestic veto players and did not end the norm violations in this way.

The equal access case: an example of an effective judgment

As in the UK collective redundancy case, governmental non-compliance interests were very strong in the UK equal access case. The Conservatives opposed market intervention in general because they regarded liberalization as the key to constant macro-economic growth. In addition, they were against the equal access directive because it imposed costs on employers and industry and considered voluntary agreements far superior

[13] The minister stated, 'We have no wish to bring the law governing public employment relationships into people's private living arrangements (. . .) we still question whether it is really appropriate to seek the objective of equal treatment by applying to all small firms a law designed to meet the circumstances of larger employers' (House of Commons 1986b: 570–1).

to legal means in combating discrimination against women (House of Commons 1975a).

Unlike the collective redundancy case, in the equal access case, the judicial discourse was not effective in ending the norm violation. In its judgment, the ECJ clarified that the UK was in violation of the directive by exempting non-binding collective agreements, independent professions, rules of undertakings, and private households as well as small undertakings from the equal access principle. This empowered societal norm entrepreneurs, such as the Fawcett Society, the Women's National Commission and the EOC, to the disadvantage of employer associations and trade unions, who constituted the major opponents to compliance. The fit between the ECJ judgment and already institutionalized domestic ideas was high and norm proponents successfully shamed the government for violating the UK's position of a leading international proponent of equality, and for preventing the greater protection of women as the weaker sex. The government reacted to the increasing domestic non-compliance costs and changed the SDA in 1986 in a minimalist fashion, excluding two of five issues. Nevertheless, this shift into minimalist compliance simultaneously avoided reputational losses vis-à-vis women and allowed for further liberalization. Conversely, as predicted by the constructivist hypothesis, re-framing strategies had low prospects of success. The dominant liberal deregulative frame was deeply institutionalized and did not complement a more demanding equality approach.

Similar to the collective redundancy case, neither the rationalist nor the constructivist pathway of sanction-threats induced compliance. The 1986 SDA changes were not the result of the UK yielding to the ECJ nor of the differential empowerment of the employment ministry.

5.II The case on the residence of foreign workers – shaming Germany into compliance

Directive 90/364 on the residence of EU citizens and their families as workers in member countries is part of the European social policy. Against the background of the realization of the internal market, member states sought the foreign workers directive as a means to harmonize national provisions to ensure freedom of movement. More concretely, the foreign workers directive aimed to enhance the legal certainty of affected persons, by creating transparent and clear standards and conditions for the provision of residence entitlements to foreign workers and their families within the EU. The directive was relatively strongly contested among the member states. As a result, even the preface of the directive stated that 'beneficiaries of the right of residence must not become an unreasonable burden on the public finances of the host Member State'.

Compared to other member states, such as the UK or Italy, German legal acts on migration and the residence of foreigners were highly complex (e.g. distinguishing between different categories of foreigners) and procedures were strongly bureaucratized (Morris 2001: 406–9). Basically, the residence of foreign workers and their families was regulated by two legal acts: the law on foreigners (Ausländergesetz) and the law on residence in the EEC (Aufenthaltsgesetz/EWG). The law on foreigners dates back to the year 1965, when the booming German economy, also known as the 'economic miracle', created so many new jobs that additional foreign workers were needed. Reacting to this situation, Germany developed a policy of inviting foreigners, mainly from Southern European countries, as guest-workers. Against this background, and due to the dominant self-perception that Germany was not a country of immigration, the law on foreigners was not designed for long-term residence, but only for short-term stays (Green 2001, Minkenberg 2003, Social Democratic Party (SPD) 1988: 1). As a consequence, it only vaguely regulated the terms under which residence was permitted and under which families were allowed to settle in Germany. This opened wide windows of opportunity for diverging administrative interpretations and created uncertainty among foreign workers (Committee for Internal Affairs 1990: 2–3, SPD 1988: 1–2). In addition to the law on foreigners, which concerns all foreigners, the law on residence/EEC specifies residency issues for EC members. This law was also designed for short-term stays of foreign workers and dealt only barely with long-term issues, such as entitlements of relatives.

Since the European foreign workers directive prescribes criteria for obtaining permissions as well as the content and durations of such authorizations, it filled gaps in the German legal landscape and created a demand for legal changes. The misfit was on a medium scale. On the one hand, the directive did not challenge core administrative ideas and required no fundamental reforms of the German legal landscape. On the other hand, German laws on foreigners were not designed for long-term stays, while the directive regulated issues of particular relevance to foreign workers who intended to reside permanently.

When in opposition, the Social Democrats made a legislative proposal

[14] In 1988, the SPD proposed a reform of the 1965 Ausländergesetz, arguing that Germany had responsibilities for foreign workers, since they had contributed to Germany's prosperity (Bundestag 1988a: 8197, Social Democratic Party (SPD) 1988: 1). Its basic aim was to increase the transparency and establish clear criteria for residence permissions for foreign workers and their families.

similar to the directive in 1988 (Bundestag 1988a, SPD 1988).[14] Already then, the CDU/FDP government and the leading interior ministry were skeptical, arguing that Germany was not an immigration country and claiming that foreign workers were short-term guests instead of long-term residents (Mr Zimmermann, in Bundestag 1988a: 81799, cf. Minister of the Interior, Wolfgang Schäuble, in Bundestag 1990e: 16281, also Minister of the Interior, Manfred Kanther, in Bundestag 1996e: 10261). Moreover, the government opposed the directive because of cost considerations. Foreign workers and their relatives would have benefited from German social security schemes, such as health care, unemployment benefits, or pension funds, if they obtained permission for residence. Although the government in Bonn regarded the free movement of workers as generally positive, they argued that it should not violate principles of distributional justice. They feared that a law on foreigners with far-reaching residence permissions would allow foreigners and their relatives to profit from German social security schemes without having properly contributed in the past (Bundestag 1990f: 16893–5).[15] Apparently, the Kohl government was not guided by the same beliefs on social justice as the SPD, according to which all contributors to the overall welfare should profit, but focused on ideas of national identity and of citizenship as criteria for entitlements of social benefits (Bundestag 1990f: 16892–5). In line with these compliance-averse interests, the transposition of the foreign workers directive followed an unobtrusive approach: the interior minister, Rudolf Seiters, merely issued a circular letter informing the administration of the presence of the foreign workers directive in June 1992, but did not implement the directive through regulations or laws. As a consequence, foreign workers and their families coming from other member states to Germany were less protected than in other member states. While this opened a window of opportunity to save public resources (e.g. costs of social security schemes), it prevented a harmonization of residency procedures in the internal market and limited the freedom of persons.

Already in October 1992, the European Commission suspected a violation of the directive (European Court of Justice 1997: 9). Although the government changed the EWG Aufenthaltsgesetz in April 1993 and authorized the federal minister of the interior to enact decrees and

[15] Some Members of the CDU even referred to the danger of 'social security tourism' (Bundestag 1990f: 16894–5) and argued that residence permissions should be restricted, in order to prevent 'that the aunt of a foreigner, who lives here, is sent to a nursing home at the expense of the German taxpayer' (Bundestag 1990f: 16892, translation DP).

regulations for the implementation of directive 90/364 (and others), the Commission was not satisfied. The former also repeatedly signalled its willingness to introduce legal adaptations to the European Commission, but failed to do so (European Court of Justice 1997: 13). In response, the Commission sent a reasoned opinion in 1993 and finally referred the case to the ECJ in 1995 (C-96/95). Two years later, the ECJ ruled that the foreign workers directive was not correctly transposed in Germany because the transparency and legal certainty of residence entitlements for foreign workers was not increased (European Court of Justice 1997).

The pattern of legal changes

The German 1990 law on foreigners explicated the principle of supremacy of European over national law, in stating the possibility that an EC directive provides for detailed rules related to foreigners. It also emphasized that the law on foreigners applies to all EU and non-EU foreigners – as far as there is no other EC secondary law. In 1993, Germany changed §15a III of the law on residence (EWG Aufenthaltsgesetz). According to this act, the law on foreigners concerned not only foreigners, but also EU citizens who lived and worked within other countries. The law also authorized the federal interior minister to enact decrees on the implementation of EC directives on the residence of foreign workers and their families with the consent of the Bundesrat.

Germany revised the law on foreigners in June 1997, less than a year after the Court judgment. The reform dealt with removals of criminal resident foreigners from German territory. It did not increase the transparency and precision of residence permission rules for foreign workers and their families and therefore did not transpose the ECJ judgment.

In the same year, the interior minister, Manfred Kanther, issued a free-movement regulation (Freizügigkeitsverordnung). This regulation addressed the issue contested in the infringement procedure, in large parts resembled the wording of the European directive and slightly increased legal certainty of foreigners seeking residence in Germany. However, while it ensured that regional administrations (Länder) recognized the European foreign workers directive as part of the legal landscape, it only slightly increased the transparency of rights and obligations vis-à-vis affected individuals. Germany did not adapt the two relevant laws and therefore did not systematically nor comprehensively strengthen the visibility of residency rules. Moreover, due to overlaps with other legal acts and since the free-movement regulation encompassed some windows of opportunity for deviations from a demanding norm interpretation in the applicatory stage, it resembled a minimalist form of compliance.[16] Thus, foreign EC citizens still faced difficulties of getting to know and claim their rights in 1997.

Table 5.2 Legal changes on the residence of foreign workers

Date	*Title*	*Initiated by*	*Content*
1990	Ausländergesetz	Opposition (SPD)	Minimalist legal act
1993	EWR Aufenthalsgesetz	Federal Government (CDU and FDP)	§15a III authorizes the Federa Minister of Internal Affairs to enact decrees on the implementation of directive 90/364 (and others), minimal legal adaptation, below the transparency requirements of the directive
1997	Revision of the Ausländergesetz	Federal Government (CDU and FDP)	Specifies removals of foreigners from German territory
1997	Freizügigkeits-verordnung	Federal Ministry of the Interior, CDU FDP government	Formal legal transposition, but purpose of the directive (higher transparency for affected individuals) still not fully achieved

How can these policy changes be explained? Why did the Kohl government adapt legal acts in 1997, although they strongly and rigidly opposed such changes during the earlier stages of the EU infringement procedure? Was the judicial discourse, the differential empowerment of the ECJ judgment, or the threat of sanctions effective in facilitating policy changes from non-compliance into minimalist compliance?

The judicial discourse

The European Commission criticized the initial German transposition with the ministerial note, as well as the Ausführungsgesetz, and claimed that both violated the foreign workers directive since they hindered transparency and legal certainty for affected foreigners. According to the Commission, foreign workers could not identify their rights due to the

[16] During their incumbency, the Kohl government maintained minimalist compliance. As late as 2000, the Social-Democratic/Green government under the chancellor Gerhard Schröder launched a revision of the law on foreigners, which broadened the grounds for granting residency permissions and thereby simplified the issue and increased the transparency.

complicated legal construction and the mere naming of the directive in the law on foreigners. On the contrary, the Kohl government argued that they had completely and correctly transposed directive 90/364 with a ministerial circular letter and also with the law on foreigners. Since their policy interests pointed rigidly towards non-compliance with the European Commission's idea of what the foreign workers directive had been about, the Commission referred the case to the ECJ (C-96/95) and a judicial discourse took place between March 1995 and March 1997. Did the judicial discourse end the norm violation and, if so, did it work through arguing or through bargaining-based mechanisms?

Judicial discourse: ideational entrapment or threats of reputational losses?

Unlike in most of the ECJ cases, there was only one single issue at stake. During the two years of the judicial discourse, the parties debated whether the circular letter of 1992, together with a general clause in the law on foreigners of 1990, which stated that European directives might specify residence entitlements, was a sufficient transposition (European Court of Justice 1997).

In the judicial discourse, the German advocate argued that the circular letter, the general clauses in the law on foreigners and in the law on residence sufficiently transposed the directive. In order to substantiate this claim, he firstly used pragmatic arguments to justify the German transposition, instead of applying legal methods of interpretation in order to analyse the obligations of the European directive. The advocate stated that the foreign workers directive could be directly implemented by national administrations without requiring a transposition into German law because it was already very precise and did not need further specifications and guidelines (European Court of Justice 1997: 33). Secondly, the German advocate pragmatically stressed that general references in German laws to the possibility that future EC directives might specify rules and procedures, as stated in the 1990 law on foreigners, are sufficient transpositions, since directives are publicly accessible and sufficiently clear (European Court of Justice 1997: 34). Thirdly, without using a legal technique of interpretation, the German advocate claimed that Article 189 III ECT expresses the supremacy of EU law and that §2 II of the German law on foreigners articulates this principle as well. Based on this, he concluded that a formal transposition of the directive into national law is not necessary (Advocate General 1996b: 30, European Court of Justice 1997: 32–4, 37).

The European advocate disagreed with his German colleague (Advocate General 1996b: 11, 34, European Court of Justice 1997: 30). He did not use the same pragmatic arguments, but instead applied a wider array of different judicial techniques of interpretation. Based on the narrow wording device, the European advocate claimed that the law on foreigners (§2) as well as the EWG residence law (§15) insufficiently transposed the directive (European Court of Justice 1997: 17). Yet the goodness of fit between the interpretational issue and the wording method was low. Germany had not been completely inactive, but had notified the Commission of the decree and the general clause in the law on foreigners as transposition measures. However, the wording instrument was too narrow to allow inquiry into whether the German transposition included all necessary measures, since no paragraph of the foreign workers directive explicated the concept of a sufficient transposition. The broader directive-immanent teleological method revealed that the main aim of the directive was to increase transparency and legal certainty of foreigners from other EU member states (European Court of Justice 1997: 33–4, 36). Yet affected foreign workers could not even inform themselves about entitlements, which contradicted the very purpose of the directive. The European advocate highlighted that the German construction thwarted the increase of transparency and legal certainty because the circular did 'not produce direct legal effects vis-à-vis individuals' and could not ensure 'that individuals are fully acquainted with their rights so that they can seek their protection before the national courts' (Advocate General 1996b: 35). In addition, transparency was hampered though the complex German legal construction of a general clause in the law on foreigners.[17]

During the judicial discourse, both parties talked at cross purposes. Germany did not use legal methods of interpretation, but presented general and pragmatic arguments. Hence, the advocates of the parties did not mutually accept their claims as valid, and therefore did not incrementally develop a common notion of how to best interpret the disputed element. Consequently, the ideational entrapment and the reputation costs hypotheses expect that the judicial discourse would fail.

Even before the judicial discourse had started, the government was aware of the fact that foreigners were often uninformed about their rights, although the Ausländergesetz should have created legal certainty (Bundesregierung 1994c: 44). A governmental dossier indirectly admitted that the transposition of the foreign workers directive could be incomplete (Bundesregierung 1994c: 44). Yet, between 1994 and 1997, the government

[17] Paragraph 2 of the law on foreigners incorporated non-EC *and* EC foreigners, which multiplied the difficulties of affected individuals to claim their rights (European Court of Justice 1997: 36).

and the leading interior ministry remained completely inactive. They did not alter compliance-averse policies during or in response to the judicial discourse. The Minister of the Interior, Manfred Kanther, continuously denied the necessity of making changes to the law on foreigners (e.g. Bundestag 1996c: 12379–81, Bundestag 1997e). While integration of foreigners was crucial, the government emphasized that Germany was not an immigration country so that long-term residences were exceptions rather than the rule (compare e.g. Bundesregierung 1994a, Bundestag 1982: 4959–60, 4968–70 with Bundestag 2000b: 8562). Instead of changing policy ideas on foreigners as short-term guests towards a long-term residence approach in response to the judicial discourse, Germany maintained its restrictive foreigners' policy. This was economically justified by arguing that foreign workers were 'a burden for the German job market and the economy' (Bundestag 1996c: 12365–6, similar 12377–80, also Finance Minister, Mr Theo Waigel, in *Süddeutsche Zeitung* 1997f). These policy ideas remained stable even after the Kohl government was no longer in office (e.g. Bundesrat 1998, Bundestag 1997e).[18] In line with their minimalist foreign workers policy preferences, the government did not introduce legal changes during the ongoing judicial discourse. Even after the ECJ judgment, the government only pursued minimalist legal changes, but no comprehensive shift towards a demanding foreign workers approach that was fully committed to increasing legal certainty and transparency.

Summing up, as expected, the judicial discourse was ineffective because the advocates of the parties talked at cross purposes. Consequently, the first compliance instrument did not trigger a policy change favourable to foreign workers' social and economic integration and reflecting either comprehensive or minimalist compliance.

The second rationalist alternative: compliance bargaining in the shadow of the ECJ

An alternative to arguing in front of the ECJ is bargaining in the shadow of the judicial discourse. Did Germany and the Commission construct a compromise through informal compliance bargaining and was it

[18] In 1998, the newly elected Social-Democratic/Green coalition under Gerhard Schröder initiated a reform of the law on foreigners. The CDU and FDP fractions strongly opposed the easing of permissions requirements for the residence of foreigners (e.g. Bundesrat 1998, Bundestag 1997e). As in the early 1990s, the CDU and FDP still argued that the danger of abusing residence permissions is too high, they emphasized countervailing economic elements, and they opposed broader residence entitlements to dependents of foreign workers (Bundestag 2000b: 8569, 8568, 8572). The CDU and FDP maintained their convictions about social justice and about foreigners as short-term guests rather than immigrants (e.g. Bundesrat 1998, Bundesregierung 1998a, Bundesregierung 1994a, Bundestag 1997e, *Süddeutsche Zeitung* 1997f).

responsible for the shift into minimalist compliance in 1997, only a few months after the ECJ judgment?

Compliance bargaining leaves no paper trails on processes and outcomes (Advocate General 1996b, e.g. European Court of Justice 1997). As a consequence, we cannot examine whether bargaining took place and whether the actors shared a conception of what power is about, so that they could exchange concessions and demands and thereby incrementally develop a compromise. While we cannot directly inquire into possible bargaining dynamics, we can counterfactually examine whether bargaining could have been possibly successful, fostering a compromise and resulting in the shift into minimalist compliance. Given the high importance of foreign worker rules for one of the four core principles of the common market, the free movement of workers, the European Commission might have had a strong incentive to settle the case quickly and thereby reinforce one of the four fundamental freedoms. In order to avoid a continued norm violation at the expense of affected foreigners and their families, the European Commission might have offered Germany concessions and/or the possibility of withdrawing the case if Germany quickly improved its foreign workers legislation. Such a deal might have been beneficial to Germany as well because a compromise might have allowed Germany to get away with a legal act with backdoors for lax implementation. Furthermore avoiding a judgment could save reputational losses vis-à-vis other member states with more liberal foreign worker rules. Yet the very fact that the ECJ issued a judgment shows that the European Commission did not withdraw the case, which is not too surprising given that Germany did not change its legal acts during the two years of the ongoing judicial discourse. Even if compliance bargaining had taken place in the shadow of the Court, it was not successful since neither side fulfilled practical concessions. In sum, informal compliance bargaining cannot explain why Germany shifted into minimalist compliance with the 1997 regulations.

The differential empowerment effect of the judgment

In March 1997, almost exactly two years after the referral to the ECJ, the latter issued a ruling against Germany. It stated that the directive's very purpose of creating transparency and increasing legal certainty was jeopardized by the German legal transposition (European Court of Justice 1997). Did the ECJ judgment empower pro-compliance actors in domestic society and did they induce compliance via bottom-up strategies? This section argues that differential empowerment did indeed take place. It shows that churches, together with trade unions, succeeded in shaming the government for violating core values of Christian charity and basic norms of solidarity among workers. In response the government quickly shifted into a minimalist form of compliance. This allowed them to pacify the domestic compliance constituency and to prevent damages to the governmental reputation on the one hand, and to pursue a less demanding foreign workers approach in the stage of practical implementation on the other.

In the foreign workers case, the compliance constituency was mainly composed of churches and trade unions (Bundestag 1988a: 8197, Checkel 2001: 568–9). They supported integration and opposed sentiments against foreigners (Bundesregierung 1995, Gemeinsame Synode der Bistümer in der Bundesrepublik Deutschland 1976: 367–410, Minkenberg 2003, Prantl 1991).[19] Similar to the government, the broader public did not regard Germany as an immigration country and was sceptical about residency and social security entitlements of foreigners. However public opinion also clearly opposed discrimination, in particular as violent xenophobic acts of radical right-wing activists made headlines in the early and mid 1990s (e.g. Bundesregierung 1991: 3243–9, Falter 1994, Funke 2001: 62–5, Raijman, Semyonov and Schmidt 2003). While churches and trade unions supported foreigner-friendly policies, societal compliance opponents were rare. While the three biggest right-wing parties, the Republikaner, the DVU (Deutsche Volksunion) and the NPD (Nationaldemokratische Partei Deutschland), opposed immigration and integration, they were marginal actors and never gained more than two per cent of votes in federal elections (Lubbers, Gijsberts and Scheepers 2002: 431).

Prior to the ECJ judgment of 1997, the societal context was not fertile for successful shaming or re-framing campaigns, since there was no consensus on whether Germany was in violation of the directive. In addition, public opinion shifted towards stronger scepticism concerning the residence of foreign workers in 1996. In this year, an ECJ preliminary ruling on foreign workers provoked negative public sentiments (e.g. *Frankfurter Allgemeine Zeitung* 1996). The case centered on an Italian guest-worker family (Paletta), who sent sick certificates from Italy, where they were on vacation, to their German employer several summers in a row (Advocate General 1996a). In 1989, their employer doubted that all four workers (husband, wife, and the two children) had simultaneously

[19] As early as 1976, the Catholic Church criticized laws on foreigners for leaving overly wide administrative margins and insufficiently regulating long-term residencies (Gemeinsame Synode der Bistümer in der Bundesrepublik Deutschland 1976: 394).

fallen ill again and stopped the wage payments (cf. Reicherzer 1993). In 1996, the ECJ stated in the 'Paletta case' that employers must accept sick certificates which were issued within the EC and that it was not lawful to deny wage payments on the basis of serious doubts of whether the persons concerned had really been ill (European Court of Justice 1996). This preliminary ruling received high media attention and created the public perception that the ECJ forced German employers to accept implausible sick certificates, which reinforced public sentiments against the residence of foreign workers (Bundesregierung 1994c, Bundestag 1996d: 12352–4, 12377–81, *Frankfurter Allgemeine Zeitung* 1996, *Frankfurter Rundschau* 1996, Ostner 1996: 559). Against this background, it was very difficult to successfully shame the Kohl government as a compliance laggard, violating domestically institutionalized norms and, thereby, creating a threat to reputational and electoral losses.

The domestic context was not fertile for successful reframing activities either. Unlike the SPD and the Green Party, the governing CDU and FDP considered foreign workers not as long-term residents or even as immigrants (Bundestag 1988a: 8197, Bundestag 1990e, Bundestag 1996a: 7586–90). The idea that aliens are short-term guest-workers was deep-seated. It fitted well with governmental liberal economic and distributional justice approaches, according to which participation in social security schemes should be limited to prevent overstraining. An alternative policy frame, conceptualizing Germany as an immigration country, would have fitted with a more demanding interpretation of the foreign workers directive, acknowledging that foreign workers and their families usually stayed for long periods. Yet such an approach would not have resonated well with the already strongly institutionalized policy ideas (Bundesregierung 1994a, Bundestag 1988a: 81799, Bundestag 1990e: 16281): 'I tell you explicitly, to make it completely clear: The government, the coalition does not define Germany as an immigration country – and I definitely don't either' (Minister of the Interior, Manfred Kanther, in Bundestag 1996e, translation DP).

In this context, the compliance constituency was mostly inactive and requested reforms in the legal landscape only in a few instances. In spring 1996, for example, the churches and the German peak association of trade unions (DGB) argued that the short term focus of the law on foreigners was inadequate for concerns of foreigners living in Germany for longer periods and also for matters of immigration (*Süddeutsche Zeitung* 1996). Besides this reframing initiative, norm proponents hardly engaged at all in public debates on issues related to the residence of foreigners and their families and did not stipulate that they were entitled to German welfare schemes (e.g. *Die Welt* 1996, Gemeinsame Synode der Bistümer in der Bundesrepublik Deutschland 1976: 393–409, *Süddeutsche Zeitung* 1997d, *TAZ* 1997a, *TAZ* 1997b). Before the ECJ judgment of 1997, both bottom-up hypotheses do not expect that Germany could have been pushed into ending the norm violation. In line with this, the CDU/FDP coalition maintained their minimalist foreign worker policy (compare e.g. Bundestag 1990e: 1620 with Bundestag 1996d: 12377–81).

In 1997, the ECJ judgment empowered churches and trade unions. They obtained additional ideational resources such as causal, normative and judicial arguments on the case, greater public attention and an authoritative interpretation on what constitutes compliance with the foreign workers directive. Yet the domestic environment was still not conducive to the successful adoption of new frames. Foreigners were widely regarded as short-term guest-workers. This perception was reinforced by the CDU/FDP's conception of social justice, according to which social security benefits should be protected from exploitation by non-citizens. Moreover, in the context of perceived economic decline, the government identified no need for foreign workers and preferred not to encourage long-term stays (Bundestag 1990e: 16894, Falter 1994, Lubbers and Scheepers 2001). These developments reduced the chances for Catholic and Protestant churches, together with the Green Party and parts of the SPD, to successfully launch a more demanding immigration approach (Green 2001, Minkenberg 2003, interview Green Party#1, 17–11–06). Thus, although churches continuously emphasized that short-term stays no longer reflected the empirical reality of foreigners living in Germany, reframing the domestic debate was not possible (Ausschuss für Innere Angelegenheiten 1990, Barth 1997, Bischof Dr Engelhardt, Bischof Dr. Dr. Lehmann and Augoustinos 1997, Bundestag 1997b, Green 2001). Consequently, the government kept their compliance-averse policy interests throughout the 1990s (e.g. Bundestag 2000b).

Prior to the ECJ ruling in 1997, the domestic context was unreceptive for shaming campaigns, not least due to the highly contested Paletta case (European Court of Justice 1996). As time passed and attention to the Paletta ruling and related sentiments waned, the conditions for successful shaming improved considerably. The ECJ judgment increased public attention and highlighted that German foreigner laws were insufficient (*Die Welt* 1997, *Frankfurter Allgemeine Zeitung* 1998, *Süddeutsche Zeitung* 1997e). In addition to the judgment, the government was under stress because the interior ministry had issued a regulation on foreigners to prevent immigration through the backdoor in 1997, shortly before the ECJ issued its judgment. This regulation considerably tightened visa requirements for children of foreigners, even if they were born in Germany and had lived there all their lives (Bundestag 1997e: 14700–1). It received a lot of attention by the media and created public resentments towards the government (*Süddeutsche Zeitung 1997c*, *Süddeutsche Zeitung* 1997d, *TAZ* 1997b). The opposition to legal acts preventing integration and immigration reached its peak in March 1997, when public demonstrations against the harsh governmental foreigners' policy took place in several German cities (Bundestag 1997e, *Süddeutsche Zeitung* 1997a *Süddeutsche Zeitung* 1997b). At the same time, church associations intensified their criticism of existing laws on foreigners and emphasized that they violated the Christian norm of charity (Bischof Dr Engelhardt, Bischof Dr. Dr. Lehmann and Augoustinos 1997, *Die Welt* 1997, *Süddeutsche Zeitung* 1997e, interview organized interests#17, 15–11–06). Churches were important actors, because of their relatively broad membership in Germany and because the governing CDU identified itself strongly with Christianity (the commitment to Christian Democracy is even part of the party's name) and it was therefore very difficult for them to ignore the position of the churches altogether (Barker 2004: 170, Pombeni 2000, interview organized interests#17, 15–11–06). Trade unions also publicly emphasized that foreign workers had been and still were an integral and important part of the German economy, which the laws on foreigners failed to acknowledge (Bundestag 1997g). This created an environment in which the government could have easily lost their good reputation vis-à-vis their Christian constituency, if they had continued non-compliance with the European foreign workers directive. Especially in anticipation of the upcoming federal elections, the government could no longer ignore societal compliance-pushes.

In response to shaming campaigns, the government, and especially the interior ministry, became increasingly sensitive to the position of the churches and strategically adapted their position accordingly. Since Christian democracy is an integral element of the CDU's party ideology (Pombeni 2000) and Catholics are part of the CDU's constituency (Jung and Roth 2002: 16), the government started to put strong rhetorical emphasis on the importance of integrating foreign workers and their families (e.g. Bundesregierung 1997, Bundestag 1997d: 14696–7). Moreover, they publicly promised to promote transparency of residency requirements to increase the legal certainty of foreigners and their families (Bundestag 1997f: 11478–9, Bundestag 1997g: 18078–9). At the same time the Christian-Democrats did not change their substantive policy ideas and continued to strongly oppose a 'dual citizenship', although this could have secured residency permission for foreigners and facilitated long-term integration (e.g. the Green Party in Bundestag 1997g: 18082–3, Bundestag 1997g: 18078, 18086–7, Checkel 2001: 568–9). The Kohl government also maintained its protectionist attitude towards the German employment market and the social security insurance schemes vis-à-vis foreigners and their families. They continued to argue that restrictions on attracting foreign workers were necessary and that limits on their access to the German employment market were important and fair (Bundestag 1997c: 16062–4, Bundestag 1997f: 11478–9).[20] In line with its adapted strategic positions, the leading ministry issued a regulation in 1997 that minimally transposed the judgment and circumvented domestic reputational costs, while keeping a backdoor open for future less demanding norm applications (e.g. Bundestag 1997f). The freedom of movement regulation resembled the wording of the foreign workers directive, but the laws on foreigners had not been changed at all. While this adaptation pacified the domestic compliance constituency, it did not improve the transparency and legal certainty for foreigners. Rather, the 1997 regulation provided a window of opportunity for pursuing less demanding norm interpretations in the stage of practical implementation, since foreigners, who are generally unaware of their and especially their families' legal entitlements, are unlikely to apply for permission for residence.

Summing up, the interior ministry and the government were reluctant to change legal acts and their underlying policy ideas before the ECJ made use of its second compliance instrument. The judgment differentially empowered domestic norm advocates who succeeded in shaming campaigns and created domestic non-compliance costs to which the government strategically adapted with a shift into minimalist compliance.

The threat of sanctions

While the judgment differentially empowered societal actors who then shamed the government into minimalist compliance, the third compliance instrument at the disposal of the ECJ, a sanction-threat, was not effective.

The rationalist hypothesis: credible sanction-threats increase non-compliance costs

In the first months after the ECJ judgment of 1997, the shadow of sanctions was not looming. Germany could have continued the norm violation for at least another year, before the Commission would have issued a second letter of formal notice as a first measure towards the

[20] Even after the case was closed, the CDU and FDP fractions still opposed the broadening of residency permissions for dependents of foreign workers and evoked economic arguments (Bundestag 2000b: 8562, 8566, 8572, *Frankfurter Allgemeine Zeitung* 1998, *Die Welt* 2000).

imposition of non-compliance penalties. Sanction-threats were therefore hardly credible in the aftermath of the judgment, because it was unlikely that the government in Berlin would be subject to sanctions in the near future. Furthermore the amount of potential sanctions would most likely not have been sufficiently high to act as a deterrent once European authorities had made first steps towards enforcement. Breaching the foreign workers directive was a serious issue in two regards. The infringement indirectly affected the free movement of persons, since the German legislation hindered foreign workers and their families from residing in Germany. The norm violation was also serious because of its financial implications. By indirectly preventing the residence of foreign workers' families, Germany forestalled increasing social insurance expenses. However, based on the other criteria, non-compliance with the European directive was not serious, because it did not impact on the functioning of the Community, did not seriously harm human health or the environment, did not affect huge parts of the population, did not harm other member states and was not a repeated norm violation. Even if the government had been highly risk-averse and had heavily discounted potential future sanctions, external norm violation costs were very low in 1997. Hence, we would not expect Germany to shy away from the third compliance instrument and quickly minimally adapt its legal acts in order to avoid becoming penalized.

In 1997, the European Commission neither issued a second letter of formal notice nor a second reasoned opinion (based on Art. 228 ECT) and did not threaten the government with negative consequences of persistent non-compliance. Nevertheless, we observe that the interior ministry quickly issued a regulation that transposed the European directive almost completely, resembling its wording but also constructing loopholes in the German legal landscape that practically reduced the transparency and legal certainty for affected foreigners. This policy change was accompanied by a change in rhetoric, according to which the government accepted the need to promote transparency on residency conditions (Bundestag 1997f: 11478–9, Bundestag 1997g: 18078–79). However, as soon as the public attention declined after the legal change of 1997, the government and the interior ministry rhetorically shifted back into promoting policies based on the idea of foreigners as short- or medium-term guests rather than long-term members of society (e.g. Bundestag 2000b: 8562, 8566, 8572). Although Germany shifted into minimalist compliance, this was not caused by the anticipation of possible future penalties. If Germany had changed its foreign workers policy in order to avoid potential penalties, the government and the interior ministry would most likely have blamed the ECJ as being ultimately responsible for the need to change legal acts. Finger pointing would have allowed them to highlight that the government still did not regard Germany as an immigration country and would have avoided losses in domestic support amongst those who feared that social security schemes were threatened by foreign workers and their families living in Germany. The government could have rhetorically demonstrated that they had preferred non-compliance, if the ECJ had remained inactive. Empirically, there is no evidence of blame shifting. Not in a single newspaper article or in a parliamentary speech did the government stress that the ECJ or the EU were responsible for the legal adaptation.[21] Indeed, blaming Europe would have thwarted the very purpose of minimally adapting policies, which was to pacify the churches and trade unions as compliance proponents and, thereby, avoid domestic reputational losses for violating not only the European foreign workers directive, but also basic values of Christian charity and solidarity among workers.

The constructivist hypothesis: sanction-threats empower pro-compliance ministries

Neither the judgment nor the possibility of future sanction-threats strengthened a logic of appropriateness, according to which withholding residency information from foreigners was deemed unacceptable, thus allowing the ECJ to differentially empower the interior ministry vis-à-vis other ministries and help, thus, to end the norm violation. Most importantly, the leading interior ministry was not in favour of a demanding interpretation of the European foreign workers directive throughout the infringement proceeding and maintained its policy preference afterwards. For example, the Minister of the Interior, Manfred Kanther, explicitly denied the necessity of changing the law on foreigners (e.g. Bundestag 1996c: 12379–81, Bundestag 1997e) and the key actors upheld their policy convictions after becoming the opposition in the 1998 elections (Bundestag 1997e, Bundestag 2000b: 8568–9). Since the leading ministry did not wish for a more demanding policy on the residence of foreign workers and their families, it could not have been held back from compliance by other ministries. Hence, there was no sanction-threat that strengthened a logic of appropriateness to which the interior ministry referred in order to overcome the resistance of veto players and realize compliance.

[21] e.g. Bundesregierung 1997, Bundesregierung 1998b, Bundestag 1997d: 146969, Bundestag 1997f: 11478–9, Bundestag 1997g: 18078–81, *Frankfurter Allgemeine Zeitung* 1998, *Süddeutsche Zeitung* 1998.

Summary of the German foreign workers case

While the judicial discourse was effective in the German drinking water case, it failed in the foreign workers case. Both parties talked at cross purposes, since the European advocate used judicial arguments and the German advocate general and pragmatic ones. Yet the ECJ judgment successfully abolished the norm violation. Churches and trade unions formed a powerful compliance constituency after gaining additional ideational resources through the judgment. In a fertile societal context, they employed their resources successfully in shaming campaigns. Due to already institutionalized ideas of Christian charity and ideas on foreign workers as an integral part of the German economy, domestic non-compliance costs increased considerably. The government responded with strategic concessions and legal changes that reflected minimalist compliance, in order to avoid damages to reputation and losses in electoral support. Reframing strategies, by contrast, had little prospect of success. The idea of Germany as an immigration country did not resonate well with the strongly institutionalized approaches of foreigners as short-term guest-workers and identity-based conceptions of social justice, according to which citizenship should be the defining criterion for participation in social security schemes. Similar to the German drinking water case, the remote threat of sanctions failed to induce compliance.

The German foreign workers and the UK equal access cases are instances in which the ECJ differentially empowered domestic norm entrepreneurs with its judgments. The latter used the additional publicity and the authoritative judgments which clarified that the governments were in violation of EU law, to shame them into minimalist forms of compliance. This worked out well, because both judgments resonated with already institutionalized domestic norms and considerably increased the domestic costs arising from the norm violations. Shifting into minimalist compliance served two purposes. It enabled the governments in both cases to circumvent losses in reputation and electoral support, while the creation of legal backdoors allowed for future norm deviations and less costly implementations of both contested norms after public attention declined.

5.III The UK drinking water case – how reframing fosters compliance

The UK has a long history of environmental policy with a special emphasis on nature conservation and, consequently, regarded itself as an environmental leader (Jordan 2004: 208, 213). Due to 'environmental chauvinism' in the 1970s and 1980s, British governments were convinced that European policies would not disrupt British practices and, as a result, they underestimated their impact (Lowe and Ward 1998: 18, Sharp 1998: 34).

The European Drinking Water Directive (DWD) of 1980 aimed to protect human health and the environment, by specifying quality standards that water must fulfil, in order to be suited for human consumption. The DWD defined more than 60 quality parameters and combined public health and environmental aspects (Börzel 2003a: 77, Knill 2001: 129, see also 4.II). The policy misfit was high. The UK's administrative, flexible approach to drinking water was based on flexible quality objectives and best practical means (Liefferink and Jordan 2004: 37–8, Ward, Buller and Lowe 1995: 19, Wurzel 2004: 103). In contrast, the 1980 DWD was legalistic, geared towards problem-solving and relied on maximum emission standards and the best available technology (Jordan 1998: 18). Thus, UK had to change legal acts to implement the DWD.

The Thatcher government informed the Commission of its transposition via a series of statutory instruments and legal acts. However, the quality of drinking water remained poor in many parts of the country afterwards (*Financial Times* 1989, Lowe and Ward 1998: 21, Ward 1998: 248). In the 1990s, Friends of the Earth and public health activists informed the European Commission about compliance deficits in the UK (Atkinson 1999). The Commission sent a letter of formal notice to the Major government in 1991, followed by a reasoned opinion in 1993 (European Court of Justice 1999a: 13). This letter made explicit the suspicion that the poor quality of drinking water might be due to the 1992 Water Industry Act (WIA)'s extension of exceptions beyond those allowed in the DWD and toleration of water suppliers exceeding water quality parameters without penalizing them (Atkinson 1999, European Court of Justice 1999a, Macrory 1990). In particular, the European Commission criticized the system of undertakings in the WIA, which de facto tolerated quality derogations due to a lack of state supervision, and the fact that it did not oblige water suppliers to develop and execute plans to improve water quality (European Court of Justice 1999a). During the infringement proceeding, the Conservatives and the Labour Party opposed the directive, mainly because of its high domestic implementation costs.[22] As a consequence of the privatization of the water industry in 1989 and the end-of-pipe approach of the UK, which shifted the costs for high water

[22] See also House of Commons 1992a: 1163–1166, House of Commons 1994a: 97, House of Commons 1994h: 878, House of Commons 1995c: 813, Parliamentary Office of Science and Technology (POST) 1993.

quality from polluters to water suppliers and ultimately to the customers, private water supplying companies and their customers were affected by costs arising from the quality parameters of the DWD (Knill and Lenschow 2001: 133, House of Commons 1998a:40–6, Ward 1998: 247). Hence there were many well-organized compliance opponents, while environmental groups, as proponents of a demanding water quality approach, faced broad public opposition (Thairs 1998: 156).

In line with this compliance-averse domestic context, the Conservatives and the Labour Party framed drinking water quality primarily as a public health affair.[23] This had important consequences: deviations from quality standards were unacceptable if they harmed human health, but combating environmental pollution more broadly, by meeting all quality standards, was deemed an unnecessarily costly burden to all water customers. Thus, the UK allowed derogations from the DWD's quality standards through the backdoor, whenever human health was not in danger (Foundation for Water Research 1998, House of Commons 1997). Most importantly, based on the WIA, water suppliers could continue derogations if they rhetorically committed themselves to future water quality measures. Since the UK had strong and rigid preferences for undemanding and cost-saving interpretations of the European directive, dissent with the Commission continued and the case was referred to the ECJ in October 1996 (Atkinson 1999). In April 1999, the ECJ issued a judgment, ruling that the UK had failed to correctly transpose the DWD (C-340/96, European Court of Justice 1999a).

Legal changes in the drinking water sector

The government in London transposed the DWD (80/778) together with the revised DWD (98/083) in 2000.[24] To this end, they issued the Drinking Water Regulations (DWR) and the Water Supply Regulations (WSR) (Department of the Environment 2000b: 69–70, 90). The 2000 DWR completely restructured the system of undertakings without providing loopholes for future lax applications. As required by the ECJ judgment,

[23] See also Foundation for Water Research 1996, House of Commons 1994a: 97, House of Commons 1996e: 814–15, the Minister for the Environment and Countryside, Mr Robert Atkins, in House of Commons 1994g: 205–7, Porter 1998: 197.

[24] The revised DWD (1998/083) had to be transposed by December 2000. After entering into force in December 2003, it substituted the old DWD 1980/778. The new DWD incorporated scientific improvements, especially on the measurement of parameter values, and introduced detailed rules on deviations. These issues were not at stake in the ECJ case. Hence, the ECJ judgment and its norm interpretation of 1999, which stated that the system of undertakings de facto delimited the enforceability of quality parameters of the DWD, were not obsolete after the new DWD entered into force.

Table 5.3 Legal changes in the drinking water sector

Date	*Title*	*Initiated*	*Outcome*
1989	The Water Act	Conservative government	Privatization of regional water authorities and creation of the National River Authority
1990	The Environment Protection Act	Conservative government	Did not specify quality parameters for drinking water
1991	Water Industry Act	Conservative government	Specifies duties and obligations of water suppliers, restricts the drinking water directive, introduced extended exceptions from quality standards through the backdoor (undertakings)
1999	Water Industry Act	Labour government	No transposition of the judgment, introduces price limits
2000	The Drinking Water (Undertaking) (England and Wales) Regulations	Labour government	Statutory Instrument 2000, No. 1297; 14 June 2000, regulations were a compliance measure for the ECJ ruling
2000	The Water Supply (Water Quality) Regulations 2000	Labour government	Statutory Instrument 2000, No. 3184, completely transposed the 1998 DWD

the Secretary of State for Environment became responsible for setting binding criteria to restore the quality of water. Moreover, the DWR set indicators and benchmarks to be reached within specific time periods. In instances where the water quality did not meet the standards of the European directive, the contracts between water companies and the Secretary of State could no longer entail vague commitments of water suppliers and be sufficient. The DWR completely and comprehensively transposed the ECJ judgment, entailed no unspecified complex concepts and contained no uncertainties or overlaps with other legal acts. Thus it closed any windows of opportunity for future lax norm interpretations without using the transposition of the new DWD with the WSR as an opportunity for creating new ones. Hence, the 2000 DWR represented comprehensive compliance. This is reflected in the number of national court cases dealing with drinking water issues. While there were 27 court cases on drinking water issues in the five-year period before the UK achieved comprehensive compliance, there were only six cases in the five-year period after the legal changes (see also Table1, Annexe).

How can we explain the UK's shift into a demanding form of compliance in 2000 after having violated the DWD for several years? Which of the three compliance instruments had been effective? The subsequent sections demonstrate that the judgment differentially empowered societal actors who reframed domestic debates and succeeded in talking the government into comprehensive compliance, while all other instruments failed to induce compliance.

The judicial discourse

This section analyses three questions: Did the judicial discourse ideationally entrap the UK government and the Department for the Environment, Transport and the Regions and did it quickly foster a comprehensive form of compliance similar to the UK collective redundancy case (H1)? Did the UK shy away from the ECJ and the Commission and end the norm violation in order to avoid losses in reputation (H2a)? Or did compliance bargaining in the shadow of the judicial discourse promote compliance (H2b)?

In 1991, the Commission opened an infringement proceeding against the UK criticizing the legal implementation of the DWD through the WIA (C-340/96) (European Court of Justice 1999a: 33–40).[25] The Commission also accused the UK of omitting judicial remedies, but only included this issue when referring the case to the ECJ in October 1996. The European Advocate General and the ECJ dismissed this complaint for procedural reasons (European Court of Justice 1999a: 40). Hence, only the legal transposition through the WIA was at stake in the judicial discourse.

Judicial discourse: Ideational entrapment or threats of reputational losses?

The Commission criticized the UK for tolerating broad derogations, and consequently, for failing to enforce all water quality parameters vis-à-vis water supplying companies (European Court of Justice 1999a). The interpretational issue at stake was highly complex since many partially overlapping rules in both concerned legal acts were relevant and involved several imprecise concepts. The DWD (Articles 18 and 19) required states to ensure that the quality of drinking water complied with the quality standards (Article 7 I and VI, Annex 1 DWD). Derogations from quality

[25] In April 1987, the European Commission had opened an infringement proceeding on the incorrect practical implementation the directive (Art. 226 ECT) (European Court of Justice 1992a). In November 1992, the ECJ ruled that implementation failures to meet certain quality parameters (e.g. lead) violated the 1980 DWD (European Court of Justice 1992a). Both the 1987 and the 1991 infringement procedures were independent from one another, because they concerned different types of violation.

standards for drinking water are dealt with in Articles 18 and 19, as well as 7 and Annex I and were also specified in articles 9, 10 and 20 of the DWD. The European directive does not allow general exceptions from quality standards and requires that states introduce measures to end derogations. To this end, the WIA stated 'Section 68(1)(a) of the Water Industry Act 1991 (hereinafter 'the Act') requires water undertakers, when supplying water to any premises for domestic or food production purposes, to supply only water which is wholesome at the time of supply' (cited in European Court of Justice 1999a: 5, 14). If the quality of drinking water failed to meet the criteria as defined in the Water Supply Regulations (WSR), the WIA required the Secretary of State to publicly issue enforcement orders specifying problems and accompanying measures to be taken (Section 20 I) (see also European Court of Justice 1999a: 7). The problem started with the exceptional clause of the WIA. The wording of section 19 I regulated that

> the Secretary of State is not required to make an enforcement order in relation to any company if he is, inter alia, satisfied that the company in question has given an undertaking to take all such steps as it appears to him for the time being to be appropriate for the company to take for the purpose of securing or facilitating compliance with the relevant rules. (Cited in European Court of Justice 1999a: 11)

In a nutshell, according to Section 20, where the water quality was poor, the Secretary of State could issue enforcement orders and specify problems and subsequent measures to combat them. Yet the exceptional clause of the WIA (Section 19 I) allowed the Secretary of State to substitute enforcement orders with the imprecise undertakings of private water companies without notifying the public or the Commission. The WIA did not oblige the Secretary of State to specify contents, aims or procedures to restore compliance with the parameter values of the DWD in the undertakings. Thus, despite the phrasing of the DWD exceptional clause, derogations could be continued in the UK, as water suppliers were not required to introduce proper measures to increase the water quality. Against this background, the European Commission argued that the British system of undertakings opened wide windows of opportunity for norm violations and did not effectively rectify failures to meet quality parameters (European Court of Justice 1999a: 11, 19).

In the judicial discourse, the European advocate focused on both legal acts in question and applied a narrow wording and a broader systematic method of judicial reasoning. At the very beginning, the European advocate highlighted that the DWD specified binding quality parameters for drinking water. Based on a systematic analysis of the WIA, the advocate claimed that in instances of quality deviations, the WIA allowed for two pathways: the UK Secretary of State had to either directly enforce quality standards where derogations from the water quality were observed (enforcement orders) or agree on an undertaking, according to which water suppliers would commit themselves to increase the water quality (Advocate General 1998b: 10, 17, European Court of Justice 1999a: 20–1). Yet the wording of the WIA lacked clarity. Hence, the European advocate argued that WIA declarations did 'not adequately specify the conditions to which acceptance of the undertakings is subject' and violated the DWD (European Court of Justice 1999a: 22). Moreover, the European advocate highlighted that the WIA did not prescribe specific aims, procedures and timetables to restore high drinking water quality for undertakings, but tolerated postponed deadlines by water supplying companies so that they could continue to supply low quality water that did not meet the standards of the DWD (Advocate General 1998b: 17–20, 29; European Court of Justice 1999a: 14, 18).

The UK disagreed and argued that the WIA and its embedded system of undertakings ensured that quality standards were met. In defending its initial transposition and the system of undertakings, the UK used pragmatic arguments. The British advocate made the general claim that 'the Water Industry Act 1991 also imposes a primary obligation on the water companies, requiring them to supply water which meets the standards laid down by the Directive. That obligation subsists at all times and in all circumstances – even, therefore, after an undertaking has been accepted' (Advocate General 1998b: 23). The UK advocate further defended the rules on undertakings in claiming that 'the fact that undertakings do not necessarily set out the applicable standards does not therefore in any way mean ... that the water company concerned is not required to conform to those standards' (Advocate General 1998b: 24). Moreover, the British advocate made the general argument that the water suppliers were in a better position to identify the measures required to comply with the DWD than the Secretary of State and should therefore be responsible for the content and aims of the undertakings (Advocate General 1998b: 31, 32, European Court of Justice 1999a: 26). Furthermore, he stated that 'undertakings may be amended, as regards both the nature of the works to be carried out and the time allowed for completing them. However, this does not constitute a flaw in the system' (Advocate General 1998b: 29). While the European Commission suspected that this allowed water supplying companies to postpone deadlines according to their liking, the UK pragmatically argued 'that it in fact affords a certain flexibility enabling undertakings to be adapted to technological progress, in that they can be modified as more effective solutions to a company's problems become available' (Advocate General 1998b: 29).

During the judicial discourse, British and European advocates argued at cross purposes. While the UK made pragmatic and general arguments, the European advocates used judicial ones. As expected, the Blair government that came to office in May 1997, which was responsible for the late stage of the infringement process, neither became ideationally entrapped nor adjusted policies in order to avoid a bad reputation vis-à-vis the European enforcement authorities. Consequently, they did not change their compliance-averse policies. During the judicial discourse, the UK argued that the WIA was a sufficient transposition and that the system of undertakings was superior to other solutions since it incorporated the expertise of water supplying companies (Advocate General 1998b: 49, European Court of Justice 1999a: 26). Before and after the ECJ judgment and in debates on the revision of the WIA in 1999, cost–benefit calculations were very important (Atkinson 1999, compare House of Commons 1997 with Select Committee on Environmental Audit 2000: 45–6, House of Commons 2000a). In order to prevent increased water bills, the Blair government introduced a system of price limits in the 1999 WIA (House of Commons 1998a: 40, 73, 110). During this process, quality issues were off the table (e.g. Select Committee on Delegated Powers and Deregulation 1999) and even the environmental ministry wanted 'to ensure that hard-pressed customers were not faced with unreasonably high bills' (Minister for the Environment, Mr Meacher, in House of Commons 1998a: 40). Consequently, the WIA revision of 1999 did not deal with derogations or the system of undertakings and did not legally transpose the issue at stake before the ECJ (House of Commons 1998b: 772–3, House of Commons Standing Committee 1998, Select Committee on Environmental Audit 2000).

The second rationalist alternative: compliance bargaining in the shadow of the ECJ

Did the European Commission and the UK engage in compliance bargaining in the shadow of the judicial discourse and can this account for the legal change in the year 2000? Due to the lack of available information, we cannot preclude the possibility of informal bargaining between the parties. However, we can counterfactually inquire whether the parties compromised during the judicial discourse and how far this is reflected in the pattern of ideational and legal changes. In the drinking water case, margins for compromise were limited because there was only one main issue (undertakings) since the ECJ dismissed the Commission's complaint on the lack of judicial remedies in the UK for procedural reasons. In line with that, it is unlikely that the parties reached an agreement outside the Court. Firstly, the European Commission did not withdraw its complaints, not even the one which it had added before referring the case to the ECJ (judicial remedies), although it was relatively obvious that the Court would not rule on it. Secondly, the European advocate did not accept any of the arguments of the UK advocate, but made the same claims in the late as in the early stage of the judicial discourse. Thirdly, the UK did not give in concerning the undertakings issue and continued to defend the WIA throughout the entire written and oral stages of the judicial discourse (see also Advocate General 1998b, European Court of Justice 1999a). Thus, if bargaining took place, it most likely failed to produce a compromise. Hence, the 2000 DWR legal change, which resolved the issue of undertakings, was not the result of informal negotiations in the shadow of the judicial discourse.

The judgment

Although the judicial discourse proved ineffective in ending the norm violation, the UK did not remain inactive but introduced a Drinking Water Regulation (DWR) in 2000, which addressed the system of undertakings. Did the ECJ judgment differentially empower societal norm proponents who pushed the government into compliance? This section argues that the Court ruling differentially empowered societal compliance proponents who reframed the drinking water debate in promoting a shift from an 'end-of-pipe' into a 'polluters-pay' approach.

In its judgment of April 1999, the ECJ followed the European Advocate General and sided with the European Commission. The ECJ concluded that 'by accepting undertakings from water companies for the purpose of ensuring that water complies with the requirements of Council Directive 80/778/EEC of 15 July 1980 relating to the quality of water intended for human consumption, without the conditions governing the acceptance of such undertakings being specified in the Water Industry Act 1991, the United Kingdom of Great Britain and Northern Ireland has failed to fulfil its obligations under the EC Treaty and under that directive' (European Court of Justice 1999a: operative part 2).

In 1988, Prime Minister Thatcher made a commitment to environmental protection in her programmatic 'green speech', which was followed by several White Papers, finally leading to the creation of the Environment Agency in 1996 (Lowe and Ward 1998: 23). The latter disseminated water quality information and alerted environmental groups, such as FoE or WWF, of any problems (Jordan 2004: 216–17, Knill 2001: 192, Knill and Lenschow 2001: 134, Lowe and Ward 1998: 27, Thairs 1998). Yet prior to the ECJ ruling of 1999, the context was neither favourable for successful shaming nor reframing campaigns. Successful shaming was difficult for two reasons. Firstly, domestically there was no consensus on whether the system of undertakings, which shifted the responsibility for creating measures to end derogations to water supplying companies, indeed violated the DWD. Secondly, the British public believed that high water quality standards required immense investments in water companies (for filters, pipes etc.), which would, in turn, considerably increase the water bills of all consumers (*Financial Times* 1996c, *The Times* 1989, Ward *et al.* 1993: 10). Hence, public opposition to the DWD was widespread (*Financial Times* 1996a, *Financial Times* 1996b, *Financial Times* 1996c, *Guardian* 1992b, *Herald* 1996). Prior to the ECJ judgment, the domestic context was also not conducive to successful reframing campaigns. Firstly, the cost-based approach, according to which high quality standards were considered an unnecessary burden to water customers as long as the water did not harm human health, was deeply institutionalized (English Nature 1999, Office of Water Services (OFWAT) 1998). Secondly, this frame did not fit with a demanding drinking water approach which abolished cost-saving loopholes in the WIA-tolerated quality derogations (Foundation for Water Research 1996, Foundation for Water Research 1998). Due to the enormous domestic benefits of an undemanding drinking water approach and to the low resonance between the two frames, neither Conservative nor Labour governments introduced policy shifts in reaction to criticisms by WWF and FoE.[26] On the contrary, the Blair government was responsive to water consumers and introduced a system of price limits that prevented increases in water bills (OFWAT 1998). This, rather than an increase of the water quality, was widely regarded as appropriate, especially since the government and OFWAT simultaneously argued that the quality of British drinking water was good (OFWAT National Customer Council 1999, interview organized interests#12, 24–04–05).

The judgment of 1999 created publicity, provided an authoritative norm definition, reduced the complexity of the contested issue and, thereby, differentially empowered environmental organizations. Nevertheless, the domestic context remained unfertile for effective shaming

[26] See also House of Commons 1992a: 1163–6, House of Commons 1996e: 814–5, House of Commons 1997, the Minister for the Environment and Countryside, Mr Atkins, in House of Commons 1994g: 205–7.

campaigns. The media coverage of the ECJ case was low,[27] and governmental non-compliance with the EU directive was portrayed positively (e.g. *The Times* 1999, interview organized interests#12, 24–04–05). Although the judgment authoritatively stated that the WIA violated the DWD, it resonated poorly with domestically institutionalized norms on water quality, end-of-pipe environmental approaches and market liberalization. The British water quality system was oriented towards the provision of drinking water at reasonable water prices (House of Commons 2000a, OFWAT National Customer Council 2000: 4, Select Committee on Environmental Audit 2000: 45–6). Shaming the government for not pursuing a demanding drinking water quality approach, which legally enforced costly quality measures, would have found low resonance, in particular since the domestic non-compliance constituency – composed of water suppliers and the public – was strong (Drinking Water Inspectorate 1999, *Financial Times* 1996a, *Financial Times* 1996b, *Financial Times* 1996c). Moreover, the UK perceived itself as an environmental forerunner and the government did not regard EU policies as superior to UK ones (Jordan 2004: 208). Against this background, it is not surprising that environmental organizations did not invest their scarce resources in shaming campaigns and abstained from blaming the government for violating institutionalized domestic norms.

In contrast, the domestic environment became increasingly conducive to a redirection of the domestic debate to a demanding drinking water approach via a re-framing campaign. The ECJ judgment of 1999 reduced the complexity of the issue at stake in three regards. On a general level, the ECJ firstly clarified that minimal drinking water quality approaches that tolerate broad derogations are not acceptable. Secondly, the ECJ stressed that the UK was responsible for ensuring that the quality parameters were fulfilled, although the drinking water sector had been privatized in 1989 (European Court of Justice 1999a: 1–2). More concretely, the Court resolved difficulties concerning legal technicalities of the complicated system of undertakings and enforcement orders and spelled out which elements were problematic and not in line with the DWD (European Court of Justice 1999a: 27–31). This severely simplified the subject matter, itself a precondition for successful reframing campaigns. However, the reduction of complexity through the judgment did not automatically redirect the domestic debate in the UK. The predominant cost frame, according to which high water bills had to be

[27] Remarkably, none of the 21 press releases of the Drinking Water Inspectorate in 1999 even mentioned the judgment (e.g. Drinking Water Inspectorate 1999).

avoided, still pointed towards an undemanding drinking water quality approach with broad margins for exceptions (Financial Times 1996b, Financial Times 1996c, OFWAT 1998). Hence, demanding drinking water quality approaches with few backdoors for derogations were incompatible with the cost frame as long as the end-of-pipe approach prevailed. According to the latter, consumers ultimately have to pay for reducing pollution. In this context, the core task of environmental organizations was to emphasize that high drinking water quality is not necessarily achieved at the expense of individual customers (interview organized interests#12, 24–04–05). The ECJ judgment coincidently overlapped with discussions on the Water Framework Directive (WFD) that introduced ideas on a polluters-pay instead of an end-of-pipe approach as a means to achieve environmental and public health protection. The former charged water polluters instead of water supplying companies to clean water to meet the DWD quality standards (Select Committee on Environment 2002b: 35). The idea that water quality could also be enhanced by an approach that passes quality costs on to polluters disseminated from WFD discussions into the UK. This idea became rapidly prominent among environmental organizations, consumer organizations (e.g. Water Voice), and water suppliers alike (*Aberdeen Press* 2002a, Environmental Audit Committee 1999, *Sunday Times* 2002a, Water Voice 2002, World Wide Fund for Nature (WWF) 2000). Water supply companies and customers' organizations sought to minimize water charges though the polluters-pay approach, while environmental organizations were interested in the prevention of pollution in the first place in order to protect the environment. Hence, even the former joined the camp of compliance proponents and launched the new environmental water quality frame, linking high water quality to the prevention of pollution by polluters, and opting for a drinking water approach that did not tolerate quality deviations (interview organized interests#12, 24–04–05). The new water frame resonated well with the complementary cost frame and, in turn, incrementally promoted demanding drinking water quality policies (Government of the UK 2000a, House of Commons 2000a, Office of OFWAT 2000, Water Voice 2002). Based on the polluters-pay principle, high quality water no longer placed enormous compliance costs on the governmental constituency. In response to these reframing activities, the Blair government adopted the polluters-pay approach to water quality issues and changed substantial policy interests accordingly (Government of the UK 2000a, Government of the UK 2001, Select Committee on Environmental Audit 2001). References to high costs arising from high water quality requirements vanished. The government increasingly referred to a broader environmental approach, pursuing high water quality while also combating water pollution (Government of the UK 2000a, House of Commons 2000a, Government of the UK 2001, House of Commons 2001a: 255f., Select Committee on Environmental Audit 2003). These ideational shifts cumulated in a revised quality drinking water policy that pursued high quality standards, included a strict enforcement system, pre-empted possible quality exceptions and no longer tolerated broad derogations. They found legal expression firstly in the 2000 DWR, which represented complete transposition of the judgment that forestalled windows of opportunity for lax water approaches in the implementation stage. Secondly they were expressed in the comprehensive reform of the UK water *aquis* through the new Water Act in 2003 (Department of the Environment 2001, Government of the UK 2003: 26, Select Committee on Environmental Audit 2002, Select Committee on Environment 2003a).

In sum, in line with the reframing hypothesis, the ECJ judgment abolished non-compliance in a two-step process. It empowered norm proponents, who then restructured the domestic debate and facilitated comprehensive compliance.

Sanction-threats

If judicial discourses and judgments are unsuccessful in inducing domestic changes reflecting compliance, the ECJ can apply sanction-threats as a third instrument. Since this is public knowledge, states could theoretically anticipate future penalties and therefore end norm violations even before the European Commission or the ECJ introduced the first measures towards enforcement. In the drinking water case, sanction-threats were not applied. Therefore, this section inquires whether the remote possibility of future penalties induced compliance with the 1999 Court ruling or whether it differentially empowered a pro-compliance ministry vis-à-vis domestic veto players.

The rationalist hypothesis: credible sanction-threats increase non-compliance costs

The British transposition of the DWD was based on an end-of-pipe approach which meant that high water quality standards severely increased the water bills of private households. The WIA system of undertakings reduced water costs by providing loopholes for lax applications. Before the ECJ judgment, non-compliance benefits were high and customers, as well as the water supply industry, opposed the DWD (see also Thairs 1998). One year after the judgment, the Blair government issued the 2000 DWR as a measure to shift into comprehensive compliance (Government of the UK 2000b). Did the government anticipate future sanction-threats and therefore give in as early as 2000? Most likely not: the rationalist sanction-threat hypothesis expects that states only yield to penalties if they are due to become realized in the near future during the incumbency of the government and if they are sufficiently high to be deterrent. This requires, firstly, that the European Commission sends a second reasoned opinion to the state (Art. 228 ECT) and, secondly, that the infringement is serious according to the criteria of the Commission. The infringement was serious. While the norm violation did not negatively affect the four freedoms, the Community resources, and the way the EU functions, the infringement was serious concerning its damages to the environment and to human health, the size of the affected population, the economic gains from non-compliance and the fact that the UK had already been convicted for violating the DWD by another ruling of the ECJ (European Court of Justice 1992a). However, the European Commission did not threaten the government in London with a second reasoned opinion (Art. 228 ECT) in 1999 nor in 2000. Therefore, it does not appear that the adaptation of policies in 2000 was the result of the UK shying away from potential future sanctions.

In line with this expectation, members of government never mentioned the potential threat of financial penalties in any of the public debates on the DWR (Department of the Environment 2000a, Department of the Environment 2000b). They did not shift the blame to the ECJ by portraying it as being ultimately responsible for the policy adaptations, in order to prevent domestic losses in reputation vis-à-vis the governmental non-compliance constituency. Instead of approaching drinking water quality issues in cost–benefit terms and instead of focusing on a minimalist water quality approach, the government shifted into comprehensive compliance (Government of the UK 2000a, House of Commons 2000a, OFWAT National Customer Council 2000: 4, Select Committee on Environmental Audit 2000: 45–6). Thus, remote sanction-threats were not effective and did not induce adaptations towards minimalist compliance in 2000.

The constructivist hypothesis: sanction-threats empower pro-compliance ministries

Did the possibility of sanction-threats differentially empower a pro-compliance ministry vis-à-vis domestic veto players and thereby foster the shift into comprehensive compliance? Again, the short answer is no. The Department for the Environment, Transport and the Regions was not in favour of a demanding drinking water approach during the infringement procedure. Instead, it followed a cost frame and was, thus, mainly concerned with preventing water from becoming too expensive for consumers (House of Commons 1998a: 40, 73, 110). Consequently, the leading environmental ministry was not prevented from pursing demanding policies by the government or other ministries as veto players. Accordingly, the 1999 WIA reflected the concern of the environmental ministry, as well as the whole government, to limit the negative consequences of the privatization of the drinking water sector for private customers by introducing a system of price limits that de facto tolerated non-heath related compromises of water quality. Only after the polluters-pay frame had successfully challenged this end-of-pipe approach, did the environmental ministry as well as the government change its underlying ideas and policies and consequently support the demanding drinking water policies.[28] This policy change was not due to differential empowerment effects towards the lead ministry. This is evidenced by the fact that, firstly, in 2000 the European Commission had not introduced first steps towards enforcement, which could have highlighted the inappropriateness of the DWD violation, and secondly because the government changed its policy ideas simultaneously with the environmental ministry and did not turn into a veto player.

Reframing and compliance in the UK drinking water case

The DWD specifies quality requirements for water intended for human consumption. Some of the parameters were more demanding than the UK approach, which increased the water bills throughout the UK, since water supply companies passed on expenses to their customers. Therefore, and due to differences in policy styles between the European and the UK drinking water policies, the latter opposed the DWD. Consequently, the UK opted for an undemanding water approach with wide margins for quality deviations to save domestic compliance costs. The European Commission criticized the Water Industry Act (WIA) for its system of undertakings, which essentially left it up to water suppliers to introduce measures and timetables to remedy failures to meet the quality parameters of the DWD. As in the UK collective redundancy and the equal access cases, governmental non-compliance preferences were very strong, so that pre-judicial settlement failed and the Commission finally referred the case to the ECJ.

The judicial discourse could not end the norm violation, because neither

[28] See also Department of the Environment 2001, Government of the UK 2000a, House of Commons 2000a, House of Commons 2000a, House of Commons 2001a: 255–333, OFWAT 2000.

arguing nor bargaining in the shadow of the judicial discourse had been effective. As predicted, the parties did not produce a consensual norm interpretation and neither ideationally entrapped the government, nor did the judicial discourse create a pressure of reputational losses because the advocates talked at cross purposes.

The second instrument of the ECJ, its judgment, created publicity by putting water issues on the public agenda. It also simplified the complex issue at stake and thereby differentially empowered societal pro-compliance actors. Unlike in the equal access case, this was not conducive to successful shaming strategies because the judgment did not resonate well with the already institutionalized domestic norms. It was, however, conducive to effective reframing. In 1999 and 2000, environmental organizations, water customer organizations and water suppliers launched a polluters-pay approach and linked it to the deeply embedded, but complementary, cost frame. Once it became apparent that high water quality could be achieved without increasing the bills of private customers, the Blair government changed its policy interests and shifted into comprehensive compliance with the regulations on drinking water one year after the ECJ ruling. In 2000, the possibility of a future sanction-threat was remote and not responsible for the shift into comprehensive compliance. Accordingly, the UK did not yield to the ECJ because they anticipated costs of penalties on a relatively serious infringement. Likewise, the possibility of sanctions did not differentially empower the environmental ministry over domestic veto players, not least because the lead ministry only came around to the demanding water quality approach in 2000.

5.IV The German equal access case – reframing domestic debates

Among the first European social policy measures was directive 76/207, which aimed for equal access of men and women in employment related matters. In its preface, the members of the Council of Ministers framed the equality directive as a measure to harmonize living and working conditions across the member states. To this end, the directive regulated the equal treatment of men and women as regards access to employment, vocational training and promotion and working conditions. Article 2 specifies that 'the principle of equal treatment shall mean that there shall be no discrimination whatsoever on grounds of sex either directly or indirectly by reference in particular to marital or family status' but also introduces the exceptional clause according to which those activities 'for which, by reason of their nature or the context in which they are carried out, the sex of the worker constitutes a determining factor' can be exempt from the equality principle.

Although the equality of men and women was addressed by the German constitution, Germany had no secondary law regulating equal treatment issues for the private sector. Hence, the directive created a demand for legal adaptation. Germany transposed the directive in 1980 with the EC employment adaptation law (the 'Arbeitsrechtliches EG Anpassungsgesetz'). It introduced two new paragraphs into the German civil code (Bürgerliches Gesetzbuch – 'BGB') and regulated equal access issues concerning private sector employment, educational training and promotion. This law was highly contested. The governing Social Democrats (SPD) regarded it as useful and emphasized that gender equality was no invention of Brussels, but an essential and widely acknowledged principle in Germany (Bundesrat 1979: 300, Bundestag 1979: 14928, Bundestag 1980: 18242). The Minister for Labour and Social Policy, Dr Ehrenberg, even framed equal treatment as part of the SPD's party ideology: in 1863, the founder of the German Social Democrats, August Bebel, had emphasized equal liberation and also the party programme of Erfurt (1893) had pushed for abolishing all women-discriminating laws. In this sense, 'the European Commission supports the current federal government's aspirations as regard the equal treatment of the sexes' (Bundestag 1979: 14928–9, translation DP). The Christian Democrats (CDU) and employers' associations, by contrast, preferred a narrow interpretation of the directive restricting its applicatory scope to protect freedom of enterprise and of contract, so as to avoid costs for employers (Bundesrat 1979: 302, Bundestag 1979: 14932, Bundestag 1980: 18238, Gottfried and O'Reilly 2002). Trade unions were also not in favour of the equality directive, but reproduced a role model according to which men and not women are the breadwinners (Bundestag 1980: 18238, Gehrhard 2004, Kodré and Müller 2003: 96, Lewis and Ostner 1994).

In a reasoned opinion issued in October 1982, the Commission suspected that the 1980 EC employment adaptation law only transposed the equal treatment provision for private matters, leaving public administrations and free professions aside, and failing to provide transparent information on granted exceptions to the equal access principle (European Court of Justice 1985: 3). The Christian Democratic/Liberal coalition under Chancellor Kohl replaced the Social Democratic/Liberal government in 1982 and stayed in office during the complete infringement proceeding. Due to the preference for an undemanding equal access approach of the new government, the disagreement with the Commission prevailed. Consequently, Germany continued to pre-empt the harmonization of living and working conditions, although the preface of the directive stated this as the general aim. Moreover, women facing discrimination in the employment realm in Germany were de facto less protected than women in other member states. In November 1983, the European Commission referred the case to the ECJ. Two years later, the Court ruled the German transposition to be incomplete, since exceptions to the equal access principle were not transparent and there was no oversight of whether they complied with the directive (European Court of Justice 1985: 3). Hence, Germany had to introduce domestic changes.

The pattern of legal changes

The ECJ judgment of 1985 clarified that Germany had failed to adequately transpose the equal access directive. Hence, Germany had to introduce domestic changes in order to comply with the equal access directive. In 1985, the SPD opposition proposed a bill to revise the 1980 law, which was dismissed. Thereafter, government initiatives dominated the process of domestic change. In 1987, the Kohl government proposed a bill on working hours (Arbeitszeitgesetz). However, it never turned into a law, but was postponed after the first reading in the Bundestag in 1988 (Bundestag 1988b). Also in 1987, the government prepared a report on the experiences with the equality principle. It concluded that discriminations were few and the 1980 law was a success (Bundestag 1990d). This report was sent to the Commission as a reaction to the ECJ ruling and resembled minimalist compliance since it merely created transparency ex-post facto, but did not legally prescribe monitoring and communication systems, which allowed for loopholes for future lax applications of the equal access principle.[29] In 1990, another governmental proposal entailed incremental improvements of the legal standing of women. Again, the legislative period ended and the bill was not reintroduced after the re-election of the government. In 1994 Germany finally passed the equal treatment law and the law on working hours. Together they completely and comprehensively legally implemented a demanding equal access approach and, in this respect, resembled a comprehensive form of compliance. Since legal uncertainties were reduced considerably, the number of national court cases on equal access matters was reduced by two-thirds to

[29] Thus, the number of preliminary references (based on Art. 234) dealing with the exceptional clause of the equal access directive was relatively high in the first five years after the ECJ judgment.

just four cases in the five-year period after compliance had been achieved (see also Annexe, Table 1).

Table 5.4 Legal changes concerning equal access

Date	*Title*	*Initiated by*	*Outcome*
1980	EG-Arbeitsrechtliches Anpassungsgesetz	SPD/FDP government	Law, below the standards of directive 76/207
1985	Proposal for a revised EG Anpassungsgesetz	SPD opposition	Bill failed
1987	Report to the Commission	CDU/FDP government	The report was not a legal act
1987	Arbeitszeitschutzgesetz	CDU/FDP government	No legal act, proposal was initiated just before the legislative period ended
1990	Gesetz zur Verbesserung der Gleichbehandlung von Frauen und Männern am Arbeitsplatz	CDU/FDP government	No legal act, proposal was initiated just before the legislative period ended
1994	Gleichberechtigungsgesetz	CDU/FDP government	Legal act, above the standards of the directive
1994	Arbeitszeitgesetz	CDU/FDP government	Legal act, above the standards of the directive

Before the Commission referred the case to the ECJ, the Kohl government strongly preferred a narrow equal access approach and violated a more demanding interpretation of the equality directive. Against this background, the following sections examine which of the instruments successfully ended the violation of European law.

The judicial discourse

Did the ECJ manage to put a stop to the violation of the equal access directive through a judicial discourse?

In November 1983 at the date of the Court referral, seven issues were contested (European Court of Justice 1985: 2–5). Firstly, the parties disputed whether the German constitution sufficiently legally implemented the directive regarding the public administration. Secondly, the same question emerged for the independent professions. The third issue at stake was the extent to which member states could exclude certain occupational activities from the directive's scope. In this context, the parties also disagreed on transparency requirements for granted exceptions. A fourth issue of contention was whether the directive also covered job postings. The fifth complaint concerned maternity leave, but the Commission withdrew this issue during the ongoing procedure, because the ECJ had already resolved this aspect in a preliminary ruling (184/83). Finally, the Commission accused Germany of incorrectly transposing the equal pay directive (75/117) (European Court of Justice 1985: 46). In its 1985 judgment, the ECJ declared the German transposition as incompatible with the directive only with regard to the third point: the usage of the directive's exceptional clause was not sufficiently transparent.

Judicial discourse: ideational entrapment or threats of reputational losses?

The following discussion focuses exclusively on the first four issues, since the last two complaints were related to the equal pay directive or withdrawn by the Commission.

Is the public sector subject to the equal access principle?

The parties disputed whether Germany sufficiently applied the equal access approach to public services (European Court of Justice 1985: 12). Germany claimed that the Constitution (Grundgesetz) together with the federal law on civil servants (Bundesbeamtengesetz) adequately legally implemented the European directive. The European Commission, by contrast, argued that Germany restricted the scope of the directive.

At the very beginning of the judicial discourse, Germany pointed out that its initial transposition was sufficient. The advocate based this claim on a wording interpretation of the relevant German legal acts, Articles 3 II and 33 II of the Grundgesetz and §8 Bundesbeamtengesetz (European Court of Justice 1985: 13). The European advocate also used the wording method of judicial reasoning, but applied it to Article 3 I of the equal treatment directive (European Court of Justice 1985: 12). Article 3 enumerates areas to which the equality principle has to be applied. It does not distinguish between private and public sectors, but explicitly states that equal treatment is obligatory for '*all* jobs or posts, *whatever the sector* or branch of activity' (European Court of Justice 1985: 12, emphasis added). Based on this line of argumentation, the European advocate concluded that the equal access principle also applied to the public sector (European Court of Justice 1985: 16). After the European advocate had also used the wording method and had demonstrated that the equal access principle was relevant to all jobs, the German advocate gave up his sole focus on the German acts (European Court of Justice 1985: 13–15). As a result, the German advocate conceded that the directive applied to public and private employment relationships and that the initial transposition through the constitution and the law on public servants might inhibit an element of legal uncertainty (European Court of Justice 1985: 13–15). Thus Germany's initial 'reservation has not in fact been maintained' (European Court of Justice 1985: 15).

In the judicial discourse, both parties actively exchanged judicial arguments and they analysed the same legal acts. In addition, the commonly applied narrow wording method matched the narrow interpretational scope of the contested issue. Since Article 3 I of the directive was very precise and did not overlap with other articles or paragraphs, excluding the public sector from the equal access principle, or delimiting the latter, could not be defended with the wording-based reasoning. Thus, a consensus emerged that the private and the public sector had to be subject to the equal access principle and that German legal acts were required to express the equal access principle evenly across both sectors (European Court of Justice 1985: 12–15).

As expected by the ideational entrapment hypothesis, governmental actors responded to the effective judicial discourse and no longer denied that the equal access directive had to be applied to the public sector and abstained from contrary cost-saving arguments. Instead, they took for granted that the public sector was subject to the directive (Bundesregierung 1993b, Bundestag 1986b, Bundestag 1993g: 15432–5, 15444–5, Bundestag 1994f: 19152–3, 19159–61). In line with this, in February 1986 the leading Ministry for Youth, Family, Women and Health issued a guideline on occupational opportunities for women in the public service, which explicitly recommended the promotion of women in the public administration (Bundesregierung 1987a).

At the same time, it is highly unlikely that the government introduced these changes in order to avoid a bad reputation vis-à-vis the Commission and the ECJ due to continuing non-compliance despite the interpretational ambiguities having been resolved. In 1986, the ECJ had already sided with Germany on this issue and did not demand further legal changes. Hence, there was no need for the German government to adapt strategic positions and shift into minimalist compliance in order to avoid a bad reputation vis-à-vis the European enforcement authorities.

After this scope issue had been resolved, the judicial discourse shifted to the related question of whether the German equality related laws sufficiently promoted equal access to employment, vocational training and career opportunities in the public sector.

The European advocate argued that the phrasing of Article 33 II of the German constitution opened a window of opportunity for exceptions, since the 'aptitude' of applicants for public offices could be used to re-introduce sex-related criteria to discriminate against individuals (European Court of Justice 1985: 12, 20–1). Yet the wording method was not suited to solving this issue because it was too narrow to specify the crucial concept ‘aptitude’. The German advocate also used the wording instrument, but combined it with a broader method and consequently arrived at a different conclusion than his European colleague. According to the systematic line of interpretation, the wordings of Article 33 II of the constitution and also of §7 and §8 of the 1957 framework law on the Public Administration (Beamtenrechtsrahmengesetz, 1 July 1957) explicitly prohibited unequal treatment on the basis of sex (European Court of Justice 1985: 14). Paragraph 7 of the 1957 framework law stated: ‘appointments shall be made on the basis of professional aptitude, achievements and qualifications, without any distinction on grounds of sex’. Paragraph 8 proceeded to state that ‘applicants shall be chosen by competition. Selection shall be on the basis of professional aptitude, achievements and qualifications, *without any distinction on grounds of sex*’ (see BGBL I S 551, 667, emphasis added, translation DP). The broad systematic technique of legal reasoning was not shared by the European advocate but fitted much better with the high complexity of the interpretational problem. It allowed the advocate to examine cross-linkages and to interpret the term in question in its broader legal context, in particular in the context of Aticle 33 Grundgesetz and the framework law on the public administration.

The ECJ also engaged in systematic interpretation and, consequently, sided with Germany. Thus, there was no need for Germany to introduce legal changes to clarify that the aptitude criterion did not discriminate against female applicants for jobs in the public service (European Court of Justice 1985: 23). In line with this, Germany did not change the framework law on the public administration along the lines that the European Commission had initially demanded.

Are the German equal access provisions on independent professions sufficient?

The Commission also accused Germany of limiting the scope of the equality directive by excluding independent professions. In the judicial discourse, the European advocate used the wording method of legal interpretation and stated that articles three to five of the directive explicitly required the application of the equal access principle to independent professions (European Court of Justice 1985: 24). The German advocate also used this instrument and applied it not only to articles three to five of the directive, but also to Article 12 I of the German constitution

(European Court of Justice 1985: 25, 26). The advocates came to the same conclusion: regardless of whether the wording instrument was first applied to article three, four or five of the directive, the result was the same: both sectors were subject to the directive. However, the wording method applied to the EC directive could not infer whether German law completely transposed it. This required an analysis of the German legal acts in question – which the European advocate failed to do. In contrast, based on the narrow wording and the broader systematic methods, the German advocate argued that Article 3 in combination with Article 12 I[30] of the constitution sufficiently transposed the issue of independent professions and additionally guaranteed individuals access to courts (European Court of Justice 1985: 25–6).

The advocates of both parties engaged in the judicial discourse, but talked at cross purposes since they did not analyse the same legal acts. Hence, the judicial discourse should not succeed in ideationally entrapping the German government or in creating reputational costs in the case of Germany continuing the norm violation. As expected, the Kohl government did not change strategic positions or substantial policy interests during the ongoing judicial discourse or after the ECJ ruling and did not deny that the private sector was subject to the equal access principle (e.g. Bundestag 1986a: 2–5; Bundestag 1988b: 3736–9, Bundestag 1990d: 14–16). Since the ECJ also adopted the broad systemic method and followed the German line of argumentation further adaptations were not required and did not take place (European Court of Justice 1985: 30–1, also, e.g. Bundestag 1993g; Bundestag 1994f).

Permitting exceptions to the equal access principle

The parties disagreed further on the extent to which states were permitted to exclude single occupational activities from the equal access directive (European Court of Justice 1985: 3, 32). In this regard, they focused on three questions: Does the directive require states to develop a catalogue of grounds on which deviations from the equal access principle were allowed? Is it necessary to put this catalogue into a legal act? Does the German transposition create sufficient transparency to allow the European Commission to monitor granted exceptions? The issues at stake were important, since broad exceptional rules and lax practices could severely undermine the effectiveness of the directive. Similar to the

[30] Paragraph one of this Article states: 'all Germans have the right to freely choose their profession, their place of work, and their place of occupational training' (translation DP).

German drinking water case, opaque practices and incomprehensive reports on granted exceptions from the directive invited lax norm applications. This limited compliance costs at the expense of affected women and restricted the protective aim of the directive.

The Commission accused Germany of failing to comply with Articles 2 II and 9 II of the directive, in not listing allowed exceptions in the respective legal act (§611 a of the German civil code, BGB) (European Court of Justice 1985: 32). The European advocate used the wording method of interpretation to highlight that Article 9 II of the European directive requires member states to oversee granted exceptions to the equal access principle and communicate them to the European Commission (European Court of Justice 1985: 32). This method of interpretation also revealed that the wording of the German civil code (§611 a BGB) did not enumerate exceptions. Yet the narrow wording instrument did not match the high complexity of the issue at stake: Article 9 II of the directive was silent on the question of whether possible exceptions have to be enumerated and whether this has to be put into a legal act. As a consequence, the absence of such a wording could have been interpreted in two ways: transparent legal rules are a prerequisite for the exercise of the Commission's monitoring function (position of the Commission) or the list of possible exceptions in legal acts are not required (German position). Indeed, the German advocate analysed the wording of Article 2 II of the directive and §611 a BGB and emphasized that the former did not specify whether legal acts should enumerate possible exceptions (European Court of Justice 1985: 33).

In a further step, the European advocate used the slightly broader directive-immanent systematic method to put Article 9 on monitoring of exceptions into the context of Article 2 of the equal access directive which states that member states can grant exceptions (European Court of Justice 1985: 32). However, the analysis of the relationship of these two articles could not solve the questions at stake, since this only revealed that member states can grant exceptions to the equality principle, but have to monitor them. The directive-immanent systematic method did not match the high complexity of the issue at stake: Article 9 of the European directive in combination with Article 2 did not prescribe whether exceptions to the equal access principle have to be enumerated and put into a legal act in order to allow for monitoring through the European Commission. In addition to the use of legal techniques of interpretation, the European advocate made the pragmatic argument that most other member states did issue legal acts to ensure that data on granted exceptions are collected and accessible for the European Commission (European Court of Justice 1985: 32). On this basis, the European advocate concluded that Germany violated the directive (European Court of Justice 1985: 32).

The narrow wording instrument did not fit the high complexity of the issue at stake and subsequently the German advocate switched to the broader directive-immanent teleological method: the directive sought to promote equal access of men and women, but also allowed for exceptions, in particular if they reflected societal values. Thus, the directive demanded that the exceptional clause would be rarely evoked, which was procedurally reflected in the monitoring function of the Commission. The German advocate further argued that listing exceptions in a legal act was not a precondition of the Commission's ability to control whether they were in line with the directive (European Court of Justice 1985: 33). Accordingly, Germany concluded that 'the existence of a list established by law is not essential for the exercise by the Commission of its right of supervision' (European Court of Justice 1985: 33). However, the European advocate disagreed in arguing that Germany failed to enable 'the Commission to exercise its right of supervision' (European Court of Justice 1985: 32). Hence, although the directive-immanent teleological method of judicial reasoning was broader than the directive-immanent systematic and the wording method, it did not match the high complexity of the issue at stake. At the same time, none of the advocates used the considerably broader historical method of interpretation to reconstruct the original will of the norm creators or the also relatively broad systematic interpretational technique that would have allowed comparing the equal access directive to other EU directives concerning the enumeration of exceptions to European directives in domestic legal acts.

The judicial discourse failed. The advocates of the parties only commonly applied the narrow wording instrument that did not match the high complexity of the issue at stake. Also they continued to talk at cross purposes until the very end since they mutually contested the results of somewhat broader methods of interpretation and since none of the advocates used a very broad technique of legal reasoning. Dissent prevailed. Consequently Germany was not ideationally entrapped and did not have to pay lip-service to enforcement authorities in the course of the judicial discourse. The Kohl government did not change its strategic positions, policy ideas and legal acts during or shortly after the judgment. In debates prior to the judicial discourse neither the permission of exceptions, nor their transparency requirements, were explicitly discussed. In general, the Kohl government preferred a narrow interpretation of the directive, restricting its impact on the German *aquis* and compliance costs for the governmental, well-organized constituency as far as possible (e.g. Bundesrat 1979: 303, Bundestag 1980: 18239). Therefore, they argued that 'the EG-adaptation law is better than its reputation' so that 'based on experiences heretofore, it would be premature to change the law after such a short period of time' (Bundesregierung 1983: 19, translation DP). In 1983, the SPD proposed a bill, strengthening the equal treatment principle (SPD 1983). It entailed increasing transparency measures, such as the duty to make the EC employment adaptation law public in all companies and enterprises (SPD 1983: 2–3). Yet majorities in the Committee on Employment and Social Policy and in the Bundestag rejected it (Ausschuss für Arbeit und Soziales 1986: 2, Bundestag 1986c). More than two years after the judgment, the government continued to opt for the restricted applicatory scope of the equal treatment principle, although the ECJ judgment had clarified that Germany was required to improve its reporting system on granted exceptions (Ausschuss für Arbeit und Soziales 1986: 4, European Court of Justice 1985: 37–40).

In sum, since the judicial discourse was ineffective, it is not surprising that the government did not become increasingly pro-equal treatment (e.g. Bundestag 1986c),[31] a stance which was reflected in the absence of legal changes in response to the judicial discourse. In its judgment, the ECJ noted that 'it is not clear from the application whether the Commission requires those exceptions to be legally determined or whether a list or a catalogue of such exceptions is to be established by other means' (European Court of Justice 1985: 32). The ECJ also stated that the equal access directive neither explicitly mentioned, nor teleological required, national legal acts with enumerative lists of exceptions (European Court of Justice 1985: 35–6). However, the ECJ sided with the European Commission and concluded that Germany violated Article 9 II in not allowing for the transparent and comprehensive monitoring of granted exceptions through the European Commission. At the same time, the ECJ did not prescribe how Germany should remedy this violation (European Court of Justice 1985: operative part 1).

[31] The FDP even shifted from moderate support for the EC employment adaptation law and the principle of equal treatment to greater scepticism after the ECJ ruling (Bundestag 1989b, Bundestag 1990d). This programmatic change went along with other internal quarrels, which were reflected by losses in more than 20% of the FDP's 86,500 party members (Gnad *et al.* 2005).

Does the directive apply to job postings?

The debate finally focused on the question of whether the equal access directive prescribed gender-neutral job postings (European Court of Justice 1985: 41). The European Commission accused Germany of not making a binding provision of §611 a of the civil code (BGB), according to which jobs *should* be posted neutrally (European Court of Justice 1985: 41, emphasis added). Based on a pragmatic argumentation, the European advocate claimed that 'since offers of employment precede access to employment they come within the scope of directive no 76/207' (European Court of Justice 1985: 41). Yet although this was the crucial disputed element, the European advocate did not use judicial means of interpretation in order to substantiate the claim that the directive also applies to job postings. Instead, the European advocate argued further that Article 6 prescribed legal remedies for persons who have been discriminated against, and highlighted that the wording of §611 a of the German civil code was not in line with the EU directive (European Court of Justice 1985: 41).

The German advocate, by contrast, used the narrow wording method to emphasize that the directive was silent on posting jobs. Yet, since the interpretational scope of the issue was broad, due to the absence of specified rules within the legal act in question, the narrow wording instrument was not suited to solve the former. The German advocate also used the much better fitting broader directive-immanent systematic technique, which revealed that the directive covered the stage 'access to employment' as the earliest stage in an application process but did not mention 'offer of employment' as subject to the equality principle (European Court of Justice 1985: 42). Hence, Germany concluded that the directive did not apply to the stage of job postings and that the non-mandatory phrasing of §611 a BGB did not breach the European directive (European Court of Justice 1985: 42).

While the wording method was too narrow, the directive-immanent systematic method of interpretation fitted well to the medium complexity of the issue at stake. Hence, the judicial discourse should be effective. However, the German government did not have to adjust policies since the directive-immanent systematic approach led to a conclusion that was completely in line with the initial German position. Therefore, it does not come as a surprise that the ECJ ruled in favour of Germany.[32] As a conse-

[32] The ECJ accepted that the stage of job postings could be relevant for 'the application of Article 9 II in full effect' (European Court of Justice 1985: 43). In line with the German advocate, the ECJ climbed up the hierarchy of judicial methods and applied

quence, legal adaptations were unnecessary after 1985 and did not take place. In line with this, the Kohl government maintained its restrictive interpretation of the directive concerning job postings in the first five years after the judicial discourse (Ausschuss für Arbeit und Soziales 1986: 4, Rosenfeld, Trappe and Gornick 2004).[33]

The second rationalist alternative: compliance bargaining in the shadow of the ECJ

The German infringement of the equal access directive is an instance of a packed ECJ case, in which a total of seven issues were at stake. This would allow for a broad scope for compromises, which the parties could informally negotiate in the shadow of the ECJ. Did compliance bargaining between the German government and the European Commission foster the German shift into compliance three years after the ECJ judgment? In short, the answer is no. None of the parties made any adjustments that could possibly imply that a compromise agreement was brokered. The European Commission did not withdraw a single issue before the ECJ ruled on it. Likewise, Germany did not initiate legal changes during the ongoing judicial discourse and did not adapt its legal acts to the ECJ judgment quickly, but delayed compliance for three more years.

The judgment

After the judicial discourse ended in 1985, the ECJ issued a judgment. In this judgment, the ECJ sided on all but one issue with the German advocate. The only issue in which the ECJ convicted Germany for violating the equal access directive concerned the question of domestic compliance monitoring. According to the ECJ, Germany had failed to fulfil its obligations, as defined in Article 9 II of the equality directive, and 'prevented the Commission from exercising effective supervision' (European Court of Justice 1985: 39, 40). While this created a demand for domestic adaptation, the ECJ did not specify how Article 9 II, combined with Article 2, should be transposed in order to guarantee efficient control of granted exceptions (European Court of Justice 1985: 37–40).

This section analyses whether the 1985 judgment differentially empowered societal norm proponents who then pushed the reluctant

---

the wording as well as the broader systematic interpretation. Hence, the Court concluded that the equal access directive did not cover job postings (European Court of Justice 1985: 45).

[33] In 1990, the government initiated a legislative proposal on the improvement of the equal treatment through legally binding neutral job postings (Bundesregierung 1990a: 10).

German government out of non-compliance. It identifies the relevant actors and inquires into the contextual preconditions for effective shaming and reframing campaigns. This reveals that the government could not successfully be shamed into compliance, but that shaming attempts contributed to an incremental normative change and later on enabled effective reframing. Accordingly, Germany shifted into a comprehensive form of compliance, but did so with a serious time lag.

German employment policy was and still is characterized by corporatist arrangements. Trade unions and employers' associations are highly organized and represented by peak associations at the federal level who negotiate employment-related issues, such as minimum payments, in tripartite settings. The Federal Association of Employers (BDA) and the Federal Association of the Industry (BDI) represent employers, while the German Trade Union Association (DGB) represents employees. Until the early 1980s, those associations were dominated by male perspectives, not least because their main constituency consisted of men (Abendroth 1989, Hassel 1999). The BDI and the BDA, and to a lesser extent the DGB, opposed a demanding equality approach because of countervailing values, such as the freedom of contract and enterprise, and because of the associated compliance costs (e.g. Bundestag 1980: 18238–9, Bundesvereinigung der Deutschen Arbeitgeberverbände 1976, Kodré and Müller 2003: 96, Rosenfeld, Trappe and Gornick 2004). Societal compliance proponents, by contrast, were relatively weak. If women were party members, they worked within the party but not too much in societal organizations.[34] Demokratischer Frauenbund, Deutscher Landfrauenverband, and the Katholischer Deutscher Frauenbund dealt mostly with everyday problems of women and were less interested in legal changes (Gehrhard 2004: 309, Kodré and Müller 2003: 97, interview SPD#1, 03–02–05). One of the few exceptions was the politically active women's organization, the Deutsche Frauenrat, which lobbied the Committee for Labour and Social Policy and the Bundestag as an umbrella organization (Bundestag 1980: 18243, Icken 2002).

Prior to the ECJ judgment of 1985, the domestic context was not conducive to successful shaming campaigns. Firstly, there was no consensus on the extent of the obligations that the equality directive encompassed so that the government could not easily be blamed for violating equal access measures. Secondly, the case attracted only limited

[34] The most prominent organization with a political party was the social-democratic women's consortium (ASF). Although the ASF promoted a broad interpretation of directive 76/207 in the early 1980s, they failed to win over a majority in the SPD (Kodré and Müller 2003: 95–6, interview SPD#1, 03–02–05).

public attention, so that it was difficult for women's organizations to create significant threats of electoral and reputational losses for the government (interview organized interests#9, 21–02–05). The domestic context was equally unfavourable for successful reframing endeavours that could have restructured the domestic debate to promote a more demanding understanding of equality between men and women. Gender-related role models were deeply institutionalized (e.g. Bundestag 1984, Rosenfeld, Trappe and Gornick 2004). So too was the dominant liberal economic approach and its embedded principle of the freedom of enterprise and of contract. Against this background, it is not surprising that societal compliance campaigns did not take place prior to the ECJ ruling. In 1983, the Kohl government prepared an internal report and evaluated the initial impact of the 1980 adaptation law (Bundesregierung 1983). This would have been an opportunity for shaming or reframing activities, in particular since state and federal labour ministries, trade unions, employer organizations and women's groups provided detailed information. Yet women's organizations hardly even used this platform, with the result that the report did not systematically present data on all exceptions from the equality directive.[35]

After 1985, the context became increasingly fertile to shaming campaigns because the judgment differentially empowered women's organizations to the disadvantage of trade unions and employer associations. Firstly, the judgment increased the media attention together with a preliminary ruling on the remotely related postage case (Schreiber, Grunwald and Hagemann-White 1994).[36] Both rulings clarified that deviations from the equality principle had to be exceptional, so that sex cannot generally be a relevant criterion in the employment sphere. Also, the ECJ authoritatively clarified that Germany violated the equal access directive, because it lacked notification procedures on granted exceptions. In this context, the Deutsche Frauenrat and the ASF blamed the government for tolerating the continuation of discrimination and highlighted that this was highly inappropriate, given the prominent constitutional status of the equality principle (Gottfried and O'Reilly 2002, Schreiber, Grunwald and Hagemann-White 1994). In addition, while individual

[35] See also Bundesregierung 1984, Bundestag 1983, Bundestag 1984, Bundestag 1985a, interviews organized interests#2, 03–02–05, organized interests#3, 08–02–05, organized interests#10, 11–03–05.

[36] The most prominent ECJ preliminary ruling concerned compensation for discrimination in employment affairs on grounds of sex (postage case). In this ruling, the ECJ stated that compensation should exceed purely symbolic gestures (e.g. in only refunding postage costs) (European Court of Justice 1984, 14/83; 79/83).

women were less eager to sue discriminators in Germany than in the USA (Zippel 2006), the former increasingly went to courts in the late 1980s and early 1990s (Gottfried and O'Reilly 2002, Icken 2002). With every national court judgment and every ECJ preliminary ruling, women's organizations could draw additional public attention to the deficient German approach to the equality of men and women (Icken 2002, interviews organized interests 10, 11–03–05, organized interests#3, 08–02–05, also, e.g. *Süddeutsche Zeitung* 1992a).

Even during the judicial discourse, the government in Bonn had accepted the importance of the equal access principle in public employment (see judicial discourse on issue one, Bundestag 1986a: 2–5; Bundestag 1988b: 3736–9, Bundestag 1990d: 14–16). After 1985, they no longer argued that the equality principle only applied to very restricted circumstances or should be subordinate to the countervailing values 'freedom of enterprise' and 'freedom of contract' (compare Bundestag 1979: 14932, Bundestag 1980: 18238 with Bundesregierung 1989, Bundesregierung 1990a). Against this background, the government risked a loss in public credibility if they were to perpetuate their old undemanding equality policies, while women's organizations publicly emphasized how insufficient and inappropriate they were. In response, the government made strategic concessions. They engaged in window-dressing pro-women activities to avoid reputational losses vis-à-vis the broader public (Bundesrat 1990, Bundesregierung 1990a, Bundestag 1990b: 16620–6). At the same time, they did not risk losing the support of industry or employers' associations, who anticipated additional administrative costs and increasing wages, nor of conservative rural voters, who strongly adhered to the male breadwinner and female caregiver role models. Similar to the survey on anti-discrimination experiences of 1983, in 1987, the Kohl-government collected data on approved exceptions to the directive. The survey revealed that the equal access principle was increasingly applied and that inequity was on the decrease in employment affairs. Germany transmitted the results to the European Commission, which considered that the form and substance of the report, as well as the practice of gathering data in cooperation with the Länder in the subsequent years, represented sufficient transposition and closed the case (Bundestag 1990d: 16). The 1987 survey was not based on a legal act that specified possible grounds for allowing exceptions (in line with Article 2 II of the directive) and that created transparency in specifying how and how often information on granted exceptions has to be collected and presented. This did not create transparency and allowed Germany to practically pursue a very undemanding equal access approach. The 1987 survey did not differ from the information collection and reporting practices of Germany before the ECJ judgment. Hence, it did not reflect even a minimalist form of compliance with the judgment, which had emphasized that the handling of exceptions to the equality principle was inadequate and opaque. In addition to the survey, the government initiated a bill on working hours in 1987, which was framed as transposing the equal access directive, although this aspect had not been at stake in the infringement proceeding (Bundesregierung 1987c: 1–2, 16). However, the government did not proceed to pass the bill in the subsequent years, although no domestic veto players blocked it. Similarly in 1990, several months prior to the federal election, the Kohl government proposed a draft law on the improvement of the equal treatment principle in employment affairs, but did not re-introduce it after their re-election (Bundesrat 1990, Bundesregierung 1990a: 10, Bundestag 1990d).[37] In all three instances, the government adapted cost–benefit calculations prior to elections in response to the incrementally growing domestic pro-equality constituency and talked about strengthening pro-equality legislation. Yet they were not persuaded and still favoured unpretentious equality policies. Although shaming campaigns facilitated rhetorical commitments to end discrimination, these commitments did not manifest themselves in legal changes. The tactic of promising pro-equality laws before elections and withdrawing them afterwards minimized political costs. On the one hand, the government circumvented losses in reputation and electoral support vis-à-vis the broader public. On the other hand, they avoided losses in support from employers' associations because bills could not be passed during ongoing legislative periods, while the government did not re-introduce bills once the re-election was secured, and continued to argue that equal treatment was important, but costly in practice and should therefore be applied cautiously (e.g. Bundesregierung 1990a: 5–7, Bundestag 1990b: 16620–6).

After the 1990 elections, the context again became less conducive to successful shaming endeavours. The media attention declined, because the ECJ judgment was more than five years old and because there were no longer prominent preliminary rulings on the equal access directive (Kodré and Müller 2003). The next federal elections were scheduled for 1994. Thus the threat of a damage of reputation and a loss of electoral support had become less severe by 1991 (Gottfried and O'Reilly 2002). Hence, the government continued non-compliance.

[37] Among other things, the bill prescribed gender-neutral job postings and stated that women discriminated against should get compensation of up to four months' salary.

The judgment also differentially empowered women's organizations in terms of their abilities to reframe domestic debates. Most importantly, the judgment considerably reduced the complexity of the case. Instead of seven elements, the ECJ authoritatively ruled that Germany had incorrectly transposed the directive in only one respect, namely by failing to comprehensively and transparently monitor and report exceptions to the equal access principle. This simplification made it much easier for societal actors to engage in pro-compliance campaigns. Nevertheless, in the first period after the ECJ judgment, successful reframing was impossible since the context was hostile to such attempts. The role models of male breadwinners and female caregivers were still strongly institutionalized and not losing traction. Moreover, the government, as well as employer and employee organizations, followed a cost approach, suggesting that equality promotion should be pursued with caution since it could easily become costly for individual employers and could negatively affect the economy (e.g. Bundesregierung 1989, Bundesregierung 1990a, Bundestag 1990b: 1662). While a restricted equal treatment approach was compatible with the old role model and the cost approach, a demanding equality policy was not. In this domestic environment, women's organizations did not invest resources in reframing domestic debates to promote a more demanding equal treatment approach. If they were active at all, women's organizations invested their energies in shaming the government for not living up to the constitutionally prescribed equality standards. Consequently, the domestic debate was not redirected towards new policy ideas and the government did not shift into a comprehensive form of compliance before 1990.

Normative change needs time and the various shaming campaigns incrementally strengthened the prescriptive status of the equal access norm and thereby created a domestic context that became increasingly conducive to reframing endeavours. In addition, the German unification triggered the degeneration of the traditional caregiver and breadwinner role models, in particular since these models had never been as prominent in the German Democratic Republic as in the Federal Republic of Germany (Ebner 1992, Fink 1994). After the federal election of 1990, the old reference systems abated gradually and the idea that equality policies should be pursued with great care to avoid economic costs and that equality meant liberation from traditional role models lost their importance (Icken 2002, Koenig 1993, Limbach 1993, Puelsch 1993, *Süddeutsche Zeitung* 1993). In this context, women's organizations as well as trade unions, most notably the DGB, reframed the equality debate by drawing on the more advanced gender equality approach of the former

German Democratic Republic (Bundestag 1994c: 15444, Kodré and Müller 2003: 112, Liebert 2003: 270, *Süddeutsche Zeitung* 1992a). Instead of focusing on role models, norm entrepreneurs promoted a much broader concept of gender equality, which also facilitated an ambitious policy with very limited possibilities to deviate from the equal access principle and grant exceptions (Bundesregierung 1996, Bundestag 1993h: 15433–5, Bundestag 1994d: 18969–71, Icken 2002, interview organized interests#9, 21–02–05). The new gender equality frame comprehensively covered discrimination in the economic, societal and political sub-systems and pushed for gender mainstreaming as a cross-cutting policy (Morgenroth 1996, Schmidtke 1996, von Wahl 2006). This frame succeeded because it was linked to and resonated well with the deep-seated human rights approach. While the Kohl government had initially claimed that legal changes were not urgent since psychological discrimination of women was much more severe than legal inequality (Chancellor Kohl in Bundestag 1984: 4671, similar Bundestag 1986b: 19952), their stance on this issue changed fundamentally in the post-reunification period. In response to the new frames, the government and the lead ministry no longer denied their responsibility to legislate, but went as far as to argue that the German constitution obliged government and parliament to promote gender equality (Minister for Family and Youth in Bundestag 1993h: 15433–5). As a result, the role models and cost-related restrictive arguments were almost completely off the table. Instead, within the new gender equality frame, political and societal actors focused on truth (causal ideas on how to improve the standing of women in the economic, the societal and the political sub-system), rightfulness (line-drawing between discrimination and positive action), and appropriateness (equality of human beings) (e.g. Bundestag 1993g: 15431–3, Holzamer 1994, Koenig 1993, Limbach 1993, Puelsch 1993). In line with this new frame, the head of the lead ministry stated that the equal treatment law should seek to abolish structural discrimination of women and referred to human rights for its justification, but did not refer to the liberation from role models at all (Angela Merkel in Bundestag 1993h: 15433–5, *Süddeutsche Zeitung* 1993).[38] Thus, in response to the reframing campaigns of the Deutsche Frauenrat and trade unions, the government

[38] The SPD and the Green party also adopted the frame of gender equality and no longer blamed the Kohl government, the economy or society for existing discriminations (Bundestag 1994d). Instead, they emphasized the cross-cutting character of gender issues and justified the necessity for legal action through recourses to human rights (e.g. Bundestag 1993g: 1545, Bundestag 1994d, Bundestag 1994f, Bundestag 1998a: 21618–9, Bundestag 1998b).

changed its ideas and policies towards a demanding gender equality approach (Bundesregierung 1996, Bundestag 1997a, Bundestag 1998b, Süddeutsche Zeitung 1994a, von Wahl 2006). They also abandoned minimalist interpretations of the equality directive and even former approaches aiming at liberating women from the caregiver's image (Bundesregierung 1996, Bundestag 1998a, Morgenroth 1996). At the same time, blame-shifting dynamics between political, economic and societal actors, about who was ultimately responsible for discriminations, stopped (compare Bundesregierung 1984, Bundestag 1985a, with Bundesregierung 1996, Bundestag 1994i, Bundestag 1997a).

After the gender equality frame was adopted, the government changed its policy ideas accordingly and initiated a comprehensive equal treatment reform in 1993. The latter expressed the moral obligation to 'combat the structural discrimination of women' (Minister Merkel in the Bundestag 1993g: 15432, translation DP). The renunciation of the minimalist approach found expression in two legal acts. Germany eventually passed a law on working hours in June 1994, after it had been initiated and withdrawn in 1986 and again in 1987 (Bundestag 1994i). At the same time, Germany finalized the equal treatment law, which included both transparency measures for discrimination and the active promotion of women in employment affairs in June 1994. The 1994 reforms not only completely transposed the ECJ judgment, they also actively endorsed gender equality in the economic and the political spheres, which was not at all required by EU law. For example, the reforms established gender equality officers in public administrations, who promoted gender equality and comprehensively monitored the application of the equal access principle. Hence, the 1994 reforms introduced a complex and decentralized system that allowed the collection of detailed information on the practical application of the equality principle and, therefore, resembled comprehensive compliance.

The threat of sanctions

Germany only shifted into compliance in 1994, although the ECJ judgment dated back to 1985. Was this due to a looming sanction-threat? Did European enforcement authorities induce a policy change via a credible threat with potential future financial penalties? Did the shadow of sanctions underline the inappropriateness of governmental non-compliance and thus differentially empower a pro-compliance lead ministry vis-à-vis domestic veto players?

The rationalist hypothesis: credible sanction-threats increase non-compliance costs

In the equality case, the ECJ did not induce compliance through sanction-threats. Prior to 1993, the enforcement system was decentralized. The only way to punish the most reluctant states was an ECJ referral to a violation of article 171 ECT. This could have facilitated informal decentralized sanctions in the form of losses of credibility – especially if other member states invested more resources and complied better than the free-riding state. Yet the shadow of external costs was not looming. The ECJ had never blamed Germany for free-riding and violating Article 171 ECT. Moreover, the equal access directive was problematic in other member states as well. The UK, Italy and Greece also faced ECJ judgments and France had been subject to judgments three times.[39] Hence, the German government had nothing to fear as regards reputational losses among the other member states, thus possibly facing disadvantages in future EU negotiations.

Was Germany nevertheless threatened by potential penalties? The government was not inactive after the ECJ ruling in 1985. They compiled an equal access report and drafted a bill on working hours and another on equal treatment in employment affairs. These actions were strategic adaptations and not expressions of changed policy ideas.[40] In line with the hypothesis, none of these activities were induced by threats of decentralized sanctions. Firstly, the government did not turn any of the legislative proposals into legal acts (Bundesregierung 1987c, Bundestag 1988b), did not transpose the judgment, and would not have hoped to pacify the ECJ, preventing the latter from taking enforcement measures. Secondly, if the government was indeed yielding to the ECJ, it would not only have issued a regulation or passed a minimalist law, but it would have accompanied its legislative activities with references to the ECJ. Through blame-shifting, the Kohl government could have justified policy changes vis-à-vis its compliance-averse constituency: employer associations. However, in 1987 and 1990 the government did not refer to pressures emanating from the

[39] The government highlighted that 'the European Commission opened similar infringements to almost all Member States' (Bundesregierung 1983: 20, translation DP), which indicates that they did not fear a damage of reputation vis-à-vis other EC member states for violating the equal access directive.

[40] Firstly, the government was not fully committed to the equal treatment principle. They did not regard legal instruments as suitable for combating discrimination in the societal sphere (e.g. Bundestag 1986b: 19952). Secondly, even later on, as the government accepted its responsibility to act, unconditional normative commitments to the equal access principle were extremely rare, since there were still references to cost in order to justify scope restrictions of the equality principle (e.g. Bundesrat 1990, Bundesregierung 1989, Bundesregierung 1990a: 5–7, Bundestag 1990b: 16620–6).

EU level.[41] Thus, as expected, Germany was not deterred by potential sanctions.

In 1994, Germany finally and completely complied with the ECJ judgment and increased transparency measures for equal access practices. This comprehensive policy change was not induced by threats from above, because the Commission had already closed the case several years earlier in response to the 1987 survey (Bundestag 1990d: 16). Hence, a sanction-threat could not have triggered compliance.

The constructivist hypothesis: sanction-threats empower pro-compliance ministries

Did a potential sanction-threat induce a demanding form of compliance in differentially empowering one pro-equality ministry vis-à-vis domestic veto players?

Ever since the CDU together with the FDP came into power in 1982, the government and the lead ministry opposed a demanding equal treatment policy not least because it followed a liberal rather than an interventionist economic policy and because of strongly institutionalized role models (Mr Blüm, Federal Minister for Labour and Social Policy, in Bundestag 1988b: 3736–3739, Bundesregierung 1987c: 16). Even female Conservative MEPs pointed out that detailed legally binding provisions, such as the draft of the EG Anpassungsgesetz, violated the employer's rights and the social partners' spheres of influence (Mrs Hürland in Bundestag 1979: 14932, 14938, Bundestag 1985b: 8782). Against this background, it is not surprising that none of the ministries pursued a demanding equality approach during and in the period after the ECJ judgment (Bundesregierung 1990a). Hence, the ruling of 1985 did not empower the leading ministry and in no way paved a way towards comprehensive compliance before the European Commission formally closed the case.

Nor did a sanction-threat induce compliance. Since the ECJ did not refer to a violation of Article 171 ECT, a decentralized sanction-threat was not present. Hence, the ECJ did not remind the government of the fact that a demanding equal access policy would be more appropriate than a minimalist one. Differential empowerment was not possible and, in line with the constructivist version of the sanction-threat hypothesis, Germany did not shift into comprehensive compliance in response to an enforcement instrument.

[41] The only exception was a statement by the government on the 1987 survey, in which the ECJ ruling was mentioned, but not used as justification for policy changes (Bundestag 1990d: 16).

Reframing and compliance: the German equal access case

In the German equal access case, it took many years for the government to finally and fully comply. The judicial discourse was ineffective, because the advocates of the parties argued at cross purposes. Nevertheless, the ECJ sided with Germany on all but one issue. This issue concerned reporting requirements for granted exceptions to the equal access directive. The German transposition allowed the pursuit of lax and undemanding interpretations of the equality principle through the backdoor – which left women less protected than the directive would have required. Although this could have thwarted the very purpose of the directive, the Kohl government persisted with its interests and was reluctant to change legal acts. The ECJ judgment differentially empowered women's organizations. They conducted shaming campaigns in the years after the judgment. The domestic context was favourable and the government reacted to anticipated damages of reputation and reduced electoral support with adaptations of strategic positions. However, the context changed rapidly. After the elections, threats of domestic non-compliance costs lost their credibility and shaming activities lost their power over the government. The latter was able to recalculate domestic costs and benefits, and shift back into non-compliance, as preferred by employer associations (e.g. the majority of trade unions and the conservative rural constituency). While the government had initiated legal changes prior to the election, they opted for silent deaths of both bills after having been re-elected.

Successful societal reframing campaigns took place in the early 1990s. Women's organizations and also trade unions launched a gender equality frame, which stressed that anti-discrimination must be a cross-cutting enterprise in the political, the economic and the societal sphere. This approach was successfully promoted, because the old role models became gradually deinstitutionalized. In addition, the new gender-equality approach fitted well with the powerful human rights frame. Societal norm entrepreneurs emphasized the linkages between both approaches, which additionally strengthened gender-equality ideas. In line with the reframing hypothesis, the Kohl government adapted policy ideas and comprehensively changed legal acts, so that Germany finally transformed non-compliance into a comprehensive form of compliance in 1994. While the government shifted into a comprehensive form of compliance in response to differential empowerment processes triggered by the ECJ judgment, sanction-threats were not effective.

5.V Summary: the power of judgments

The four case studies have exemplified that judgments are indeed an important tool for restoring compliance with law beyond the nation-state. They foster compliance in a two-step process. Firstly, judgments provide an authoritative norm definition, clarify that the state in question was indeed breaching law, reduce the complexity of the issue at stake and create publicity. This differentially empowers societal compliance proponents to the disadvantage of opponents who can no longer make legitimate arguments against compliance. In a second step, societal norm proponents can make use of the increased public attention and the additional ideational resources in pushing the government into compliance from below. This requires the presence and willingness of civil society actors to invest own resources, which is contingent and can vary from case to case. Once organized interests are willing to push for compliance, they have two strategies at their disposal. Shaming induces quick shifts into minimalist compliance, while reframing takes longer and brings about comprehensive compliance. In line with the rationalist and the constructivist hypothesis, each strategy is only effective under certain scope conditions. The British equal access and the German collective redundancy case showed that shaming is effective to create reputational costs for the government, if the judgment not only increases the public attention, but can also be linked to institutionalized domestic norms, so that the government can be blamed for violating the latter. If these scope conditions are absent, shaming fails as all other case studies in this book demonstrate. The British drinking water and the German equal access cases illustrated how effective reframing induced a long-term policy shift resembling comprehensive compliance. Yet the studies showed that domestic debates can only be restructured effectively if judgments reduced the complexity of the issue and if the issue is embedded in a new frame that can subsequently be linked to a complementary policy frame. If these scope conditions are absent, domestic debates cannot be restructured, which is what all the other six case studies in this book demonstrate.

6

Effective sanction-threats

This section offers two examples of how sanction-threats successfully foster compliance. It tests the rationalist and the constructivist variant of the sanction-threat hypothesis and finds evidence for the former, but not for the latter. Thus, sanction-threats do not differentially empower pro-compliance ministries vis-à-vis domestic veto players by highlighting that non-compliance is inappropriate. Instead, sanction-threats pose costly threats to governments who shy away from these costs if the issue is serious so that they anticipate becoming subject to high penalties during their incumbency.

6.1 The UK nitrates case

The nitrates directive (91/676) protects the environment by reducing the level of nitrates in drinking and other fresh water and groundwater. It especially focuses on nitrates from agricultural sources, which are the main water polluter. Unlike the drinking water directive, the nitrates directive does not clearly define maximum emission concentrations. Instead, it prescribes the designation of Nitrate Vulnerable Zones (NVZ) and Action Programmes as instruments to protect water from nitrates, and additionally includes new modes of governance, such as the development of codes of good agricultural conduct. Apart from these new modes of governance, it follows a legalistic, interventionist problem-solving approach. Since the nitrates directive encompasses consultation and self-regulation mechanisms in the implementation stage, it fits better with the UK environmental approach than the 1980 DWD did (Lowe and Ward 1998: 9).

Pesticides and fertilizers in water gained public attention in the UK after the Royal Commission on Environmental Pollution published a report in 1979. At that time, nitrates from agricultural sources were not at the centre of the debate, since it was widely believed that water pollution was caused by other sources, including the disposal of containers or spray tank washings (Ward *et al.* 1993: 5). The Ministry of Agriculture, Fisheries and Food (MAFF) pursued an unobtrusive nitrates policy. For example, they gave no direction on the use of fertilizers so that farmers were usually guided by commercial instructions on how to use them (Ward *et al.* 1993: 1). Although water quality was low, and nitrates played an important role in it, the major political parties shared a concern about costs arising from the cleaning of water (House of Commons 1996g, Pretty *et al.* 2000). In addition they framed water quality as an issue of protecting public health rather than the environment and therefore had few water-related policies preventing pollution in the first place (Ward *et al.* 1993: 7). Farmers also opposed the nitrates directive because they feared restrictions in the use of fertilizers and pesticides and, in turn, a decrease in agricultural production (House of Commons 1994f). In this context, the UK opted for a narrow and cost-saving interpretation of the nitrates directive that focused only on drinking water sources, and not on other groundwater and fresh water.[1]

British legislation already encompassed water quality laws and regulations as well as specific rules on nitrates,[2] though these only related to drinking water. The misfit between the European and the UK nitrates *aquis* was limited, but still required some legal adaptations. The government in London reported that they transposed the directive with three regulations in 1996. In line with previous legislation and the framing of water quality as a public health issue, these legal acts exclusively referred to drinking water instead of applying the nitrates directive to all groundwater and fresh water (House of Commons 1994a: 9, House of Commons 1994g: 205–7, House of Commons 1996e: 814–15).

While this implementation saved compliance costs, it did not satisfy the European Commission. In October 1997, the Commission sent a letter of formal notice, followed by a reasoned opinion in June 1998, accusing the UK of severely restricting the applicatory scope of the directive (Advocate General 2000: 9). The Blair government disagreed and the Commission referred the case to the ECJ in February 1999 (case C-69/99). Almost two years later, the Court ruled that the UK had violated EU law by incorrectly transposing the nitrates directive (European Court of Justice 2000a).

[1] See also Foundation for Water Research 1996, Foundation for Water Research 1998, House of Commons 1994a: 9, 97, House of Commons 1994g: 205–7, House of Commons 1994i, House of Commons 1996e: 814–15, House of Commons 1997, House of Lords 1996: 1161, Ward *et al.* 1993: 14.

[2] e.g. the Control of Pesticides Regulation 1986, the Code of Good Agricultural Practice for the Protection of Water (England and Wales) 1991, the Code of Good Agricultural Practice for the Protection of Water (Scotland) of March 1992.

The pattern of legal changes in the nitrates case

Almost two years after the ECJ judgment, the UK still continued in non-compliance. The Blair government merely planned a consultation with farmers in January 2002 as a first measure in the transposition process. This process additionally delayed legal changes, with the result that the Commission sent a second reasoned opinion to the UK in spring 2002. After this sanction-threat, the government quickly transposed the ECJ

Table 6.1 Legal changes in the nitrates sector

Date	*Title*	*Initiated by*	*Outcome*
1996	The Protection of Water against Agricultural Nitrate Pollution Regulations (Northern Ireland) 1996 S.I. Northern Ireland no. 217 of 1996	Conservative government	Legal transposition of the nitrates directive, below the directive
1996	The Protection of Water against Agricultural Nitrate Pollution (England and Wales) Regulations 1996 S.I. no. 888 of 1996	Conservative government	Legal transposition of the nitrates directive, below the directive
1996	The Protection of Water against Agricultural Nitrate Pollution (Scotland) Regulations 1996 S.I. Scotland no. 1564 of 1996	Conservative government	Legal transposition of the nitrates directive, below the directive
1999	Water Industry Act	Labour government	Legal transposition of the nitrates directive, below the directive
2002	The Nitrate Vulnerable Zones (Additional Designations) (England) (No. 2) Regulations 2002, S.I. 2614. Came into force on the 18 October and 19 December 2002	Labour government	Reported as legal transposition of the nitrates directive, complies with the ECJ judgment
2002	The Protection of Waste Against Agricultural Nitrate Pollution (Amendment) (Wales) Regulations 2002 S.I 2002 No. 2297 (W.226) 11/09/2002	Labour government	Reported as legal transposition of the nitrates directive, complies with the ECJ judgment
2002	The Designation of Nitrate Vulnerable Zones (Scotland) Regulations 2002 S.I 2002 No. 276 01.07.2002	Labour government	Reported as legal transposition of the nitrates directive, complies with the ECJ judgment

judgment, with the 2002 nitrates regulations, within a couple of weeks. While the regulations included all water and not only water intended for human consumption, they contained several loopholes for lax practical applications with regard to the designation of NVZs (Department of the Environment 2002b). The regulations of 2002 introduced windows of opportunity for pursuing less demanding and less costly nitrates policies in the stage of practical implementation and therefore resembled minimalist compliance.[3]

How can these policy changes be explained? Which instrument triggered compliance?

The judicial discourse

The Commission accused the UK of violating the nitrates directive in three respects (Advocate General 2000: 13–19). It was firstly contested whether all surface water and groundwater were subject to the directive, or only water intended for human consumption. Secondly, the parties differed over the UK's designation of nitrate vulnerable zones as delimiting the applicatory scope of the nitrates directive. The third disagreement was whether the British action programmes required for the NVZs were sufficient. Did the judicial discourse that took place between February 1999 and December 2000 trigger ideational entrapment, which translated into policy change in 2002? Did compliance bargaining in the shadow of the judicial discourse foster legal adaptations?

Judicial discourse: ideational entrapment or threats of reputational losses?

Scope of the nitrates directive – all surface water and groundwater or only water intended for human consumption?

The parties were in disagreement over whether or not the UK had applied the nitrates directive to too few instances. The Commission argued that the Water Industry Act (WIA) focused on surface water intended for the abstraction of drinking water, but excluded all non-consumption waters (European Court of Justice 2000a: 14). The UK, by contrast, claimed that the WIA did not restrict the applicatory scope of the European directive.

The European advocate applied the narrow wording method of legal reasoning and applied it to Article 3 I of the directive. It states that 'waters affected by pollution and waters which could be affected by pollution if

[3] Since the legal changes hardly reduced legal ambiguities, the number of national court cases dealing with these issues increased from three to five in the five-year period after compliance was achieved compared to the five-year period before the 2002 changes (see also Annexe, Table 13).

action pursuant to Article 5 is not taken shall be identified by the Member States in accordance with the criteria set out in annex I.' Hence, the phrasing of Article 3 I did not exclude all surface water from the directive's scope (European Court of Justice 2000a: 15, 23). Yet the wording-based approach had a low match with the relatively high complexity of the interpretational problem, which was dealt with in different parts of the directive and did not specifically discriminate between types of water intended for human consumption. In particular, Article 3 I did not distinguish between drinking water, fresh water, and groundwater. Thus, the wording instrument did not reveal which types of water were subject to the directive. In order to analyse Annexe I, which specified the directive's applicatory scope, the European advocate used the broader systematic method of legal interpretation. It matched the interpretational scope of the contested issue, since paragraphs A1 and A2 of the Annexe explicitly specified the scope of Article 3 I. Thus, the nitrates directive applied to all surface water, regardless of whether or not it was intended for the abstraction of drinking water (European Court of Justice 2000a: 15, 17). The European Commission also accused the UK of delimiting the scope of application of the nitrates directive, in only subsuming groundwater that was intended for human consumption as falling under the nitrates directive (European Court of Justice 2000a: 16). In applying the wording method to Article 3 I and, in combination with the systematic interpretational technique, to Annexe A2, the European advocate argued that all groundwater, regardless of its future use, was subject to the nitrates directive (European Court of Justice 2000a: 17, 23).

In both instances, the UK advocate did not defend the British restrictive reading of Article 3 I and Annexe 1 before the ECJ by applying any devices of legal interpretation. Instead of engaging in judicial arguments, the UK claimed that it 'had initially interpreted the scope of the Directive differently with regard to the identification of "waters affected by pollution" under Article 3(1) and that the transposition of the Directive into national law was based on that interpretation' (European Court of Justice 2000a: 20, similar Advocate General 2000: 19).

We do not expect that the Blair government would become argumentatively entrapped and pursue comprehensive compliance or become subject to pressures of reputational losses and pursue minimalist compliance because the UK advocate did not engage in legal argumentation at all so that the judicial discourse could not produce a common norm definition.

In Court, the UK stated that the Commission was right (Advocate General 2000: 19). Also, in December 1999, only ten months after the referral to the ECJ, the Secretary of State for the Environment, Transport and the Regions, Mr Mullin, declared: 'Following a reference to the European Court of Justice, the Government have now widened their interpretation of the EU Nitrates Directive, beyond monitoring nitrate levels in drinking water sources, to include monitoring in non-drinking water freshwaters' (House of Commons 1999a). At first glance, this statement could indicate that the government had accepted that restricting the scope of application to drinking water violated the European nitrates directive. Also, it could be interpreted as paying lip service to the European actors in order to avoid a bad reputation. Alternatively, it might have been a strategy to circumvent a judgment altogether.

The third explanation is the most likely one, also because the UK did not introduce any legal changes at all. The British advocate did not even try to defend the narrow British nitrate approach to the ECJ. This could indicate that the UK did not hope to persuade the ECJ. If the responsible ministry assumed that the ECJ would side with the Commission, it might have been strategically rational for the government to circumvent an adverse judgment by avoiding a judgment altogether. To this end, they might have admitted that the British interpretation had been too narrow and might have stressed their willingness to instigate legal changes to fully comply with the nitrates directive before the Court. In line with this interpretation, the government did not consistently argue in favour of a demanding interpretation of the nitrates directive before the case had been closed. While they verbally supported a broad applicatory scope in 1999 before the ECJ, the government in London shifted back to a narrow interpretation in 2000. After the ECJ judgment, the government and the lead ministry did not refer to the appropriateness, rightfulness or scientific soundness of the nitrates directive, but restricted its applicatory scope geographically through restrictive nitrate vulnerable zones approaches and repeatedly referred to high domestic compliance costs and to the need to avoid burdening farmers.[4] This is not in line with either the constructivist ideational entrapment mechanism which would have expected stable policy ideas or the rationalist reputation-cost mechanism which would

[4] See also House of Commons 2002b: 472, House of Commons 2002c, House of Commons 2002f, House of Commons 2002g, House of Commons 2002h, Select Committee on Environment 2002a: 552, Select Committee on Environment 2003b: 14. Moreover, the Blair government adhered to a health, rather than an environmental frame and consequently were reluctant to broaden the scope of application from drinking water, to fresh water and groundwater (e.g. Department of the Environment 2000a, House of Commons 1998a, House of Commons 2001c). Even the environmental ministry pursued a narrow approach and maintained that nitrates were not very important because phosphates were the main source of eutrophication (Secretary of State for Environment, Food and Rural Affairs, Mr Meacher, in House of Commons 2002e).

have expected shifts into the old rhetoric only once the Commission has closed the case. Also, the UK introduced no measures towards legal adaptation during the judicial discourse, nor in the months after the ECJ judgment. In fact, the UK was reluctant to comply with the nitrates directive until the European Commission issued the second reasoned opinion and suggested a daily penalty of £135,000 in spring 2002. Subsequently, the Minister for the Environment admitted 'we have delayed implementation as long as possible (...) we now risk fines and therefore have to act' (Mr Meacher, in House of Commons 2002d).

Scope of application – designation of 'Nitrate Vulnerable Zones' across the UK
The second dispute centered on the question of whether the UK had correctly transposed Article 3 II of the directive, which concerned the designation of affected areas or areas in danger as 'Nitrate Vulnerable Zones' (NVZs). In particular, the Commission accused the UK of not designating any NVZs in Northern Ireland (Advocate General 2000: 17, European Court of Justice 2000a: 18). The British advocate did not defend the exclusion of Northern Ireland from the designation of vulnerable zones by using legal methods of reasoning. Rather than engaging in judicial interpretation, the UK again stated that they had initially misinterpreted Articles 3 II and III, as well as Article 5, of the nitrates directive (Advocate General 2000: 19). Conversely, the European Advocate General applied the narrow wording method to Article 3 II (Advocate General 2000: 18). It explicitly stated that member states were responsible to 'designate as vulnerable zones all known areas of land in their territories which drain into the waters identified in accordance with Article 3(1) and which contribute to pollution (Article 3(2))' (Advocate General 2000: 23, 18). However, the match between the issue and the judicial method was low because Article 3 did not clarify the central concepts of areas which 'drain into water' and which 'contribute to pollution'.

Again, the UK did not engage in judicial argumentation at all. Hence we would expect that the judicial discourse was ineffective and that the UK maintained non-compliance. In December 1999, the government had planned to extend NVZs across the UK and initiated a mapping process for the designation of areas and consultations for the year 2000 (The Secretary of State for the Environment, Transport and the Regions, in House of Commons 1999a). However, this rhetorical commitment was not followed by any formal action, other than considerations concerning the delegation of recommending designations of NVZs to the Environmental Agency (Select Committee on Environment 2000). In response to the judicial discourse, nothing happened. The British government did not change its policy approach from a narrow focus on health towards a more demanding environmental approach (House of Commons 1999a). For this reason and also because domestic compliance costs were considerably high, nitrate reductions outside the public health approach were not discussed after the ECJ judicial discourse (House of Commons 2000c, House of Commons 2002d). Only after the Commission threatened the UK with a second letter of formal notice in October 2001 and a second reasoned opinion in early 2002, did the government finally consult farmers and stakeholders in England (Department of the Environment 2002a: 3, House of Commons 2002d). Only then, almost four years after the UK first conceded that the NVZs were insufficient, did the leading ministry finally become active. At first, the baseline for the consultations with stakeholders in 2002 was that 'all regions of England are potentially at risk from agricultural nitrogen pollution of water supplies' (Secretary of State for Environment, Food and Rural Affairs Mr Meacher, in House of Commons 2002g). At the beginning, the consultations for the NVZs were based on an interpretation of the applicatory scope which included surface water and groundwater (House of Commons 2002g, House of Commons 2002i). However, the Department for Environment, Food and Rural Affairs (DEFRA) changed the options up for consultation with farmers and other stakeholders after the process had already started: option one was to turn 100 per cent of the British territory into an NVZ and option two was to turn 80 per cent. However, DEFRA as the leading ministry reduced the second option post hoc to 55 per cent (Department of the Environment 2002b, House of Commons 2002f). Against the advice of farmers and other stakeholders, who opted by majority for 100 per cent NVZ designation for reasons of fairness, DEFRA designated 55 per cent of the territory as an NVZ (Department of the Environment 2002c: 4–5, 14). Thus, as expected, the judicial discourse failed and non-compliance prevailed.

Third issue: action programmes

The European Commission suspected that the UK had violated Article 5 of the directive which required action programmes for all designated NVZs (Advocate General 2000: 19, European Court of Justice 2000a: 19–23).

As in the first two complaints, the UK abstained from using judicial or pragmatic arguments to defend its narrow norm interpretation. Instead of engaging in judicial reasoning to persuade the Court of its restricted interpretation of the nitrates directive, the British advocate simply declared that the UK intended to change its corresponding implementation measures (European Court of Justice 2000a: 20).

The European advocate applied the wording method to the nitrates directive (European Court of Justice 2000a: 19). The wording of Article 5 'obliges the Member States to establish, by 20 December 1995 at the latest, action programmes for avoiding the problems of water pollution caused by nitrates from agricultural sources relating to the vulnerable zones designated under Article 3(2) of the Directive or for remedying those problems' (Advocate General 2000: 24). Thus member states were undoubtedly responsible for the development of action programmes in vulnerable zones, as a measure to prevent or defeat nitrate pollution.

Again, due to the inactivity of the British advocate, the judicial discourse did not induce compliance. The government did not change its rhetoric: they did not actively pursue or argumentatively promote more demanding action programmes to combat nitrate pollution in designated NVZs after the 2000 judgment. Rather, members of government emphasized the domestic compliance costs for farmers who were already suffering severe problems due to the BSE or foot-and-mouth disease crises (House of Commons 2002a). In this context, the Labour government avoided additional burdens for farmers and, instead of launching costly action programmes, chose to financially support farmers in designated NVZs (House of Commons 2000b, House of Commons 2000d, House of Lords 2000). In line with these strategic considerations, the government never mentioned that action programmes were required for all areas designated as NVZs, nor did the government refine existing programmes or adopt additional action programmes in response to the judicial discourse (House of Commons 2002f, House of Commons 2002g, House of Commons 2002i).

The second rationalist alternative: compliance bargaining in the shadow of the ECJ

Did the UK shift into minimalist compliance in 2002 to fulfil its share of a compromise reached with the European Commission in the shadow of the judicial discourse? Did informal compliance bargaining take place and was it successful? The major bargaining chip of the European Commission is to withdraw cases during ongoing judicial discourses. On the other side, the bargaining power of the UK would have been more limited, because the number of possible concessions was limited. In the nitrates case, the UK could have offered to shift quickly into compliance instead of continuing the nitrates violations for one to two or even three additional years, thereby saving on domestic implementation costs at the expense of the environment and possibly also the public health. The government in London might indeed have calculated that a compromise with the European Commission that avoided an ECJ ruling, which might possibly be more demanding than a compromise with the Commission, was strategically preferable. One indicator underlying this assertion is that the UK explicitly stated during the early stages of the judicial discourse that they had initially misunderstood the nitrates directive concerning all three contested issues (e.g. Advocate General 2000: 19). For example, the UK stated: 'The United Kingdom Government accepts that in the present case the submissions of the Commission are well founded (...) it had initially interpreted the scope of the Directive differently (...) and that the transposition of the Directive into national law was based on that interpretation' (European Court of Justice 2000a: 20). Moreover, the UK promised to change its policies: 'It also sets out the implementing measures which it has adopted or are in the process of being adopted in order for it to comply with its obligations under the Directive' (European Court of Justice 2000a: 20). However, even if compliance bargaining did take place between the parties, it certainly did not produce a compromise to which the parties lived up. Despite its promises, the UK did not initiate legal changes during or shortly after the judicial discourse ended. Similarly, the European Commission did not withdraw a single complaint prior to the ECJ judgment. Hence, compliance bargaining in the shadow of the ECJ was not causally responsible for the UK's shift into minimalist compliance in 2002.

The judgment

On 7 December 2000, the ECJ issued a judgment according to which the UK was deemed to have incorrectly transposed the nitrates directive concerning all issues at stake (European Court of Justice 2000a). The ECJ followed the argumentation of the European advocate concerning the application of the directive to all surface water and groundwater and concerning the action programmes to combat and prevent nitrate pollution (European Court of Justice 2000a: 23, 26). With regard to the second issue, the designation of NVZs, the ECJ ruled that the UK approach violated the nitrates directive, but based its legal reasoning on different grounds than the ones of the European advocate, who had applied an overly narrow technique of legal reasoning to convincingly solve the interpretational problem II (European Court of Justice 2000a: 23).[5]

[5] Since the interpretational problem was rather complex, the ECJ moved up in the hierarchy of judicial methods and used the broader systematic method of judicial reasoning, putting Annexe I (§§A1 and A2) into the context of Article 3 II (European Court of Justice 2000a: 23). On this basis, the Court concluded that member states have to designate NVZs as required and specified by Article 3 I and the wording of Annexe I of the nitrates directive, which the UK failed to do.

Did this judgment differentially empower environmental organizations, the most important societal norm advocates, at the expense of the agricultural lobby and farmers? Was this instrument effective in fostering a policy shift resembling minimalist compliance in 2002? With its binding judgment, the ECJ provided the preconditions essential for successful bottom-up campaigns in issuing an authoritative interpretation on what the nitrates directive was (not) about and in reducing the complexity of the issues at stake. The judgment also increased the publicity, but did so only to a limited extent. While British newspapers continually and frequently reported on nitrates and water pollution, the ECJ ruling itself received very little attention (*Belfast Newsletter* 2001, *Express* 2001a, *Farmers Guardian* 2000, *Western Morning News* (Plymouth) 2001).

In this context, shaming strategies had limited prospects of successfully inducing minimalist compliance. The judgment did not resonate well with domestic norms. The former rested on an environmental-based nitrates approach while the latter focused on safeguarding public health and regarded a nitrates policy aiming at environmental protection as an unnecessary costly burden for farmers. In particular after the ECJ ruling, the agricultural sector feared being exposed to immense implementation costs: 'The total cost to farmers could be up to GBP 2.9 billion, and the overall cost of the directive is estimated to be up to GBP 9.2 billion. George Dunn, chief executive of the Tenant Farmers' Association, described the predicted additional costs, of up to GBP 175 per hectare, as "frightening"' (*Western Morning News* (Plymouth) 2001).[6] Farmers' associations demanded financial support schemes for members affected by the nitrates directive. The public, as well as politicians from both major parties, acknowledged a need to financially support workers in the agricultural sector, whether in the context of the BSE crisis (House of Commons 2002a, House of Commons 2002b, House of Lords 2002), in the context of the foot-and-mouth epidemic (early 2001) (Nerlich 2003, Taylor 2003, Ward, Donaldson and Lowe 2004, Wouter *et al.* 2004), or with regard to action programmes for reducing nitrate pollution (House of Commons 1999b, House of Commons 2000b, House of Commons

[6] Farmers were organized in the National Farmers Union (NFU) and, together with the fertilizer industry (British Agrochemical Association – BAA), opposed the nitrates directives, because they associated high compliance costs with the directives (Ward *et al.* 1993: 8–11). In particular, they feared restrictions of fertilizers and pesticides and, in turn, decreased agricultural production and lower sales numbers, as well as a potential policy shifts towards the polluters-pay principle (European Court of Justice 1999b: 15–18, House of Commons 1994f).

2000d, *Western Mail* 2001).[7] Against this background, environmental organizations were inactive and did not shame the government into compliance directly after the ECJ ruling.

More than one year later, the Royal Society for the Protection of Birds criticized the Labour government for its 'half-hearted attempt to implement the directive' and its failure to comply with the ECJ ruling (*Financial Times* 2002b). During this period, which coincided with a second reasoned opinion (Art. 228 ECT) of the European Commission, the government launched consultations with farmers and stakeholders on how to implement the nitrates directive. Was this policy adaptation due to effective shaming? The agricultural and in particular the fertilizer industry preferred a narrow approach and emphasized high implementation costs (*Guardian* 2002b). On the contrary, water companies together with Water UK supported a demanding nitrate approach, in order to forestall ever-increasing water charges stemming from the necessity to clean up water from nitrates (*Guardian* 2002a). As the consultation process came to an end in 2002, the UK designated 55 per cent instead of 80 per cent or 100 per cent of the territory as NVZs (*Guardian* 2002b). This did not reflect a compromise, which the government constructed in response to successful shaming campaigns of environmental organizations. Firstly, there was only one attempt to shame the government into compliance, while most of the environmental organizations remained inactive. Secondly, even if there were more shaming campaigns, they were likely to fail due to the unfavourable domestic context. Firstly, public debates were still dominated by farmers' associations and their concerns about implementation costs (*Farmers Guardian* 2002b, *Financial Times* 2002b). Secondly, the media coverage increased after the second reasoned opinion, but British newspapers overwhelmingly opposed a demanding nitrates approach (*Aberdeen Press* 2002b, *Daily Telegraph* 2001, *Farmers Guardian* 2002a, *Sunday Times* 2002b, *Western Morning News* (Plymouth) 2002). Thirdly, due to BSE and the foot-and-mouth epidemic, public opinion strongly sympathized with farmers (House of Commons 2002a, House of Commons 2002b, House of Lords 2002, House of Lords 2001a).[8] Hence, while solidarity with farmers

[7] Environmental activists, such as Friends of the Earth, WWF, the Royal Society for the Protection of Birds, English Nature and governmental agencies, such as the Environment Agency, the Farming and Rural Conservation Agency and Water Voice, promoted high water quality and environmental protection (Maloney 2001: 637).

[8] 'The government has delayed taking action for years because it feared a backlash from the farming industry, which has been hit by a succession of crises, culminating in last year's foot-and-mouth epidemic (...) Mr Meacher added that the government was "not wishing to bash the agricultural community (...) We are trying to do it in a manner which is the least oppressive and the most co-operative"' (*Financial Times* 2002a).

was widely considered as appropriate, there was no strongly institutionalized norm of appropriateness on the basis of which the government could have been shamed for non-compliance. In this context of high domestic implementation costs, the shaming campaign was ineffective. Consequently, the government did not emphasize the environmental merits of the nitrates directive and the 2002 regulation, but made it clear that they would have preferred their old nitrates approach (House of Commons 2002b: 472, House of Commons 2002c, House of Commons 2002g, Select Committee on Environment 2002a: 552, Select Committee on Environment 2003b: 14). Rather than giving in to domestic shaming endeavours and defending policy changes in a window dressing manner as the appropriate thing to do, the government and DEFRA explained to their non-compliance constituency that their minimalist policy changes of 2002 were the fault of the ECJ and were necessary to avoid the possibility of sanctions to the tune of to £50 million a year (e.g. *Daily Telegraph* 2002, *Financial Times* 2002a, *Financial Times* 2002a, *Financial Times* 2002a, *Guardian* 2002b).

In sum, directly after the ECJ judgment and in the subsequent two years, the societal context was characterized by broad public scepticism towards the nitrates directive and a lack of a norm of appropriateness, to which compliance with the nitrates directive could have been linked and against which non-compliance could be shamed as inappropriate. Against this background, it is not surprising that environmental organizations invested so few of their resources in shaming campaigns and that the one endeavour to shame the government into compliance, by the Royal Society for the Protection of Birds, was a failure.

The domestic environment was also unfavourable to effective reframing endeavours. With the judgment, the ECJ reduced the complexity of the issues at stake and summarized the judicial arguments. This empowered societal norm proponents, who could use these ideational resources to refocus domestic debates. The World Wide Fund for Nature (WWF) aimed to restructure the debate on water pollution in the UK in more general environmental terms. To this end, they stressed the merits of sustainable agriculture and 'issued a six-point rural recovery challenge to the United Kingdom Government to halt the environmental decline in the countryside' (*Belfast Newsletter* 2001). However the WWF was unsuccessful. In 2001 and 2002, the cost frame was strongly institutionalized and constantly re-invoked through references to farming catastrophes (BSE, foot-and-mouth disease). The public and both major parties perceived farmers as the victims of agricultural crises (House of Commons 2002b, House of Lords 2001a, Nerlich 2003, Taylor 2003). Moreover, the public health approach, on which the narrow interpretation of the nitrates directive rested, was deep-seated in the UK (House of Commons 2001c, House of Commons 2002a). Hence, a nitrates prevention policy which exclusively focused on drinking water resonated well with the public health and the cost frames (House of Commons 2002b, House of Commons 2002c). Conversely, a more demanding interpretation of the nitrates directive which included all fresh water and groundwater was not compatible with the cost-concerns of the government, farmers, the fertilizer industry, and the broader public and did not fit prominent public health and agricultural approaches (e.g. House of Commons 2000b, House of Commons 2000d, House of Lords 2001a). At the same time, alternative focal ideas, to which an environmental nitrate approach could have been linked for successful promotion, were absent. Hence, the WWF did not succeed in reframing the domestic debate and the government as well as DEFRA maintained their non-compliance policy preferences for a minimalist nitrates approach (House of Commons 2002b: 472, House of Commons 2002c, House of Commons 2002g, Select Committee on Environment 2002a: 552, Select Committee on Environment 2003b: 14).

In conclusion, in line with the shaming and the reframing hypotheses, the ECJ judgment did not end the norm violation. Rather than being pushed into compliance from below, the government introduced the nitrates regulations of 2002 against severe domestic resistance.

The sanction-threat

Since the two judicial compliance instruments, judicial discourses and judgments, were ineffective, sanction-threats came into play. Did they finally end non-compliance and if so through which of the two causal pathways?

The rationalist hypothesis: credible sanction-threats increase non-compliance costs

The rationalist version of the sanction-threat hypothesis expects that governments will strategically adapt to rising external non-compliance costs and pursue a policy resembling a minimalist form of compliance that avoids punishment through the ECJ. This presupposes that sanction-threats are credible which, in turn, depends on the likelihood that a government will be penalized during their incumbency (a second reasoned opinion) as well as on whether the sanctions are sufficiently high to act as a deterrent (a serious infringement according to the Commission).

In the immediate aftermath of the ECJ judgment, sanction-threats were not looming. Since the European Commission did not introduce any measures towards enforcement, the British government introduced no preparatory steps towards legal change (House of Commons 2000b,

House of Commons 2001c). The Commission reacted to continued non-compliance by sending a letter of formal notice in autumn 2001 (*Daily Telegraph* 2001, *Express* 2001b). While this increased external non-compliance costs, a second ECJ judgment issuing financial penalties was still two procedural steps and several months or even a year away (House of Commons 2001c, House of Commons 2002b: 426). In addition, the European Commission had not publicized its calculations on the amount of the daily penalty and the lump sum. The government was therefore uncertain about whether the future sanction-threat would be a deterrent, and still would have had time to react to the sanction-threat once the Commission announced the concrete amount. Hence, the hypothesis expects that the UK would not yield and not shift into compliance in response to the second letter of formal notice. However, the UK did not remain inactive, but began to prepare for a consultation process with farmers on the designation of NVZs. Although this endeavour was publicly labelled as a preparatory step towards legal change (House of Commons 2001c, House of Lords 2001b), it delayed domestic legal changes even further. The ECJ judgment had already specified the content and scope of the nitrates directive so that consultation with farmers was not necessary in order to transpose the directive. Moreover, the consultations were useless, as the responsible ministry altered the available options during the ongoing process without providing farmers with an update (Department of the Environment 2002c).[9] Since the consultations were neither required nor subsequently pursued, this endeavour was mere window-dressing and not a serious reaction to a credible threat of sanctions.

The situation changed after the European Commission sent a second reasoned opinion to the UK and proposed a daily penalty of £135,000 in May 2002 (*Financial Times* 2002a, *Financial Times* 2002b, House of Commons 2002d). This sanction-threat was instantly credible because the government could be penalized while still in office and because the amount was sufficiently high, due to the seriousness of the infringement. According to at least five indicators, the European Commission considered the violation of the nitrates directive as relatively serious. While persistent non-compliance of the UK did not impede the four fundamental freedoms of goods, services, capital and persons, it harmed human health

[9] After consultations were completed in summer 2002, DEFRA opted for a narrow option (55% designation), which was not consulted upon with farmers at all. DEFRA did so even though farmers and other stakeholders had opted for 100% designation (Department of the Environment 2002c) and thereby introduced a narrow approach through the backdoor.

as well as the environment. Secondly, the size of the affected population was very high, including the general public and farmers. Thirdly, the financial sums involved in the infringement were relatively high: farmers' associations stated that 'the overall cost of the directive is estimated to be up to GBP 9.2 billion' (*Western Morning News* (Plymouth) 2001). Fourthly, the UK could realize financial gains from not complying with the judgment, since the broad use of fertilizers improved agricultural production while a demanding nitrates policy would have imposed considerable direct and indirect costs on the fertilizer and the water industries, as well as on farmers (House of Commons 1998c: 474, Ward *et al.* 1993: 10). Fifthly, the nitrates case constituted a serious infringement because water policy is a sector in which the UK repeatedly violated EU laws. Hence, the sanction-threat hypothesis would expect the UK to quickly shift into a minimalist form of compliance in order to avoid penalties. In line with this, the government immediately reacted to this threat:

> We are subject to infraction proceedings if we do not implement it in full, and non-compliance fines could run as high as £135,000 a day (...) Those constraints are unavoidable, and we have delayed implementation as long as possible (...) we now risk fines and therefore have to act' (Mr Meacher, the Minister for the Environment, in House of Commons 2002d: 906)

Thus, the credible sanction-threat which was looming large increased non-compliance costs. In response, the government and the lead ministry adapted their strategic cost–benefit calculations and a minimalist move towards compliance became more beneficial than continuing non-compliance. The Blair government no longer claimed that the nitrates directive applied exclusively to drinking water in 2002, but still emphasized that compliance would be very costly (House of Commons 2002b: 426, Select Committee on Environment 2002a: 552; Select Committee on Environment 2003b: 14). Moreover, the normative ideas underlying the initial non-compliance interests of the government were not changed by the sanction-threat. Hence, they did not suddenly consider nitrates reduction as a means of environmental protection, but rather continued to apply public health and cost approaches to nitrates issues (House of Commons 2002f, House of Commons 2002h). Also, government officials never mentioned the appropriateness, righteousness, or scientific correctness of a demanding nitrate approach or of the fight against nitrates-based environmental pollution in their public speeches (Department of the Environment 2002b, House of Commons 2001c, House of Commons 2002b, House of Commons 2002c).

In response to the deterrent sanction-threat, the UK adapted strategic positions and quickly issued the 2002 nitrates regulations, which had originally been scheduled for at least a year later (being based on the autumn survey results) (Department of the Environment 2002c, House of Commons 2002d). The 2002 regulations had a broader applicatory scope than those of 1996, and included all fresh water and groundwater, regardless of whether it was intended for human consumption (House of Commons 2002g). This policy change did not reflect a comprehensive, but only a minimalist transposition of the ECJ judgment,[10] because the UK introduced a less demanding nitrate approach through the backdoor. Against the advice gained during the consultation with farmers to designate 100 per cent of the territory as NVZs, the government opted only for 55 per cent (Department of the Environment 2002c, House of Commons 2001c). This saved governmental expenditure arising from the various financial support schemes for affected farmers, but pre-empted a thorough environmental protection approach (e.g. House of Commons 2001c, House of Commons 2002d). Moreover, the 2002 regulations, the NVZ designations and the action programmes all entailed a number of ambiguities. For example, they introduced considerable uncertainty as to which territories were subject to action programmes and codes of good agricultural conduct (House of Commons 2002d). Hence, the sanction-threat fostered a policy shift towards minimalist compliance once sanctions were looming because the Commission issued a second reasoned opinion, and acted as a deterrent, because the proposed penalty was high due to the high seriousness of the norm violation. In order to justify these minimalist but still unwanted legal changes to their non-compliance constituency and to avoid electoral sanctions ex-post facto and losses in reputation, the government repeatedly referred to the Court judgment and sanction-threats, thus shifting the blame for unpopular policy changes to the ECJ (House of Commons 2002f, House of Commons 2002g, House of Commons 2002i): 'The Department's current proposals to reduce nitrate pollution from agriculture arise from the requirement to comply with the European Court of Justice judgment that implementation of the Nitrates Directive is currently incomplete in the UK' (House of Commons 2002e).

In sum, as expected by the rationalist hypothesis, the government adapted its strategic policy preferences and introduced a policy reform

[10] 'Only "minimal" new measures to tackle nitrate pollution in England will be introduced because the farming industry is in bad financial shape, Michael Meacher, the environment minister, announced yesterday. "Nitrate vulnerable zones" to cut pollution in water supplies will cover just 55 per cent of the country, rather than the 100 or 80 per cent discussed previously by ministers' (*Financial Times* 2002b)

that resembled minimalist compliance once sanction-threats were looming and became deterrent.

The constructivist hypothesis: sanction-threats empower pro-compliance ministries

The constructivist alternative predicts that sanction-threats emphasize the inappropriateness of norm violations and thereby differentially empower lead ministries, which fosters a shift into comprehensive compliance if the lead ministry preferred compliance from the outset, but was prevented from proposing or passing demanding policies by domestic veto players. Yet the explanatory value of this theoretical claim is limited. In the nitrates case, MAFF and later on DEFRA, as the lead ministries, had been against a demanding and costly nitrates approach throughout the infringement procedure.[11] The same holds true for other ministries involved in nitrates issues.[12] Hence, the UK did not persist in the nitrates violation until 2002 because political veto players prevented a shift into more demanding policies. Instead, non-compliance prevailed because it allowed the government to save considerable implementation costs and was in line with substantial policy ideas of the government which focused on public health rather than environmental aspects of nitrates policies. Since the necessary condition for differential empowerment of lead ministries was absent, the constructivist sanction-threat hypothesis cannot account for ideational and policy shifts in the nitrates sector.

Sanction-threats at work: the UK nitrates case

The nitrates directive combats the over-use of fertilizers and protects the environment. Although the legal misfit was lower in the nitrates than in the drinking water case, the UK had strong and rigid compliance-averse policy interests. The government and especially DEFRA were highly sensitive to the problems of farmers and assisted them financially in NVZs (House of Commons 2000c, House of Commons 2002d). Similar to the UK collective redundancy, the UK equal access and the UK drinking water cases, the European Commission appealed to the ECJ for action. Before the Court, the parties argued over issues on the scope (drinking water vs.

[11] See also Department of the Environment 2002b, *Financial Times* 2002b, House of Commons 1994e, House of Commons 1995c, House of Commons 1999b, House of Commons 2000b, House of Commons 2000d, House of Commons 2001b, House of Commons 2001d.

[12] See also House of Commons 2001c, House of Commons 2002b: 426, House of Commons 2002c, House of Commons 2002f, Select Committee on Environment 2002a: 552; Select Committee on Environment 2003b: 14.

all fresh water and groundwater, designation of NZV) and content of the European directive (action programmes to combat nitrate pollution in NVZ). The UK did not actively engage in the judicial discourse and the advocates did not commonly apply judicial methods matching the interpretational scope of the problems at hand. As a consequence, the judicial discourse remained ineffective. The judgment was also unsuccessful. Unlike in the British equal access case, the societal context was not conducive to shaming campaigns, because the judgment did not resonate with already institutionalized norms. In addition, in the nitrates case – as in the UK drinking water case – the broad public opposition to a demanding interpretation of the directive was responsible for high domestic non-compliance benefits. Unlike the drinking water case, however, the context did not become conducive to successful societal reframing strategies. The public health and cost frames were strongly institutionalized, reinforced each other, and were repeatedly re-invoked through external farming-related crises. In this ideational context, nitrates prevention was considered as subordinate to costs and public health issues, while a demanding interpretation which included also environmental aspects did not fit either of the frames. Hence, reframing failed and non-compliance continued.

The instrument of financial penalties came into play, but it did not differentially empower a pro-compliance ministry vis-à-vis domestic veto players. Instead, in line with the rationalist sanction-threat hypothesis, the last compliance instrument of the ECJ fostered ideational and legal change into minimalist compliance. Due to the UK's complete inaction after the ECJ judgment, the sanction-threat began gradually to loom. Once the Commission issued a second reasoned opinion in spring 2002 and proposed a financial penalty that reflected the seriousness of the norm violation, non-compliance ended. The UK adapted strategic positions and quickly transposed the Court ruling with a series of regulations. While the 2002 nitrates regulations included all waters and not only water intended for human consumption, the designation of NVZs as the territory on which action programmes were applied was minimized (Department of the Environment 2002b, *Financial Times* 2002b). As expected, the 2002 regulations resembled a minimalist form of compliance.

In essence, the nitrates case exemplifies that the ECJ's toolbox is sufficient to induce compliance even against the strong will of member states' governments and domestic actors. Sanction-threats are a last resort and are seldom evoked but they are effective once high daily penalties are proposed and are likely to be implemented during the incumbency of a government. In such instances, it is the government in office and not their successors that have to bear the costs of continued non-compliance. In order to avoid these costs, the UK finally abandoned their norm violation and introduced policy changes – even against the opposition of the domestic constituency.

6.II The German environmental impact assessment case

The environmental impact assessment directive (EIA, 85/337) is part of the European environmental policy. Its aim was to prevent environmental damage as a result of construction processes and sites. The EIA directive prescribed mandatory procedures, according to which construction projects may only be approved if they do not harm the environment. The European directive followed an integrated environmental protectionist approach, covering all environmental media (air, water and soil) at once. The EIA was alien to German environmental law (Liefferink and Jordan 2004: 37). The latter was highly fragmented and based on media specific approaches (Knill 2001: 144, 147, Wurzel 2004: 103). In addition, German law relied on quality aims, while the EIA was based on procedural regulations (Bundestag 1994b, Bundestag 1994h). Due to these mismatches, the directive created a demand for legal change, to which the Kohl government was reluctant to respond. Sentiments against the EIA were, firstly, rooted in the belief that German media-specific environmental law was superior to European environmental approaches (Bundestag 1989c: 13404, Bundestag 1993d, Héritier, Knill and Mingers 1996).[13] Secondly, German industry strongly opposed the directive because they anticipated high costs and because of perceived negative effects for the international competitiveness of the German economy (e.g. *Süddeutsche Zeitung* 1994b, *Süddeutsche Zeitung* 1994c). Thirdly, the ministerial bureaucracy was organized along the different environmental media and disliked the directive since it required institutional reforms to cope with an integrated approach (Bundestag 1989b: 9231, 9237, 9239).

The government was sensitive to these concerns (Bundestag 1989b: 9221, 9231, Bundestag 1999a, *TAZ* 1994, *TAZ* 1995). The federal environmental minister, Klaus Töpfer, constructed a compromise between 'EC law and environmental necessities on the one hand and practical implementation-related considerations on the other hand' (Bundestag 1989b: 9239,

[103] Even the Minister for the Environment, Klaus Töpfer, stated that 'the EU falls short of German environmental standards. Therefore, EU actions do not constitute calls for action' (Bundestag 1994g: 20625, translation DP).

translation DP). Hence, Germany legally implemented the EIA directive with a two-year delay with the minimalist Umweltverträglichkeitsprüfungsgesetz in 1990 (UVPG). This law allowed German industry to save considerable implementation costs, but did so at the expense of the environment and affected individuals. Moreover, the UVPG violated one of the very aims of the EIA directive as outlined in its preface: 'the disparities between the laws in force in the various Member States with regard to the assessment of the environmental effects of public and private projects may create unfavourable competitive conditions and thereby directly affect the functioning of the common market'. Against this background, the European Commission voiced its suspicion that the German transposition was not fully in line with European law because its narrow applicatory scope thwarted the purpose of the EIA directive almost immediately after Germany introduced the 1990 UVPG. The Kohl government never responded to the reasoned opinion in 1994 and the Commission referred the case to the ECJ in September 1995. On 22 October 1998, the ECJ ruled that the UVPG did not comply with the directive (European Court of Justice 1998).

In the same year, federal elections took place and a Social-Democratic/Green coalition, whose policy interests were already in line with a demanding interpretation of the EIA, came into office. Accordingly, they opted for a demanding comprehensive reform, abolishing the German media-specific environmental approach. An environmental code was planned to completely transpose the EIA, but failed due to lacking competencies. As a result, they kept the deficient UVPG for two years after the ECJ ruling. As a response to continued non-compliance, the Commission applied sanction-threats by sending a reasoned opinion based on Article 228 ECT to Germany in winter 2000/2001.

The pattern of legal changes

Germany initially transposed the EIA directive with the 1990 environmental impact assessment law (UVPG) in 1990. It left the German media-specific environmental approach largely unaltered and restricted the applicatory scope of EIAs. In response to the ECJ judgment, the new Social-Democratic/Green government pursued a comprehensive reform through an environmental code, of which the EIA was set to become an essential part. Yet this law was never passed and non-compliance continued. In 2001, Germany introduced a compound law. It resembled a minimalist form of compliance, since it entailed several ambiguities, mainly arising from overlaps with media-specific environmental laws. Moreover, imprecise procedures, unspecified thresholds and ambivalent measurements opened windows of opportunity for future incomplete or incoherent norm applications in the implementation stage (Bundestag 2001b, Bundestag 2001d: 16071–3, 16076–7).[14]

Table 6.2 Legal changes concerning the EIA in Germany

Date	*Title*	*Initiated by*	*Outcome*
1990	Umweltverträglichkeit-sprüfungsgesetz (UVPG, environmental impact assessment law)	CDU/FDP government	Below the EIA directive, concerning scope and content
1998	Vorschlag für ein Umweltgesetzbuch (UBG) (proposal for an environmental code)	SPD/Green government	More demanding than the EIA directive and the judgment, but the project failed
2001	Artikelgesetz (compound law)	SPD/Green government	Legal transposition of the EIA directive, but various overlaps between legal acts, new and imprecise concepts, complex exceptional clauses

To date, a unitary EIA approach based on a legal framework that encompasses all media is lacking. Because of the remaining legal ambiguities, so far six national court cases have dealt with the applicatory scope of the EIA directive after the compound law entered into force.

The judicial discourse in operation

The discourse between the advocates of both parties lasted from September 1995 until October 1998 and covered six complaints. These were the undue transposition of the directive, failures in notification, incomplete applications after 1988, incorrect transposition of Annexe II, incomplete transposition of Article 5 II and non-application of Article 5 II (European Court of Justice 1998: 9). The first, second, and third issues concerned procedural failures (delayed legal transposition, incomplete notification, incomplete application due to an exceptional period), which the government could not fix after the judgment. In all three instances, the

[14] Although the new law entailed 275 instead of 45 types of projects to which the EIA procedure had to be applied, there were several ambiguities that created loopholes for lax and less costly implementation (DNR 2000: 21). For example, wind farms were defined as having at least three wind turbines and were subject to EIAs. However, due to the federal emission control act, wind farms were in fact only subject to EIAs if at least three turbines belonged to a single carrier (interview state ministry#3, 09–03–05).

European and German advocates did not arrive at consensual norm definitions. The ECJ sided with the Commission, while the Kohl government maintained compliance-averse positions (e.g. compare Federal Government 1995: 2–3 with Bundestag 1999b, Bundestag 2001e). However, Germany did not need to adapt policies in response to the judicial discourse, or after the judgment, since it would have been impossible to correct delayed transpositions or incomplete notifications in hindsight. Also, the issue of whether the introduction of a transitional period was in fact legal or violated the EIA directive lost its importance afterwards since the period had already ended (in 1995) at the time of the ECJ judgment (1998) so that no further legal changes were required. Therefore, the following discussions focus exclusively on the fourth and fifth issue at stake, for which changes in the domestic legal order were important.

Judicial discourse: ideational entrapment or threats of reputational losses?

Scope of application, incorrect legal transposition of Annexe II

The German 1990 law on the environmental impact assessment (UVPG) enumerated construction projects for which impact assessments were required before permissions could be granted. Many classes of projects mentioned in Annexe II of the EIA directive were not part of the UVPG. This considerably reduced compliance costs and put German industry at a competitive advantage at the expense of the environment and of other member states. Against this background, the Commission accused Germany of severely restricting the applicatory scope of the EIA. In the three years of the judicial discourse, the German and the European advocate applied several judicial methods of interpretation to substantiate their claims on the status of Annexe II as either obligatory (Commission) or voluntary (Germany).

Germany considered the application areas out of Annexe II of the EIA directive as voluntary and excluded some 'classes of projects' from the obligation to conduct environmental impact assessments before permitting construction to take place. Thus, the German advocate applied the narrow wording method to Article 4 II and to Annexe II of the EIA directive (European Court of Justice 1998: 36–7). Annexe II explicitly differentiated between classes and projects, and listed twelve 'classes of projects' in which single projects were incorporated as subtypes (European Court of Justice 1998: 36). Since the wording of the annexe did not specify the status of the classes and projects in the enumerative list as being obligatory or voluntary, the German advocate applied the wording instrument also to article 4 II of the directive (European Court of Justice 1998: 37). It states

> Projects of the classes listed in Annexe II shall be made subject to an assessment, in accordance with Articles 5 to 10, *where Member States consider that their characteristics do require*. To this end Member States may inter alia specify certain types of projects as being subject to an assessment or may establish the criteria and/or thresholds necessary to determine which of the projects of the classes listed in Annexe II are to be subject to an assessment in accordance with Articles 5 to 10. (Emphasis added)

Article 4 II allowed member states to define projects and attribute certain assessment procedures to them, which in turn, permitted the exclusion of pre-defined projects from the application of EIA procedures. Based on this systematic line of judicial reasoning, Germany put Article 4 into the context of Annexe II of the EU directive and concluded that environmental impact procedures are not obligatory for the projects listed in Annexe II, but are subject to member states' discretion (European Court of Justice 1998: 37).

The European advocate also applied the broad directive-immanent systematic instrument in addition to the wording one (European Court of Justice 1998: 34). Accordingly, Article 2 I specified an obligatory assessment duty. Like the German advocate, the European advocate emphasized that the wording of Article 4 II EIA allowed for applicatory choices of member states. Since Article 4 itself gave no indication of which options should be subsumed under the directive, the European advocate applied the broader directive-immanent systematic method of legal reasoning and compared the structures of Part I and II of Article 4, referring to Annexe I and II respectively (European Court of Justice 1998: 39–43). Annexe II was very similar to Annexe I, and, therefore, had to be obligatory. Hence Annexe II was not an 'annexe a la carte', which supported the claim that Article 4 II could not be interpreted as a general exceptional clause.

The advocates of the parties both actively engaged in the judicial discourse, analysed the same legal acts, and shared the wording method. However, this narrow instrument of legal interpretation did not allow for the development of a consensual norm definition. Due to the high complexity of the interpretational problem (unspecified concepts, overlapping rules, different relevant provisions and complex exceptional clauses), the wording method could lead to two different conclusions, depending on which article (2 or 4) was given priority. It allowed one to defend either restricted (primacy of the exceptional clause, Article 4) or broad applicatory scopes (primacy of Article 2). Hence, the high complexity of the contested issue required a broader method of judicial reasoning than the narrow wording instrument. The advocates of the parties both applied the broader systematic method of interpretation. However, they came to two different conclusions because they compared different aspects of the very complex directive with each other. In this sense, they argued at cross purposes. Since they did not use the even broader directive immanent teleological or the very broad historical method of interpretation, the parties failed to develop a consensual norm interpretation.

As a consequence, the judicial discourse did not promote compliance. In line with this expectation, even two years after the ECJ judgment, former members of government from the CDU and FDP still argued against the appropriateness and virtue of the EIA directive (Bundestag 2001c, Bundestag 2001d, Bundestag 2001f). Instead of favouring a demanding reading of the EIA, they pointed to the high investments and countervailing economic aims (e.g. Bundestag 1998d, Bundestag 1999a, Bundestag 2000d, Bundestag 2001c, Bundestag 2001d). The FDP even claimed that financial penalties were preferable to sanctions due to the enormous anticipated compliance costs for the economy (Ausschuss für Umwelt 2001b: 124). The Kohl government neither changed their policy ideas nor strategically adapted their rhetoric in response to the judicial discourse and consequently did not change legal acts during their incumbency.

Informational requirements

In order to assess whether projects harm air, water and soil and pass the EIA, the collection and distribution of relevant data was deemed crucial. To this end, Article 5 of the directive regulated the informational requirements associated with environmental impact assessment procedures. The Commission and the Kohl government dissented on whether the UVPG violated this provision. The debate centred on the interpretation of §6 II UVPG that specified what information project-organizers must provide before impact assessments can be carried out.

Initially, the Commission claimed that the UVPG violated the informational requirements of project organizers as outlined by Article 5 I of the EIA directive (Advocate General 1998a: 67–9, European Court of Justice 1998: 48, 49). This was important, since insufficient information could easily affect the outcomes of impact assessments and bias them to the disadvantage of environmental protection. The European advocate applied the wording method of judicial interpretation to the UVPG and argued that the 'second sentence of Paragraph 6(2) of the UVPG states that those provisions are applicable only if the information listed in subparagraphs 3 and 4 is not defined in detail by a statutory provision' (European Court of Justice 1998: 48). Hence, the European advocate concluded that the UVPG violated the EIA 'by failing to lay down a general requirement in respect of the information to be supplied under the Directive' (European Court of Justice 1998: 49).

The German advocate did not agree with his European colleague and argued that the German UVPG used the discretion allowed by Article 5 of the directive,[15] which specifies informational requirements (Advocate General 1998a: 70). More concretely, the German advocate claimed that §4 together with §6 UVGP regulate data collection and dissemination requirements in line with Article 5 of the EIA directive (European Court of Justice 1998: 50). The interpretational issue at stake was highly complex, not least because it included a series of different articles and paragraphs with many cross-references. Hence, the wording instrument of judicial reasoning alone would have been too narrow to provide a coherent interpretation of whether the UVPG introduced backdoors for EIAs based on fewer data on the project and its impact on air, water and soil, since §4 and 6 UVPG allowed for different conclusions if they were not read in conjunction. Accordingly, the German advocate applied the directive-immanent systematic method of reasoning: while §6 UVGP opened doors for other legal acts to specify which data requirements the body responsible for a project has to fulfil before impact assessment procedures start, the advocate highlighted that §4 UVGP specified the relationship between the UVPG and other German laws and clarified that 'if the requirements laid down by such statutory provisions fall short of those of the UVPG, then the latter take precedence' (European Court of Justice 1998: 50). Hence, based on the combined wording and directive-immanent systematic interpretation that connects all relevant paragraphs and puts them into the context of the EIA directive, Germany argued that the 1990 UVPG did not violate the European directive.

Neither of the judicial discourse hypotheses would expect a consensual norm interpretation to emerge from the judicial discourse on whether Germany indeed requested as much data from builders as demanded by

[15] Article 5 stated: 'In the case of projects which, pursuant to Article 4, must be subjected to an environmental impact assessment in accordance with Articles 5 to 10, Member States shall adopt the necessary measures to ensure that the developer supplies in an appropriate form the information specified in Annexe III in as much as: (a) the Member States consider that the information is relevant to a given stage of the consent procedure and to the specific characteristics of a particular project or type of project and of the environmental features likely to be affected; (b) the Member States consider that a developer may reasonably be required to compile this information having regard inter alia to current knowledge and methods of assessment.'

the European directive. The advocates of the parties both applied the wording method of judicial reasoning, but this narrow device did not match the broad interpretational scope of the contested issue. While Germany also used the somewhat broader systematic method in order to put the three central rules into the context of one another, the European advocate did not do so, but did also not apply an additional broad method. Hence, the parties stopped talking at cross purposes towards the end of the judicial discourse. The ECJ joined the German line of argumentation and, in turn, declared that the UVPG did not violate the directive in this regard (European Court of Justice 1998: 53). Since the ECJ sided with Germany, there was no need for further ideational and legal changes in this regard. As expected, members from the CDU and the FDP did not change their policy ideas during the judicial discourse and did not opt for broader and more demanding informational requirements later on (compare Bundestag 1989b with Bundestag 2001c, Bundestag 2001e). Moreover, the Kohl government did not even undertake first steps to initiate legal changes during the three years of the judicial discourse.

The second rationalist alternative: compliance bargaining in the shadow of the ECJ

The judicial discourse did not argumentatively resolve the German EIA case. Did bargaining as an alternative to arguing foster compliance? In a nutshell, the answer is no. The European Commission did not drop any of the issues at stake, not even the ones that no longer required any adjustments from Germany, since a failure of timely notification cannot be undone. The same can be observed for Germany which did not introduce first measurements to comply with the EIA directive according to the interpretation of the European Commission. Hence, even if compliance bargaining did take place, it did not produce a compromise to which the parties mutually adjusted.

The judgment and societal campaigns

In its judgment of 1998, the ECJ authoritatively stated that Germany had violated the EIA directive. The Court emphasized that the German UVPG incorrectly transposed the directive in restricting its applicatory scope though considering the classes of projects listed in Annexe II as voluntary rather than obligatory (European Court of Justice 1998: 45–6). Concerning the other issue at stake, the informational requirements for conducting impact assessment procedures properly, the ECJ joined the German line of argumentation and declared that the UVPG did not violate the directive in this regard (European Court of Justice 1998: 53).

Thus, the judgment clarified that there was a demand for domestic change. The new SPD/Green government introduced minimalist legal adaptations in 2001 and broadened the applicatory scope of the environmental impact assessment procedures to include all projects as specified in Annexe II of the directive. Did the ECJ judgment empower societal compliance proponents who pushed the Schröder government into minimalist compliance?

Prior to the ECJ judgment, environmental organizations, such as BUND, NABU, Gesellschaft für Umweltrecht, Deutsche Umwelthilfe, DNR, or Greenpeace, only had limited incentives to push the government into compliance, since they were organized alongside media-specific lines and specialized on EIA matters dealing with air, water and soil at once (e.g. Börzel 2006, interview organized interests#4, 08–02–05). While the compliance constituency was fragmented, norm opponents were many and highly organized. Almost all sectors of German industry opposed the directive due to expected implementation costs and argued that the EIA would bring about negative effects on the international competitiveness of German firms.

With its 1998 judgment, the ECJ created publicity, diffused new ideas and provided an authoritative norm definition (e.g. *Süddeutsche Zeitung* 2000b). This strengthened the ideational resources of environmental organizations, whereas industry still strongly opposed the EIA but had increasing difficulties in backing up their opposition with legitimate arguments (see also BDI 2005: 17, Fürst 2004: 160).

Nevertheless, successful shaming or reframing campaigns were unlikely. Pushing the government into compliance from below was difficult for two reasons. Firstly, the judgment on the cross-media EIA did not fit well with the German sectoral environmental law that deals with water, soil and air issues separately rather than in an integrated approach (Knill 2001: 144, 147, Liefferink and Jordan 2004: 37, Wurzel 2004: 103). Secondly, the Schröder government had turned into a forerunner and no longer discussed environmental issues exclusively in media-specific terms. The new SPD/Green government was committed to complying with the EIA directive in a demanding manner (Trittin 1999, Trittin 2000). The Green party (GP) ensured that a comprehensive reform of the environmental law took place, unifying the formerly sector-specific rules in one comprehensive environmental codebook. The environmental code was to be based on the EIA directive as an integral element and was an important part of the coalition agreement between the SPD and the GP (Bundestag 1998c, Bundestag 1998d, Trittin 1999, Trittin 2000). Hence, the policy ideas of the Schröder government, in general, and of the Green coalition partner, in particular, were already in line with a demanding form of compliance

(Bundesregierung 1999c) so that societal shaming or reframing strategies would have unnecessarily spent scarce resources.

In line with this, environmental organizations did not engage in reframing or shaming campaigns in the immediate period after the ECJ judgment of 1998. Although environmental organizations supported a comprehensive reform of the German environmental law, some bigger and sector-specific organizations were sceptical regarding individual issues, such as the lacking legal standing of environmental organizations as collective actors (Verbandsklage) (BUND für Umwelt und Naturschutz Deutschland 1999, Greenpeace 1999: 2–3, *TAZ* 1999c). Thus, rather than shaping domestic EIA debates and setting high standards in the environmental field, societal activities were rather limited (e.g. interview organized interests#4, 08–02–05).

The environmental code was never realized, most importantly because federal competencies were lacking. In order to complete the comprehensive reform and to unify all environmental laws into one book, a constitutional reform strengthening the environmental competencies of the federal state would have been required in the first place (Bundestag 2001d: 16066). Yet the Länder would not agree to give up some of their competencies. As a consequence, the environmental code project failed, the legal landscape was not altered within two years after the ECJ judgment and non-compliance continued. Although administrators at state and federal levels opposed the integrated approach, the Schröder government still preferred an environmental code (Umweltgesetzbuch, UGB) as a comprehensive time consuming reform over faster and less demanding patchy legal changes (Bundestag 2000a).

The domestic context remained hostile to reframing campaigns. The government still preferred a demanding environmental reform and could not possibly be pushed further along this line, while environmental organizations had no incentives to reframe the debates in media-specific terms in order to prevent a demanding environmental protection policy (Bundesrat 2000: 625, Bundestag 2001d: 16076). The government itself had turned into a reform forerunner. Therefore, shaming campaigns would have had low prospects of success, since threats of reputational losses would have failed to be credible. As in 1998, environmental organizations did not push their government after the environmental code had failed because they preferred a comprehensive reform (UGB) over minimalist changes (e.g. BUND für Umwelt und Naturschutz Deutschland 1999, DNR 2000, Greenpeace 1999, *Süddeutsche Zeitung* 2000b, *Süddeutsche Zeitung* 2001).

Summing up, the ECJ judgment failed to end the norm violation.

Differentially empowered environmental organizations did not induce policy changes through either shaming or reframing campaigns, mainly because of the ideational entrepreneurship of the government, their pro-compliance interests and their far-reaching reform plans.

The sanction-threat

In the German EIA case, the judicial discourse and the judgment had been unsuccessful, so that threats of penalties became important. Did the Schröder government strategically adapt positions to costly sanction threats and, thereby, transform continued non-compliance into minimalist compliance? Alternatively, did the sanction-threat differentially empower the environmental ministry and thereby open doors for a demanding form of compliance?

The rationalist hypothesis: credible sanction-threats increase non-compliance costs

In the first years after the 1998 judgment the shadow of sanctions was not yet highly imminent since the Commission did not introduce a sanction-threat. Germany did not shy away from the ECJ at this early stage but favoured the time-consuming comprehensive environmental code reform, because the possibility that the government could have been punished while still being in office was remote (Bundesregierung 1999d, Trittin 1999). Due to their pro-compliance policy interests, the Schröder government pushed for an environmental code that would have resembled comprehensive compliance, although this would take time and require many resources (Bundestag 1998d, Bundestag 2000d, Trittin 1999, Trittin 2000). Accordingly, cost considerations played no role during the environmental code debates. Instead of highlighting the expenses associated with the directive (as the CDU and the FDP did), the government argued that the EIA and an environmental code were important, scientifically sound and appropriate (Bundesregierung 1999e, Bundesregierung 1999d, Bundestag 1999a, Bundestag 1999b, Bundestag 2000d).

In winter 2000 the environmental code project failed, since a constitutional reform strengthening environmental competencies of the federal state would have been required in the first place (Bundestag 2001d: 16066). As a consequence, the legal landscape was not altered within two years after the ECJ judgment and non-compliance continued. After this became obvious, the European Commission issued a second reasoned opinion based on Article 228 ECT (Bundesrat 2000: 62, Bundestag 2001d: 16067). In spring 2001, the European Commission calculated and proposed €237,600 as a daily penalty to the ECJ (Bundestag 2001d: 16076). This considerably increased the costs for further transposition delays. The sanction threat became a deterrent: not only was it very likely that the government could be penalized during their incumbency, but also the amount of sanctions was considerable because the infringement was serious. Breaching the EIA directive harmed the environment and could have led to irreparable damage. Moreover, the infringement was serious for several reasons. The norm violation involved big financial sums, put the non-complying state and industry into an advantageous positions vis-à-vis the industry of other states, was already part of EU case law and basically affected all economic sectors as well as a large number of the population. Moreover, the infringement was serious because Germany violated one of the very purposes of the EIA directive, the abolishment of unfavourable competitive conditions that affect the functioning of the common market (see also preface of the EIA directive).

Since the Schröder government expected to be penalized during their incumbency, if the norm violation had been further continued, external non-compliance costs exceeded the benefits for further delaying legal changes (e.g. Bundesrat 2000: 624, Bundestag 2001d: 16076). Thus in reaction to the sanction-threat, the government adapted their strategic positions and opted for a minimalist, fast reform in 2001. The compound law (Artikelgesetz) allowed the government to circumvent the financial penalty associated with a second Court judgment, but compromised a demanding but very slow environmental code reform, which the government would have preferred, but which would have required cumbersome, time-consuming constitutional changes before being passed. The Artikelgesetz entailed ambiguities and unspecified concepts and had several overlaps with the still fragmented media-specific environmental law so that numerous deviations from a demanding norm interpretation occurred in the stage of practical implementation.[16] This minimalist legal reform was not in line with the more demanding governmental policy preferences, but prevented the ECJ from imposing penalties. Environmental organizations also did not applaud the new law, since they preferred demanding changes to a minimalist patching-up reform (e.g. BUND für Umwelt und Naturschutz Deutschland 1999, DNR 2000, Greenpeace 1999, *TAZ* 1999b). Moreover, even German industry disliked the compound law, because it quickly brought about implementation costs, while the continuation of the norm violation would have allowed them to save these costs for some additional time. In order to defend the minimalist reform vis-à-vis environmental organizations and industry and

[16] Within the first five years after the Artikelgesetz was passed, already six national court cases dealt with the applicatory scope of the EIA directive.

minimize reputational losses and losses in electoral support of their constituency, the government blamed the ECJ for the minimalist legal changes (Bundesrat 2000: 625, Bundestag 2001d: 16066–7, 16076). The leading environmental ministry repeatedly emphasized that quick adaptations were necessary in order to avoid financial penalties of the ECJ: 'the legislative procedure is under immense time-pressure (...) henceforth we are threatened by considerable financial penalties from the EU Commission. While we debate here, the European Commission decides the question of whether a financial penalty shall be imposed upon the Federal Republic of Germany' (the Minister for the Environment, Mr Trittin, in Bundesrat 2000: 624–5, translation DP).

Although the probability of a second ECJ judgment increased as time went by, the Länder governments in the second chamber (Bundesrat) did not speed up the legislative process (Bundestag 2001d: 16076). The opposition in the Bundestag also opposed the legal changes. FDP members even argued that financial penalties were the lesser of two evils, since compliance expenses for German industry were extraordinary high (Ausschuss für Umwelt 2001b: 124, Bundestag 2001d: 16073). The CDU joined the FDP in warning of comparative disadvantages for German companies in international competition (Ausschuss für Umwelt 2001b: 123–4, Bundestag 2001d: 16072–3). Yet despite this broad political and societal resistance, the government finally managed to quickly shift into a minimalist form of compliance (the compound law – Artikelgesetz) in September 2001 to avoid financial penalties. Thus, three years after the ECJ judgment in 1998, Germany complied with the EIA directive.

The constructivist hypothesis: did sanction-threats empower pro-compliance ministries?

The constructivist alternative to the rationalist sanction-threat hypothesis expects that the latter empowered pro-compliance ministries, but not domestic veto players since the former can highlight how inappropriate the continuation of the norm violation would be and use this as an asset in internal negotiations.

In the German EIA case, the environmental ministry under Mr Trittin from the Green Party was indeed strongly in favour of complying with the European EIA directive. In fact, from the very beginning, the SPD and the GP opted for a more demanding legal transposition than the 1990 UVPG, which they criticized for its scope restrictions, while the CDU and the FDP favoured a less costly EIA approach (Bundesrat 1988: 327, Bundestag 1989b: 9238, Bundestag 1989c: 13398, 13402, Green Party 1991: 2). Only weeks after the ECJ judgment, federal elections brought about a change in government. The Social-Democratic/Green coalition under Chancellor Schröder succeeded the Kohl government in October 1998. Since the CDU and FDP coalition did not introduce steps towards further legal adaptations prior to the ECJ ruling, the following analysis puts emphasis on the environmental code project (1999–2000) and the Artikelgesetz (2000–2001).

The GP wanted to transpose the judgment with a comprehensive reform turning the highly fragmented, media-specific German environmental law into an integrated and coherent approach (Bundesregierung 1999b, Bundesregierung 1999c). To this end, the environmental ministry pursued an environmental code reform (Trittin 1999: 3). The UGB project had high salience and was an important issue in the coalition agreement (Fürst 2004: 160–1, *TAZ* 1999a, compare Ausschuss für Umwelt 2001a, Bundesregierung 1999a, Bundesregierung 2000, Bundestag 2001d). Although they were less enthusiastic about an environmental code than the GP, members of the Social-Democratic coalition partner repeatedly highlighted the righteousness and appropriateness of such an integral environmental approach (e.g. Bundestag 2000c, Bundestag 2001d: 16078). Yet the economic and the transport and traffic ministries were veto players. Because they were sensitive to cost-related concerns of industry they did not fully support the environmental code project (Bundesregierung 2000, *TAZ* 1999a, *TAZ* 1999b, *TAZ* 1999d, *TAZ* 2000). These ministries were not the only political actors against a comprehensive reform as envisaged by the GP and the leading environmental ministry. The CDU and FDP opposed a demanding interpretation of the EIA directive in both chambers. Yet their potential for changing or preventing an environmental code was restricted, since the government acted in concert with the Ministry for the Environment and possessed the majority in the Bundestag. In addition, the SPD/Green governed Länder had the majority in the Bundesrat between November 1998 and October 1999 (35 vs. 16 votes and 18 neutral votes). This constellation prevented party politics in both chambers from blocking or radically changing the environmental code bill effectively. Yet regional concerns facilitated opposition in most of the CDU and SPD Länder governments (interview state ministry#5, 15–03–05).

Although the opposition in the Bundestag, the Bundesrat, and the economic and the transport ministries did not welcome the draft environmental code, none of these actors substantially altered the proposal. Nevertheless, the UGB project was delayed at the federal level and finally failed in winter 1999/2000 (*Süddeutsche Zeitung* 1999, *TAZ* 1999d, Trittin 1999, Trittin 2000). The Bundesrat did not cause a breakdown of the environmental code project, although the opposition of the Länder was often blamed for the maintenance of the highly fragmented media-specific German environmental law (Trittin 2000: 1). The failure was not due to veto players in both chambers, who bargained in several committees for concessions, and tried to delay the legislative process. Rather, the environmental code reform came to a standstill after a substantial shift of discussions towards legal aspects within the federal interior ministry and the ministry of justice (see also Bundesministerium für Umwelt 2005, Bundestag 2001a: 16078). This revealed that the vertical distribution of competencies prohibited a comprehensive environmental law reform altogether (Börzel 2003a: 112, Bundestag 2001a: 16074, 16078). The enactment of the environmental code would have required a constitutional reform shifting water issues from framework competencies into the area of competing competencies (Bundestag 2001a). Yet the Länder refused to give up their competencies on water, prescribed in Article 75 of the constitution (framework competencies) (Trittin 2000: 1). Consequently, the environmental ministry came to realize that the constitutional vertical fragmentation was an insurmountable barrier to comprehensive transposition of the ECJ judgment (Trittin 2000).

In the meantime, the parameters of action changed. The European Commission issued first a second letter of formal notice, followed by a second reasoned opinion. In this context, the government in Berlin basically faced two options. In line with its policy interests, the SPD/Green coalition could have further pursued the UGB project, which would have required further pushing for a constitutional reform. In this regard, they could have used the sanction-threat to highlight that non-compliance was inappropriate and that a constitutional reform of competencies would be necessary to end the norm violation. This would have been in line with the constructivist sanction-threat hypothesis. Alternatively, in line with the rationalist sanction-threat hypothesis, the government could have compromised on the comprehensive reform and opted for a minimalist, but much faster, legal adaptation in order to avoid the looming financial penalties.

Contrary to the expectations of the constructivist version of the hypotheses, the environmental ministry did not become differentially empowered by the sanction-threat, but instead shifted into a minimalist form of compliance. The environmental ministry drafted a minimalist compound law, quickly submitted it to the Bundesrat, and pointed towards its urgency (Mr Trittin, in Bundesrat 2000: 624). In order to speed up the process of legal change, the government also emphasized the threat of financial penalties and of potential external reputational losses within the EU (Mr Trittin in Bundesrat 2000: 625, Bundestag 2001d: 16076). Despite the looming shadow of sanctions, the opposition in the Bundestag strongly opposed the bill on the Artikelgesetz – even though the latter was far less demanding than the (not immediately realizable) environmental code project (Ausschuss für Umwelt 2001b: 124, Bundestag 2001d: 16072–3). Compliance-averse Länder governments reacted to governmental hints of looming financial penalties by arguing that European threats should not lead to careless handling of the issue (e.g. Bavaria, in Bundesrat 2000: 626). Nevertheless, the Bundesrat did not manage to substantively alter or even block the proposed bill of the environmental ministry.[17] In the Bundestag, the CDU and the FDP were also against the compound law because of compliance costs and accompanying comparative disadvantages of German companies in the international economy (Ausschuss für Umwelt 2001b: 123, 124; Bundestag 2001d: 16070). Despite this resistance, the Bundestag finally passed the compound law on 27 June 2001 without considerable delay and, more importantly, without fundamental substantial changes to the governmental draft (Bundestag 2001b: 214).

Hence, the sanction-threat did not differentially empower the environmental ministry to push their preference for a comprehensive reform through the legislative process.

Summary of the German environmental impact assessment case

As in the German equal access and in the German foreign workers cases, the ECJ could not facilitate comprehensive compliance with the judicial discourse in the EIA case. For one of the two issues at stake, the advocates of the two parties failed to develop consensual norm definitions.

[17] After the compound bill was sent to the Bundesrat, the Länder had initiated no fewer than 350 proposals for changes before December 2000 (Bundesrat 2000: 626). A lack of coordination of the proposals in the Bundesrat severely decreased the bargaining power of EIA opponents. Since the Bundesrat and its committees were over-loaded, the second chamber did not manage to formulate a coherent proposal for changes in the compound law. This slowed down the process of legal adaptation, but at the same time undermined the bargaining power of the Bundesrat vis-à-vis the Bundestag majority and the government. The Bundestag committee on the environment dealt with the immense workload of more than 300 remaining proposals to the draft compound law and instantly rejected almost two-thirds of them (Ausschuss für Umwelt 2001a, Bundestag 2001b, Bundestag 2001d: 16080). In reaction to that, the Bundesrat called for a Conciliation Committee (Bundesrat 2001: 216). Not least because of different protective interests among the Länder, the Bundesrat did not negotiate with a single voice, and the Conciliation Committee finally rejected almost all substantive Länder proposals which would have restricted EIA procedures (Bundesrat 2001: 216, Vermittlungsausschuss 2001).

Consequently, they continued to talk at cross purposes and the Kohl government maintained its initial stance towards the status of Annexe II of the directive and continued non-compliance in not requiring environmental impact assessment procedures for projects listed in Annexe II of the EIA directive. This reduced the applicatory scope of the directive severely.

Similar to the UK nitrates case, the ECJ judgment was ineffective in the German EIA case. The German media rarely reported on the ECJ ruling, but focused instead on instances of practical application of the EIA procedures (e.g. *Süddeutsche Zeitung* 2000a). After the 1998 elections, a Social-Democratic/Green government came into office, whose substantial policy interests were already in line with a demanding environmental approach (Bundestag 1998d). In addition, the domestic context was not fertile for successful societal compliance campaigns. The high misfit between the German environmental law and the EIA judgment rendered successful shaming campaigns difficult. Reframing strategies also had low prospects of success, since the government was a forerunner of the integrated environmental approach. In addition, due to restricted resources and fragmentation, environmental organizations often specialized in media-specific issues, instead of pursuing an encompassing media-overarching approach, on which the EIA was based (DNR 2000). Hence, differentially empowered societal norm proponents did not induce domestic changes after the ECJ ruling via either shaming or reframing campaigns. Non-compliance continued after the judgment, because the newly elected SPD/Green government planned a comprehensive and time-consuming reform, which would have completely restructured the German environmental law, had it been passed.

As long as the shadow of sanctions was not looming and the European Commission abstained from sending a second reasoned opinion, the government did not adapt strategic positions to potential penalties. Accordingly, the government recurred neither to the ECJ ruling nor to a possible sanction-threat, in order to shift the blame for legal adaptations and its associated costs to the EU. Yet, the environmental code was never passed, since federal competencies were lacking and a constitutional change would have been required. As a consequence, non-compliance prevailed for two years after the ECJ judgment. In response, a sanction-threat came into play. Similar to the UK nitrates case, the infringement was relatively serious and the European Commission had already taken first steps towards enforcement so that the governments in both cases could reasonably expect to be punished while still in office. In order to avoid that, the governments in London and Berlin suddenly and swiftly adapted their legal acts. The immediate possibility of high penalties induced changes in governmental strategic positions almost at once and outweighed domestic cost–benefit considerations. The government wished to avoid becoming the subject of severe financial penalties while still being in office and pursued quick legal changes – although this meant giving up the environmental code project and their own initial policy interests. The result was a compound law, which changed several pre-existing laws at once, but resembled minimalist and not comprehensive compliance because it entailed many uncertainties and ambiguities. Thus, the instrument 'sanction-threat' successfully put an end to the norm violation in the EIA case. While the dynamics of policy change were in line with the rationalist sanction-threat hypothesis, the alternative constructivist differential empowerment hypothesis was not confirmed.

6.III Summary: the power of sanction-threats

If judicial discourses and judgments fail to end norm violations, sanction-threats come into play. The UK nitrates and the German environmental impact assessment case studies have illustrated that sanction-threats induce quick shifts into minimalist compliance, if the threat is high and looming so that the government is likely to be punished while still being in office. The other six case studies have shown that the mere anticipation of possible high sanction-threats in the remote future does not trigger compliance. The UK nitrates and the German environmental impact assessment case studies also showed that the issuing of sanction-threats does not differentially empower pro-compliance lead ministries vis-à-vis other ministries and does not induce shifts from non-compliance into comprehensive compliance. Hence, the rationalist version of the sanction-threat hypothesis finds empirical confirmation, while the constructivist one does not.

Since the European Commission takes not only the economic power of a country, but also the seriousness of the infringement into consideration when proposing concrete sanctions to the ECJ, and since most of the cases in which member states rigidly resist compliance are indeed serious, sanction-threats are likely to be successful. This is in line with the empirical observation that penalties are very rare exceptions. Between 1993 and 2000, the ECJ did not issue financial penalties for instances of incorrect legal transpositions at all.[18] Hence, the three compliance instruments studied in this book are highly effective.

[18] From 2000 to 2009, the ECJ issued penalties in only four instances of incorrect transpositions.

7

Comparing the UK and Germany

The previous chapters analysed the most important legalized compliance instruments and inquired into their operation as well as the scope conditions for their success. This revealed, firstly, that judicial discourses can ideationally entrap governments, if they engage in judicial discourses, if a judicial method of interpretation is applied with a high match to the interpretational scope of the issue at stake and if the advocates of the parties do not talk at cross purposes (H1). Secondly, judgments differentially empower pro-compliance constituencies that can shame governments into compliance, if the judgment resonates well with present domestic norms (H3), or induce compliance through reframing domestic debates, if the issue at stake in the infringement can be incorporated into an alternative frame and linked to a complementary policy approach (H4). Thirdly, sanction-threats end norm violations, if the infringement is serious and the penalties are looming so that the government is likely to get punished while still being in office (H5). Fourthly, none of the alternative hypotheses (H2a, b, H6) could account for the observed compliance dynamics.

A glance at EU infringement proceedings revealed that a compliance instrument is not always successful in ending norm violations. Each state reacts sometimes to judicial discourses, sometimes to judgments and sometimes to sanction-threats in settling infringement cases. The effectiveness of compliance instruments varies considerably within states, since one and the same judicial instrument is sometimes successful but fails in other instances, even against one and the same government. The previous chapters theoretically and empirically showed that the effectiveness of judicial discourses, judgments and sanction-threats crucially depends on issue-specific scope conditions. Even though the UK and Germany differ in a variety of ways, for example concerning their judicial cultures, their support for European Integration, or the number of veto players to name but a few, the governments in London and Berlin did not react differently to the any of the three compliance instruments whenever the very specific scope conditions for its success were met.

This chapter takes a closer look at the role of country-variables and discusses why the UK and Germany respond to the same stimuli in the same manner, although both states differ in some respects. The next paragraph provides short summaries of the UK and the German infringements and their settlement dynamics. This shows that although country-specific variables are constant in the four UK cases and in the four German cases respectively, judicial discourses, judgments and sanction-threats are only sometimes successful vis-à-vis each of the two states. This is completely in line with the hypotheses developed in this book. But is it surprising for state of the art compliance theories? The short answer is 'yes'. The remainder of this chapter takes a closer look at managerial, cultural and enforcement approaches. It specifies their expectations on the effectiveness of compliance instruments and inquires as to how far they can explain settlement dynamics in the eight UK and German cases. This reveals firstly that country-variables play a minor role when it comes to hard cases of non-compliance. For example, capacity or cultural differences do not translate into different settlement dynamics. Each compliance instrument works in exactly the same way, regardless of whether it is applied in a German infringement case or in a case of the UK. Secondly, a closer look at the variables featured by state-centred theories shows that some of them vary within countries as well. For example, veto players shape the political capacity of states and one could assume that Germany has per se more difficulties in transposing judgments, because more actors have a say. Yet the number of effective veto player differs from case to case in both of the countries, for example depending on whether the oppositional parties in the parliament or other ministries have preferences to block or delay legislation. Nevertheless, in none of the eight cases did veto players delay transpositions and prevent governments from reacting to compliance instruments.

7.1 The German and the UK case studies

If we are comparing the responses of member states to the compliance instruments of the ECJ, the first notable observation is that the Westminster government as well as their German counterpart responded in a similar fashion to judicial discourses, judgments and sanction-threats.

In the drinking water case, the Kohl government was argumentatively entrapped by the judicial discourse. Non-compliance could no longer be defended with compelling arguments and Germany quickly shifted into comprehensive compliance. Similarly, the UK government became argumentatively entrapped in the collective redundancy case. In both cases, the advocates engaged in legal argumentation, applied judicial methods of interpretation that matched the interpretational scope of the problem and stopped talking at cross purposes once a legally valid norm interpretation had been developed.

The German case on the residence of foreign workers, the UK drinking water case and the UK and German equal access cases demonstrated that judicial discourses always risk dissent and can fail to induce settlements. After judicial discourses end, ECJ judgments come into play. Judgments authoritatively define the content and scope of the disputed norm, create publicity and diffuse new ideas into domestic spheres. This differentially empowers societal norm proponents vis-à-vis opponents. In the German foreign workers case, churches and trade unions shamed the government into minimalist compliance by constructing reputational threats for violating the institutionalized domestic norm of Christian charity. Similarly in the UK case, the resonance between the ECJ judgment and domestically institutionalized norms was high and shaming campaigns induced minimalist compliance. In the UK drinking water and the German equal access cases, shaming failed because the judgment resonated poorly with already institutionalized domestic norms. Yet, with some delay, reframing campaigns were successful. In the German equal access case, women's organizations and trade unions reframed the domestic debate in terms of gender equality. This new policy approach resonated well with the deeply entrenched frame of human rights and, therefore, succeeded in facilitating comprehensive compliance. In the UK drinking water case, environmental organizations reframed domestic water debates from a narrow health-oriented frame into a broader environmental protection approach. The new approach incorporated the polluters-pay principle, through which it could easily be linked to the prominent cost frame, according to which private water bills should not considerably increase because of quality issues.

In none of the six above cases were sanction-threats effective and responsible for the observed compliance dynamics. This is due to the fact that penalties were not perceived as deterrents. These infringements were not too serious and European authorities had not yet introduced first enforcement measures, so that governments did not anticipate being penalized during their incumbency and did not shy away from the ECJ. In the German EIA and the UK nitrates cases, by contrast, sanction-threats were effective after judicial discourses and judgments could not facilitate compliance, since none of the issue-specific scope conditions had been present. Non-compliance carried on after the judgment and sanction-threats came into play. In both instances, the norm violations were serious according to the criteria of the European Commission. The proposed penalties were high and deterred both governments once the second reasoned opinion had been issued so that they both could expect to become subject to the fines while still in the office. As a consequence, the Schröder government made strategic concessions and quickly pursued an undemanding legal reform resembling minimalist compliance – even against their own substantial policy interests and against the preferences of environmental organizations and industry. Similarly in the UK nitrates case: once the government received the second reasoned opinion, they quickly adjusted their preferences and shifted into minimalist compliance in order to avoid sanctions.

Reflecting on the eight case studies, we can further observe that the Westminster government responded differently to the three compliance instruments in the four UK cases. The same observation holds true for Germany: judicial discourses, judgments and sanction-threats were each only sometimes successful in fostering domestic changes. The very fact that one and the same state can sometimes be talked into compliance with, for example, a judicial discourse, while this instrument fails in other instances already indicates that country-variables cannot carry the explanatory workload in accounting for the varying success of compliance instruments. In the four German cases, country-specific variables, such as economic and political power, administrative and political capacities, or the judicial and political culture to name but a few, are constant and can consequently not explain why each of the instruments was only sometimes effective in ending the norm violations. The same holds true for the role of country-specific variables in the four UK cases.

Even though country-specific variables are constant in the four UK cases and in the four German cases respectively, judicial discourses, judgments and sanction-threats are only sometimes successful vis-à-vis each of the two states. This is completely in line with the featured four main hypotheses developed in this book. But it is surprising for state of the art compliance theories. Therefore the subsequent section takes a closer look at the most prominent cultural, capacity-related and power-based approaches and inquires in detail why their explanatory powers are limited when it comes to the transformation of hard cases of non-compliance into compliance, although their explanatory power is relatively high in explaining why member states violate EU law in the first place (Börzel *et al.* 2007).

7.II Country-specific compliance approaches

In the four UK cases as well as in the four German cases country-specific variables are constant, while each of the compliance instruments is only sometimes successful vis-à-vis each of the two states. This is completely in line with the hypotheses developed in this book, but is puzzling for country-centred state of the art compliance theories.

Although the primary focus of prominent compliance theories is on the emergence of norm violations in the first place, all of them at least implicitly refer to specific compliance instruments and provide hypotheses on prospects to end norm violations. Legalization approaches focus on institutional mechanisms such as voluntary or obligatory arbitration and adjudication by more or less independent third parties that can issue binding rulings or non-binding opinions.[1] However, since institutional variables are constant in each of the stages of the EU infringement procedure, the presence of these institutions themselves cannot explain why some cases are settled in a particular stage of the infringement procedure, in response to a particular compliance instrument, while others continue. In contrast to cultural approaches, legalization approaches, management approaches, and enforcement theories focus on the characteristics of member states (capacities, judicial culture, and power). They seek to explain differences in transformational performances between states. The subsequent sections introduce the prominent country-based approaches and discuss their hypotheses in the context of the German and UK cases.

Political capacities

The management school contends that non-compliance is involuntary, caused by lacking capacities or misinterpretations of norms (Chayes and Handler-Chayes 1993, Chayes and Handler-Chayes 1995). No matter how strongly a government wants to comply, if it lacks the required resources for timely and correct transpositions and implementations, norm violations will occur. Compliance requires four types of capacity: knowledge and expertise (cognitive capacity), monetary means (financial capacity), bureaucratic efficiency (administrative capacity), and the autonomy of governments vis-à-vis domestic veto players (political capacity) (see also Börzel *et al.* 2007, Falkner *et al.* 2004, Haverland 2000, Steunenberg 2006).

[1] See also Abbott *et al.* 2000: 401–16, Goldstein *et al.* 2000: 401, Kahler 2000: 663, Keohane, Moravcsik and Slaughter 2000: 461–2.

While the implementation of laws can be financially costly, the transposition as such hardly requires financial means. Thus, we can safely assume that the EU members basically possess sufficient financial means to correctly transpose EU law, but must eventually be willing to redistribute resources accordingly. The same holds for administrative capacity[2] and cognitive capacities: if states are challenged with too few executive staff members or too few experts, this more severely hampers the implementation and eventually the initial transposition of EU laws, but not the process of legal adaptation to ECJ compliance instruments. Once governments want to settle infringements, they can prioritize the one or two necessary bills and command bureaucrats and experts to work on them with full energy. Hence, we would not expect that the effectiveness of judicial discourses, judgments, and sanction-threats is systematically biased if states lack these three types of capacities. This is in line with the eight case studies, in none of which any ministerial member, no matter whether he or she belonged to a big economic or a small environmental ministry, argued that the process of legal change as such is too costly, requires more bureaucratic staff to be completed or cannot be carried out due to lack of expertise.

By contrast, high numbers of effective veto players more plausibly pose obstacles to legal changes in reaction to ECJ compliance instruments. Therefore, this section analyses this capacity type in greater detail. At first glance, the UK and Germany vary in terms of their political capacities, since the number of veto players is much higher in the latter due to federalism, the much stronger role of the Bundesrat compared to the rather weak House of Lords and the fact that Germany is usually governed by a coalition and not a one-party government. Hence, in the adjusted veto player index, Germany scores 4.76 and the UK 4.05 (Tsebelis 2002a, Tsebelis 2002b). Domestic veto players are sometimes responsible for delayed transpositions of EU law (see also Falkner *et al.* 2004, Haverland 2000, Steunenberg 2006). Can they also influence settlement dynamics and the effectiveness of judicial discourses, judgments and threats of sanctions? Theoretically, it is possible that veto players bias processes of legal adaptation through which governments respond to compliance instruments. Veto players could block a particular bill or delay transpositions, thus forcing the ECJ to apply a subsequent instrument, or they

[2] The UK and Germany differ in their administrative capacities, since the UK has three incentives to make individuals work effectively (performance-related pay, the absence of permanent tenure and public announcement of vacancies) while the German civil service is less competitive and only faces two of these variables (Auer, Demmke and Polet 1996).

could substantively alter the outcome of legal change pushing towards minimalist or towards comprehensive adaptations. Did Germany receive the sanction-threat in the EIA case because domestic veto players inhibit the government from reacting to judicial discourses and judgments? Did the judicial discourses fail in the German foreign workers and the equal access cases because the government could not push for comprehensive legal changes against the will of domestic veto players? Is the UK government better equipped to adapt legal acts in order to transpose consensual norm definitions developed in judicial discourses or judgments? All answers are negative, as the remainder of this section will show and as the eight case studies illustrated, demonstrating that once governments changed their preferences from non-compliance into compliance in response to a judicial instrument, they introduced and completed domestic changes. The following paragraphs show firstly that the number of effective veto players is case sensitive and, therefore, varies within each of the countries and, secondly, that governments in London and Berlin have not been prevented from pursuing legal adaptations against the preferences of domestic veto players, even in the two most likely cases.

Veto players in the UK

The UK concentrates power in the government. The electoral system is disproportional, which facilitates a low number of effective parties and one-party governments instead of multi-party coalitions (Lijphart 1999). The Prime Minister as head of the executive (and most often also the leader of his party) is elected by the majority of the House of Commons, on whose support the government depends. Party discipline is high and additionally concentrates power in the government. In line with this logic, parliamentary instruments of scrutiny are restricted to oral requests, questions and select committees. The parliamentary opposition in the House of Commons lacks a majority and cannot block, substantially alter nor fundamentally delay governmental bills. With laws and regulations, the Westminster government can choose between two different instruments for legal adaptations. While laws require the consent of the first chamber, decrees and regulations are executive acts and are passed by the government without the involvement of the House of Commons. Hence power fragmentation is lower for regulations than for laws. Unlike in the other three case studies featured in this book, the parliamentary opposition had no chance to influence or delay the transposition in the nitrates cases where the government opted for legal changes via a regulation.

Although the UK is a bicameral system, composed of the House of Commons and the House of Lords, legislative power is hardly dispersed between both chambers. The House of Commons is solely responsible for legislation, the election of the head of government, scrutinizing the government and creating publicity, while the second chamber has fewer competencies (e.g. delaying a veto in legislative matters with a maximum of one year) (Ashford 1981: 10–13, Craig 1998). The majority in the House of Commons can overrule a veto of the House of Lords (Smith 1988). Yet in none of the four UK case studies did the House of Lords issue a veto, thus it was not an effective veto player in the processes of legal adaptation.

The extent of horizontal and vertical power fragmentation varies between policies. Horizontal fragmentation is crucially influenced by the number of involved ministries which represent different positions. Environmental policies are traditionally cross-cutting in character, so the number of ministries which have issues at stake is, on average, higher than for social policy.

Yet in the UK drinking water and nitrates cases, the environmental ministry adopted public health and cost frames, so that other affected and involved ministries (such as the health ministry or the agricultural ministry) represented very similar positions to the environmental ministry (in 1970, Department for the Environment and Countryside, in 1997, Department for the Environment, Food and Rural Affairs). During both processes of legal adaptation, all involved ministries acted in concert and promoted additional policy goals which would have compromised the policy of the environmental ministry. In the equal treatment case, the economic ministry welcomed the narrow approach of the employment ministry. The horizontal dispersion of power was slightly higher in the redundancy case. Two other ministries were involved, but represented less restrictive approaches concerning collective workers' rights. In response to the effective judicial discourse, the Department for Education and Employment changed its policy from opposition to support of collective worker rights. However, the Department of Trade and Industry opted for deregulation and was rather sceptical with regard to intervention in employment affairs (House of Commons 1992b: 167–73, House of Commons 1993b: 325–56). Hence, the horizontal power fragmentation was highest in the collective redundancy case, although social policies are not, per se, cross-cutting in character.

Unlike in the social policy field, there is vertical power dispersion in environmental policy. Due to devolution, the importance of sub-national government has increased in the regulation of water issues (in particular in Scotland). Yet regions are mainly responsible for specifying the practical application of the DWD and the nitrates directives. In all four case studies, legal transpositions were at stake. Consequently, in spite of devolution in the environmental sector, regional bodies were not involved in the process of legal adaptation after the ECJ compliance instruments and were not effective veto players. Hence, the power fragmentation varied to some extent over the four case studies and was strongest in the collective redundancy case.

Among the four UK case studies featured in this book, the collective redundancy case is the most likely instance for successful domestic veto players, since the extent of power fragmentation was higher than for the other three cases. Moreover, unlike the nitrates case, the drinking water case, and to a lesser extent, the equal access case, the cleavage between government and opposition was clear-cut and stable during most of the infringement procedure. While the Conservative government strongly opposed collective trade union rights and the obligatory recognition of workers' representatives in the context of collective redundancies, the Labour opposition sided with trade unions and opted for strengthening trade union rights in general and specifically for obligatory recognition during processes of collective redundancies. While Labour favoured comprehensive compliance from the beginning, the Conservatives changed their position after over 15 years of firm resistance. Accordingly, the Major government introduced demanding legal changes during the judicial discourse in 1993 and immediately after the judgment in 1995.

The bill on trade union reform and employment (TURERA) restricted trade unions severely, but strengthened individual and collective protective rights by transposing three of the four issues at stake before the ECJ. It broadened the applicatory scope of the collective redundancy legislation to encompass all collective dismissals instead of only redundancies for economic reasons. Moreover, the TURERA introduced the notion that consultations must aim for agreements between employees and employers and established prohibitive sanctions for disobedient employers. Did domestic veto players influence these changes?

Horizontally, the trade and the competition ministries had interests at stake. Both, but specifically the Department of Trade and Industry, strongly endorsed deregulation and liberalization. Hence they opposed state intervention into industrial affairs, except in work safety and public health measures (e.g. House of Commons 1993b: 331–56). Counterfactually, if these ministries had had a greater say, the collective redundancy issues would not have been included in the TURERA in a demanding manner and non-compliance would have either been continued or transformed into minimalist compliance. The very fact that the collective redundancy reforms were introduced in the TURERA, despite the fact that they did not fit particularly well with this legal act (as the TURERA restricted trade union rights), indicates that both ministries were not effective veto players. Thus, the Department of Employment's policy change was not substantially altered by other ministries. Rather the opposite is likely: the ECJ proceeding empowered the employment ministry within the cabinet.

Vertically, the Labour opposition in the House of Commons had strong interests at stake in the TURERA, because it would restrict the rights of their core constituency, trade unions. Members of the Labour Party preferred to strengthen trade union rights and, therefore, strongly opposed the TURERA as a whole (e.g. House of Commons 1992b: 173, House of Commons 1993b: 355). For the same reasons, the Labour opposition did not welcome the transposition of collective redundancy issues. Counterfactually, if the opposition had been able to substantially alter the TURERA, they would have opted for trade union rights instead of merely strengthening collective employee entitlements. However, the opposition in the House of Commons was a weak veto player. They possessed only the minority of seats and could not outvote the governmental TURERA draft, nor use their potential veto as a bargaining asset in order to negotiate demanding approaches. Hence the collective redundancy reforms were adopted without substantial changes to the bill (see also House of Commons 1993b: 360, Skidmore 1995). This is not very surprising. Among the reforms introduced with the TURERA, the collective redundancy elements were the least threatening issues for trade unions. Hence Labour focused more on the severe restrictions of trade unions, such as the requirement to give seven days' notice before calling a strike or the issue of financing trade unions (e.g. House of Commons 1992b: 196–7, 207–8). Due to the fact that they lacked the competency to block or alter the TURERA, the parliamentary opposition could not even prevent the restriction of essential trade union rights (see also House of Commons 1996b: 210–13). Neither other ministries, nor the Labour Party, managed to substantially influence the legal act. Thus, in line with the Conservative agenda, the TURERA constrained trade unions and strengthened individual and collective rights – in spite of parliamentary opposition.

In 1995, the Major government passed collective redundancies and transfers of undertaking regulations which transposed compulsory recognition of workers' representatives in processes of collective redundancies. This resembled a demanding transposition of the recognition issue without restricting mandatory recognition rules through the backdoor by creating overlaps with other legal norms, or introducing broad exceptional clauses, or referring to new and ill-defined concepts.

The only potential veto player with diverse interests at stake was the

Labour Party. In the House of Commons, they strongly opposed the regulations (e.g. House of Commons 1996b: 210). In particular, they criticized them as an insufficient legal adaptation of the ECJ judgment, because the regulations restrained trade union rights and allowed employers to choose between dealing with trade unions or with elected worker representatives during collective redundancies. Since regulations do not require the consent of the House of Commons, the opposition had no chance to formally alter the drafts before they were passed. Therefore, they initiated a parliamentary debate after the regulations had already entered into force. Again, Labour pushed for trade union rights and compulsory recognition of trade unions by employers (House of Commons 1996b: 197–9). Yet, as in 1993, the parliamentary opposition was a weak veto player. The Labour Party lacked the majority of votes which would have been necessary to change, replace, or even abolish the regulations. Hence the opposition failed to change the regulation in the 1996 debate, even though they had strong reasons to attempt to do so. After the debate, the House of Commons voted on whether to change the regulation. There were 258 Ayes and 295 Nos and the 1995 regulation remained unchanged (House of Commons 1996b: 231). Hence in the collective redundancy case comprehensive compliance was not due to the strength and activities of the Labour opposition in the House of Commons, but to the effectiveness of the judicial discourse which facilitated complete legal changes.

In conclusion, even in the most likely case for changes in governmental drafts during processes of legal adaptation in the UK, veto players did not slow down or substantially alter legal adaptations. Consequently, changes of governmental policy ideas could have been translated into a comprehensive form of compliance without further modifications and biases towards either compliance-averse preferences of other ministries or more demanding policy approaches of the parliamentary opposition. The extent of fragmentation of political decision-making power did not influence the effectiveness of ECJ compliance instruments. Consequently, judicial discourses, judgments and sanction-threats did translate into the compliance outcomes predicted by the respective hypothesis without delays or content-related biases.

Veto players in Germany

Compared to the UK, the German political system shows a higher level of power fragmentation. Vertically, power is dispersed between the Bund (federal state) and the 16 regions (Länder), which have their own constitutionally guaranteed legislative competencies and are additionally responsible for the implementation of state and federal laws. Horizontally, power is divided in the coalition government and between the Bundestag and the Bundesrat. Unlike the House of Lords, the Bundesrat is a strong second chamber, since it is incongruent and symmetrical.[3] The parliamentary opposition in the Bundestag and the Bundesrat can refer to oral and written questions, debates and committee work in order to scrutinize the government and participate in the policy-making process. The Bundesrat is a strong veto player, which can put up conciliation committees and even completely block legal acts requiring the consent of the Länder. At first glance, the institutional framework is constant across the four cases and cannot explain variation in compliance outcomes.

As in the UK, however, there is variation in the horizontal and vertical distribution of power between policy fields and even between single issues. Vertically, social policy is much more centralized than the traditional cross-cutting environmental issues, in which the Länder have more competencies. The consent of the Bundesrat was not required in the equal access case and in the foreign workers case only in so far as residency procedures were affected. In the drinking water and in the EIA cases consent had been necessary – especially since legal changes affected the practical implementation, for which the Länder were responsible. Horizontally, there are more similarities than differences between the policies. In the EIA case, horizontal power fragmentation within the government was the strongest. The environmental ministry was leading, but others, such as the economic ministry, were also involved and represented substantially different policy interests. In the foreign workers case, the interior ministry was mainly responsible. While the interests of the economic and the finance ministries were also at stake, they did not turn into veto players, because all affected ministries represented similar policy interests. In the equal access case, the leading ministry was the ministry for labour and employment, while the economic ministry and the ministry for youth, family, and health were also involved, but represented mostly similar positions. Horizontal fragmentation was the lowest in the drinking

[3] The Bundesrat possesses wide legislative competencies, since its consent is required for all federal legal acts that affect the Länder, which is frequently the case, since the Länder are responsible for the execution of federal acts ('Verbundföderalismus', see also Scharpf 1989b, Scharpf 1991). The membership in the Bundesrat is based on a different principle than the first chamber. The Bundesrat is composed of the Länder governments who most often pursue regional interests rather than federal party-politics. In addition, the party-political majority in the second chamber can be different from that in the first chamber.

water case. Prior to and even after the creation of a ministry for the environment in 1986, drinking water quality was primarily dealt with by the ministry for health. The environmental ministry was consulted, but represented similar policy ideas to the ministry for health (Bundestag 1988c).

The role of Bundestag and Bundesrat as veto players crucially depends on the type of legal act. While laws require the consent of the Bundestag and for certain issues also of the Bundesrat (Art. 70–5, 80, 84–5 Grundgesetz),[4] executive regulations do not need the approval of the Bundestag and only seldom need that of the Bundesrat. In the four German cases, laws have been used as frequently as regulations as means to respond the ECJ compliance instruments.

Summing up, the likelihood that domestic veto players might have influenced compliance dynamics and outcomes varies across the cases. It was the lowest in the drinking water case, followed by the equal access and the foreign workers case. In the EIA case, the horizontal and vertical fragmentation and the number of potential veto players were very high. It is also the only instance in which comprehensive legal changes, as originally planned by the government, failed.

The following paragraphs focus on the role of veto players in the dynamics and outcomes in the EIA case, which is the most likely case for successful veto players due to the high extent of vertical and horizontal power dispersion and due to the fact that no executive acts, but only laws, were used as means of legal changes. It demonstrates that not even in this most likely case were domestic veto players responsible for persistent non-compliance in the first three years after the ECJ judgment and for minimalist compliance afterwards.

From the very beginning, the SPD and Green Party opted for a more demanding legal transposition than the 1990 UVPG, which they criticized for its scope restrictions, while the CDU and FDP favoured a less costly EIA approach (Bundesrat 1988: 327, Bundestag 1989b: 9238, Bundestag 1989c: 13398, 13402, Green Party 1991: 2). Only weeks after the ECJ judgment, federal elections brought about a change in government. The SPD/GP coalition under Chancellor Schröder succeeded the Kohl government in October 1998. Since the CDU and FDP coalition had not introduced steps towards further legal adaptations prior to the ECJ

[4] Recently, a comprehensive constitutional reform ('Föderalismusreform', 2006) severely reduced the share of legal acts that require the consent of the Bundesrat (Gunlicks 2007).

judgment, the following analysis focuses on the environmental code project (1999–2000) and the Artikelgesetz (2000–2001).

The Green Party wanted to transpose the ECJ judgment with a comprehensive reform which would turn the highly fragmented German environmental law into an integrated and coherent approach (Bundesregierung 1999b, Bundesregierung 1999c, interview organized interests#4, 08–02–05). To this end, the environmental ministry pursued an environmental code reform (Trittin 1999: 3). The UGB project had high saliency and was an important issue in the coalition agreement (Fürst 2004: 160–1, *TAZ* 1999a). The Green Party supported the environmental code project to a greater extent than the SPD (compare Ausschuss für Umwelt 2001a, Bundesregierung 1999a with Bundesregierung 2000, Bundestag 2001d). Although they were less enthusiastic, the Social-Democratic coalition partner repeatedly highlighted the righteousness and appropriateness of such an integral environmental approach (e.g. Bundestag 2000c, Bundestag 2001d: 16078). The economic and the transport and traffic ministries were sensitive to cost-related concerns of the industry and did not fully support the environmental code project, but did not substantially alter the environmental ministry's draft (Bundesregierung 2000, *TAZ* 1999a, *TAZ* 1999b, *TAZ* 1999d, *TAZ* 2000).

At the beginning of the legal adaptation, several veto players had adverse interests. The CDU and FDP opposed a demanding interpretation of the EIA directive in both chambers. Yet their potential for changing or preventing an environmental code was restricted, since the government acted in concert with the Ministry for the Environment and held the majority in the Bundestag. In addition, the SPD/GP-governed Länder had the majority in the Bundesrat between November 1998 and October 1999 (35 vs. 16 votes and 18 neutral votes). This constellation prevented party politics in both chambers from blocking or radically changing the environmental code bill effectively. Yet regional concerns facilitated opposition in most of the CDU and SPD Länder governments. Although the UGB reform was not substantially altered in Bundestag and Bundesrat, the process of legal adaptation was not smooth. The UGB project was delayed at the federal level and finally failed in winter 1999/2000 (*Süddeutsche Zeitung* 1999, *TAZ* 1999d, Trittin 1999, Trittin 2000). The Bundesrat did not cause the breakdown of the environmental code project, although the opposition of the Länder was often blamed for the maintenance of the highly fragmented media-specific German environmental law (Trittin 2000: 1). The failure was not due to veto players in both chambers, who bargained in several committees for concessions and tried to delay the legislative process. Rather, the failure of the UGB became apparent after a shift of substantial discussions within the federal interior ministry and the ministry of justice towards legal aspects (see also Bundesministerium für Umwelt 2005, Bundestag 2001a: 16078), which revealed that the vertical distribution of competencies prohibited a comprehensive environmental law reform (Börzel 2003a: 112, Bundestag 2001a: 16074, 16078). A constitutional reform shifting water issues from framework into the area of competing competencies would have been required for the enactment of the environmental code (Bundestag 2001a). This would have been difficult to achieve, since the Länder could have refused to give up their competencies on waters prescribed in Article 75 of the constitution (framework competencies) (Trittin 2000: 1). The federal environmental ministry realized that the constitution might become an insurmountable barrier and pushed for a legal adaptation of the ECJ judgment via a single law ('Artikelgesetz') in late 2000 (Trittin 2000).

Summing up, the environmental code project failed because the necessary competencies were lacking at the federal level from the very beginning. Hence incomplete information on the distribution of competencies of the federal government was responsible for the delay in the transposition, rather than the activities of domestic veto players.

After the federal government was confronted with the lack of competencies, they basically faced two options. Firstly, in line with its substantial policy interests, the SPD/Green coalition could have further pursued the UGB project, which would have required pushing for a constitutional reform. Secondly, they could have compromised the comprehensive reform and opted for a minimalist, but much faster legal adaptation to the ECJ judgment. As the pressure from above increased in November 2000, the government chose the second alternative (Ausschuss für Umwelt 2000).

In October 1999, regional elections had shifted the majority in the Bundesrat to the advantage of the CDU (28 CDU votes, 23 SPD/Green votes, 18 neutral votes). This transformed the second chamber into a much stronger domestic veto player. Party politics aside, most of the 16 Länder governments opposed a demanding interpretation of the European directive due to high compliance expenses and the negative impact on the competitiveness of regional industries. In 2000, the Länder in the Bundesrat all opted for minimalist legal adaptations with less demanding criteria for environmental impact assessment procedures, restricted applicatory scopes and broad exceptional clauses (e.g. Bundesrat 2000). The different regional environmental and economic situations contributed to a high number of diverse policy interests and strategic preferences in the

Bundesrat. After the compound bill was sent to the Bundesrat, the Länder initiated no fewer than 350 proposals for changes before December 2000 (Bundesrat 2000: 626). The lack of coordination of the proposals in the Bundesrat severely decreased the bargaining power of EIA opponents. Since the CDU-dominated Bundesrat and its committees were overburdened, the Bundesrat did not manage to formulate a coherent proposal for changes in the compound law (state ministry#3, 09–03–05). This slowed down the process of legal adaptation, but at the same time undermined the bargaining power of the Bundesrat vis-à-vis the Bundestag majority and the government. The Bundestag committee on the environment dealt with the immense workload of more than 300 remaining proposals to the draft compound law and instantly rejected almost two-thirds of them (Ausschuss für Umwelt 2001a, Bundestag 2001b, Bundestag 2001d: 16080). In reaction to that, the Bundesrat called for a Conciliation Committee (Bundesrat 2001: 216). Not least because of different protective interests among the Länder, the Bundesrat did not negotiate with a single voice and the Conciliation Committee finally rejected almost all substantive Länder proposals which would have restricted EIA procedures (Bundesrat 2001: 216, Vermittlungsausschuss 2001).

As soon as the draft compound law was submitted to the Bundesrat, the environmental minister pointed towards its urgency (Mr Trittin, in Bundesrat 2000: 624). In order to speed up the process of legal change, he emphasized the threat of financial penalties and of potential external reputation losses within the EU (Mr Trittin, in Bundesrat 2000: 625). Yet, the Bundesrat did not speed up the legislative process. Rather, compliance-averse Länder governments reacted to the hint of financial penalties by emphasizing that European threats should not lead to careless handling of the issue (e.g. Bavaria, in Bundesrat 2000: 626).

Despite the looming shadow of sanctions, the opposition in the Bundestag strongly opposed a fast legal adaptation of the ECJ judgment with the compound law – even though the latter was far less demanding than the (not immediately realizable) environmental code project (Ausschuss für Umwelt 2001b: 124, Bundestag 2001d: 16072–3). The CDU and FDP were still against the Artikelgesetz because of compliance costs and arising comparative disadvantages of German companies in the international economy (Ausschuss für Umwelt 2001b: 123, 124; Bundestag 2001d: 16070). Despite this resistance, the Bundestag finally passed the compound law on 27 June 2001 without considerable delay and, more importantly, without fundamental substantial changes to the governmental draft (Bundestag 2001b: 214).

The EIA case was characterized by a high level of vertical and horizontal fragmentation and, respectively, a relatively high number of domestic veto players. The governmental plans for legal reforms were oriented towards a comprehensive and demanding legal change, which would have resembled comprehensive compliance – if the environmental code reform had been successful. The policy interests and strategic preferences of the domestic opposition, by contrast, were strongly pointing towards continuing the norm violation. Since the government needed the consent of the Bundestag and the Bundesrat, the EIA case has been a most likely instance for successful domestic veto players to block, delay, or alter governmental drafts. Yet not even in such a likely scenario were domestic veto players responsible for the continued non-compliance in the first three years after the ECJ judgment and for the change into minimalist compliance afterwards.

Hence, we can conclude that veto players might become important in individual cases and might indeed delay or substantially alter governmental bills, but veto players do not generally nor systematically influence settlement processes. High power fragmentation in a country or in a certain policy area does not systematically bias the effectiveness of judicial discourses, judgments and sanction-threats because it does not automatically influence speed and outcomes of legal transpositions. Once a compliance instrument has altered the governmental preferences from non-compliance into compliance, the cases studied here show that governments facing domestic veto players have managed to pursue legal changes – even against the will of domestic constituencies.

Judicial cultures

Cultural approaches assume that decision-makers are socially constituted and thus socialized into the particular legal and political culture of their states, which affects how they deal with non-compliance and how they respond to the instruments of international courts (Gibson and Caldeira 1996, Visegrády 2001, Wendt 1999). What is culture and what is judicial culture? If we take the assumption that law cannot be discussed separately from issues of righteousness and appropriateness (Habermas 1992a) as a starting point, judicial culture can be defined as a structure of meaning, which is constituted, reproduced and changed through social practices that are related to perceptions on the procedural and substantive fairness and appropriateness of legal interventions into political, economic, societal and private spheres.

There are two types of judicial culture approaches. One distinguishes between popular and professional attitudes towards the law (MacAulay 1989), the other between different legal traditions (Van Hoeck and Warrington 1998). The former focuses on intra-state attitude differences (e.g. social classes) toward the law (Gibson and Caldeira 1996: 68–71), and can neither provide state-specific, nor issue-specific scope conditions for the effectiveness of compliance instruments.[5] The second body of literature is more promising. It often distinguishes between common law systems and continental or Roman systems (e.g. Legrand 1996). In common law systems, legal rules are less abstract and generalized than in continental legal systems where formalism dominates over pragmatism (Slaughter, Stone Sweet and Weiler 1998). As a consequence, common law systems grant judges wider margins for the interpretation and the development of case-law, while continental legal systems tend towards a strict separation between law-making and application of laws (Visegrády 2001). On the one hand, these approaches expect states with a continental legal culture, such as Germany, to respond well to judicial compliance instruments, since the European legal system resembles their judicial culture in procedural and substantial terms and the margins of the ECJ as 'law-making' actor are restricted (e.g. Garrett 1995, Stone Sweet and Sandholtz 1998, Weiler 1981).[6] On the other hand, common law systems resonate well with the European legal culture in one important respect: they accept the quasi law-making powers of judges and are familiar with the idea that political decision-makers agree upon a certain rule, which courts may apply beyond their original scopes and

[5] These approaches are grounded in sociological empiricism and focus on professional attitudes to the status of law and judges (Hunt 1999) as well as popular attitudes towards the rule of law and its fairness and their impact on obedience (MacAulay 1989). They hypothesize that strong popular commitments to the rule of law and a perception of the law as fair prevents states from violating European law in the first place. Yet studies have demonstrated that attitudes differ more strongly within than between states (e.g. between different social groups and classes) (Gibson and Caldeira 1996: 68–71) and cannot explain inter-state variation (Börzel *et al.* 2007).

[6] There are instances in which the ECJ extended its competencies (e.g. the supremacy doctrine) or created new law (e.g. the doctrine of mutual recognition) (Alter 1998, Alter 2001). In these cases, the ECJ created new law by relying on extensive interpretation of existing legal acts (teleological interpretation oriented towards the Community goal of intensified integration). Yet in almost all cases, the ECJ sticks to a much narrower approach of judicial interpretation and does not create new law with its judgments (e.g. Garrett 1995, Garrett, Kelman and Schulz 1998, Rasmussen 1986). As a consequence, the ECJ uses narrow judicial techniques of legal reasoning, such as the directive-immanent wording method, for the interpretation of European secondary law in its daily operation (Gulmann 1980: 198, Snyder 1993: 40–3) and cases in which the ECJ created new norms are few (such as the doctrine of direct effect or of supremacy, see also Alter 2001).

thereby create case-law.[7] In this respect, states such as the UK should have very good compliance records with ECJ compliance instruments. Thus, the distinction between common law systems (UK and Ireland) and continental legal cultures (the other member states) is too imprecise, since it leads to indeterminate predictions on settlement performances.

Two further distinctions allow for fine-grained propositions on the effectiveness of judicial discourses and judgments. The dimensions of judicialization vs. politicization and internationalization vs. state-centeredness conceptually grasp differences in the substance and strength of logics of appropriateness vis-à-vis the ECJ as a judicial authority. Through judicial discourses and in judging whether national legal acts are in line with EU secondary law, the ECJ intervenes into the political sphere of member states. States with strongly internationalized and judicialized (as opposed to state-centered and politicized) cultures are more likely to consider the ECJ as a legitimate extra-territorial authority and are more strongly inclined to comply with ECJ judicial discourses and judgments, due to logics of appropriateness (Gibson and Caldeira 1996).

The judicialization–politicization dimension grasps different perceptions on the legitimate role of the judiciary within states. In systems with strong parliamentary sovereignty, the legislature is perceived as the democratically elected, ultimate authority (Steffani 1983). In line with this logic, the parliament is not restricted by a written constitution or by judicial review, which could annul legislative acts (Lijphart 1999). Conversely, in judicial review systems, the balance of power requires a constitution and also a judicial branch that oversees legislative activities and intervenes if basic principles are violated (Diamond 1978).

The distinction between internationalized and state-centred member states reflects differences in substantial doctrines on the acceptance of authorities beyond the nation state. Internationalized legal cultures are monist,[8] accept the supremacy of EU law over national law from early on and attribute the Kompetenz-Kompetenz[9] to the EU level (Slaughter, Stone

[7] In addition, the European legal culture has incorporated principles of 'natural justice' (right of hearings, right of due process, etc.) that have traditionally been associated with common law systems (Visegrády 2001).

[8] This means that international treaties enter into force without an intermediate step of parliamentary approval.

[9] While the supremacy doctrine was only disputed until the mid 1990s (Slaughter, Stone Sweet and Weiler 1998), it is still contested whether national courts or the ECJ are the supreme judicial authorities regarding Community acts outside the designated sphere of competence (Kompetenz-Kompetenz) (Slaughter, Stone Sweet and Weiler 1997).

Sweet and Weiler 1997). State-centered legal cultures are dualistic[10] and sceptical regarding the strengthening of competencies of the ECJ (opposed the supremacy doctrine for a long time, oppose the issue of a European Kompetenz-Kompetenz).[11]

Both dimensions can be combined in a two by two matrix. Judicial discourses and ECJ judgments should be the most successful in facilitating compliance for states with judicialized and internationalized legal cultures, such as Germany.[12] They should be inclined to accept the authority of the ECJ as a judicial non-state actor and consider compliance with it as appropriate. On the contrary, states combining politicization with state-centrism (e.g. the UK)[13] should be the least inclined to abolish norm violations in reacting to the ECJ. State-centred-judicialized[14] and internationalized-politicized[15] legal cultures form intermediate categories with no clear inclination towards either compliance or non-compliance as the appropriate response to ECJ activities.

[10] This means that international treaties and provisions require parliamentary approval.

[11] Monist states are Spain, Greece, France, the Netherlands, and Germany (since 2001). Belgium, Germany (before 2001), Denmark, Luxembourg, and the UK are dualist. Italy and Ireland have characteristics of both, because they are monistic in regard to international law and dualistic regarding international treaties.

[12] Highly judicialized and internationalized legal cultures are present in Germany (strongest between 1980 and 1993, see also Cartabia 1998: 143, Kokott 1998: 89–90), Spain (supremacy was explicitly accepted in a decision in 1989, see also Barrios 2003: 640), Greece (the supremacy doctrine was explicitly accepted in 1986, see also Zervakis 2003: 721), France (after 1989, see also Kempf 2003: 320), Ireland (after 1983, see also Elvert 2003: 290), and Belgium (after 1983, see also Woyke 2003: 410). On the dualism–monism dimension, both Germany and Italy are ambiguous. However, both states differ in their handling of the doctrine of the supremacy of European law. Germany belonged to the internationalized type from the beginning, whereas Italy opposed the supremacy doctrine until 1984.

[13] States with a politicized and state-centred legal culture are the UK (Craig 1998: 200), Belgium (before 1971, see also Bribosia 1998), Luxembourg (1956–1984), and Denmark (Nannestad 2003: 86).

[14] States with state-centered-judicialized legal cultures are Italy (strongest before 1984, Cartabia 1998: 135–40) France (before 1989 not all three supreme courts accepted the supremacy doctrine, see also Plotner 1998: 51–3) and Portugal (strong monist constitution, see also Merkel and Striehl 2003: 677). Italy is judicialized because it has a written constitution and a strong and active constitutional court with competencies for judicial review (Trautmann and Ulrich 2003: 589).

[15] Belgium (1971–1983, see also Bribosia 1998), Luxembourg (after 1984, see also Schroen 2003: 438–41) and the Netherlands (from the beginning, see also Claes and De Witte 1998: 187) belong to the internationalized-politicized type of legal culture.

Table 7.1 Types of judicial cultures

	Judicialization	*Politicization*
Internationalized	D, E, EL, F (after 1989), IR, B (after 1983)	B (1971–1983), L (after 1984), NL
State-centered	I (strongest before 1984), F (prior to 1989), P	UK (strongest before 1991), B (prior to 1971), L (1956–1984), DK

Key:
B – Belgium; D – Germany; DK – Denmark; E – Spain; EL – Greece; F – France; I – Italy; IR – Ireland; L – Luxembourg; NL – Netherlands; P – Portugal; UK – United Kingdom

The corresponding hypothesis states: the higher the degree of judicialization and the more internationalized a legal culture is, the higher the likelihood that states settle norm violations in response to compliance instruments. Hence we would expect that Germany would respond better to compliance instruments than the UK and would settle more cases in earlier stages of the infringement procedure. We would also expect that domestic debates on transpositions would more often be accompanied by references to the legitimacy of the ECJ, to the appropriateness of its judgments or to the need for compliance in order to be 'good European citizens' in Germany than in the UK.

If we look at the first indicator, we see that Germany has a withdrawal rate of 73 per cent relative to all of its ECJ referrals for incorrect and delayed transpositions, while the UK only settles 61 per cent of all its ECJ referrals prior to a judgment. By contrast, only 5 per cent of all ECJ referrals receive sanction-threats in the UK, whereas the figure is 13 per cent for Germany. While Germany settles more cases earlier than the UK, Germany also has a higher share of cases exposed to a sanction-threat. The correlations are not robust and cannot give us a hint that judicial cultures as a background variable indeed influence the responses of states to judicial compliance instruments of international courts.

Having a look at the domestic debates that accompanied the legal adaptations in the eight cases studied in this book shows that German decision-makers did not refer to the appropriateness of the ECJ and its judicial instruments, to the general obligation to comply with ECJ rulings or to the need for Germany to be a 'good European citizen' in order to end norm violations. Not even in the German EIA case, in which the newly elected coalition of SPD and GP had policy preferences in line with a demanding form of compliance and tried to pursue a comprehensive reform (an environmental code), did governmental members refer to the appropriateness of complying with EU law in order to strengthen their position. Instead, the lead minister shed a negative light on the ECJ in order to speed up legislative processes: 'we are threatened by considerable financial penalties by the EU Commission. While we debate here, the European Commission decides whether a financial penalty shall be imposed upon the Federal Republic of Germany' (the Minister for the Environment, Mr Trittin, in Bundesrat 2000: 624–5, translation DP). By contrast, UK government officials made not many but nevertheless more, and indeed positive, references to the ECJ: 'The European Court of Justice must be supported in its judgment' (Minister for Competition and Consumer Affairs, Mr Taylor, in House of Commons 1996b: 205).[16] Hence, contrary to the expectation of the judicial culture approach, governmental members in Germany do not seem to more often use pro-European references, which would indicate that their judicial culture urges them to comply with EU law and settle infringement cases, than governmental members of the UK.

In sum, the successful application of compliance instruments is not influenced by the judicial cultures of the states concerned. The judicial discourse did not foster quick shifts into comprehensive compliance in the German drinking water case because the German judicial culture demanded obedience, but because the advocates developed a common norm definition due to the engagement of both parties and the fact that they both analysed all essential legal acts and that they used judicial interpretational techniques that matched the interpretational scope of the debated issue, which argumentatively entrapped the government. Likewise, the UK did not respond to the judicial discourse in the collective redundancies case in spite of its judicial culture, but simply because the UK government became argumentatively entrapped. Moreover, the judicial culture is constant across all four German case studies and also across all four UK cases, but the effectiveness of the compliance instruments varied in the countries. Hence, as Germany and the UK differ in their judicial culture, this variable did not systematically influence the reactions of the governments in Bonn and Berlin as well as in Westminster to judicial discourses, judgments and sanction-threats. Although the UK resembles a common law and a state-centered politicized culture, while Germany has a continental and an internationalized judicialized legal culture, both countries react in similar ways to impetuses of the ECJ.

[16] Similarly, 'I do not need to look behind the judgment to find out what the intention was, because I accept the judgment' (Mr Taylor, Minister for Competition and Consumer Affairs, in House of Commons 1996b: 210).

Whenever the issue-specific scope conditions for the success of the compliance instruments were present, the governments in office abandoned the norm violation, irrespective of whether they considered the European judicial intervention as appropriate or not.[17]

Economic and political power

A third branch of compliance theories focuses on the role of political or financial power of states. Enforcement theory basically assumes that states calculate costs and benefits before adapting domestic acts in accordance with law beyond the nation-state (see also Fearon 1998, Martin 1992). If costs exceed benefits, states opt for norm violations. These calculations can be influenced by compliance instruments that impose additional costs on reluctant governments. Accordingly, states should respond to the instruments of the ECJ if they make norm violations more expensive than compliance. Yet, the more powerful states are, the more easily they can afford to bear additional costs. Thus, powerful states should be less inclined to respond to judicial discourses, to judgments and even to sanction-threats than weaker states.

Germany and the UK are powerful states in the EU, because they both have many votes in the Council and they both have big and strong economies. On the aggregate level, they should be able to afford to not respond to judicial discourses, judgments and sanction-threats. In this sense, they are least likely cases for the ECJ and its instruments to foster compliance. Yet, although their power does not vary, the responses of the governments in London and Berlin each varied across the cases and each infringement was successfully settled in the end. Moreover, if we compare the settlement dynamics of both countries across the stages, we see that they differ, although the political power is constant across both countries (29 votes in the Council). Germany shifts more frequently into compliance before the ECJ issues a judgment (73 per cent of all German ECJ referrals) than the UK (61 per cent), while Germany has a higher share of sanction-threats (13 per cent) than the UK (5 per cent) (see also Figure 7.1). Yet if we have a closer look at economic power, we see that Germany has a higher GDP than the UK (see also Annexe). In this regard, the enforcement approach would expect the UK to settle more cases in anticipating judgments than Germany, while the German government should have a

[17] Moreover, the judicial culture approach has another important shortcoming: it offers no predictions on the effectiveness of each of the compliance instruments individually and can, therefore, not address the empirical puzzle of why one and the same instrument can sometimes be successful but fails in other instances, even against one and the same government.

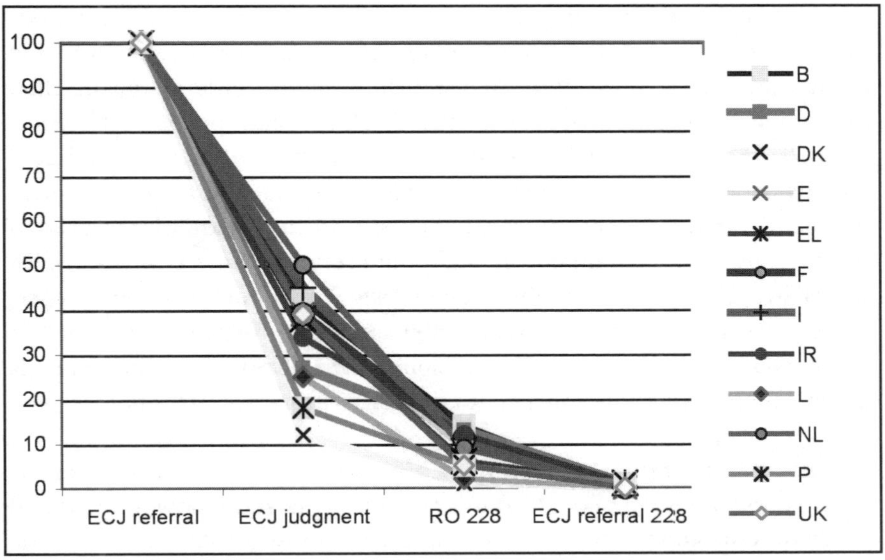

Figure 7.1 Open infringement cases in per cent of ECJ referrals

Key:
B – Belgium; D – Germany; DK – Denmark; E – Spain; EL – Greece; F – France; I – Italy; IR – Ireland; L – Luxembourg; NL – Netherlands; P – Portugal; UK – United Kingdom

higher share of sanction-threats than the UK. The empirics are inconclusive, since only the second but not the first indicator shows the expected correlations.

In the case-studies, power was not a decisive factor either. Governments and their constituencies associated high expenditures with the transposition and implementation of demanding interpretations of the European law at stake in all eight infringement cases. Consequently, they all opted for incorrect transpositions that saved compliance costs. Within the four German cases and within the four UK cases, power was constant. Yet, the effectiveness of compliance instruments showed in-country variation. The governments not only reacted differently to one and the same stimuli but also did not highlight compliance costs in domestic debates in the context of judicial discourses and judgments. One could argue that this is not too surprising since the costs associated with the two judicial instruments are limited (e.g. losing parties have to carry the costs of the ECJ procedure). Among the three compliance instruments, sanction-threats impose the highest costs on states. The anticipation of sanctions played no role in most studies, except the UK nitrates and the German EIA cases, in which the shadow of penalties was looming. Yet, the very fact that Germany is economically more powerful than the UK did not influence the reactions in those two cases. Both governments finally ended non-compliance as it became clear that they would be subject to high sanctions during their incumbencies. Hence, the case studies show that power differences between the two countries did not translate into different compliance dynamics. While at first glance this might be surprising for enforcement theory, in particular concerning sanction-threats, a closer look reveals that the ECJ and the Commission include the economic power of states into their calculations of the amount of penalties (Panke forthcoming). Hence, more powerful Germany receives higher sanction-threats than the slightly less powerful UK (ceteris paribus). Thus, in the EU, weaker states are not per se more deterred by sanction-threats than more powerful ones.

In sum, the operation of compliance instruments is not influenced by country variables. Although state capacity and state power are good predictors in accounting for the occurrence of norm violations in the first place (Börzel *et al.* 2007), they do not bias the effectiveness of judicial discourses, judgments and sanction-threats.

Part IV

Conclusions

8

Compliance with law beyond the nation-state

Every international institution grapples with instances of norm violations. This is problematic, since states' compliance is the very precondition for the effectiveness of international law, while norm violations severely reduce its power. In order to cope with compliance deficits, international institutions have developed monitoring and compliance restoring mechanisms. In particular, in the last fifteen years, many international institutions have either strengthened existing international courts and tribunals or created new ones (see also Smith 2000). Although only the most serious and persistent norm violations reach international courts, we know very little about how they operate and under which conditions they successfully foster compliance. This book filled this gap in relation to the EU and investigated how the ECJ manage to talk states into compliance. How and under which conditions are judicial discourses, judgments and threats of sanctions effective in facilitating policy changes?

In answering these questions this book contributes to several strands of the current research in political science, legal studies and sociology. Firstly, the legalization literature focuses on judicial means to abolish non-compliance. However, legalization approaches are largely under-theorized and expect judicial discourses either to be effective, once they are in place, or once states possess the necessary capacities to comply. Based on a comprehensive analysis of the operation of the ECJ, this book showed that the explanatory value of legalization theory is limited. In order to account for the empirical puzzle that the success of compliance instruments significantly varies in each of the member states, this book developed a fine-grained theoretical approach and demonstrated that the presence of compliance instruments is only the necessary condition for their success, which ultimately depends on issue-related variables. Secondly, compliance approaches of International Relations (IR) often focus on sanctions as a means to abolish norm violations and tend to overstate the impact of power-variables (e.g. Downs, Rocke and Barsoom 1996, Martin 1992, Martin and Simmons 1998). In contrast, this book argued that sanction-threats do not facilitate compliance, as long as governments cannot be sure that they might be sanctioned while they are still in office. In contrast to the IR literature with its strong emphasis on country-variables as explanatory factors, this book focused on the interplay between the ECJ and domestic politics. It demonstrated that governments can become argumentatively entrapped by judicial discourses, that domestic compliance constituencies crucially influence whether judgments succeed, and that sanction-threats end violations of EU law if they are looming and high. Thirdly, while prominent EU compliance studies mainly analyse compliance dynamics in early stages of the EU infringement procedure (e.g. Falkner *et al.* 2005, Tallberg 1999), this book focused only on ECJ cases. It analysed hard cases of norm violations, in which states stubbornly resisted introducing sufficient domestic changes and in which the very preconditions for the effectiveness of EU law had been severely impaired. In addition, this book complements prominent compliance and Europeanization approaches and provides a gap-bridging approach, which coherently combines rationalism and constructivism in order to fully account for the complex reality of social interactions.

This chapter summarizes the argument and the major findings and points to lessons learned from studying the European Union and its institutionally embedded compliance instruments.

8.1 The argument and major findings

If member states do not comply with EU law, the European Commission can refer infringement cases to the ECJ. Just like any other international court, the ECJ lacks a legitimate monopoly of force. Hence, it is very important to talk states into compliance with judicial discourses, judgments and threats of sanctions. Yet although these instruments are always applied in the same order, their success varies significantly, in particular within but also between states. Sooner or later, all cases get settled, but the required time differs. The records of member states are very mixed. All show cases that were quickly settled and others that dragged on for a while before compliance was ultimately achieved. Why is the application of a compliance instrument successful in some cases but a failure in others? How can we explain differences in the transformational prospects? Why are some infringements settled swiftly after the ECJ referral, while others take several additional years?

This book shows that the ECJ, similar to other international courts, has three different instruments to push reluctant states into compliance. The Court applies judicial discourses, judgments and sanction-threats, always in the same order. The presence of the toolbox and the use of the instruments is a necessary but not sufficient condition to end norm violations. All three compliance instruments are only successful in inducing compliance despite the initial resistance of the responsible ministries, if issue-scope conditions are met. By contrast, the book showed that country-variables, such as economic and political power, political or administrative capacities or judicial culture did not shape responses to compliance instruments. These factors are more or less constant in the four German cases, while the success of judicial discourses, judgments and sanction-threats varies. The same applies to the four UK cases.

Judicial discourses can foster comprehensive forms of compliance. If both parties actively engage in the judicial discourse, exchange judicial arguments, relate to the same legal acts and if the judicial methods of interpretation fit to the interpretational complexity of the issue at stake, the advocates stop talking at cross purposes in the course of the discourse and are likely to resolve the interpretational ambiguity and develop a legally superior interpretation of the contested norm. Through regular contacts between ministries and advocates, states get argumentatively entrapped. They learn that the norm violation can no longer be defended with good arguments and shift into comprehensive compliance because they could not argumentatively defend the old norm interpretation any longer without violating norms of consistency, credibility and appropriateness. As hypothesized, judicial discourses are based on constructivist dynamics, while none of the eight case studies found any evidence of compliance bargaining in the shadow of judicial discourses or of reputational-threats, as the two rationalist approaches would expect (see also Table 8.1).

Judgments do not directly foster compliance top-down. They do not carry new arguments other than those already voiced in the judicial discourse and cannot directly induce policy changes since the same arguments in the original judicial discourse had no effect on the state. Nor do judgments themselves pose a costly threat on non-compliant governments or enable states to engage in compliance bargaining. Judgments provide authoritative norm definitions, increase the publicity, diffuse new ideas or arguments into the society and thereby differentially empower domestic compliance constituencies to the disadvantage of compliance opponents. Differentially empowered norm-advocating actors can use the additional resources to push their governments into compliance from below with shaming or reframing strategies. Shaming is based on a rationalist causal mechanism. If the judgment resonates with already institutionalized domestic ideas, shaming the government for inappropriately violating its own norms increases domestic non-compliance costs, to which governments respond with minimalist adaptations in order to avoid reputational and electoral losses. Unlike shaming, the reframing of domestic debates does not directly address the ECJ case but indirectly relates to the legal norm in question. It is based on a constructivist mechanism. If differentially empowered societal actors launch a new frame that affects the handling of the issue at stake in the infringement case, it brings about comprehensive compliance if a complementary frame is present to which the new frame can easily be linked. Hence, judgments can operate on an argumentative and a bargaining basis and, depending on which strategies are applied, can foster either minimalist or comprehensive forms of compliance. In addition, the timing of when norm violations will be abolished differs. Shaming strategies work best immediately after the ECJ judgment, since they rely on public attention to generate reputation costs for the government. Reframing domestic debates, by contrast, is a time-consuming process in which an old reference system is incrementally replaced by a new one, which paves the way for comprehensive policy change.

Sanction-threats come into play once judicial discourses and judgments have proven ineffective. The eight case studies did not find any support for the constructivist hypothesis. Sanction-threats do not reinforce a logic of appropriateness to comply with the ECJ and thus do not differentially empower pro-compliance ministries vis-à-vis governmental veto-players. Rather, this compliance instrument operates on a rationalist basis. Whenever a government can expect to become subject to high penalties during their incumbency because first steps towards enforcement have been introduced and the infringement is serious, governments adapt their strategic cost–benefit calculations and shift into minimalist compliance.

Overall, the ECJ possesses a rich toolbox in order to restore the effectiveness of European law – even against the initial resistance of affected states. In the broader picture, the application of judicial discourses, judgments and sanction-threats is a great success story. Since 1993 there have only been four cases of incorrect transpositions in which these compliance instruments did not suffice, meaning that the ECJ actually had to issue penalties (see also footnote 2, Chapter 1). Thus, the EU has an effective legal system and manages to induce compliance. Even if it might take up to 15 years, in the end all infringement cases are settled and states comply with previously contested law.

This book introduced a distinction in two types of domestic change in response to compliance instruments: minimalist and comprehensive compliance. Why should we be interested in whether a case ends in minimalist or in comprehensive compliance? The answer is simply that the nature of domestic change affects the effectiveness of EU law. In minimalist legal changes, states adapt legal acts in some respects but incorporate backdoors (e.g. through overlapping rules, complex exceptional clauses, undefined new concepts, broad legal terms) allowing them to shift into lax and less costly norm interpretations for the application stage. By contrast, the more comprehensive domestic legal changes are, the fewer legal uncertainties and norm divergences can emerge in the process of practical implementation. As a consequence, EU law that was subject to comprehensive legal changes is better equipped to fulfil its regulatory or protective purpose. On the other hand, EU law subject to minimalist transpositions is more likely to still entail a high number of legal uncertainties leading to applicatory margins of manoeuvre for implementation authorities. Such minimalist transpositions foster less effective and less coherent applications of EU law and restrain some of its regulatory ambitions. Cases ending in comprehensive compliance, by contrast, are less prone to domestic legal conflicts, which reduces the probability that they become referred to the ECJ via the decentralized preliminary ruling procedure (Art. 234) in subsequent years. The UK collective redundancies, the UK and the German drinking water cases and the German equal access case were all instances in which states shifted from non-compliance into comprehensive forms of compliance in response to the judicial discourses and reframing campaigns triggered by judgments respectively. In all four cases, the numbers of domestic court cases dealing with similar interpretational difficulties as the EU infringement proceeding dropped drastically after the legal changes were completed. By contrast, in the cases in which states shifted into minimalist forms of compliance, as in the German foreign workers and environmental impact assessment cases as well as in the UK cases on equal access and nitrates, the number of national court cases on very similar issues was more or less constant or hardly declined at all after states adopted their legal acts in response to judgment-induced shaming or sanction-threats respectively (see also Annex, Table 1).

Table 8.1 Findings

	Hypothesis	*Findings*
Judicial discourse	**H1 ideational entrapment (constructivist mechanism):** Judicial discourses are likely to foster comprehensive compliance, if the advocates actively engage in the judicial discourse, if they analyse the same legal norm, and if they use a judicial method of interpretation with a high goodness of fit to the complexity of the interpretational problem at stake.	Confirmed
	H2a reputation costs (rationalist mechanism): Judicial discourses are likely to induce minimalist compliance if the advocates actively engage in the judicial discourse, if they analyse the same legal norm, and if they use a judicial method of interpretation with a high goodness of fit to the complexity of the interpretational problem at stake.	Not confirmed
	H2b compliance bargaining (rationalist mechanism): Informal compliance bargaining in the shadow of judicial discourse fosters quick legal adaptations and minimalist compliance, if the European Commission and the state mutually accept their bargaining capacities and incrementally arrive at a compromise norm interpretation.	Not confirmed
Court judgment	**H3 shaming (rationalist mechanism):** ECJ rulings strengthen societal norm proponents to the disadvantage of opponents. This is conducive to successful shaming and a minimalist form of compliance, if the judgment resonates well with domestically institutionalized norms.	Confirmed
	H4 reframing (constructivist mechanism): Judgments reduce the complexity of the issues at stake. This is conducive to societal reframing strategies that induce comprehensive compliance, if new frames fit with other prominent, complementary frames.	Confirmed
Sanction threat	**H5 sanction costs (rationalist mechanism):** Minimalist compliance can be expected, if anticipated sanction costs exceed domestic non-compliance benefits. This is all the more likely if sanction-threats are looming and if the amount of sanctions is high due to the seriousness of the infringement.	Confirmed
	H6 domestic empowerment (constructivist mechanism): Sanction-threats differentially empower lead ministries and induce comprehensive compliance, if the lead ministry preferred compliance from the outset but was prevented from proposing or passing demanding policies by domestic veto players.	Not confirmed

8.II Summary of the cases

The British collective redundancy case shows how successful judicial discourses further comprehensive compliance. The collective redundancy directive (75/129) regulates information and consultation rights of workers seeking to protect them in processes of collective redundancies. While the Labour government completely complied with it, the preceding Conservative government pursued a liberal economic approach that delimited collective rights of trade unions and de facto abolished entitlements to information and consultation. Thus, the UK shifted into non-compliance. The case came before the ECJ, where both parties actively exchanged arguments and where they stooped talking at cross purposes after they used methods of legal reasoning that provided clear and unambiguous interpretations and allowed them to resolve the four contested issues. The government could no longer defend its initial preferences with valid arguments, became argumentatively entrapped and shifted into a comprehensive form of compliance – even against domestic resistance of employer associations. In the UK equal treatment (76/207), drinking water (80/778), and nitrates (91/676) cases, judicial discourses failed. The governments in Westminster maintained the norm violations, because the advocates of both parties either did not both engage in legal interpretation (e.g. the UK did not make legal arguments in the nitrates case), applied judicial interpretational methods to different legal acts (e.g. equal access case), or used judicial methods that did not fit with the interpretational scope of the contested elements (e.g. drinking water case, equal access case). ECJ judgments were effective in two of the remaining three cases. In the equal treatment case, the judgment created publicity, provided an authoritative norm definition and empowered women's organizations vis-à-vis employers and trade unions. The former succeeded in shaming the government into a minimalist form of compliance, because of the high resonance between the judgment and domestically institutionalized norms on economic deregulation. Domestic non-compliance costs increased and the Thatcher government adapted strategic positions by abolishing negative and positive discrimination against women. In the drinking water case, the judgment reduced the complexity of the issue at stake. Differentially empowered environmental and water customer organizations reframed the judgment and the public drinking water debate from a public health into a more demanding environmental issue that encompassed different types of water and thereby induced comprehensive compliance. This was possible because the polluters-pay principle allowed linkage of the environmental to the prominent cost frame, according to which private water bills should not considerably increase because of quality issues, as long as public health was not affected in a complementary manner. In the nitrates case, the government restricted the applicatory scope of the nitrates directive severely. Neither the judicial discourse, nor the judgment was successful in putting the norm violation to an end. The domestic non-compliance constituency of farmers was strong and widely supported by the public, because of the BSE and other farming crises, so that shaming strategies would not have posed effective bargaining threats of reputational losses. Environmental organizations did not successfully reframe nitrates into a demanding environment protection approach, because a complementary frame was lacking, while the discourse was dominated by public health ideas and solidarity avowals with farmers, which reinforced each other. In this context, a sanction-threat came into play. The Commission calculated the amount of penalties and took the seriousness of the infringement into consideration. Accordingly, the proposed amount of penalties was high and the government became deterred after they had received the second reasoned opinion and could expect to be subject to penalties during their incumbency. Hence, the government finally shifted into minimalist compliance.

In the German drinking water case (80/778), the Commission accused the Kohl government of allowing exceptions and tolerating derogations without transparently communicating them. During the judicial discourse, the advocates of both parties actively exchanged legal arguments in relation to the same legal acts and stopped talking at cross purposes after they applied judicial methods, which fitted well the interpretational scope of disputed elements. Both parties concluded that 'states of emergency' is a necessary precondition for granting exceptions, while not all natural events, such as thunderstorms, qualify as 'states of emergency'. They also agreed that data on all derogations and granted exceptions must be

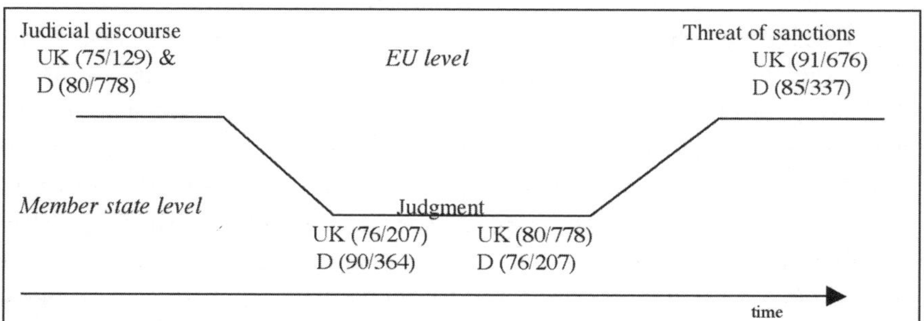

Figure 8.1 Overview of the case studies

collected and made publicly accessible. In response to the judicial discourse, the German government changed its policy ideas and transformed the norm violation into a comprehensive form of compliance – even against the strong resistance of its advisory body, the federal health office. At the same time, the judgment and the threat of financial sanctions were ineffective, the former because a pro-compliance constituency was largely absent and the latter because possible sanctions were remote since the Commission did not even introduce first steps towards enforcement. In the remaining three cases judicial discourses failed in many of the issues at stake. In the German case on the residence of foreign workers and their families (90/364), the judgment released an authoritative norm definition, highlighting that transparency of legal entitlements is essential to increase the reliability for foreign workers and their families concerning residence rights. It differentially empowered church associations and trade unions. These norm proponents successfully conducted shaming campaigns because of the match between the judgment and domestically deep-seated ideas on Christian charity, as well as on fundamental rights such as fair, transparent, and equal procedures. In response, the government in Bonn shifted into minimalist compliance. Conversely, successful reframing strategies focusing on Germany as an immigration country did not take place, because this alternative conception was not compatible with prominent ideas of foreigners as short-term guest workers. Finally, the government did not perceive potential financial penalties as threatening and did not shift into minimalist compliance in order to avoid external costs, because the shadow of sanctions was not imminent. In the German equal treatment case (76/207), the judgment reduced the complexity of the issues at stake, which empowered women's organizations. While shaming campaigns failed to induce domestic changes, because the re-elected government adjusted its policy preferences once the threat declined, reframing campaigns succeeded. Societal norm proponents launched a new gender equality frame, which could be linked to the complementary, prominent human rights approach. This created a more demanding definition of the equal treatment principle and triggered policy changes. As a result, more than ten years after the directive came into effect, a comprehensive form of compliance was finally achieved. Threats of sanctions had no effect on compliance dynamics, in particular because first steps towards enforcement measures were not introduced and because external reputational losses were unlikely since many member states violated the equal access directive. The environmental impact assessment case was an example of successful sanction-threats. The judicial discourse failed to resolve all interpretational questions. The ECJ judgment was also not effective, due to a lack of societal actors specialized in an integrated instead of a media-specific environmental approach. Thus, only after the Commission sent a second reasoned opinion to the SPD/Green government and, due to the seriousness of the infringement, specified a deterrent daily penalty, did a second ECJ judgment issuing financial sanctions become very likely in the near future. In order to avoid becoming subject to these high financial penalties during their incumbency, the Schröder government quickly abandoned their comprehensive and time-consuming plans to reform the whole environmental law sector in Germany and instead shifted into minimalist compliance.

8.III Lessons learned for other member states

What can we learn about other states from studying how the UK and Germany reacted to the compliance instruments of the ECJ? Can we expect that others, for example Austria and Cyprus, react in the same manner to judicial discourses, judgments and sanction-threats? The short answer is 'yes'.

Prominent compliance theories focus on institutional design, capacity and cultural variables and cannot sufficiently account for the differential success of compliance instruments. Legalization approaches emphasize the importance of the institutional design for prospects of transforming norm violations into compliance (e.g. the independence of judges, the binding character of judgments) (see also Mitchell 1996). Yet the institutional design is constant and the ECJ applies each of the instruments in a subsequent order. Hence, institutional provisions cannot explain why some cases are settled quickly while others drag on and they cannot account for the fact that only some judicial discourses or only some judgments succeed in promoting compliance. The UK and Germany have different legal cultures and political capacities. Hence, management and cultural approaches (Chayes, Handler-Chayes and Mitchell 1998, Gibson and Caldeira 1996, Visegrády 2001) predict differences in the effectiveness of judicial discourses between Germany and the UK. While the management school expects higher success rates for the UK than for Germany, which is burdened by high numbers of domestic veto players and lower political capacities (Chayes and Handler-Chayes 1993, Chayes, Handler-Chayes and Mitchell 1998), legal culture approaches expect judicial discourses to be more effective in Germany with its judicialized-internationalized legal culture than in the UK with its politicized and state-centered culture (Gibson and Caldeira 1996; Jacob *et al.* 1996). Neither holds true. Despite their differences, Germany and the UK are principally equally responsive to judicial discourses. The German drinking water and the British collective redundancy cases demonstrated that Berlin and London can be talked into compliance, if national and European advocates both actively engage in exchanging arguments, both focus on the same legal acts, and stop talking at cross purposes once a judicial method with a good match to the complexity of the problem at stake provides a norm definition. In both cases, the governments changed policies in response to the judicial discourses. At the same time, there are numerous instances of failed judicial discourses for the UK and for Germany. Whenever the essential preconditions of active engagement, the application of juridical methods of interpretation to the same legal acts, and the acceptance of judicial interpretations that have a high match to the issue at stake are absent, the advocates talk at cross purposes, irrespective of their legal cultures, and governments do not become argumentatively entrapped. The German foreign workers, the German and British equal access, the British drinking water, the German environmental impact assessment and the British nitrates cases are all instances in which judicial discourses could not solve all interpretational questions at stake. Consensual norm definitions were not developed and subsequently the governments in London and in Berlin did not introduce legal changes in reaction to judicial discourses.

Powerful states, such as Germany or the UK, cannot deter the ECJ from issuing judgments against them – even though this is what enforcement theory would expect (Dorn and Fulton 1997, Downs, Rocke and Barsoom 1996, Fearon 1998, Martin 1992). The case studies showed that judgments automatically follow if judicial discourses do not induce very swift adaptations. Although judgments are frequent, they are only sometimes effective in fostering domestic changes even for one and the same government. In both equal access cases, in the German foreign workers case and in the British drinking water case, judgments empowered domestic norm proponents respectively, which used their additional ideational resources to push their governments into compliance from below. At the same time, judgments were ineffective in the German environmental impact and the British nitrates cases; although the legal cultures remained constant within both countries and although the political and economic powers neither deteriorated nor increased in Germany or in the UK. The UK equal access and the German foreign worker cases exemplified that societal proponents can succeed with shaming campaigns if judgments resonate well with already institutionalized domestic norms. Only then can they blame governments for inappropriate actions and threaten them with damages of reputation and losses in electoral support. In both Court cases, the governments shied away from increasing non-compliance costs and pursued incomplete legal changes that left broad loopholes for future norm deviations. Similarly, the UK drinking water and the German equal access cases illustrate that societal actors can successfully reframe domestic debates, if they launch new policy frames that can be easily linked to complementary prominent ones. In both instances, the governments in London and Berlin adopted new policy approaches, abandoned non-compliance and pursued comprehensive compliance instead.

For sanction-threats, enforcement theories expect that powerful states will shy away from penalties less frequently (Dorn and Fulton 1997, Downs, Rocke and Barsoom 1996, Fearon 1998, Martin 1992). Yet the British nitrates case and the German environmental impact assessment cases prove the opposite. In both cases sanction-threats became effective once the Commission proposed deterrent penalties to the ECJ, which the government would have faced during their incumbency. Then, non-compliance costs became prohibitive and the governments in London and Berlin transformed continued non-compliance into a minimalist form of compliance.

In sum, country-specific variables cannot explain why one and the same compliance instrument is sometimes effective in facilitating domestic change, but fails to end norm violations in other instances, even if the same government is concerned. If we wish to explain under which conditions judicial discourses, judgments and sanction-threats succeed in restoring compliance, we must shift our attention to issue-specific variables, such as the interpretational scope of the issue, prior existing domestic norms, domestic policy frames or the seriousness of the infringement.

Hence, we can generalize the findings of this study on the effectiveness of judicial discourses, judgments and sanction-threats also to other EU member states. Although this book does not analyse new member states or countries with lower administrative or financial capacities, such as Bulgaria or Greece, its conclusions apply to this group of states as well. This book focused on compliance problems arising from the transposition of EU law into domestic law but did not analyse problems of incorrect practical applications of EU law in member states. While the latter requires many financial and administrative capacities, but fewer political capacities, the opposite applies to instances of incorrect transpositions. For the adaptation of legal acts, governments need to be able to pass laws and regulations, while the need for financial means and the demand for bureaucratic support are limited. Thus, if capacity differences matter at all for the prospects of international courts to settle hard cases of non-compliance, political capacities should have influenced compliance-restoring dynamics and outcomes. Yet, as Chapter 7 showed, veto players do not negatively influence the operation and effectiveness of compliance instruments, even in most likely cases. Moreover, while administrative and financial capacity shortcomings are important for the occurrence of norm violations in the first place (Börzel *et al.* 2007), their relevance declines across the stages of the infringement procedure. Once cases reach the ECJ, each of the EU members principally possesses the necessary administrative or financial capacities to correctly transpose EU law into their domestic orders. If states should run into capacity shortcomings during the process of legal adaptation, they can redistribute financial resources internally and they can push their bureaucracy to be more effective in order to cope with governmental priorities. In particular, since only a few cases are usually in front of the Court at a given time, member states can adjust their resource investments to the cases in which legal transpositions are of utmost importance.

8.IV Lessons learned for other policy fields

What can we learn from studying environmental and employment policies for other policy areas? Are the insights of this book also applicable to the policy field 'transport and energy', for example? Again, the short answer is 'yes'.

The chances of compliance instruments of international courts settling cases and restoring the effectiveness of law beyond the nation-state are strongly influenced by issue-related variables, such as the interpretational scope of the problem at stake or the seriousness of the infringement. These variables can neither be equated with policy fields, nor do they correlate with specific policies. Hence, the insights of this book can be applied to all policy fields.

The most prominent compliance instrument, judicial discourses, effectively and comprehensively ends norm violations if the advocates of the parties do not talk at cross purposes in Court. This requires that they engage in the exchange of judicial arguments, analyse the same legal acts, and apply a judicial method of interpretation, which must fit the complexity of the interpretational problem. For example, the narrow wording method of legal reasoning inquires into the exact phrasing of contested issues. If the interpretational problem at hand is complex, a wording method cannot provide a single interpretation. If crucial concepts are not specified, different paragraphs are relevant but differ in their literal meaning, or contested issues are not mentioned at all, investigating the wording of norms provides no solutions of how to interpret them. Hence, only if the issue-specific scope condition is present, as in the German drinking water and in the UK collective redundancy cases, can judicial discourses succeed in completely abolishing norm violations. As these two and the other six case studies showed, policy fields did not influence the complexity of the interpretational questions at stake and thus do not affect the effectiveness of judicial discourses.

Likewise, judgments are effective if differentially empowered societal actors engage in bottom-up compliance strategies and if the contextual preconditions for effective shaming or reframing campaigns are present. Empirically, judgments ended norm violations in four cases, three of which belonged to the social policy field (the German and the UK cases on the equal access directive and the German foreign workers case). In order to be effective, judgments require organized societal domestic norm proponents, which push their governments into compliance from below, after becoming differentially empowered. The domestic structure of interest representation differs between the social and environmental policy fields. While the latter is characterized by interest group pluralism and a high number of specialized organized interests, social policy is characterized by corporatism and the presence of peak associations (Falkner 1999). The presence of highly organized norm proponents is conducive to successful shaming or reframing strategies, since peak organizations represent a high number of individuals and speak with one voice. This is not to say that judgments are in principle less effective in the environmental policy field and are in general more successful in employment policies. Firstly, trade unions, just like employer associations, are not per se compliance proponents in all social policy cases, but might well be opponents in some cases. Secondly, interest group pluralism delimits the power of environmental organizations as compliance proponents if we compare them to peak associations. Nevertheless, they can turn into important actors and succeed with compliance-inducing strategies. This requires that the contextual preconditions are present, as the UK drinking water case demonstrated, in which reframing was possible as the new environmental frame was linked to the complementary cost frame.

Finally, sanction-threats induce domestic changes once governments anticipate that they will become subject to high penalties during their incumbency, which requires that the European authorities introduce first steps towards enforcement and that the infringement is serious so that sanctions act as a deterrent. The criteria for the seriousness of an infringement are issue-specific and encompass among others the relative gains of a member state from violating a particular norm and the damage of the norm violation for other member states and the operation of the EU. Does this introduce a policy field related bias in the effectiveness of sanction-threats? Can sanction-threats induce compliance if a distributive or redistributive issue instead of a regulative or reregulative one is at stake? In a nutshell, the answer is 'no'. Firstly, all cases that reach the ECJ are instances in which governmental non-compliance preferences are very strong; otherwise they could have settled the case in the pre-judicial stage of the infringement procedure. Thus, severe gains and losses are at stake for the governments and the issue salience is high across all ECJ cases. Secondly, negative externalities arising from the norm violation for other member states or the EU as a whole do also not systematically vary over policy fields or between regulative and (re)distributive issues.

In sum, the scope conditions for the success of the compliance instruments are not influenced by policy field variables. Judicial discourses, judgments and sanction-threats can be as effective in distributive and redistributive domains (e.g. agricultural policy, social policy) as in regulative ones (e.g. transport and energy, enterprise, environment).

Moreover, rule-specific variables, such as the precision of the contested secondary law (Kaeding 2006: 236, Mastenbroek 2003), the complexity of the directive (Krislov, Ehlermann and Weiler 1986), the number of disputed issues at stake in Court or the extent of misfit (Falkner *et al.* 2005), did not influence whether cases could have been settled quickly or slowly. For example, the EIA and the equal access directive as such have broad interpretational scopes, because they are based on abstract concepts and broad and complicated exceptional clauses, whereas the DWD and the foreign workers directives are more precise. Yet this did not causally influence the durations of infringement procedures and settlement dynamics, because the overall precision of a norm does not determine the precision of the interpretational issues at stake. Precise and vague directives can entail very specific or very complex issues, each of which can possibly turn into an interpretational dispute. Thus the high complexity of the nitrates and the equal access directives did not cause longer durations of infringement procedures in the corresponding UK and German cases. Once non-compliance had been detected by the Commission, it required a total of nine years in both of the UK cases before domestic changes took place that resembled compliance, while the more precise collective redundancy and the drinking water directives needed a total of 15 and 19 years respectively to be settled in the UK. This is not surprising, since the eight

Court cases encompassed issues with narrow, as well as broad, interpretational scopes. The qualitative studies showed that complex interpretational problems, such as the status of midwives in the equal access directive, do not per se take longer and are not generally less suited to being resolved via judicial discourses than precise interpretational issues, as for example the inclusion of small undertakings in the equal access case.

The extent of policy misfit does not influence the duration of infringement proceedings either. The resonance between European and already present domestic policies was lower in the German drinking water and the German equal access cases than in the German cases on the foreign workers and the EIA directives, but the latter two did not take more time (6 and 14 years) than the former (10 and 15 years) from the detection of the norm violation until compliance was finally achieved. In the UK, the legal mismatch was higher in the drinking water and the collective redundancy cases, in which relatively precise directives were at stake, than in the nitrates and the equal access cases, in which rather ambivalent directives were contested. Yet neither the precision of the European law as such, nor the degree of misfit, influenced the success of ECJ compliance instruments. Norm violations were not quickly resolved through judicial discourses in cases with low misfit or precise directives and it also did not take longer until cases were settled in those instances with high misfit or complex directives. The UK nitrates case, for example, was an instance with relatively limited misfit, but it required a sanction-threat in order to foster compliance.

Thus, the very fact that the ECJ has been very successful in facilitating compliance with its three compliance instruments, even against the strong initial resistance of affected governments, is not too surprising: neither country, nor policy field nor rule-specific characteristics systematically bias the operation of the instruments and do not prevent judicial discourses, judgments and threats of sanctions from effectively ending norm violations. Hence, there is no reason why the compliance instruments should be less or more effective in other policy areas.

8.V Outlook – international institutions and the settlement of norm violations

What can we learn from the EU and its toolbox of compliance instruments for the prospects of other international organizations to transform norm violations into compliance? Due to its supranational features, the EU is often regarded as a system of its own kind (e.g. Wallace and Wallace

2000).[1] Yet, this does not preclude lessons from the EU for other international institutions. Whether one can generalize from the EU experience to institutions, such as the EFTA, the Andean Community, the ASEAN, the WTO, the IMF, or the UN, depends on the properties we look at.

The EU infringement system – particular concerning hard cases of persistent non-compliance – is clearly not unique. Judicial discourses, binding judgments or threats of sanctions are prominent compliance instruments can also be found in other international institutions, such as the Andean Tribunal of Justice, the EFTA Court, the new GATT/WTO, the ECHR, the ICC, the ECOWAS Court or the COMESA Court, to name but a few (see also Alter 2008, Alter, Helfer and Guerzovich 2009, Smith 2000). Since 1993, the EFTA member states Norway, Iceland and Lichtenstein are under the jurisdiction of the EFTA Court, which expands market creating and regulating principles of EU law to non-EU members of the European Economic Area. In the EFTA Court, similar to the EU, ECOWAS, the EAC and the CACM, the first judicial compliance instrument is a judicial discourse, which is followed by binding judgments (Smith 2000). In many international institutions, such as the WTO/GATT, the Andean Pact, the CACM, the COMESA and the MERCOSUR, threats of sanctions subsequently come into play, if states do not comply with binding rulings (Garrett and Smith 2002, Petersmann 1997, Steinberg 2002). However, can we apply the insights from the compliance instruments of the ECJ to other international institutions as well? At first glance, the level of legalization might operate as a background variable for compliance and varies between international institutions. Highly legalized international institutions delegate competencies for the making of rules, their implementation, and the resolution of disputes to third parties, whereas international institutions with very low degrees of legalization retain the power of states to act independently (Abbott *et al.* 2000: 416). In terms of third party delegation, the EU almost resembles an empirical extreme case. Other international institutions, such as the WTO/GATT, the CACM, the COMESA and the MERCOSUR, less strongly delegate competencies to make and enforce decisions – possibly against the will of an affected state – to supranational bodies. While the general level of legalization could influence the extent to which norm violations occur in the first place, the main variable influencing the prospects to transform

[1] Among the most prominent supranational elements is the supremacy doctrine, according to which European breaks national law. Moreover, there is the preliminary rulings procedure, based on which national courts can refer cases in which they are uncertain whether national law complies with EU law to the ECJ (Alter 2000, Conant 2001, Conant 2006, Stone Sweet and Brunell 1998a).

detected instances of norm violation into compliance would be the extent to which the dispute resolution is legalized. This ranges from pure political bargaining, over conciliation, non-binding arbitration, and binding arbitration to the presence of courts with unlimited authority and the competence to make binding decisions (Abbott *et al.* 2000: 416). Thus, courts that can apply a judicial discourse, make a binding judgment, or issue a sanction threat or sanctions even against the will of affected states, are all highly legalized. To these courts, the insights of this study can be applied. While several courts have been developed according to the blueprint of the ECJ, the Andean Tribunal of Justice not only closely resembles the ECJ, but is also the fourth most active court in the world (Alter, Helfer and Guerzovich 2009). Another example of a court that can recur to the three compliance instruments is the EFTA Court.

Hence, judicial discourses should be as successful in the EFTA and the Andean Community as they are in the EU. Judgments should, however, be slightly less effective vis-à-vis authoritarian than democratic states since shaming by societal actors presupposes the presence of active civil society actors as well as a responsive government.[2] Hence, the transformational pattern in the EFTA should closely resemble that of the EU, while judgments by the COMESA Court are probably less successful. Finally, threats of sanctions most likely balance the somewhat decreased effectiveness of judgments vis-à-vis non-democratic regimes, because sanctions should be more of a deterrent for regimes with high government stability.[3]

[2] The shaming mechanism implicitly presumes that regimes are democratic, so that governments depend on popular support, which can be deprived in elections. If states are not sufficiently democratic, reputational losses created in shaming campaigns are less severe, since electoral ex-post sanctions are impossible. Authoritarian governments have fewer incentives to respond to the public and their electorate than their democratic counterparts. In addition, civil societies with independent presses and resource-prone, active societal organizations are weaker in authoritarian regimes. Thus, comparing democracies and authoritarian systems, the latter are likely to be less responsive to shaming campaigns so that judgments of international courts might be less successful in abolishing norm violations.

[3] The rationalist sanctioning hypothesis rests on the idea that governments discount costs arising from future penalties and shift into compliance once penalties become deterrent, which requires that they are high and likely to be issued while the government is still in office. If governments change more or less regularly because they are subject to popular elections every four, five or six years, it is possible that a government currently in office is eventually not subject to penalties, once they are issued and, therefore, does not respond to threats in the remote future but only to immediate ones. If, on the contrary, governmental compositions remain considerably more stable over time, it becomes more likely that a government will become subject to penalties during its incumbency. In general, governmental stability is higher in authoritarian than in democratic systems, not least because of the number of competing bigger political

Thus, given their heterogeneous membership, threats of penalties in the COMESA, ECOWAS, and the Andean Community should be slightly more prohibitive than in the EU, in which all members are democratic.

Ultimately, every political system becomes *sui generis*, if it is analysed in great depth. For example, the ECJ developed decentralized enforcement mechanisms in its case law. These include the doctrine of state liability, according to which individuals can sue states that violated EU law in not transposing or implementing it and claim compensation (Tallberg 2000: 110), as well as the doctrine of the indirect effect, according to which citizens can rely on EU law, even if states fail to correctly transpose or practically implement it (Stone Sweet and Brunell 1998b: 66). Both doctrines can exert a general compliance push in the first place, since member states seek to avoid paying financial compensations to their citizens. Nevertheless, no state is completely deterred from non-compliance, since all states violate some EU law (Börzel *et al.* forthcoming). Hence, the important question is whether these two very specific background conditions influence the operation of the ECJ compliance instruments. Can we generalize the findings on the scope conditions for the success of judicial discourses, judgments and sanction-threats to other IOs? This study showed that some infringement cases are settled early, while others are dragged on and reach the ECJ and might even require a judgment or a sanction-threat before states give in. The two EU-specific enforcement doctrines cannot explain this empirical variation. The indirect effect doctrine was established by the ECJ in 1984 in the *Von Colson* case and the state liability doctrine was developed in 1991 in the *Francovich* case (Stone Sweet and Brunell 1998b: 66). Thus both equal access cases were brought to Court at a time when none of the indirect enforcement doctrines were present (see also Chapter 5). Nevertheless, the German and the British governments reacted to the judgments of the ECJ and stopped their norm violations in the same way as in the German case on the residence of foreign workers and the UK case on drinking water. It was not the case that the governments were less reluctant to comply in the earlier infringement processes because of the lack of indirect enforcement doctrines. Hence, even though the presence of the indirect effect and state liability doctrines did vary across these four infringement cases, they did

parties differs and because elections tend to be less free and fair in authoritarian states. Hence, authoritarian rulers are more likely to be in office when an international court issues sanctions and should, therefore, be slightly more risk-averse than democratic governments. Ceteris paribus, this implies that penalties become more quickly prohibitive for authoritarian than for democratic governments.

not influence the effectiveness of the compliance instruments. Similarly, in the other six ECJ cases presented in this book both indirect enforcement doctrines were present while the success of compliance instruments varied. In sum, while the presence of the state liability and the indirect effect doctrines in the EU might increase the overall level of compliance compared to an international organization without these two indirect enforcement mechanisms, we can safely conclude that both doctrines do not influence the operation and the success of judicial discourses, judgments and sanction-threats in the EU.

Each and every international institution faces instances of norm violations, some of which endure for many years and hamper the effectiveness of international law. Against this background, this study has demonstrated that institutional engineering that introduces highly legalized compliance instruments can combat severe non-compliance cases. The current trend towards increasing legalization created several highly legalized judicial institutions (e.g. the EFTA Court, the Andean Tribunal of Justice, the ICC, the ECOWAS Court or the COMESA Court). The hope associated with those institutions has been that they prevent norm violations and restore compliance. This study suggests that institutional provisions are indeed important for detecting and abolishing breaches of international law, as the very precondition for its effectiveness. Moreover, this book argues that whether judicial discourses, binding judgments or sanction-threats will ultimately be successful does not causally depend on the judicial or political culture of a state, nor on the economic or political power or political or administrative capacities of the respective state, but is crucially influenced by issue-specific scope conditions (e.g. the interpretational scope of the issue, the fit between judgments and domestic norms, the seriousness of the infringement). Hence, establishing independent courts with a broad toolbox of compliance instruments, such as in the EFTA, the COMESA or in the Andean Community, is indeed necessary, but this alone will not be sufficient to remedy norm violations. The ECJ experience teaches us that issue-specific variables are crucial for successful settlements of hard non-compliance cases. This indicates that there are no structural, country-specific obstacles of why the might of the law cannot prevail in the longer run over the strength of powerful states.

Annex

Data sources for the dependent variable

All data on non-compliance stem from the Annual Reports of the European Commission and were compiled and updated by a research project funded by the German Research Council (DFG). The project 'Compliance. Wenn Staaten sich (nicht) an die Regeln halten' ('Compliance. Member States' (Non-)Compliance with EU Law') is headed by Prof. Dr Tanja A. Börzel (project number 0015031102; BO 1831/1–2, duration 2002–2007).

The data set on which the empirical puzzle is based encompasses all incorrect or delayed legal transpositions of EC directives and regulations into national legal acts between 1978 and 2000 in the EU-12. The total number of violations is 3,918. Using this subset has several advantages. Firstly, the subset encompasses all violations for delayed and incorrect transpositions of EC directives and regulations, but not failures in practical implementation. This reduces the total number of infringements (3,918 instead of 6,096 cases), but has the advantage of limiting the number of crucial actors as respondents to ECJ compliance instruments to governments, instead of including also regional and local governments and administrations. Secondly, it covers all cases for which the ECJ issued rulings between 1978, the date of the first published Annual Report, and 2000. The time-lag of nine years allows observing states' reactions to ECJ compliance instruments. Thirdly, the subset used includes the EU-12 member states and avoids a bias concerning newer member states. Research on the occurrence of non-compliance revealed that states have higher shares of norm violations in the years following their EU accession (Börzel 2001). Due to the high amount of secondary law in force, which new members must transpose, capacity problems can arise and might affect the ability to react to compliance instruments. Restricting the dataset to the EU-12 allows observing regular non-compliance records and transformational performance rates for at least 10 years for all states in the subset.

In order to categorize legal changes as comprehensive or minimalist, this study analysed the relevant legal acts. What issues were problematic in the original legal acts? Did the government introduce changes and were they comprehensive or incomplete (e.g. were all issues at stake before the ECJ legally transposed, did the legal acts introduce new concepts and complex interconnections within the norm, and did the legal acts introduce broad and complex exceptional clauses?). Finally, it was analysed how the adapted legal act fits into the broader legal landscape (where there many or few overlaps with other legal acts?). The data stem from the DIP database of the German Bundestag (http://dip.bundestag.de/cgi-bin/dip), from the database provided by the Office of Public Sector Information www.opsi.gov.uk/si/si199324.htm), and for the social policy fields additionally from the NATLEX database (www.ilo.org/dyn/natlex/natlex_browse.search?p_lang=en).

Furthermore, the type of domestic changes correlates with the number of court cases before and after the ECJ has been successful in fostering compliance. Comparing minimalist and comprehensive forms of compliance, we see that the number of domestic cases drops more sharply in instances in which the ECJ achieved transformations into comprehensive compliance. This is due to the fact that minimalist forms of compliance give rise to judicial contestation, due to ambiguities, abstract and undefined concepts, complex exceptional clauses, or overlaps within and between legal norms.

Preliminary reference data stem from the EUREX database (available at: http://europa.eu.int/eur-lex) and from the jurisprudence database, provided by the Association of the Councils of State and Supreme Administrative Jurisprudence of the European Union i.n.p.a. (1959–2006) (available at: http://193.191.217.21/en/jurisprudence/jurisprudence_en.lasso?page=results). Data on British court cases also stem from the Association of the Councils of State and Supreme Administrative Jurisprudence of the European Union i.n.p.a. as well as from Her Majesty's Courts Service database (1996–2006) (www.hmcourts-service.gov.uk/judgments.htm) and the BAIL II database provided by the British and Irish Information Institute (www.bailii.org/databases.html). Data on German court cases also stem from the Association of the Councils of State and Supreme Administrative Jurisprudence of the European Union i.n.p.a. as well as from the Bundesverwaltungsgericht (www.bverwg.de), Bundesarbeitsgericht (juris.bundesarbeitsgericht.de/cgi-bin/rechtsprechung/list

.py?Gericht=bag&Art=en) and Bundessozialgericht (www.jura.uni-sb.de /Entscheidungen/Bundesgerichte/BSG/).

Annexe Table 1 Preliminary ruling references and domestic court cases*

Case	*Number of court cases in the 5-year period before compliance was achieved*		*Outcome after compliance instrument was effective*	*Number of court cases in the 5-year period after compliance was achieved*	
	Art. 234 references	National court cases		Art. 234 references	National court cases
UK collective redundancy	0	4	Comprehensive compliance	0	0
Germany DWD	0	4	Comprehensive compliance	0	0
UK DWD	1	27	comprehensive compliance	0	6
Germany equal access	4	11	Comprehensive compliance	2	4
UK equal access	12	54	Minimalist compliance	10	38
Germany foreign workers	3	4	Minimalist compliance	1	2
UK nitrates	1	3	Minimalist compliance	0	5
Germany EIA	1	7	Minimalist compliance	1	6

*Court cases dealing with issues related to the 226 ECJ case

Data sources for the independent variables

This study draws on a broad variety of data sources. It analysed primary documents on judicial discourses, parliamentary debates, and newspaper articles, as well as public statements and strategy papers of involved public and societal actors. It also used a series of questionnaires on perceptions of involved organized interests regarding the case, their own role, the role of ECJ compliance instruments, and the domestic impact of the Court case. The empirical material includes a series of interviews with UK and German politicians and public administrators, organized interests, members of the European Commission, and former European Advocates General.

Primary documents in the respective parliaments and committees allow the tracing of rhetorical changes in domestic debates. The data stem from the Office of Public Sector Information for the House of Commons and the House of Lords (www.opsi.gov.uk/acts.htm). The parliamentary speeches in the German Bundestag and the Bundesrat were accessed though the DIP (Dokumentations- und Informationssystem für Parlamentarische Vorgänge) database of the Bundestag (http://dip.bundestag.de/cgi-bin/dipweb). All documents related to the issue area at stake before the ECJ were examined, covering periods from initial transpositions until five years after the first legal response to ECJ compliance instruments. The documents were subject to a content analysis in order to reconstruct initial governmental substantial policy interests and strategic positions as well as changes over time.

The newspapers selection includes the prominent as well as smaller, conservative/liberal and social-democratic papers, and regional as well as national papers. All newspapers were accessed in their electronic version, as available through the Lexis-Nexis database (http://web.lexis-nexis.com/professional/).

Aberdeen Press
Belfast Newsletter
Berliner Zeitung
Daily Mail
Daily Telegraph
Deutsche Presse Agentur (DPA)
Die Welt
Die Witschafts Woche
Express
Farmers Guardian
Financial Times
Frankfurter Allgemeine Zeitung
Frankfurter Rundschau
Guardian
Herald
Independent
Observer
Presswire
Scotsman
Stuttgarter Nachrichten
Stuttgarter Zeitung
Süddeutsche Zeitung
Sun
Sunday Herald
Sunday Times
TAZ
The Times
Western Daily Press
Western Mail
Western Morning News

In addition to the analysis of parliamentary speeches, discussions in committees, public speeches and newspaper reports, this book is also based on a variety of interviews that were conducted between 2004 and 2006. The interview partners were selected in order to triangulate information. Hence, they include state officials, MPs and party members, organized interests (pro and contra the directive at stake) and European actors (ECJ, Commission, and European Parliament). Since ECJ cases are sensitive issues, most of the officials agreed to give background information only. This information is not cited in the work. As a consequence interview data are rarely used throughout the study.

Annexe Table 2 List of interview partners

Affiliation	*Topic*	*Date and type of interview*	*Cited as*
Former member of the European Commission	Procedural issues	25/02/05 phone	COM#1, 25–02–05
Former member of the European Commission, DG Environment	Infringements, legal issues, procedural issues, environmental policy	02/03/05 phone	COM#2, 02–03–05
Former member of the European Commission	Equal access, procedural issues	03/03/05 phone	COM#3, 03–03–05
Former member of the European Commission	Environmental issues	22/11/05 phone	COM#4, 22–11–05
Former member of the European Commission	Environmental issues, legal issues, procedural issues	25/11/05 phone	COM#5, 25–11–05
Member of the European Commission	Environmental issues	6/12/05 phone	COM#6, 06–12–05
Member of the European Commission	Environmental and procedural issues	7/02/06 phone	COM#7, 07–02–06
Member of the Conservative Party, UK	Collective redundancies	11/10/06 phone	Conservative Party#1, 11–10–06
Member of the Conservative Party, UK	Nitrates	20/10/06 phone	Conservative Party#2, 20–10–06
Former Advocate General, European Court of Justice	Procedural issues	09/03/05 face to face	ECJ#1, 09–03–05
Former Advocate General, European Court of Justice	Procedural issues	16/03/05 phone	ECJ#2, 16–03–05
Former Advocate General, European Court of Justice	Procedural issues	23/03/05 phone	ECJ#3, 23–03–05
Former Advocate General, European Court of Justice	Procedural issues	02/10/08 face to face	ECJ#4, 02–10–08
Member of the European Parliament	Collective redundancies	22/10/04 phone	EP#1, 22–10–04
Member of the European Parliament	Collective redundancies	23/10/04 phone	EP#2, 23–10–04
Member of the European Parliament	Environmental impact assessment, nitrates, drinking water issues	02/02/05 phone	EP#3, 02–02–05

Affiliation	*Topic*	*Date and type of interview*	*Cited as*
Member of the European Parliament	Procedural issues	08/02/05 phone	EP#4, 08–02–05
Member of the European Parliament	Drinking water, nitrates.	04/02/05 phone	EP#5, 04–02–05
Member of the European Parliament	Drinking water, environmental policy	06/03/05 phone	EP#6, 06–03–05
Member of the European Parliament	Nitrates	03/06/05 phone	EP#7, 03–06–05
Federal Ministry of Finance, Germany	Procedural issues	08/10/04 face to face	Federal ministry#1, 08–10–04
Federal Ministry of Health and Social Security, Germany	Procedural issues, social policy issues	13/10/04 face to face	Federal ministry#2, 13–10–04
Federal Ministry of the Environment, Germany	Environment, procedural issues	15/10/04 face to face	Federal ministry#3, 15–10–04
Federal Ministry of Health and Social Security, Germany	Equal access, foreign workers, employment policy in general, procedural issues	01/02/05 phone	Federal ministry#4, 01–02–05
Federal Ministry of Labour and Social Affairs, Germany	Equal access	08/02/05 phone	Federal ministry#5, 08–02–05
Federal Ministry of Labour and Social Affairs, Germany	Equal access	08/02/05 phone	Federal ministry#6, 08–02–05
Federal Ministry for Health and Nuclear Safety, Germany	Drinking water, environmental policy, procedural issues	08/03/05 face to face	Federal ministry#7, 08–03–05
Member of the Green Party	Residence of foreign workers	17/11/03 phone	Green Party#1, 17–11–06
Member of the House of Commons, UK	Equal access	12/10/05 phone	House of Commons#1, 12–10–05
Member of the House of Commons, UK	Equal access	12/10/05 phone	House of Commons#2, 12–10–05
Member of the House of Commons, UK	Nitrates, environmental issues	02/11/05 phone	House of Commons#3, 02–11–05
Member of the House of Commons, UK	Nitrates	3/11/2005 phone	House of Commons#4, 03–11–05

Member of the House of Commons, UK	Employment policy, collective redundancies	10/10/06 phone	House of Commons#5, 10–10–06
Member of the House of Commons, UK	Collective redundancies	11/10/06 phone	House of Commons#6, 11–10–06
Member of the Labour Party, UK	Nitrates, environmental issues	02/11/05 phone	Labour Party#1, 02–11–05
Member of the Labour Party, UK	Drinking water issues	21/09/06 phone	Labour Party#2, 21–09–06
Department for Work and Pensions, UK	Collective redundancies	25/10/05 phone	Ministry#1, 25–10–05
DEFRA, UK	nitrates and drinking water	02/11/05 phone	Ministry #2, 02–11–05
Sustainable Development Commission, UK	Nitrates	09/12/05 phone	Ministry#3, 09–12–05
DEFRA, UK	Nitrates and water quality issues	09/12/05 phone	Ministry#4, 09–12–05
Department for Work and Pensions, UK	Collective redundancies	07/02/06 phone	Ministry#5, 07–02–06
Government Equality Office, UK	Equal access	02/03/06 phone	Ministry#6, 02–03–06
Department for Business, Enterprise and Regulatory Reform, UK	Equal access	03/03/06 phone	Ministry#7, 03–03–06
Deutscher Landfrauen-verband, Germany	Equal access	04/02/05 phone	Organized interests#1, 04–02–05
Deutscher Frauenrat, Germany	Equal access	04/02/05 email	Organized interests#2, 03–02–05
Deutscher Juristinnenbund, Germany	Equal access in Germany and the UK	08/02/05 phone	Organized interests#3, 08–02–05
UVP Gesellschaft, Germany	Environmental impact assessment	08/02/05 phone	Organized interests#4, 08–02–05
Demokratischer Frauenbund, Germany	Equal access	09/02/05 phone	Organized interests#5, 09–02–05
Deutscher Frauenring, Germany	Equal access	10/02/05 phone	Organized interests#6, 10–02–05
Bundesverband Deutscher Gas- und Wasserindustrie, Germany	Drinking water	09/02/05 phone	Organized interests#7, 09–02–05

Affiliation	*Topic*	*Date and type of interview*	*Cited as*
Deutscher Juristinnenbund, Germany	Equal access	15/02/05 phone	Organized interests#8, 15–02–05
Deutscher Gewerkschaftsbund, Germany	Equal access in Germany and the UK	21/02/05 phone	Organized interests#9, 21–02–05
Katholischer Deutscher Frauenbund, Germany	Equal access	11/03/05 email	Organized interests#10, 11–03–05
Bundesverband Deutscher Gas- und Wasserindustrie, Germany	Drinking water	16/03/05 phone	Organized interests#11, 16–03–05
Friends of the Earth, UK	Drinking water	24/04/05 phone	Organized interests#12, 24–04–05
Confederation of British Industry, UK	Collective redundancies	13/09/05 phone	Organized interests#13, 13–09–05
Trade Unions Congress, UK	Employment policy, collective redundancies	20/03/06 phone	Organized interests#14, 20–03–06
Trade Unions Congress, UK	Employment policy, collective redundancies	20/03/06 phone	Organized interests#15, 20–03–06
Equal Opportunity Commission, UK	Equal access	21/03/06 phone	Organized interests#16, 21–03–06
Evangelische Kirsche Deutschlands, Germany	Foreign workers	15/11/06 phone	Organized interests#17, 15–11–06
Former Member of the Arbeitsgemeinschaft Sozialdemokratischer Frauen, Germany	Equal access	03/02/05 phone	SPD#1, 03–02–05
Employment ministry, Sachsen-Anhalt, Germany	Social policy, collective redundancies	03/02/05 phone	State ministry# 1, 03–02–05
Finance ministry, Baden-Würtemberg, Germany	Procedural issues	11/02/05 phone	State ministry#2, 11–02–05
Environmental ministry, Baden-Würtemberg, Germany	Environmental impact assessment	09/03/05 face to face	State ministry#3, 09–03–05
Economic ministry, Brandenburg, Germany	Procedural issues, state-regions	10/03/05 phone	State ministry#4, 10–03–05

Affiliation	*Topic*	*Date and type of interview*	*Cited as*
Environmental ministry, Sachsen-Anhalt Germany	Environmental impact assessment	15/03/05 phone	State ministry#5, 15–03–05
Finance ministry, Brandenburg, Germany	Procedural issues, state-regions	15/03/05 phone	State ministry#6, 15–03–05
Environment ministry, Baden-Würtemberg, Germany	Environmental impact assessment, nitrates	10/05/05 phone	State ministry#7, 10–05–05
Economic ministry, Hessen, Germany	Foreign workers, equal access	30/06/05 phone	State ministry#8, 30–06–05
Umweltbundesamt, Germany	Drinking water	18/02/05 phone	UBA#1, 18–02–05
Umweltbundesamt, Germany	Drinking water, environmental impact assessment	21/02/05 phone	UBA#2, 21–02–05
Umweltbundesamt, Germany	Drinking water, environmental impact assessment	21/02/05 phone	UBA#3, 21–02–05
Umweltbundesamt, Germany	Drinking water	01/03/05 phone	UBA#4, 01–03–05
Umweltbundesamt, Germany	Drinking water in Germany and UK	18/03/05 phone	UBA#5, 18–03–05
Umweltbundesamt, Germany	Drinking water in Germany and UK	06/05/05 face to face	UBA #6, 06–05–05

Independent variables of country-specific approaches

Power

Within the EU, power resources of states are either economic or political in character, but not military. Economic capacity (measured by the GDP) is a proxy for power, since the GDP influences the financial vulnerability of states and the number and goodness of alternative actions (e.g. unilateral) to future institutionalized cooperation within or outside the EU (Börzel *et al.* 2007). The data on GDP stem from the World Bank (World Bank 2004). In the EU, political power of states is most likely exerted in the Council of Ministers. Hence, the number of votes in the Council provides a proxy for its political power.

Capacity

Political capacity can be operationalized as the number of veto players according to the adjusted veto player index of Tsebelis (Tsebelis 2002a,

Tsebelis 2002b). The data are available at: www.polisci.ucla.edu/tsebelis/vpdata.html. Administrative capacities are operationalized by an index for bureaucratic efficiency (Mbaye 2001), which is based on data in *Civil Services in the Europe of the Fifteen: Current Situation and Prospects*, by Astrid Auer *et al.* (Auer, Demmke and Polet 1996). The bureaucratic efficiency index captures individuals' motivations to work effectively and consists of three equally weighted elements (3: highest efficiency; 1: lowest efficiency), performance-related pay, the absence of permanent tenure, and public announcement of vacancies. The bureaucratic efficiency is Belgium 1; Denmark 3; Germany 2; Greece 1; Spain 1; France 1; Ireland 1; Italy 1; the Netherlands 2; Portugal 1; United Kingdom 3. In addition to political and administrative capacity, financial means are also a capacity indicator (Börzel *et al.* 2007). It is measured by the GDP per capita. The data stem from the World Bank (http://siteresources.worldbank.org/DATASTATISTICS/Resources/GNIPC.pdf).

Judicial culture

Judicial culture is operationalized through a compound index on internationalization/judicialization and state-centrism/politicization. The indicator captures the extent to which national policy-makers accept supranational legal interventions. It is based on two dimensions, which are equally weighted. Hence, the inclination to accept ECJ judgments is highest for states, which are internationalized and judicialized, and lowest for states that are politicized and state-centered. The degree of internationalization and of state-centrism is operationalized by the legal cultures (monist or dualist), the acceptance of the supremacy doctrine (early or late), and the position on the Kompetenz-Kompetenz issues (supportive or sceptical). The degree to which states are judicialized or state-centered is operationalized by the presence or absence of a written constitution and of judicial review.

Annex Table 3 Independent variables of country-specific approaches

Country	*Votes*	*GDP (in millions of US$, IMF, 2008)*	*Adjusted veto players*	*Administrative effectiveness*	*Judicial culture*
Germany	27	3,667,513	4.76	2	Internationalized/ judicialized
UK	27	2,674,085	4.05	3	State-centered/ politicized

References

Abbott, Kenneth W., Robert O. Keohane, Andrew Moravcsik, Anne Marie Slaughter and Duncan Snidal, 'The Concept of Legalization', *International Organization*, 54: 3 (2000), 401–19.

Abbott, Kenneth W. and Duncan Snidal, 'Hard and Soft Law in International Governance', *International Organization*, 54: 3 (2000), 421–56.

Abendroth, Wolfgang, *Die deutschen Gewerkschaften: Weg demokratischer Integration* (Berlin: DVK-Verlag, 1989).

Aberdeen Press, 'Ecologists Want Tougher Water Bill', (5 April 2002).

Aberdeen Press, 'Farmers Fear High Cost of Clampdown on Nitrates', (5 January 2002).

Advocate General, 'Opinion of the Advocate General Rozès on June 7th 1983. Commission of the European Communities v UK. Failure of a state to fulfil its obligations – equal treatment for men and women. Case 165/82', *Official Journal of the European Communities*, 1983: 61982C0165 (1983).

Advocate General, 'Opinion of the Advocate General Jacobs on February 12th 1992. Incorrect Legal Transposition of Directive 80/778 by the Federal Republic of Germany; C-237/90', *Official Journal of the European Communities*, 1992 I-05973 (1992).

Advocate General, 'Opinion of the Advocate General Van Gerven on March 2nd 1994. Commission of the European Communities v United Kingdom of Great Britain and Northern Ireland, Incorrect Legal Transposition of Directive 75/129, Case C-237/90. Safeguarding of Employees' Rights in the Event of Collective Redundancies', *Official Journal of the European Communities*, 1994, I-02435 (1994).

Advocate General, 'Opinion of the Advocate General Cosmas on January 30th 1996. Brennet AG Against Vittorio Paletta. C-206/9', *Official Journal of the European Communities*, 1996: 61994C0206 (1996a).

Advocate General, 'Opinion of the Advocate General La Pergola on September 9th 1996', *Official Journal of the European Communities*,

C-96/95, I-01653 (1996b).

Advocate General, 'Opinion of the Advocate General Mischo on March 12th 1998. Incorrect Legal Transposition of Directive 85/337 by the Federal Republic of Germany; C-301/95', *European Court Reports*, 1999 I-06135 (1998a).

Advocate General, 'Opinion of the Advocate General Mischo on September 15th 1998. Incorrect Legal Transposition of Directive 80/778 by the United Kingdom; C-340/96', *Official Journal of the European Communities*, 1999, I-02023 (1998b).

Advocate General, 'Opinion of the Advocate General Leger on July 13th, 2000. Incorrect Legal Transposition of Directive 91/676 by the United Kingdom; C-69/99', *Official Journal of the European Communities*, 2000 I-10979 (2000).

Alexy, Robert, *Theorie der juristischen Argumentation. Die Theorie des rationalen Diskurses als Theorie der juristischen Begründung* (Frankfurt: Suhrkamp, 1983).

Alter, Karen, 'Who are the Masters of the Treaty? European Governments and the European Court of Justice', *International Organization*, 52: 1 (1998), 121–47.

Alter, Karen, 'The European Union's Legal System and Domestic Policy: Spillover or Backlash?', *International Organization*, 54: 3 (2000), 519–47.

Alter, Karen, *Establishing the Supremacy of European Law: The Making of an International Rule of Law in Europe* (Oxford: Oxford University Press, 2001).

Alter, Karen, 'Do International Courts Enhance Compliance with International Law?', *Review of Asian and Pacific Studies*, 25 (2003), 51–78.

Alter, Karen, 'Private Litigants and the New International Courts', *Comparative Political Studies*, 39: 1 (2006), 22–49.

Alter, Karen, 'Agent or Trustee: International Courts in their Political Context', *European Journal of International Relations*, 14: 1 (2008), 33–63.

Alter, Karen, Laurence Helfer and Maria Florencia Guerzovich, 'Islands of Effective International Adjudication: Constructing an Intellectual Property Rule of Law in the Andean Community', *American Journal of International Law*, 103: 1 (2009), 1–43.

Alter, Karen and Jeannette Vargas, 'Explaining Variation in the Use of European Litigation Strategies: EC Law and UK Gender Equality Policy', *Comparative Political Studies*, 24: 4 (2000), 535–61.

Ashford, Douglas E., *Policy and Politics in Britain* (Philadelphia, PA: Temple University Press, 1981).

Atkinson, Carl, 'The Regulation of Drinking Water Quality: Control by Co-operation Rather than Enforcement', *Environmental Law Review*, 3: 1 (1999), 1–16.

Auer, Astrid, Christoph Demmke and Robert Polet, *Civil Services in the Europe of the Fifteen: Current Situation and Prospects* (Maastricht, European Institute of Public Administration 1996).

Ausschuss für Arbeit und Soziales, *Ausschussbericht zum Gesetzentwurf der Bundesregierung zur Sicherung der Gleichbehandlung von Männern und Frauen am Arbeitsplatz*, 10/4945 (1986).

Ausschuss für Innere Angelegenheiten, *Ausschussbericht zum Gesetzentwurf des Bundesausländergesetzes, 24.04.1990* 11/6955 (1990).

Ausschuss für Umwelt, Naturschutz und Reaktorsicherheit, *Ausschussbericht zum Gesetzentwurf der Bundesregierung. Gesetz zur Umsetzung der UVP-Änderungsrichtlinie, der IVU-Richtlinie und weiterer EG-Richtlinien zum Umweltschutz. 03.04.2001* 14/5750 (2000).

Ausschuss für Umwelt, Naturschutz und Reaktorsicherheit, *Beschlussempfehlung und Bericht Ausschuss für Umwelt, Naturschutz und Reaktorsicherheit. Entschließungsantrag zum Gesetz zur Umsetzung der UVP-Änderungsrichtlinie, der IVU-Richtlinie und weiterer EG-Richtlinien zum Umweltschutz* (Drs 14/4599, 14/5204) 14/5750 (2001a).

Ausschuss für Umwelt, Naturschutz und Reaktorsicherheit *Beschlussempfehlung und Bericht zum Regierungsentwurf des Artikelgesetzes; 03.04.2001*, 14/5750, (2001b).

Axelrod, Robert A., *The Evolution of Cooperation* (New York: Basic Books, 1984).

Bamfort, Nicholas, 'The Changing Concept of Sex Discrimination', *The Modern Law Review*, 56: 6 (1993), 872–80.

Barker, Christine R., 'Church and State: Lessons from Germany?', *The Political Quarterly*, 75: 2 (2004), 168–76.

Barrios, Harald, 'Das politische System Spaniens', in Wolfgang Ismayr (ed.), *Die politischen Systeme Westeuropas* (Opladen: Lesek & Budrich, 2003), pp. 609–49.

Barth, Hermann, 'Die Christen und Europa. Der Vizepräsident des EKD-Kirchenamtes, Hermann Barth, zu Herausforderungen und Aufgaben für Christen im heutigen Europa', in Evangelische Kirche Deutschland (EKD): *Evangelische Kirche Deutschland* (EKD) (1997).

Bayern, *Antrag 24.09.1992* (1992).

BDI, Innovation und Produzieren in Deutschland, *BDI-Drucksache* 366 (2005).

Belfast Newsletter, 'It's Time to Tackle Real "Rural Crisis"', (28 April 2001).

Bischof Dr Engelhardt, Klaus, Karl Bischof Dr Dr Lehmann and Metropolit Augoustinos, 'Offen für Europa – offen für andere'. Gemeinsames Wort der Kirchen zur Woche der ausländischen Mitbürger, 1997', in Evangelische Kirche Deutschland (EKD): *Evangelische Kirche Deutschland* (EKD) (1997).

Börzel, Tanja A., 'Improving Compliance through Domestic Mobilisation? New Instruments and the Effectiveness of Implementation in Spain', in Christoph Knill and Andrea Lenschow (eds), *Implementing EU Environmental Policy: New Approaches to an Old Problem* (Manchester: Manchester University Press, 2000), pp. 221–50.

Börzel, Tanja A., 'Non-Compliance in the European Union: Pathology or Statistical Artefact?', *Journal of European Public Policy*, 8: 5 (2001), 803–24.

Börzel, Tanja A., *Environmental Leaders and Laggards in the European Union. Why There is (Not) a Southern Problem* (London: Ashgate, 2003a).

Börzel, Tanja A., 'Guarding the Treaty: The Compliance Strategies of the European Commission', in Tanja A. Börzel and Rachel Cichowski (eds), *The State of the European Union VI: Law, Politics, and Society* (Oxford: Oxford University Press, 2003b), pp. 197–220.

Börzel, Tanja A., 'Participation Through Law Enforcement. The Case of the European Union', *Comparative Political Studies*, 39: 1 (2006), 128–52.

Börzel, Tanja A., Meike Dudziak, Tobias Hofmann, Diana Panke and Carina Sprungk, 'Recalcitrance, Inefficiency, and Support for European Integration:Why Member States do (not) Comply with European Law', *Harvard University Center for European Studies Working Paper Series*, No. 153 (2007).

Börzel, Tanja A., Tobias Hofmann, Diana Panke and Carina Sprungk, 'Obstinate and Inefficient: Why Member States Do Not Comply with European Law', *Comparative Political Studies* (forthcoming).

Börzel, Tanja A. and Thomas Risse, 'When Europe Hits Home: Europeanization and Domestic Change, *European Integration On-line Papers*, 4: 15 (2000), at: http://eiop.or.at/eiop/texte/2000–015a.htm.

Boston, Sarah, *Women Workers and Trade Unions* (London: Lawrence & Wishart, 1987).

Brainard, Alfred P., 'The Law of Election and Business Interest Groups in Britain', *The Western Political Quarterly*, 13: 3 (1960), 670–7.

Brest, Paul, 'Interpretation and Interest', *Stanford Law Review*, 34 (1982), 765–74.

Bribosia, Herve, 'Report on Belgium', in Anne Marie Slaughter, Alec Stone Sweet and J. H. H. Weiler (eds), *The European Court and National Courts – Doctrine and Jurisprudence. Legal Change in Its Social Context* (Oxford: Hart Publishing, 1998), pp. 1–40.

BUND für Umwelt und Naturschutz Deutschland, Waffengleichheit für Umweltnützer und -schützer, *BUND Pressearchiv*, 04/03 (1999).

Bundesministerium für Jugend, Familie und Gesundheit, *Answer to the Green Party's Request, 02.10.1990* (1990a).

Bundesministerium für Jugend, Familie und Gesundheit, *Verordnung zur Änderung der Trinkwasserverordnung und der Minieral- und Tafelwasserverordnung. 15.06.1990*, 429/90 (1990b).

Bundesministerium für Umwelt, Naturschutz und Reaktorsicherheit, 'Informationen zum Umweltgesetzbuch', at: www.bmu.de/gesetze_verordnungen/umweltgesetzbuch/doc/3916php (2005).

Bundesrat, *Plenarprotokoll vom 28.09.1979*, 477/79, 282–3, 300–4 (1979).

Bundesrat, *Plenarprotokoll vom 23.09.1988*, 335/88 (1988).

Bundesrat, *Plenarprotokoll vom 06.04.1990*, 159D-64B (1990).

Bundesrat, *Plenarprotokoll 25.09.1992*, 646 (1992).

Bundesrat, *Plenarprotokoll vom 10.07.1998*, Plenarprotokoll 728 357A-8A (1998).

Bundesrat, *Plenarprotokoll vom 21.12.2000*, 758, 624C-7C, 49B-C/Anl (2000).

Bundesrat, *Plenarprotokoll vom 11.05.2001*, 763 (2001).

Bundesratsausschuss für Gesundheit, *Empfehlungen zur Allgemeinen Verwaltungsvorschrift über Trinkwasser, 14.09.1992*, 484/1/92 (1992).

Bundesregierung, *Unterrrichtung der Bundesregierung zur Gleichberechtigung von Mann und Frau, 31.03.1983*, 10/14 (1983).

Bundesregierung, *Antwort der Bundesregierung auf eine kleine Anfrage der Abgeordneten Steinhauer (SPD). Schriftliche Antwort Frau Karwatzki, PStSekr BMJFG Plenarprotokoll it:* 10/112 (1984), 8396–7.

Bundesregierung, *Answer of the Federal Government to the Request of the Green Party. 08.07.1985* (1985).

Bundesregierung, *Antwort der Bundesregierung (BMJFFG (federführend); Bundesministerium des Innern; Bundesministerium der Justiz) auf eine kleine Anfrage der Abgeordneten Schmidt (SPD). Förderung der beruflichen Chancen von Frauen im öffentlichen Dienst des Bundes*, 11/273 (1987a).

Bundesregierung, *Antwort der Bundesregierung auf eine kleine Anfrage der Abgeordneten Frau Grabe und der Fraktion DIE GRÜNEN – Grund- und Trinkwasser*, 11/460 (1987b).

Bundesregierung, *Gesetzentwurf der Bundesregierung zum Arbeitszeitgesetz, 24.04.1987*, 154/87 (1987c).

Bundesregierung, *Antwort der Bundesregierung auf eine kleine Anfrage der Abgeordneten Frau Kiehm und der Fraktion der SPD – Schadstoffbelastung Wasser*, 11/2285 (1988).

Bundesregierung, *Bericht der Bundesregierung an den Deutschen Bundestag über die Gleichstellungsstellen in Bund, Ländern und Gemeinden*, 11/4893 (1989).

Bundesregierung, *Gesetzentwurf der Bundesregierung vom 23.02.1990 'Gesetz zur Verbesserung der Gleichbehandlung von Frauen und Männern am Arbeitsplatz'*, 11/6946 (1990a).

Bundesregierung, *Unterrichtung der Bundesregierung 01.06.1990*, 11/7327 (1990b).

Bundesregierung, *Regierungserklärung im Bundestag am 06.09.1991*, 2/39, 3243B-9C (1991).

Bundesregierung, *Antwort Bundesregierung; BMG (federführend) 18.01.1993. Wasserversorgung; Trinkwasser; Abwasser*, 12/4143 (1993a).

Bundesregierung, *Gesetzentwurf der Bundesregierung vom 07.05.1993 'Gesetz zur Durchsetzung der Gleichberechtigung von Frauen und Männern'*, 301/93 (1993b).

Bundesregierung, *Antwort der Bundesregierung Bundesministerium des Innern (federführend) auf eine kleine Anfrage von Cem Özdemir, Bündnis 90/Die Grünen zur Ausweisung hier geborener oder aufgewachsener minderjähriger bzw. heranwachsender Ausländerinnen und Ausländer nach Strafverbüßung*, 13/158 (1994a).

Bundesregierung, *Unterrichtung der Bundesregierung 06.09.1994. Politik für eine nachhaltige, umweltgerechte Entwicklung*, 849–91 (1994b).

Bundesregierung, *Unterrrichtung der Bundesregierung vom 11.03.1994 'Lage der Ausländer in der Bundesrepublik 1993'*, 12/6960 (1994c).

Bundesregierung, *Antwort der Bundesregierung Bundesministerium des Innern (federführend) auf eine kleine Anfrage von Ulla Jelpke (PDS) vom 12.07.1995 zu Rechtsextremismus und 'Evangelische Notgemeinschaft in Deutschland e.V.' (ENiD), 'Evangelische Zentralstelle für Weltanschauungsfragen'* (EZW), 13/1969 (1995).

Bundesregierung, *Antwort der Bundesregierung, Bundesministerium für Familie, Senioren, Frauen und Jugend, auf eine kleine Anfrage der Abgeordneten Frau Monika Ganseforth, SPD zu Situation der Frauenförderung in Bund und Ländern, EU-Mittel für Frauenprojekte, geschlechtsneutrale Gesetzessprache*, 13/5192 (1996).

Bundesregierung, *Bericht der Beauftragten der Bundesregierung für*

Ausländerfragen über die Lage der Ausländer in der Bundesrepublik Deutschland 1997, 13/9484 (1997).

Bundesregierung, *Antwort Bundesregierung; Auswärtiges Amt (federführend) – Kleine Anfrage Amke Dietert-Scheuer, Bündnis 90/Die Grünen; Bündnis 90/Die Grünen 31.03.1998 zum Familiennachzug von Ausländern*, 13/10565 (1998a).

Bundesregierung, *Bericht der Beauftragten der Bundesregierung für Ausländerfragen über die Lage der Ausländer in der Bundesrepublik Deutschland 1998*, 13/9669 (1998b).

Bundesregierung, *Antwort der Bundesregierung auf eine kleine Anfrage des Abgeordneten Erich Maaß (CDU/CSU). Simone Probst, Parlamentarischer Staatssekretär Bundesministerium für Umwelt, Naturschutz und Reaktorsicherheit*, 14/1777 (1999a).

Bundesregierung, *Antwort der Bundesregierung; Bundesministerium für Umwelt, Naturschutz und Reaktorsicherheit (federführend) vom 12.04.1999 auf Kleine Anfrage Eva Bulling-Schröter*, PDS: 14/746 (1999b).

Bundesregierung, *Jahreswirtschaftsbericht 1999 der Bundesregierung – Unterrichtung (Bericht) Plenarprotokoll vom 18.03.1999*, 14/27, 2275B-6B (1999c).

Bundesregierung, *Plenarprotokoll vom 08.10.1999. Antwort Gila Altmann, Parlamentarischer Staatssekretär Bundesministerium für Umwelt, Naturschutz und Reaktorsicherheit*, 14/2121 (1999d).

Bundesregierung, *Plenarprotokoll vom 08.10.1999. Schriftliche Antwort Simone Probst, Parlamentarischer Staatssekretär Bundesministerium für Umwelt, Naturschutz und Reaktorsicherheit 08.10.1999*, 14/1777 (1999e).

Bundesregierung, *Antwort der Bundesregierung; Bundesministerium für Verkehr, Bau- und Wohnungswesen (federführend) auf eine kleine Anfrage von Frau Christine Ostrowski, PDS*, 14/3503 (2000).

Bundestag, *Plenarprotokoll vom 29.11.1979*, 08/189, 14928–41 (1979).

Bundestag, *Plenarprotokoll vom 25.06.1980*, 08/225, 18237–56, 307 (1980).

Bundestag, *Plenarprotokoll vom 04.02.1982*, 09/83, 4888A-924A, 942C-979A (1982).

Bundestag, *Plenarprotokoll vom 23.08.1983. Anfrage zur Beachtung der geschlechtsneutralen Ausschreibung von Ausbildungsstellen gemäß Arbeitsrechtlichem EG-Anpassungsgesetz durch die Arbeitsämter* 10/24 (1983).

Bundestag, *Plenarprotokoll vom 12.04.1984*, 10/67, 4639D-85B (1984).

Bundestag, *Plenarprotokoll vom 13.12.1985. Fragestunde. Gleichstellung*

der Frauen im öffentlichen Dienst; Einbeziehung von Förderungskonzeptionen CDU-regierter Bundesländer und des BMJFG in die frauenfördernden Maßnahmen 10/4564, 10992–3 (1985a).
Bundestag, *Plenarprotokoll vom 25.01.1985*, 10/118, 8778–88 (1985b).
Bundestag, *Beschlussempfehlung und Bericht AfArbSoz 29.01.1986*, 10/4945 (1986a).
Bundestag, *Plenarprotokoll vom 10.12.1986*, 10/255, 19951–71 (1986b).
Bundestag, *Plenarprotokoll vom 10.12.1986*, 10/255, 19970D (1986c).
Bundestag, *Plenarprotokoll vom 01.12.1988*, 11/113, 8197–205 (1988a).
Bundestag, *Plenarprotokoll vom 15.01.1988*, 11/53, 3736–52 (1988b).
Bundestag, *Plenarprotokoll vom 19.08.1988*, 11/2799, 2799 (1988c).
Bundestag, *Plenarprotokoll vom 27.10.1988*, 11/103, 7119–30 (1988d).
Bundestag, *Plenarprotokoll vom 16.06.1989. Anfrage zur Trinkwassergefährdung furch militärische Altlasten*, 11/4813 (1989a).
Bundestag, *Plenarprotokoll vom 16.02.1989*, 11/125, 9230–41 (1989b).
Bundestag, *Plenarprotokoll vom 16.11.1989*, 11/176, 13398–409 (1989c).
Bundestag, *Plenarprotokoll vom 31.03.1989*, 4292 (1989d).
Bundestag, *Plenarprotokoll vom 10.05.1990*, 11/210, 16549–64 (1990a).
Bundestag, *Plenarprotokoll vom 11.05.1990*, 11/211, 16618C-30A (1990b).
Bundestag, *Plenarprotokoll vom 14.02.1990*, 15097 (1990c).
Bundestag, *Plenarprotokoll vom 23.04.1990*, 11/6946 (1990d).
Bundestag, *Plenarprotokoll vom 26.04.1990*, 11/207 (1990e).
Bundestag, *Plenarprotokoll vom 31.05.1990*, 11/214, 16891–8 (1990f).
Bundestag, *Plenarprotokoll 12/64 vom 05.12.1991*, 5455C-5468A (1991a).
Bundestag, *Plenarprotokoll vom 05.12.1991*, 12/64, 5455–68 (1991b).
Bundestag, *Plenarprotokoll vom 12.03.1991*, 12/13, 644 (1991c).
Bundestag, *Plenarprotokoll vom 12.06.1991*, 12/30, 2288–302 (1991d).
Bundestag, *Plenarprotokoll vom 21.03.1991*, 12/18, 1164–75 (1991e).
Bundestag, *Plenarprotokoll vom 27.09.1991*, 12/45, 3783–94 (1991f).
Bundestag, *Plenarprotokoll vom 05.12.1991*, 5455C-68A (1991g).
Bundestag, *Plenarprotokoll vom 19.04.1991. Anfrage zu Wasserversorgungsanlagen in den neuen Bundesländern*, 13/396 (1991h).
Bundestag, *Plenarprotokoll vom 19.04.1991. Fragestunde. Anhörung der Wasserwirtschaft und der Umweltschutzverbände zu Düngemitteln in der Landwitrtschaft*, 12/694 (1991i).
Bundestag, *Plenarprotokoll vom 18.12.1992*, 650, 632–87 (1992a).
Bundestag, *Plenarprotokoll vom 16.01.1992*, 650 (1992b).
Bundestag, *Plenarprotokoll vom 24.11.1992* (1992c).

Bundestag, *Plenarprotokoll vom 14.01.1993*, 12/131, 11431–45 (1993a).

Bundestag, *Plenarprotokoll vom 22.04.1993*, 12/152, 13027–48 (1993b).

Bundestag, *Plenarprotokoll vom 04.03.1993*, 12/143, 12355C-21360D (1993c).

Bundestag, *Plenarprotokoll vom 08.04.1993. Fragestunde. Auswirkungen der UVP-Richtlinie auf Großprojekte in den Jahren 1988 bis 1992*, 12/4713 (1993d).

Bundestag, *Plenarprotokoll vom 14.01.1993*, 12/131 (1993e).

Bundestag, *Plenarprotokoll vom 19.02.1993*, 12/4404 (1993f).

Bundestag, *Plenarprotokoll vom 30.09.1993*, 12/179, 15432C-4453C (1993g).

Bundestag, *Plenarprotokoll vom 30.09.1993*, 12/179, 15432C-53C (1993h).

Bundestag, *Plenarprotokoll vom 21.09.1994*, 12/243, 21641–57 (1994a).

Bundestag, *Plenarprotokoll vom 23.08.1994. Anfrage zur Sicherstellung der Umweltverträglichkeit von noch nicht unter das UVP-Gesetz vom 1.8.1990 fallenden Projekten* 12/8536 (1994b).

Bundestag, *Plenarprotokoll vom 13.04.1994* (1994c).

Bundestag, *Plenarprotokoll vom 14.04.1994*, 12/219, 18967D-71C, 9001A-B (1994d).

Bundestag, *Plenarprotokoll vom 20.01.1994*, 17766–96 (1994e).

Bundestag, *Plenarprotokoll vom 21.04.1994* (1994f).

Bundestag, *Plenarprotokoll vom 23.06.1994*, 12/235 (1994g).

Bundestag, *Plenarprotokoll vom 23.09.1994. Fragestunde. Sicherstellung der Umweltverträglichkeit von noch nicht unter das UVP-Gesetz vom 1.8.1990 fallenden Projekten* 12/8536 (1994h).

Bundestag, *Plenarprotokoll vom 27.04.1994* (1994i).

Bundestag, *Plenarprotokoll vom 08.02.1996*, 13/86, 7586C-92B, 95B-C, 602B-604D (1996a).

Bundestag, *Plenarprotokoll vom 02.06.1996*, 13/42, 3415A-C, 25A-32D (1996b).

Bundestag, *Plenarprotokoll vom 14.11.1996*, 13/138, 12349B-C, 52B-81C, 85D (1996c).

Bundestag, *Plenarprotokoll vom 14.11.1996*, 13/138, 12352A-81C, 82C, 86B-88C (1996d).

Bundestag, *Plenarprotokoll vom 21.06.1996*, 13/114 (1996e).

Bundestag, *Plenarprotokoll vom 12.12.1997*, 13/211, 19162 (1997a).

Bundestag, *Plenarprotokoll vom 20.02.1997. Entschließungsantrag zu der Großen Anfrage betr. Gemeinsames Wort der Kirchen "Zur wirtschaftlichen und sozialen Lage in Deutschland"*, 13/157, 14083B-136D (1997b).

Bundestag, *Plenarprotokoll vom 05.06.1997*, 13/178, 16042D-64C (1997c).

Bundestag, *Plenarprotokoll vom 13.03.1997*, 13/163, 14690D-702C, 703A, 728B-730D (1997d).

Bundestag, *Plenarprotokoll vom 13.03.1997 – Entschließungsantrag zu der Großen Anfrage betr. Situation der Bundesrepublik Deutschland als Einwanderungsland* 14690D-702C, 703A, 728B-730D (1997e).

Bundestag, *Plenarprotokoll vom 27.02.1997*, 13/160, 14476B-83C (1997f).

Bundestag, *Plenarprotokoll vom 30.10.1997*, 13/200, 18078A-92B (1997g).

Bundestag, *Plenarprotokoll vom 07.05.1998*, 13/235, 21612B-9C (1998a).

Bundestag, *Plenarprotokoll vom 26.03.1998*, 13/224, 20476C-D, 7D (1998b).

Bundestag, *Plenarprotokoll vom 03.03.1998*, 13/10010 (1998c).

Bundestag, *Plenarprotokoll vom 05.03.1998*, 13/222, 20303–30326 (1998d).

Bundestag, *Plenarprotokoll vom 08.10.1999. Fragestunde. Notwendigkeit einer Umweltverträglichkeitsprüfung wegen Nichtumsetzung der EU-Änderungsrichtlinie; Wettbewerbsnachteile deutscher Unternehmen* 14/1777, 10992–3 (1999a).

Bundestag, *Plenarprotokoll vom 19.11.1999. Fragestunde. Umweltverträglichkeitsprüfung für die Nordumfahrung der Hörselberge (Thüringen) im Zuge der A 4* 14/2121 (1999b).

Bundestag, *Plenarprotokoll vom 16.03.2000. Aktuelle Stunde*, 14/ 93, 8614C-5D (2000a).

Bundestag, *Plenarprotokoll vom 16.04.2000*, 14/2368, 8555–75 (2000b).

Bundestag, *Plenarprotokoll vom 16.11.2000*, 14/133 12818 (2000c).

Bundestag, *Plenarprotokoll vom 21.12.2000*, 624–50 (2000d).

Bundestag, *Plenarprotokoll vom 05.04.2001*, 14/164 16078A-9D (2001a).

Bundestag, *Plenarprotokoll vom 11.05.2001*, 763, 214 (2001b).

Bundestag, *Plenarprotokoll vom 05.04.2001*, 14/164, 16065–79 (2001c).

Bundestag, *Plenarprotokoll vom 05.04.2001*, 14/164, 16065–80 (2001d).

Bundestag, *Plenarprotokoll vom 15.03.2001*, 14/158, 15416 (2001e).

Bundestag, *Plenarprotokoll vom 15.06.2001. Fragestunde. Stellung der Biomasse bezüglich Genehmigungen in der Europäischen UVP-Richtlinie im Vergleich zu fossilen Brennstoffen*, 14/6272, (2001f).

Bundesvereinigung der Deutschen Arbeitgeberverbände, *Jahresbericht 1976* (Bergisch Gladbach: Bundesvereinigung der Deutschen Arbeitgeberverbände, 1976).

Busch, Marc L. and Eric Reinhardt, 'The Evolution of GATT/WTO Dispute Settlement', in John M. Ciuriak and Dan Curtis (eds), *Trade Policy Research 2003* (Ottawa: Department of Foreign Affairs and International Trade, 2003), pp. 143–83.

Cameron, James, Jacob Werksman and Peter Roderick (eds), *Improving Compliance with International Environmental Law* (London: Earthscan, 1996).

Cartabia, Marta, 'The Italian Constitutional Court and the Relationship Between the Italian Legal System and the European Union', in Anne Marie Slaughter, Alec Stone Sweet and J.H.H. Weiler (eds), *The European Court and National Courts – Doctrine and Jurisprudence. Legal Change in Its Social Context* (Oxford: Hart Publishing, 1998), pp. 133–46.

Chalmers, Damian, 'The Positioning of EU Judicial Politics within the United Kingdom', *West European Politics, Special Issue*, 23: 4 (2000), 169–210.

Chayes, Abram and Antonia Handler-Chayes, 'Compliance Without Enforcement: State Behavior Under Regulatory Treaties', *Negotiation Journal*, 7: 2 (1991), 311–30.

Chayes, Abram and Antonia Handler-Chayes, 'On Compliance', *International Organization*, 47: 2 (1993), 175–205.

Chayes, Abram and Antonia Handler-Chayes, *The New Sovereignty. Compliance and International Regulatory Agreements* (Cambridge and London: Harvard University Press, 1995).

Chayes, Abram, Antonia Handler-Chayes and Ronald B. Mitchell, 'Managing Compliance: A Comparative Perspective', in Edith Brown Weiss and Harold K. Jacobsen (eds), *Engaging Countries: Strengthening Compliance with International Environmental Accords* (Cambridge, MA: MIT Press, 1998), pp. 39–62.

Checkel, Jeffrey T., 'Sanctions, Social Learning and Institutions: Explaining State Compliance with the Norms of the European Human Rights Regime', *ARENA Working Papers*, WP 99/11 (1999), 1–44.

Checkel, Jeffrey T., 'Why Comply? Social Learning and European Identity Change', *International Organization*, 55: 3 (2001), 553–88.

Checkel, Jeffrey T., 'Social Constructivism in Global and European Politics: A Review Essay', *Review of International Studies*, 30: 2 (2004), 229–44.

Checkel, Jeffrey T., 'Constructivist Approaches to European Integration', *ARENA Working Papers*, WP 06/06 (2006), 1–41.

Cichowski, Rachel, 'Courts, Rights, and Democratic Participation', *Comparative Political Studies*, 39: 1 (2006), 50–75.

Claes, Monica and Bruno De Witte, 'Report on the Netherlands', in Anne Marie Slaughter, Alec Stone Sweet and J.H.H. Weiler (eds), *The European Court and National Courts – Doctrine and Jurisprudence. Legal Change in Its Social Context* (Oxford: Hart Publishing, 1998), pp. 171–94.

Commission of the European Communities, *Communication from the Commission. Application of Article 228 of the EC Treaty. SEC (205) 1658* (Brussels: Commission of the European Communities, 2005).

Committee for Internal Affairs, *Suggestion to the Bundesausländergesetz, April 24, 1990* (1990).

Conant, Lisa J., 'Europeanization and the Courts: Variable Patterns of Adaptation among National Judiciaries', in Maria Green Cowles, James A. Caporaso and Thomas Risse (eds), *Transforming Europe. Europeanization and Domestic Change* (Ithaca, NY: Cornell, 2001), pp. 97–115.

Conant, Lisa J., *Justice Contained. Law and Politics in the European Union* (Ithaca, NY: Cornell University Press, 2002).

Conant, Lisa J., 'Individuals, Court, and the Development of European Social Rights', *Comparative Political Studies*, 39: 1 (2006), 76–100.

Craig, P.P., 'Report on the United Kingdom', in Anne Marie Slaughter, Alec Stone Sweet and J. H. H. Weiler (eds), *The European Court and National Courts – Doctrine and Jurisprudence. Legal Change in Its Social Context* (Oxford: Hart Publishing, 1998), pp. 195–225.

Dai, Xinyuan, 'Why Comply? The Domestic Constituency Mechanism', *International Organization*, 59:2 (2005), 363–98.

Daily Mail, 'Who needs a Social Charter? British Don't Says the EC' (1 April 1992).

Daily Telegraph, 'Farmers Are Hit by European Curb on Muck Spreading' (21 December 2001).

Daily Telegraph, 'Slurry Ban on Half of England' (28 June 2002).

Deitelhoff, Nicole and Harald Müller, 'Theoretical Paradise – Empirically Lost? Arguing with Habermas', *Review of International Studies*, 31 (2005), 167–79.

Department of the Environment, Food and Rural Affairs, *Implementation of the Nitrates Directive (91/676/EEC). Description of the Methodology Applied by the Secretary of State in Identifying Additional Nitrate Vulnerable Zones in England (2002)*, October 2002 (2002a).

Department of the Environment, Food and Rural Affairs, *News Release – Nitrate Controls to Spearhead Long-Term Strategy to Improve Water Quality*, 27 June 2002 (2002b).

Department of the Environment, Food and Rural Affairs, *Nitrates*

Directive Consultation. A Report Prepared by NOP Social & Political for the Department for Environment, Food and Rural Affairs (DEFRA) April 2002/ 433602 (2002c).

Department of the Environment, Transport and the Regions, *Government Response to the Consultation on Regulations for Drinking Water*, 8 December 2000 (2000a).

Department of the Environment, Transport and the Regions, *The Water Supply (Water Quality) (England) Regulations 2000 – Consultation on Regulations*, 19 April 2000 (2000b).

Department of the Environment, Transport and the Regions, *Water Bill – Consultation on Draft Legislation*, 31 January 2001 (2001).

Dewey, John, 'Logical Method and the Law', *Cornell Law Quarterly*, 10: 17 (1924).

Diamond, Martin, 'The Separation of Powers and the Mixed Regime', *Publius*, 8: 3 (1978), 33–43.

Die Welt, 'CSU fordert härtere Ausländerpolitik' (25 January 1996).

Die Welt, 'Katholische Kirche fordert Hilfe für Ausländer ohne Aufenthaltsrecht' (22 November 1997).

Die Welt, 'EU: Familiennachzug' (27 September 2000).

DNR, *DNR Deutschland Rundbrief. Naturschutz und Umweltpolitik auf Bundesebene* (Bonn, 2000).

Docksey, Christopher, 'Information and Consultation of Employees: The United Kingdom and the Vredeling Directive', *The Modern Law Review*, 49: 3 (1986), 281–313.

Dorn, A. Walter and Andrew Fulton, 'Securing Compliance with Disarmament Treaties: Carrots, Sticks, and the Case of North Korea', *Global Governance*, 3: 1 (1997), 17–40.

Downs, George W., 'Enforcement and the Evolution of Cooperation', *Michigan Journal of International Law*, 19: 2 (1998), 319–44.

Downs, George W., David M. Rocke and Peter N. Barsoom, 'Is the Good News About Compliance Good News About Cooperation?', *International Organization*, 50: 3 (1996), 379–406.

Drinking Water Inspectorate, *Press Notice -13–08–99 South East Water Plead Guilty to Breaching Water Quality Regulations* (London: Drinking Water Inspectorate, 1999).

Duina, Francesco G., *Harmonizing Europe. Nation-States within the Common Market* (New York: State University of New York Press, 1999).

Ebner, Michael, 'Gespräche mit Wolfgang Ullmann Den dritten Weg im Auge. Bundestagsabgeordneter und evangelischer Kirchenmann von drüben', *Süddeutsche Zeitung* (17 November1992).

Elvert, Jürgen, 'Das politische System Irlands', in Wolfgang Ismayr (ed.),

Die politischen Systeme Westeuropas (Opladen: Leske & Budrich, 2003), pp. 263–300.

English Nature, *Select Committee on Environmental Audit. Minutes of Evidence. Memorandum Submitted by English Nature* (1999).

Environmental Audit Committee, *House of Commons. Select Committee on Environmental Audit. First Report. Europe and the Environment: An Agenda for the Helsinki Summit*, 25 November 1999 (1999).

Equal Opportunity Commission, *The Statutes of the EOC* (Manchester, 2006).

European Commission, *Report by the Commission to the Council on Progress with Regard to Implementation of the Directive on the Approximation of the Laws of the Member States Relating to Collective Redundancies (Council Directive75/129/EEC of 17February1975), 51991SC1639, /*SEC/91/1639FINAL* (Brussels: European Communities, 1991).

European Court of Justice, 'Court Judgment of November 8th 1983. European Commission Against the United Kingdom Regarding the Incomplete Legal Transposition of Directive 76/207; C-165–82', *Official Journal of the European Communities*, 1983 03431 (1983).

European Court of Justice, 'Preliminary Ruling, Court Judgment of April 10th 1984. Sabine von Colson und Elisabeth Kamann against the Land Nordrhein-Westfalen. Preliminary Ruling Requested by the Landesarbeitsgericht Hamm, Equal Access of Men and Women', *Official Journal of the European Communities*, 1984: J0014 (1984).

European Court of Justice, 'Court Judgment of May 21st 1985. European Commission Against the Federal Republic of Germany Regarding the Incomplete Legal Transposition of Directive 76/207; C-248–83', *Official Journal of the European Communities*, 1985 01459 (1985).

European Court of Justice, 'Rules of Procedure of the European Court of Justice of the European Communities of 19 June 1991', in *Official Journal*, L 288, 29 October 2005. (Brussels: European Court of Justice, 1991).

European Court of Justice, 'Court Judgment of November 22nd 1992. The European Commission Against the United Kingdom Regarding the Incomplete Application of Directive 80/778, C-337/89', *Official Journal of the European Communities*, 1992: I-06103 (1992a).

European Court of Justice, 'Court Judgment of November 24th 1992. European Commission Against the Federal Republic of Germany Regarding the Incomplete Legal Transposition of Directive 80/778; C-237–9', *Official Journal of the European Communities*, 1992 I-05973 (1992b).

European Court of Justice, 'Court Judgment of June 8th 1994. European Commission Against the United Kingdom Regarding the Incomplete Legal Transposition of Directive 75/129, C-383/92', *Official Journal of the European Communities*, 1994 I-02479 (1994).

European Court of Justice, 'Preliminary Ruling, Court Judgment of 2 May 1996. Alberto Paletta and Others v Brennet AG. Preliminary Ruling: Arbeitsgericht Lörrach – Germany. Recognition of Incapacity for Work. – Case C-206/94', *Official Journal of the European Communities*, 1996: 61994J0206 (1996).

European Court of Justice, 'Court Judgment of March 20th 1997. European Commission Against the Federal Republic of Germany Regarding the Incomplete Legal Transposition of Directives 90/364 and 90/365; C-96/95', *Official Journal of the European Communities*, I-01653 (1997).

European Court of Justice, 'Court Judgment of October 22nd 1998. European Commission Against the Federal Republic of Germany Regarding the Incomplete Legal Transposition of Directive 85/337', *Official Journal of the European Communities*, C-301–95 I-06135 (1998).

European Court of Justice, 'Court Judgment of April 22nd 1999. The European Commission Against the United Kingdom Regarding the Incomplete Legal Transposition of Directive 80/778, C-340/96', *Official Journal of the European Communities*, 1999 I-02023 (1999a).

European Court of Justice, 'Preliminary Ruling, Court Judgment of April 29th, 1999. Case C-293/97', *European Court Reports*, 1999: I-02603 (1999b).

European Court of Justice, 'Court Judgment of December 7th, 2000. The European Commission Against the United Kingdom Regarding the Incomplete Application of Directive 91/676, C-69/99', *Official Journal of the European Communities*, 2000 I-10979 (2000a).

European Court of Justice, 'Court Judgment of July 4th, 2000. European Commission Against the Hellenic Republic Regarding the Failure of a Member State to fulfil its obligations regarding the Directives 75/442/EEC and 78/319/EEC, based on Article 171 of the EC Treaty (now Article 228 EC). Issuing of Financial penalties. Case 387/97', *Official Journal of the European Communities*, I-05047 (2000b).

European Court of Justice, 'Court Judgment of November 25, 2003. European Commission Against the Kingdom of Spain. Failure of a Member State to Fulfil Obligations Concerning the Quality of Bathing Water Based on Directive 76/160/EEC. Judgment of the Court Issuing Financial penalties based on Article 228 EC. Case C-278/01', *Official*

Journal of the European Communities, I-14141 (2003).

European Court of Justice, 'Court Judgment of July 12th, 2005. European Commission Against the French Republic. Failure of a Member State to Fulfil Obligations Concerning Fisheries (Regulations No 2847/93, No 171/83, No 3094/86, No 894/97, No 850/98), Imposition of a Penalty Payment based on Article 228 EC, Case C304/02', *Official Journal of the European Communities*, I-06263 (2005).

European Court of Justice, 'Supplementary Rules of Procedure of the European Court of Justice', in *Official Journal*, L 72, 21 February 2006. (Brussels: European Court of Justice, 2006).

European Foundation for the Improvement of Working Conditions (Marc W. Gilman), 'CBI Sets Out its Plans for 1997', *IRRU*, Warwick Business School.

Express, 'GBP 1BN Clean-Up Cost of Water Pollution by Farm Pesticides' (28 January 2001).

Express, 'GBP 50M Pollution Price' (21 December 2001).

Falk, Richard A., *Human Rights Horizons: The Pursit of Justice in a Globalizing World* (London: Routledge, 2000).

Falkner, Gerda, 'European Social Policy: Towards Multi-level and Multi-Actor Governance', in Beate Kohler-Koch and Rainer Eising (eds), *The Transformation of Governance in the European Union* (London: Routledge, 1999), pp. 83–97.

Falkner, Gerda, Miriam Hartlapp, Simone Leiber and Oliver Treib, 'Non-Compliance with EU Directives in the Member States: Opposition through the Backdoor?', *West European Politics*, 27 (2004), 452–73.

Falkner, Gerda, Oliver Treib, Miriam Hartlapp and Simone Leiber, *Complying with Europe. EU Harmonization and Soft Law in the Member States* (Cambridge: Cambridge University Press, 2005).

Falter, Jürgen W., *Wer wählt rechts? Die Wähler und Anhänger rechtsextremistischer Parteien im vereinigten Deutschland* (München: Verlag C. H. Beck, 1994).

Farmers Guardian, 'Revised Crop Input Recommendations' (22 December 2000).

Farmers Guardian, 'Nitrates Directive Worse For Others' (6 Spetember 2002).

Farmers Guardian, 'Union to Challenge Flawed Scientific Basis Behind the NVZ Directive?' (5 July 2002).

Fearon, James, 'Bargaining, Enforcement, and International Cooperation', *International Organization*, 52: 2 (1998), 269–305.

Federal, Government, *Answer of the Federal Government to the Request of the Green Party. 08.07.1985* (1985).

Federal Government, *Answer of the Federal Government to the Request of the Green Party; 23.11.1995* (1995).

Federal Ministry for Health, *Allgemeine Verwaltungsvorschrift zu Trinkwasser, 09.07.1992*, 484/92 (1992).

Federal Ministry of Youth, Family and Health, *Trinkwasserverordnung. Zustimmungsbedürftige Rechtsverordnung 09.12.1985*, 589/85, 1 (1985).

Financial Times, 'European Court on Equal Pay' (18 November 1983).

Financial Times, 'BP Oil Faces Legal Action on Job Cuts', (9 November 1985).

Financial Times, 'An End to Willful Discrimination' (10 January 1985).

Financial Times, 'Europe's Role In UK Law' (11 July 1986).

Financial Times, 'Sex Discrimination Law Under Review' (28 February 1986).

Financial Times, 'A Victory For Equality' (3 April 1986).

Financial Times, 'Why Some Are Still More Equal Than Others. Britain's Sex Discrimination Laws 10 Years On' (3 January 1986).

Financial Times, 'The Employment Bill. Moves For A Freer Labour Market' (2 December 1988).

Financial Times, 'Setback For Water Industry' (8 February 1989).

Financial Times, 'The Maastricht Treaty. Astonishing Compromise Threatens to Create a Brussels Benefit for the Legal Fraternity – The Social Charter' (12 December 1991).

Financial Times, 'Tough Penalties for Redundancy Offence Planned' (10 December 1991).

Financial Times, 'Employers Face EC Curbs on Ability to Cut Pay' (8 April 1993).

Financial Times, 'Courts Shift the Employment Goalposts: The Maastricht Opt-out May be Academic' (7 March 1994).

Financial Times, 'A Union Rallying Cry Echoes in Europe: Robert Taylor Reports on the TUC's Break with Tradition in Advocating Workplace Rights for All' (13 December 1994).

Financial Times, 'Unions Stand Up for Non-members. TUC to Debate Representation and Rights in the Workplace for All' (8 August 1994).

Financial Times, 'CBI to Reassess Policy on Union Rights' (24 July 1995).

Financial Times, 'Job Consultation' (6 April 1995).

Financial Times, 'Brussels Attacks UK on Drinking Water Quality' (3 July 1996).

Financial Times, 'Companies and Finance: UK: Drinking Water Inspectors Deny Accusations from EU' (4 July 1996).

Financial Times, 'Companies Describe EC Legal Action Over Drinking Water as Ludicrous' (4 July 1996).

Financial Times, 'Government to Implement EU Water Directive' (28 May 2002).

Financial Times, 'Nitrate Pollution Zones "Will Cover Only 55% of UK"', (28 June 2002).

Fink, Bettina, 'Wer sich nicht wehrt, landet am Herd', *taz, die Tageszeitung* (8 February 1994).

Finnemore, Martha and Kathryn Sikkink, 'International Norm Dynamics and Political Change', *International Organization*, 52: 4 (1998), 887–917.

Fisher, Roger, *Improving Compliance with International Law* (Charlottesville: University of Virginia Press, 1981).

Fiss, O., 'Objectivity and Interpretation', *Stanford Law Review*, 34 (1982), 739–63.

Foundation for Water Research, *Report on an Evaluation of the Water Quality and Health Research Programme* (Marlow: Report to the Department of the Environment, Transport and the Regions, DWI0793, 1996).

Foundation for Water Research, *Investigation of Drinking Water Quality Enforcement Procedures in Member States of the European Union* (Marlow: Final Report to the Department of the Environment, Transport and the Regions, DWI0800, 1998).

Frankfurter Allgemeine Zeitung, 'Lohnfortzahlung auch bei Auslands-Attest' (3 May 1996).

Frankfurter Allgemeine Zeitung, ' CSU macht die "Eindämmung der Zuwanderung"zum Wahlkampfthema' (10 July 1998).

Frankfurter Rundschau, 'Bundesinnenminister Kanther alarmiert durch Ausländerkriminalität, 12.12.96' (12 December 1996).

Fritzpatrick, Barry, 'The Sex Discrimination Act 1986', *The Modern Law Review*, 50: 7 (1987), 934–51.

Funke, Hajo, 'Zusammenhänge zwischen rechter Gewalt, Einsetllungen in der Bevölkerung sowie der Verantwortung von Politik und Öffentlichkeit', in Christoph Butterwegge and Georg Lohmann (eds), *Jugend, Rechtsextremismus und Gewalt* (Opladen: Leske & Budrich, 2001), pp. 61–80.

Fürst, Volker, *Umweltpolitisches Regieren im Wandel* (Berlin: Digital Library, at www.diss.fu-berlin.de/2004/192, 2004).

Garrett, Geoffrey, 'The Politics of Legal Integration in the European Union', *International Organization*, 49: 1 (1995), 171–81.

Garrett, Geoffrey, Daniel Kelman and H. Schulz, 'The European Court of Justice: Master or Servant? Legal Politics in the European Union', *International Organization*, 52 (1998), 149–70.

Garrett, Geoffrey and James M. Smith, 'The Politics of WTO Dispute

Settlement', in UCLA International Institute Occasional Paper Series (Los Angeles, 2002).

Gehrhard, Ute, 'Feminismen im 20sten Jahrhundert', in Jens Flemming, Pauline Puppel, Werner Troßbach, Christina Vanja and Ortrud Wörner-Heil (eds), *Lesearten der Geschichte. Ländliche Ordnungen und Geschlechterverhältnisse* (Kassel: Kassel University Press, 2004), pp. 302–16.

Gemeinsame Synode der Bistümer in der Bundesrepublik Deutschland, *Beschlüsse der Vollversammlung* (Freiburg: Herder Verlag, 1976).

Gibson, James L. and Gregory A. Caldeira, 'The Legal Cultures of Europe', *Law & Society Review*, 30: 1 (1996), 55–85.

Gilpin, Robert, *War and Change in the International System* (New York: Cambridge University Press, 1981).

Gnad, Oliver, Daniela Gniss, Marion Hausmann and Carl-Wilhelm Reibel, *Handbuch zur Statistik der Parlamente und Parteien in den westlichen Besatzungszonen und der Bundesrepublik* (Düsseldorf: Droste Verlag, 2005).

Goldstein, Judith, Miles Kahler, Robert O. Keohane and Anne-Marie Slaughter, 'Introduction: Legalization and World Politics', *International Organization*, 54: 3 (2000), 385–99.

Gottfried, H. and J. O'Reilly, 'Reregulating Breadwinner Models in Socially Conservative Welfare Systems: Comparing Germany and Japan', *Social Politics*, 9: 1 (2002), 29–59.

Government of the UK, *Achieving a Better Quality of Life. Review of Progress Towards Sustainable Development, Government Annual Report 2000* (2000a).

Government of the UK, *Explanatory Note to the Drinking Water (Undertakings) (England and Wales) Regulations 2000, Statutory Instrument No 1297*, Statutory Instrument No. 1297 (2000b).

Government of the UK, *Achieving a Better Quality of Life. Review of Progress Towards Sustainable Development, Government Annual Report 2001* (2001).

Government of the UK, *Explanatory Note to the Water Act* (2003).

Green Party, *Motion for a Resolution on Drinking Water, 27.09.1989*, 11/5261, (1989).

Green Party, *Request on the Draft of the Drinking Water Regulation, 04.09.1990*, (1990).

Green Party, *Request Regarding the EIA Directive* (1991).

Green, Simon, 'Immigration, Asylum and Citizenship in Germany: The Impact of Unification and the Berlin Republic', *West European Politics*, 24: 4 (2001), 82–104.

Greenpeace, 'Umweltminister Tritin macht es seinen Gegnern in Industrie und Politik zu leicht', *Greenpeace Magazin*, 99: 4 (1999), 1–3.

Guardian, 'Guardian Women: The Verdict After Ten Years – Must Try Harder. The Workings of the Equal Pay Act' (6 March 1985).

Guardian, 'Customers Promised Imported Coal as Pits Shut', (27 October 1992).

Guardian, 'News Round UK in Hot Water' (29 January 1992).

Guardian, 'EU Court Backs UK Workers' Rights to Representation' (3 March 1994).

Guardian, 'Heavy Price: Water Companies Fear That They May Be Forced to Clean Up Everyday Pollutants' (30 January 2002).

Guardian, 'Meacher Caves In On Farm Pollution' (28 June 2002).

Gulmann, Claus, 'Methods of Interpretation of the Court of Justice', *Scandinavian Studies in Law*: 24 (1980), 187–204

Gunlicks, Arthur, 'German Federalism Reform: Part One', *German Law Journal*, 80: 1 (2007), 111–31.

Habermas, Jürgen, *Faktizität und Geltung. Beiträge zur Diskurstheorie des Rechts und des demokratischen Rechtsstaats* (Frankfurt am Hain: Suhrkamp, 1992a).

Habermas, Jürgen, 'Handlungen. Sprechakte, Sprachlich Vermittelte Interaktion und Lebenswelt', in Jürgen Habermas (ed.), *Nachmetaphysisches Denken – Philosophische Aufsätze* (Frankfurt am Main: Suhrkamp, 1992b), pp. 63–104.

Habermas, Jürgen, *Theorie des Kommunikativen Handelns. Band 1 Handlungsrationalität und gesellschaftliche Rationalisierung* (Frankfurt am Main: Suhrkamp, 1995a).

Habermas, Jürgen, *Theorie des Kommunikativen Handelns. Band 2 zur Kritik der funktionalistischen Vernunft* (Frankfurt am Main: Suhrkamp, 1995b).

Habermas, Jürgen, *Faktizität und Geltung. Beiträge zur Diskurstheorie des Rechts und des demokratischen Rechtsstaats* (Frankfurt: Suhrkamp Verlag, 1998).

Hardin, Garret, 'The Tragedy of the Commons', *Science*, 162 (1986), 1243–8.

Harrison, Lowell H. and Fred E. Crossland, 'The British Labour Party in the General Elections, 1906–1945', *The Journal of Politics*, 12: 2 (1950), 383–404.

Hart, H.L.A., *The Concept of Law* (Oxford: Oxford University Press, 1961).

Hassel, Anke, *Gewerkschaften und sozialer Wandel: Mitgliederrekrutierung und Arbeitsbeziehungen in Deutschland und Großbritannien* (Baden-Baden: Nomos, 1999).

Haverland, Markus, 'National Adaptation to European Integration: The Importance of Institutional Veto Points', *Journal of Public Policy*, 20: 1 (2000), 83–103.

Henkin, Louis, *How Nations Behave: Law and Foreign Policy* (New York: Columbia University Press, 1968).

Herald, 'You Can't Keep a Euro-Law Down' (25 June 1992).

Herald, 'EU May Sue on Water Quality. Britain Could Find Itself in Dock Over Pesticide Levels' (29 June 1996).

Héritier, Adrienne, Christoph Knill and Susanne Mingers, *Ringing the Changes in Europe. Regulatory Competition and the Redefinition of the State: Britain, France, Germany* (Berlin and New York: De Gruyter, 1996).

Hill, M., 'Implementation Theory', *Policy and Politics*, 25 (1997), 375–85.

Holzamer, Hans-Herbert, 'Gespräch mit Bundestagspräsidentin Rita Süßmuth: Frauen im Job benachteiligt – Recht und gesellschaftliche Realität klaffen auseinander', *Süddeutsche Zeitung* (6 October 1994).

Horne, Christine and Anna Cutlip, 'Sanctioning Costs and Norm Enforcement', *Rationality and Society*, 14: 3 (2002), 285–307.

House of Commons, *House of Commons Hansard Debates for 12 March 1975*: Hansard Debates, 540 (1975a).

House of Commons, *House of Commons Hansard Debates for 18 June 1975*: Hansard Debates, 1429–553 (1975b).

House of Commons, *House of Commons Hansard Debates for 26 March 1975*: Hansard Debates, 511–617 (1975c).

House of Commons, *Official Report of the House of Commons from December 9th 1983*: Hansard Debates, 50, 581 (1983).

House of Commons, *House of Commons Hansard Debates for 21 March 1985*: Hansard Debates, 701–9 (1985).

House of Commons, *House of Commons Hansard Debates for 19 June 1986*: Hansard Debates, Column 1211–1234 (1986a).

House of Commons, *House of Commons Hansard Debates for 22 May 1986*: Hansard Debates, 569–626 (1986b).

House of Commons, *House of Commons Hansard Debates for 23 October 1986*: Hansard Debates, Column 1326–36 (1986c).

House of Commons, *House of Commons Hansard Debates for 24 November 1988*: Hansard Debates, Column 323–8 (1988).

House of Commons, *House of Commons Hansard Debates for 6 July 1989*: Hansard Debates, Column 475 (1989a).

House of Commons, *House of Commons Hansard Debates for 10 January 1989*: Hansard Debates, Column 726–9 (1989b).

House of Commons, *House of Commons Hansard Debates for 11 January 1989*: Hansard Debates, Column 853–933 (1989c).

House of Commons, *House of Commons Hansard Debates for 17 May 1989*: Hansard Debates, Column 342–52 (1989d).

House of Commons, *House of Commons Hansard Debates for 29 July 1989:* Hansard Debates, Column 1108 (1989e).

House of Commons, *House of Commons Hansard Debates for 20 January 1990*: Hansard Debates, Column 38–109 (1990).

House of Commons, *House of Commons Hansard Debates for 7 May 1991*: Hansard Debates, Column 476 (1991).

House of Commons, *House of Commons Hansard Debates for 16 January 1992*: Hansard Debates, Column 1163–6 (1992a).

House of Commons, *House of Commons Hansard Debates for 17 November 1992*: Hansard Debates, Column 168–242 (1992b).

House of Commons, *House of Commons Hansard Debates for 8 June1993*: Hansard Debates, Column 227 (1993a).

House of Commons, *House of Commons Hansard Debates for 17 February 1993*: Hansard Debates, Column 326–74 (1993b).

House of Commons, *House of Commons Hansard Debates for 7 February 1994*: Hansard Debates, Column 89–100 (1994a).

House of Commons, *House of Commons Hansard Debates for 9 December 1994. Commons Written Answers*: Hansard Debates (1994b).

House of Commons, *House of Commons Hansard Debates for 10 March 1994. Opposition Day. Topic: Sex Discrimination*: Hansard Debates, Column 423–98 (1994c).

House of Commons, *House of Commons Hansard Debates for 11 March 1994*: Hansard Debates, Column 431–2 (1994d).

House of Commons, *House of Commons Hansard Debates for 14 June 1994 – Commons Written Answers*: Hansard Debates (1994e).

House of Commons, *House of Commons Hansard Debates for 14 June 1994. Commons Written Answers*: Hansard Debates (1994f).

House of Commons, *House of Commons Hansard Debates for 19 July 1994*: Hansard Debates, Column 204–8 (1994g).

House of Commons, *House of Commons Hansard Debates for 20 April 1994*: Hansard Debates, Column 877–80 (1994h).

House of Commons, *House of Commons Hansard Debates for 23 March 1995*: Hansard Debates, Column 238–9 (1994i).

House of Commons, *House of Commons Hansard Debates for 5 April 1995. Commons Written Answers*: Hansard Debates, 1118 (1995a).

House of Commons, *House of Commons Hansard Debates for 14 June 1995 – Commons Written Answers* (1995b).

House of Commons, *House of Commons Hansard Debates for 14 March 1995*: Hansard Debates, Column 807–16 (1995c).

House of Commons, *House of Commons Hansard Debates for 20 January 1995. Commons Written Answers*: Hansard Debates, 729 (1995d).

House of Commons, *Written Answer by Mr. Michael Forsyth, the Secretary of State for Employment, July 27 1993*: Hansard Debates, Column 805 (1995e).

House of Commons, *House of Commons Hansard Debates for 3 July 1996. Commons Written Answers*: Hansard Debates (1996a).

House of Commons, *House of Commons Hansard Debates for 6 February 1996*: Hansard Debates, Column 197–235 (1996b).

House of Commons, *House of Commons Hansard Debates for 7 May 1996. Commons Written Answers*: Hansard Debates (1996c).

House of Commons, *House of Commons Hansard Debates for 8 March 1996. Commons Written Answers*: Hansard Debates (1996d).

House of Commons, *House of Commons Hansard Debates for 14 October 1996*: Hansard Debates, Column 814–16 (1996e).

House of Commons, *House of Commons Hansard Debates for 18 March 1996*: Hansard Debates, 27–46 (1996f).

House of Commons, *House of Commons Hansard Debates for 23 July 1996. Commons Written Answers*: Hansard Debates (1996g).

House of Commons, *House of Commons Hansard Debates for 23 July 1997*: Hansard Debates, Column 924–7 (1997).

House of Commons, *House of Commons Hansard Debates for 7 December 1998*: Hansard Debates, Column 40–114 (1998a).

House of Commons, *House of Commons Hansard Debates for 19 February 1998. Commons Written Answers*: Hansard Debates, Column 772–3 (1998b).

House of Commons, *House of Commons Hansard Debates for 25 March 1998*: Hansard Debates, Column 467–75 (1998c).

House of Commons, *House of Commons Hansard Debates for 2 December 1999. Commons Written Answers:* Hansard Debates (1999a).

House of Commons, *House of Commons Hansard Debates for 20 October 1999*: Hansard Debates, Column 444–99 (1999b).

House of Commons, *House of Commons Hansard Debates for 8 December 2000*: Hansard Debates, Column 10 (2000a).

House of Commons, *House of Commons Hansard Debates for 10 February 2000*: Hansard Debates, Column 114–53 (2000b).

House of Commons, *House of Commons Hansard Debates for 17 April 2000. Commons Written Answers*: Hansard Debates (2000c).

House of Commons, *House of Commons Hansard Debates for 29 June 2000*: Hansard Debates, Column 1043–7 (2000d).

House of Commons, *House of Commons Hansard Debates for 11 December 2001*: Column 225–33 (2001a).

House of Commons, *House of Commons Hansard Debates for 12 November 2001*: Hansard Debates, Column 574–86 (2001b).

House of Commons, *House of Commons Hansard Debates for 19 December 2001. Commons Written Answers:* Hansard Debates (2001c).

House of Commons, *House of Commons Hansard Debates for 28 February 2001*: Hansard Debates, Column 913–60 (2001d).

House of Commons, *House of Commons Hansard Debates for 6 November 2002*: Hansard Debates, Column 299–302 (2002a).

House of Commons, *House of Commons Hansard Debates for 12 December 2002*: Hansard Debates, Column 410–505 (2002b).

House of Commons, *House of Commons Hansard Debates for 14 May 2002*: Hansard Debates, Column 198–219 (2002c).

House of Commons, *House of Commons Hansard Debates for 16 May 2002*: Hansard Debates (2002d).

House of Commons, *House of Commons Hansard Debates for 28 January 2002. Commons Written Answers*: Hansard Debates (2002e).

House of Commons, *House of Commons Hansard Debates for 30 January 2002. Commons Written Answers*: Hansard Debates (2002f).

House of Commons, *House of Commons Hansard Debates for 30 January 2002. Commons Written Answers*: Hansard Debates (2002g).

House of Commons, *House of Commons Hansard Debates for 31 January 2002*: Hansard Debates, Column 480–504 (2002h).

House of Commons, *House of Commons Hansard Debates for 31 January 2002. Commons Written Answers*: Hansard Debates (2002i).

House of Commons Standing Committee, *House of Commons Hansard Debates for 6 April 1998*: Hansard Debates, 1–9 (1998).

House of Lords, *House of Lords Debates, 27 February 1986*: Hansard Debates (1986).

House of Lords, *House of Lords Debates, 4 June 1996*: Hansard Debates, Column 1161–89 (1996).

House of Lords, *House of Lords Debates, 26 October 2000*: Hansard Debates, Column 489–501 (2000).

House of Lords, *House of Lords Debates, 4 April 2001*: Hansard Debates, Column 822–997 (2001a).

House of Lords, *House of Lords Debates, Lords Written Answers. 20 December 2001*: Hansard Debates (2001b).

House of Lords, *House of Lords Debates, 11 December 2002*: Hansard Debates, Column 230–44 (2002).

Hunt, M., 'The Human Rights Act and Legal Culture: The Judiciary and the Legal Profession', *Journal of Law and Society*, 26: 1 (1999), 86–102.

Icken, Angela, *Der Deutsche Frauenrat: etablierte Frauenverbandsarbeit im gesellschaftlichen Wandel* (Opladen: Leske & Budrich, 2002).

Independent, 'Woman Seeking to Challenge the Status Quo' (25 June 1992).

Independent, 'Law Report: Case Summaries' (27 June 1994).

Jachtenfuchs, M., 'Frames and Learning', in M. Jachtenfuchs (ed.), *International Policy-Making as a Learning-Process?* (Aldershot/Brookfield USA: Avebury Ashgate Publishing Ltd, 1996), pp. 23–41.

Jacob, Herbert, Erhard Blankenburg, Herbert Kritzer, Doris Marie Provine and Joseph Sanders, *Courts, Law, and Politics in Comparative Perspective* (New Haven: Yale University Press, 1996).

Jönsson, Christer and Jonas Tallberg, 'Compliance in Post-Agreement Bargaining', *European Journal of International Relations*, 4: 4 (1998), 371–408.

Jordan, Andrew, 'The Impact on UK Environmental Administration', in Philip Lowe and Stephen Ward (eds), *British Environmental Policy and Europe. Politics and Policy in Transition* (London: Routledge, 1998), pp. 173–94.

Jordan, Andrew, 'The United Kingdom. From Policy "Taking" to Policy "Shaping"', in Andrew Jordan and Duncan Liefferink (eds), *Environmental Policy in Europe. The Europeanization of National Environmental Policy* (London: Routledge, 2004), pp. 205–23.

Jung, Matthias and Dieter Roth, 'Ablösung der Regierung vertagt: Eine Analyse der Bundestagswahl 2002', *Aus Politik und Zeitgeschichte*, 49/50 (2002), 3–17.

K.W.W., The Employment Protection Act, *The Modern Law Review*, 39: 2 (1976), 169–83.

Kaeding, Michael, 'Determinants of Transposition Delay in the European Union', *Journal of Public Policy*, 26: 3 (2006), 229–53.

Kahler, Miles, 'Conclusion: The Causes and Consequences of Legalization', *International Organization*, 54: 3 (2000), 661–83.

Kelsen, Hans, *Principles of International Law* (New York: Rinehart & Company, 1966).

Kempf, Udo, 'Das politische System Frankreichs', in Wolfgang Ismayr (ed.), *Die politischen Systeme Westeuropas* (Opladen: Leske & Budrich, 2003), pp. 301–47.

Keohane, Robert O., *After Hegemony* (Princeton: Princeton University Press, 1984).

Keohane, Robert O. and Joseph S. Nye, *Power and Interdependence* (Glenview: Scott, Foresman and Company, 1989).

Keohane, Robert O., Andrew Moravcsik and Anne Marie Slaughter, 'Legalized Dispute Resolution: Interstate and Transnational', *International Organization*, 54: 3 (2000), 457–88.

Klare, Karl E., 'Legal Culture and Transformative Constitutionalism', *South African Journal on Human Rights*, 14: 1 (1998), 146–88.

Knill, Christoph, *The Europeanisation of National Administrations. Patterns of Institutional Change and Persistence* (Cambridge: Cambridge University Press, 2001).

Knill, Christoph and Andrea Lenschow, 'Adjusting to EU Environmental Policy: Change and Persistence of Domestic Administrations', in Maria Green Cowles, James A. Caporaso and Thomas Risse (eds), *Transforming Europe. Europeanization and Domestic Change* (Ithaca, NY: Cornell University Press, 2001), pp. 116–36.

Kodré, Peter and Henrike Müller, 'Shifting Policy Frames: EU Equal Treatment Norms and Domestic Discourse in Germany', in Ulrike Liebert (ed.), *Gendering Europeanization* (Brussels: P.I.E. – Peter Lang, 2003), pp. 83–116.

Koenig, Stefanie, 'Zur Diskussion um den Gleichstellungsartikel 3: Zwischen Schein und Sein. Berufliche Nachteile der Frauen sollen ausgeglichen werden', *Süddeutsche Zeitung* (19 May 1993).

Kokott, Juliane, 'Report on Germany', in Anne Marie Slaughter, Alec Stone Sweet and J.H.H. Weiler (eds), *The European Court and National Courts – Doctrine and Jurisprudence. Legal Change in Its Social Context* (Oxford: Hart Publishing, 1998), pp. 77–131.

Krämer, Ludwig, 'Enforcement of Community Legislation on the Environment', *Journal of the Regional Science Association*, 137: March (1989), 243–8.

Krislov, S., Claus-Dieter Ehlermann and Jospeh Weiler, 'The Political Organs and the Decision-Making Process in the United States and the European Community', in M. Cappelletti, M. Seccombe and Joseph Weiler (eds), *Integration Through Law, Methods, Tools and Institutions: Political Organs, Integration Techniques and Judicial Process* (Berlin: Gruyter, 1986), pp. 3–112.

Le Moal-Ollive, I., 'Drinking Water in Germany: The Commission Decides to Refer to the Court', *European Community Press Archive* (10 January 1990).

Legrand, Pierre, 'European Legal Systems Are Not Converging', *The*

International and Comparative Law Quarterly, 45: 1 (1996), 52–81.

Lewis, Jane and Ilona Ostner, 'Gender and the Evolution of European Social Policies', *Working Paper, Center for Social Policy Research, Bremen*, 94: 4 (1994).

Liebert, Ulrike, 'Gendering Europeanisation: Patterns and Dynamics', in Ulrike Liebert (ed.), *Gendering Europeanization* (Brussels: P.I.E. – Peter Lang, 2003), pp. 255–83.

Liefferink, Duncan and Andrew Jordan, 'Measuring Europeanization of Policy Convergence. National Baseline Conditions', in Andrew Jordan and Duncan Liefferink (eds), *Environmental Policy in Europe. The Europeanization of National Environmental Policy* (London: Routledge, 2004), pp. 32–46.

Lijphart, Arendt, *Patterns of Democracy. Government Forms and Performance in Thirty-Six Countries* (New Haven: Yale University Press, 1999).

Limbach, Jutta, 'Frauen in bester Verfassung? Wie sich der Grundsatz der Gleichberechtigung umsetzen lässt – Plädoyer für eine aktive Förderungspflicht', *Süddeutsche Zeitung* (22 February 1993).

Lowe, Philip D. and Stephen Ward, 'Britain in Europe. Themes and Issues in National Environmental Policy', in Philp D. Lowe and Stephen Ward (eds), *British Environmental Policy and Europe. Politics and Policy in Transition* (London: Routledge, 1998), pp. 3–30.

Lubbers, Marcel, Mérove Gijsberts and Peer Scheepers, 'Extreme Right-Wing Voting in Western Europe' *European Journal of Political Research* 41: 3 (2002), 345–78.

Lubbers, Marcel and Peer Scheepers, 'Explaining the Trend in Extreme Right-Wing Voting: Germany 1989–1998', *European Sociological Review*, 17: 4 (2001), 431–49.

Lutz, Ellen L. and Kathryn Sikkink, 'International Human Rights Law and Practice in Latin America', *International Organization*, 54: 3 (2000), 633–59.

MacAulay, Stewart, 'Popular Legal Culture: An Introduction', *The Yale Law Journal*, 98: 8 (1989), 1545–58.

Macrory, Richard, 'The Privatisation and Regulation of the Water Industry', *The Modern Law Review* 53: 1 (1990), 78–87.

Maloney, William A., 'Regulation in an Episodic Policy-Making Environment: The Water Industry in England and Wales', *Public Administration*, 79: 3 (2001), 625–42.

March, James G. and Johan P. Olsen, 'The Institutional Dynamics of International Political Orders', *International Organization*, 52: 4 (1998), 943–69.

Martin, Lisa L., *Coercive Cooperation: Explaining Multilateral Economic Sanctions* (Princeton: Princeton University Press, 1992).

Martin, Lisa L. and Beth A. Simmons, 'Theories and Empirical Studies of International Institutions', *International Organization*, 52: 4 (1998), 729–57.

Mastenbroek, Ellen, 'Surviving the Deadline: The Transposition of EU Directives in The Netherlands', *European Union Politics*, 4: 4 (2003), 371–95.

Mbaye, Heather A.D., 'Why National States Comply with Supranational Law', *European Union Politics*, 2 (2001), 259–81.

McGinley, Gerald P., 'Judicial Approaches to Sex Discrimination in the United States and United Kingdom – A Comparative Study', *The Modern Law Review*, 49: 4 (1986), 413–45.

Mendrinou, Maria, 'Non-Compliance and the European Commission's Role in Integration', *Journal of European Public Policy*, 3: 1 (1996), 1–22.

Merkel, Wolfgang and Volker Striehl, 'Das politische System Portugals', in Wolfgang Ismayr (ed.), *Die politischen Systeme Westeuropas* (Opladen: Leske & Budrich, 2003), pp. 651–86.

Minkenberg, Michael, 'The Politics of Citizenship in the New Republic', *West European Politics*, 26: 4 (2003), 219–40.

Mitchell, Ronald, 'Compliance Theory: An Overview', in J. Cameron, J. Werksman and P. Roderick (eds), *Improving Compliance with International Environmental Law* (London: Earthscan, 1996).

Mitchell, Ronald B., 'Regime Design Matters: Intentional Oil Pollution and Treaty Compliance', *International Organization*, 48: 3 (2003), 425–58.

Morgenroth, Christine, *Die engagierte Frau: Frauen und ihre Interessenorganisationen* (Münster: Westfälisches Dampfboot, 1996).

Morris, Lydia, 'Stratified Rights and the Management of Migration. National Distinctiveness in Europe', *European Societies*, 3: 4 (2001), 387–411.

Mörth, Ulrika, 'Competing Frames in the European Commission – the Case of the Defense Industry and Equipment Issue', *Journal of European Public Policy*, 7: 2 (2000), 173–89.

Müller, Harald, 'Internationale Beziehungen als Kommunikatives Handeln. Zur Kritik der utilitaristischen Handlungstheorien', *Zeitschrift für Internationale Beziehungen*, 1: 1 (1994), 15–44.

Müller, Harald, 'Spielen hilft nicht immer. Die Grenzen des Rational-Choice-Ansatzes und der Platz der Theorie Kommunikativen Handelns in der Analyse internationaler Beziehungen', *Zeitschrift für Interna-*

tionale Beziehungen, 2: 2 (1995), 371–91.

Müller, Harald, 'Arguing, Bargaining and all that. Reflections on the Relationship of Communicative Action and Rationalist Theory in Analysing International Negotiations', *European Journal of International Relations*, 10: 3 (2004), 395–435.

Nannestad, Peter, 'Das politische System Dänemarks', in Wolfgang Ismayr (ed.), *Die politischen Systeme Westeuropas* (Opladen: Leske & Budrich, 2003), pp. 55–92.

Nerlich, Brigitte, 'War on Foot and Mouth Disease in the UK, 2001: Towards a Cultural Understanding of Agriculture', *Journal of Agriculture and Human Values* 21: 1 (2003), 15–25.

Observer, 'Little Cheer in the Rule of Euro Law' (12 June 1994).

Office of Water Services (OFWAT), *Corporate Finance Adviser: Setting Price Limits for Water and Sewerage Services* (February 1998).

Office of Water Services (OFWAT), *Annual Report of the Director General of Water Services for April 1st 1999-March 31st, 2000* (2000).

OFWAT National Customer Council, '*Water Industry Act 1999. Draft Guidance to the Director General of Water Services Under Section 4. A Consultation Paper. Response of the Ofwat National Customer Council* (Birmingham: Consumer Council for Water, 1999).

OFWAT National Customer Council, *Environmental Audit Committee inquiry 'Water price limits for 1999–2005: costing the environment' – submission by the ONCC'* (Birmingham: Consumer Council for Water, 2000).

Onuf, Nicholas, *World of Our Making: Rules and Rule in Social Theory and International Relations* (Colombia: University of South Carolina Press, 1989).

Ostner, Ilona, 'Grenzen der Gleichheit. Die EG Frauenpolitik auf dem Prüfstand', *Gewerkschaftliches Monatsheft des DGB*, 9 (1996), 549–61.

Panke, Diana, 'Why Big States Cannot Do What They Want. International Courts and Compliance', Paper presented at the Law & Society Conference, Baltimore USA 2006, at http://web.fu-berlin.de/europa/team /PankeD/Diana+Panke+big+states+and+compliance+LSA+2006.pdf (2006).

Panke, Diana, 'Why Big States Cannot Do What They Want. International Courts and Compliance', *International Politics* 47 (2010), 186–209.

Parliamentary Office of Science and Technology (POST), *Drinking Water Quality, Balancing Safety and Costs* (London: House of Commons, 1993).

Payne, Roger A., 'Persuasion, Frames and Norm Construction', *European*

Journal of International Relations, 7: 1 (2001), 37–61.

Petersmann, Ernst-Ulrich, *The GATT/WTO Dispute Settlement System. International Law, International Organizations and Dispute Settlement* (The Hague: Kluwer International, 1997).

Plotner, Jens, 'Report on France', in Anne Marie Slaughter, Alec Stone Sweet and J. H. H. Weiler (eds), *The European Court and National Courts – Doctrine and Jurisprudence. Legal Change in Its Social Context* (Oxford: Hart Publishing, 1998), pp. 41–76.

Pombeni, Paolo, 'The Ideology of Christian Democracy', *Journal of Political Ideologies*, 5: 3 (2000), 289–300.

Porter, Martin, 'Waste Management', in Philip Lowe and Stephen Ward (eds), *British Environmental Policy and Europe. Politics and Policy in Transition* (London: Routledge, 1998), pp. 195–213.

Posner, Eric A. and John C. Yoo, 'A Theory of International Adjudication', *California Law Review*, 93: 1 (2005), 1–72.

Povall, Margery, 'Positive Action for Women in Britain', *Annals of the American Academy of Political and Social Science*, 523 (1992), 175–85.

Powell, Robert, 'Anarchy in International Relations Theory: The Neorealist-Neoliberal Debate', *International Organization*, 48: 2 (1994), 313–44.

Prantl, Heribert, 'Ein scharfer Wind', *Süddeutsche Zeitung* (16 July 1991).

Pretty, J.N., C. Brett, D. Gee, R.E. Hine, C.F. Mason, J.I.L. Morison, H. Raven, M.D. Rayment and G. van der Bijl, 'An Assessment of the Total External Costs of UK Agriculture', *Agricultural Systems*, 65 (2000), 113–36.

Puelsch, Anja, 'SPD zu 75 Jahren Frauenwahlrecht. Von Wegen Gleichberechtigung. Wählerinnen sollen für Kandidatinnen stimmen', *Süddeutsche Zeitung* (18 Novermber 1993).

Raijman, Rebeca, Moshe Semyonov and Peter Schmidt, 'Do Foreigners Deserve Rights? Determinants of Public Views Towards Foreigners in Germany and Israel', *European Sociological Review*, 19: 4 (2003), 379–92.

Rasmussen, Hjalte, *On Law and Policy in the European Court of Justice. A Comparative Study in Judicial Policymaking* (Dordrecht, Boston and Lancester: Martinus Nijhoff Publishers, 1986).

Raustiala, Kal and Anne Marie Slaughter, 'International Law, International Relations and Compliance', in Walter Carlsnaes, Thomas Risse and Beth A. Simmons (eds), *Handbook of International Relations* (London: Sage Publications, 2002), pp. 538–58.

Reicherzer, Judith, 'Europäischer Gerichtshof: Am Beispiel der Sozialpolitik zeigt sich, wie stark die Richter in Luxemburg in nationales Recht eingreifen können. Dreizehn mächtige Männer; 24.09.1993', *DIE ZEIT* (24 September 1993).

Rein, Martin and Donald Schön, 'Reframing Political Discourse', in Frank Fischer and John Forester (eds), *The Argumentative Turn in Policy Analysis and Planning* (Durham: Duke University Press, 1993),

Reinhardt, Eric, 'Adjudication without Enforcement in GATT Disputes', *Journal of Conflict Resolution*, 45: 2 (2001), 174–95.

Risse, Thomas, '"Let's Argue!": Communicative Action in World Politics', *International Organization*, 54: 1 (2000), 1–39.

Risse, Thomas, 'Constructivism and the Study of International Institutions: Toward Conversations Across Paradigms', in Ira Katznelson and Helen V. Milner (eds), *Political Science as a Discipline? Reconsidering Power, Choice, and the State at Century's End* (New York: W.W. Norton, 2002).

Rosenfeld, Rachel A., Heike Trappe and Janet C. Gornick, 'Gender and Work in Germany: Before and After Reunification', *Annual Review of Sociology*, 30 (2004), 103–24.

Sacks, Vera, 'The Equal Opportunities Commission. Ten Years On', *The Modern Law Review*, 49: 5 (1986), 560–92.

Scharpf, Fritz W., 'Decision Rules, Decision Styles and Policy Choices', *Journal of Theoretical Politics*, 1: 2 (1989a), 149–76.

Scharpf, Fritz W., 'Der Bundesrat und die Kooperation auf der dritten Ebene', in Bundesrat (ed.), *Vierzig Jahre Bundesrat. Tagungsband zum wissenschaftlichen Symposium in der Evangelischen Akademie Tübingen, 11.-13. April 1989* (Baden-Baden: Nomos, 1989b), pp. 121–66.

Scharpf, Fritz W., 'Entwicklungslinien des bundesdeutschen Föderalismus', *Leviathan*, Sonderheft 12 (1991), 146–59.

Schelling, Thomas, *Micromotives and Macrobehavior* (New York: Norton, 1978).

Schreiber, Robert, Marianne Grunwald and Carol Hagemann-White, *Frauenverbände und Frauenvereinigungen in der Bundesrepublik Deutschland* (Stuttgart: Verlag W. Kohlhammer, 1994).

Schroen, Michael, 'Das politische System Luxemburgs', in Wolfgang Ismayr (ed.), *Die politischen Systeme Westeuropas* (Opladen: Leske & Budrich, 2003), pp. 415–44.

Select Committee on Delegated Powers and Deregulation, *Select Committee on Delegated Powers and Deregulation. Eighth Report*, Report of the Select Committee on Environmental Audit (3 March 1999).

Select Committee on Environment, Food and Rural Affairs, *Select Committee on Environment, Food and Rural Affairs. Select Committee Report. Memorandum submitted by Department for Environment, Food and Rural Affairs, Examination of Witnesses. 11 December 2002* (2002a).

Select Committee on Environment, Food and Rural Affairs, *Select Committee on Environment, Food and Rural Affairs. Select Committee Report. Minutes of Evidence 11 December 2002* (2002b).

Select Committee on Environment, Food and Rural Affairs, *Select Committee on Environment, Food and Rural Affairs. Fourth Report: The Water Framework Directive, 12 March 2003* (2003a).

Select Committee on Environment, Food and Rural Affairs, *Select Committee on Environment, Food and Rural Affairs. Select Committee Report. Appendices to the Minutes of Evidence. 12 March 2003* (2003b).

Select Committee on Environment, Transport and Regional Affairs, *Select Committee on Environment, Transport and Regional Affairs, First Special Report. 13 December 2000* (2000).

Select Committee on Environmental Audit, *Water Prices and the Environment, Report of the Select Committee on Environmental Audit, Seventh Report, 1 November 2000* (2000).

Select Committee on Environmental Audit, *Appendix I. Government Response to the Sixth Report From the Environmental Audit Committee, 1999–2000, HC 404, Budget 2000 and the Environment, Report of the Select Committee on Environmental Audit, Second Report, 28 February 2001* (2001).

Select Committee on Environmental Audit, *Select Committee on Environmental Audit Appendices to the Minutes of Evidence. Memorandum from The World Wildlife Fund UK (WWF UK), 22 February 2002* (2002).

Select Committee on Environmental Audit, *Select Committee on Environmental Audit Written Evidence. Memorandum from WWF-UK, 17 September 2003* (2003).

Sharp, Robin, 'Responding to Europeanization. A Governmental Perspective', in Philip Lowe and Stephen Ward (eds), *British Environmental Policy and Europe. Politics and Policy in Transition* (London: Routledge, 1998), pp. 33–56.

Sifft, Stefanie, 'Pushing for Europeanisation: How British Feminists Link with the EU to Promote Parental Rights', in Ulrike Liebert (ed.), *Gendering Europeanization* (Brussels: P.I.E. – Peter Lang, 2003), pp. 149–86.

Skidmore, Paul, 'Enforcement of Rights to Worker Representation in Community Law', *The Modern Law Review*, 58: 5 (1995), 744–51.

Slaughter, Anne Marie, Alec Stone Sweet and J.H.H. Weiler, *The European Court and the National Courts – Doctrine and Jurisprudence: Legal Change in Social Contexts* (Oxford: Northwestern University Press, 1997).

Slaughter, Anne Marie, Alec Stone Sweet and J.H.H. Weiler, 'Prologue – The European Court of Justice', in Anne Marie Slaughter, Alec Stone Sweet and J. H. H. Weiler (eds), *The European Court and the National Courts – Doctrine and Jurisprudence: Legal Change in Social Contexts* (Oxford: Hart Publishing, 1998), pp. v–xiv.

Smith, Brian, 'The United Kingdom', in Donald C. Rowat (ed.), *Public Administration in Developed Democracies. A Comparative Study* (New York: Marcel Dekker, Inc., 1988), pp. 67–86.

Smith, James McCall, 'The Politics of Dispute Settlement Design: Explaining Legalism in Regional Trade Pacts', *International Organization*, 54: 1 (2000), 137–80.

Snidal, Duncan, 'Rational Choice and International Relations', in Walter Carlsnaes, Thomas Risse and Beth Simmons (eds), *Handbook of International Relations* (London: Sage, 2002), pp. 73–94.

Snow, David A. and Robert D. Benford, 'Master Frames and Cycles of Protest', in Alan D. Morris and Carol McClury Mueller (eds), *Frontiers in Social Movement Theory* (New Haven: Yale University Press, 1992), pp. 133–55.

Snyder, Francis, 'The Effectiveness of European Community Law: Institutions, Processes, Tools and Techniques', *Modern Law Review*, 56: 1 (1993), 19–54.

Social Democratic Party (SPD), *Antrag zum Gesetz zur Sicherung der Gleichbehandlung von Männern und Frauen am Arbeitsplatz, 15.06.1983*: Bundestagsdrucksache (1983).

Social Democratic Party (SPD), *Antrag zum Bundesausländergesetz, 29.06.1988* (1988).

Social Democratic Party (SPD), *Antrag zur Sanierung der Trinkwasserversorgung in den neuen Bundesländern, 06.11.1991* (1991).

Stathopoulos, C. and E. Kaiser, 'Community Asks Germany to Adopt its Legislation on Drinking Water to Community Law', *European Community Press Archive* (13 July 1989).

Steffani, Winfried, 'Zur Unterscheidung parlamentarischer und präsidentieller Regierungssysteme', *Zeitschrift für Politikwissenschaft*, 15: 3 (1983), 390–401.

Steinberg, Richard H., 'In the Shadow of Law or Power? Consensus-Based

Bargaining and Outcomes in the GATT/WTO', *International Organization*, 56: 2 (2002), 339–74.

Steunenberg, Bernard, 'Turning Swift Policy-making into Deadlock and Delay. National Policy Coordination and the Transposition of EU Directives', *European Union Politics*, 7: 3 (2006), 293–319.

Stone Sweet, Alec and Thomas Brunell, 'The European Court and the National Courts: A Statistical Analysis of Preliminary References, 1961–95', *Journal of European Public Policy*, 5: 1 (1998a), 66–97.

Stone Sweet, Alec and Thomas L. Brunell, 'Constructing a Supranational Constitution. Dispute Resolution and Governance in the European Community', *American Political Science Review*, 92: 1 (1998b), 63–81.

Stone Sweet, Alec and Wayne Sandholtz (eds), *European Integration and Supranational Governance* (Oxford: Oxford University Press, 1998).

Süddeutsche Zeitung, 'Umweltschäden kosten Milliarden. Allein 200 Millionen DM jährlich für sauberes Wasser', (10 September 1991).

Süddeutsche Zeitung, 'Der Aufstand der Unionsfrauen. Das Gleichberechtigungsgesetz soll nicht länger vor sich hindümpeln', (29 January 1992).

Süddeutsche Zeitung, 'Gas- und Wasserwirtschaft wirft Bundesregierung Untätigkeit vor' (30 November 1992).

Süddeutsche Zeitung, 'Umweltinitiativen schlagen Alarm Naturnahe Fluesse tauchen unter' (27 November 1992).

Süddeutsche Zeitung, 'Umweltrecht ist noch nicht Umweltschutz. Der Ministerialbuerokratie fehlen Überwachungs- und Kontrollmöglichkeiten', (28 February 1992).

Süddeutsche Zeitung, 'Nach monatelanger Abstimmung zwischen den Ministerien Merkel legt Gleichberechtigungsgesetz vor. Frauenförderung ohne Quoten im Öffentlichen Dienst / Mehr Schutz vor sexueller Belästigung' (15 January 1993).

Süddeutsche Zeitung, 'Mit Frauenpolitik einen Namen gemacht. Die neue stellvertretende FDP-Chefin Ruth Witteler-Koch' (13 December 1994).

Süddeutsche Zeitung, 'Schneekanonen am Kreuzeck Die Gruenen reagieren eisig. Landtagsabgeordnete Tessy Loedermann fuer Pisten-Sperre' (5 February 1994).

Süddeutsche Zeitung, 'Urteil des Verwaltungsgerichts Lüneburg Baustop fuer Gorleben aufgehoben' (8 March 1994).

Süddeutsche Zeitung, 'Kirchen und DGB fordern Reform des Ausländerrechts' (23 April 1996).

Süddeutsche Zeitung, '3000 protestierengegen Kanther. Visumszwang fuer Kinder' (10 March 1997).

Süddeutsche Zeitung, 'Demonstrationen gegen Visumspflicht fuer Kinder.

Proteste in mehreren Staedten' (28 February 1997).

Süddeutsche Zeitung, 'Der Bock als Gaertner' (8 February 1997).

Süddeutsche Zeitung, 'Kanthers Handstreich gegen Kinder. 400 000 junge Auslaender brauchen Aufenthaltsgenehmigung' (14 January 1997).

Süddeutsche Zeitung, 'Prominente Hilfe fuer Kurdenfamilie. Kirchen und Sportler bitten um Gnade. Der Landtag soll noch im April über ein Bleiberechtder Zans in Puchheim entscheiden' (7 April 1997).

Süddeutsche Zeitung, 'Zur Finanzierung der grossen Steuerreform CSU erwägt auch höhere Mehrwertsteuer. Einnahmelücke soll aber vor allem durch Abbau von Vergünstigungen und Einsparungen geschlossen werden Waigel warnt FDP vor Profilierung zu Lasten der CSU / Glos sieht Fehler der Liberalen bei der Verbrechensbekämpfung' (8 January 1997).

Süddeutsche Zeitung, 'Kritik an Ausländerpolitik der neuen Bundesregierung' (23 October 1998).

Süddeutsche Zeitung, 'Umweltgesetzbuch verzögert sich' (3 September 1999).

Süddeutsche Zeitung, 'Genauer kontrollieren Umweltprüfung von Industrieanlagen' (26 October 2000).

Süddeutsche Zeitung, 'Naturschuetzer zwischen Hoffen und Bangen' (5 June 2001).

Sunday Times, 'A Greener View on the Home Front' (20 January 2002).

Sunday Times, 'Scots Farmers Face Pollution Crackdown' (13 January 2002).

Surel, Yves, 'The Role of Cognitive and Normative Frames in Policy-Making', *Journal of European Public Policy*, 7: 4 (2000), 495–512.

Tallberg, Jonas, *Making States Comply. The European Commission, the European Court of Justice and the Enforcement of the Internal Market* (Lund: Studentlitteratur, 1999).

Tallberg, Jonas, 'Supranational Influence in EU Enforcement: The ECJ and the Principle of State Liability', *Journal of European Public Policy*, 7: 1 (2000), 104–21.

Tallberg, Jonas, 'Paths to Compliance: Enforcement, Management, and the European Union', *International Organization*, 56: 3 (2002), 609–43.

Tallberg, Jonas and J. Christer, 'Compliance and Post-Agreement Bargaining', *European Journal of International Relations*, 4: 4 (1998), 371–408.

Tallberg, Jonas and Christer Jönsson, '*Compliance Bargaining in the European Union*, in ECSA International Conference (Madison, Wisconsin, 2001).

Taylor, I., 'Policy On the Hoof: the Handling of the Foot and Mouth Disease Outbreak in the UK 2001', *Policy & Politics*, 31: 4 (2003), 535–46.

TAZ, 'Umweltbundesamt und Bundesumweltministerium stellen den Entwurf eines ein-heitlichen Umweltgesetzbuches vor' (24 August 1994).

TAZ, 'Von der Saale zur technisch genormten Rinne. Die Bundesregierung will fuer 220 Millionen Mark die Saale schiffsgerecht ausbaggern. Doch die Verkehrsstatistiken sind falsch, die Umwelt an Saale und Elbe wird zerstoert. An der Elbe drohen wie am Rhein haeufige Hochwasser' (18 July 1995).

TAZ, 'Manfred Kanthers Überfall auf Kinder. Regierung will per Kindervisumpflicht Familienzusammenführung verhindern' (14 January 1997).

TAZ, 'Seit kurzem benötigen Kinder aus Einwandererfamilien eine Aufent-haltsgenehmigung. Diese Regelung muss weg' (28 January 1997).

TAZ, 'Das neue Umweltrecht wird zur Hängepartie' (26 May 1999).

TAZ, 'Der Sachverständige Gerd Winter zur weiteren Verschiebung des Umweltgesetzbuches. "Den Interessen der Industrie nachgegeben" (6 September 1999).

TAZ, 'Deutsches Umweltrecht veraltet' (16 March 1999).

TAZ, 'Neue Gesetzespleite von Trittin' (3 September 1999).

TAZ, 'Trittin legt Gesetzentwurf zu mehr Umweltschutz vor und stoesst auf heftige Kritik bei Wirtschafts- und Umweltverbaenden. Regierung muss EU-Richtlinien umsetzen' (31 August 2000).

Thairs, Edwin, 'Business Lobbying on the Environment. The Perspective of the Water Sector', in Philip Lowe and Stephen Ward (eds), *British Environmental Policy and Europe. Politics and Policy in Transition* (London: Routledge, 1998), pp. 153–70.

The Fawcett Society, *1975– 2005. Are We There Yet? 30 Years of Closing the Gap Between Women and Men. Economic Disadvantage* (London 2006).

The Fawcett Society, *Past, Present and Future. Fawcett's Achievements and Visions* (London, 2006).

The Times, 'Parliament: Sex Equality Law to be Widened', (7 November 1985).

The Times, 'Thatcher's Era Leaves Women Still Not Equal' (11 March 1986).

The Times, 'Water Boards Face Pesticide Clean-up Bill' (20 January 1989).

The Times, 'Women's Voices, Loud and Clear' (5 August 1991).

The Times, 'Women At Work' (6 November 1991).

The Times, 'Getting Equal' (30 June 1992).

The Times, 'I See Opportunity Denied, Potential Unfulfilled and Talent Unused', (20 July 1992).

The Times, 'UK Broke EC Work Laws' (3 March 1994).

The Times, 'UK in Breach of EC Duty to Harmonise Rights of Workers' (27 June 1994).

The Times, 'Britain in Hot Water with EU' (23 April 1999).

Trades Union Congress, *Representation at Work: The Role of Trade Unions and the Role of the Law*, Industrial Law Society Meeting (Worcester, 2002).

Trautmann, Günther and Hartmut Ulrich, 'Das politische System Italiens', in Wolfgang Ismayr (ed.), *Die politischen Systeme Westeuropas* (Opladen: Leske & Budrich, 2003), pp. 553–607.

Trittin, Jürgen, *Perspektiven der deutschen Umweltpolitik*, Speech in the German Bundestag, 29 September 1999. (Berlin: 18th Session of the Committee on Environment, Nature and Nuclear Safety, 1999).

Trittin, Jürgen, *Die ökologische Erneuerung der Bundesrepublik. Speech at the Heinrich Böll Foundation*, (Berlin: Heinrich-Böll Stiftung, 2000).

Tsebelis, George, 'Veto Players Data', at www.polisci.ucla.edu/tsebelis /vpdata.html (2002a).

Tsebelis, George, *Veto Players: How Political Institutions Work* (Princeton NJ: Princeton University Press, 2002b).

Van Hoeck, Mark and Mark Warrington, 'Legal Cultures, Legal Paradigms and Legal Doctrine: Towards a New Model for Comparative Law', *The International and Comparative Law Quarterly*, 47: 3 (1998), 495–536.

Vermittlungsausschuss, *Beschlussempfehlung Vermittlungsausschuss 20.06.2001* Drucksache 14/6357 (2001).

Victor, David G., Kal Raustiala and Eugene B. Skolnikoff (eds), *The Implementation and Effectiveness of International Environmental Commitments* (Cambridge, MA: MIT Press, 1998).

Visegrády, A., 'Legal Cultures in the European Union', *Acta Juridicia Hungarica*, 42: 3 (2001), 203–17.

von Wahl, Angelika, 'Gender Equality in Germany: Comparing Policy Change Across Domains', *West European Politics*, 29: 3 (2006), 461–88.

Wallace, Helen and William Wallace (eds), *Policy-Making in the European Union* (Oxford: Oxford University Press, 2000).

Ward, Neil, 'Water Quality', in Philip Lowe and Stephen Ward (eds), *British Environmental Policy and Europe. Politics and Policy in Transi-*

tion (London: Routledge, 1998), pp. 244–64.

Ward, Neil, Henry Buller and Philip Lowe, *Implementing European Environmental Policy at the Local Level: The British Experience with Water Quality Directives, Volume 1 Summary Report*, Research Report (Newcastle: University of Newcastle, 1995).

Ward, Neil, Judy Clark, Philip Lowe and Susanne Seymour, *Water Pollution From Agricultural Pesticides* (Newcastle: University of Newcastle Centre For Rural Economy, 1993).

Ward, Neil, Andrew Donaldson and Philip Lowe, 'Policy Framing and Learning the Lessons From the UK's Foot and Mouth Disease Crisis', *Government and Policy*, 22: 1 (2004), 291–306.

Water Voice, *Representing Water Customers: Water Voice Programme 2002–03* (Birmingham: Consumer Council for Water, 2002).

Weiler, Joseph H.H., 'The Community System: The Dual Character of Supranationalism', *Yearbook of European Law*, 1 (1981), 268–306.

Wendt, Alexander, 'The Agent-Structure Problem in International Relations Theory', *International Organization*, 41: 3 (1987), 335–70.

Wendt, Alexander, *Social Theory of International Politics* (Cambridge: Cambridge University Press, 1999).

Western Mail, 'Rescue Package Must be Part of Agriculture Reform, Says WWF. Disease Funds Must Go to Rural Economy as a Whole, Says Study' (1 May 2001).

Western Morning News (Plymouth), 'New Cost Burden of EU Water Regulations' (11 April 2001).

Western Morning News (Plymouth), 'Concern Over New Anti-Pollution Rules' (2 January 2002).

Wheeler Cook, Walter, 'Scientific Method and the Law', *American Bar Association Journal*, 13 (1927), 305–6.

World Bank, *World Development Indicators on CD-Rom* (Washington D.C.: World Bank, 2004).

World Wide Fund for Nature (WWF), *Implementing the EU Water Framework Directive* (Brussels: WWF, 2000).

Wouter, Poortinga, Karen Bickerstaff, Ian Langford, Jörg Niewöhner and Nick Pidgeon, 'The British 2001 Foot and Mouth Crisis: A Comparative Study of Public Risk Perceptions, Trust and Beliefs About Government Policy in Two Communities', *Journal of Risk Research* 7: 1 (2004), 73–90.

Woyke, Wichard, 'Das politische System Belgiens', in Wolfgang Ismayr (ed.), *Die politischen Systeme Westeuropas* (Opladen: Leske & Budrich, 2003), pp. 389–414.

Wurzel, Rüdiger K.W., 'Germany. From Environmental Leadership to

Practical Mismatch', in Andrew Jordan and Duncan Lieferink (eds), *Environmental Policy in Europe. The Europeanization of National Environmental Policy* (New York: Routledge, 2004), pp. 99–117.

Zervakis, Peter A., 'Das politische System Griechenlands', in Wolfgang Ismayr (ed.), *Die politischen Systeme Westeuropas* (Opladen: Leske & Budrich, 2003), pp. 687–730.

Zippel, Kathrin S., *The Politics of Sexual Harassment. A Comparative Study of the United States, the European Union, and Germany* (New York: Cambridge University Press, 2006).

Zürn, Michael and Christian Joerges (eds) *Law and Governance in Postnational Europe. Compliance Beyond the Nation-State* (Cambridge: Cambridge University Press, 2005).

Index